David J. Neumann earned a Ph.D. in History from the University of Southern California as a Provost's Fellow. His teaching interests focus on historical thinking, historical literacy, and the intersection between scholarship and pedagogy. A lecturer in the History Department at CSU Long Beach for eight years, he taught American history, world history, and capstone courses in elementary and secondary education. He won several awards during more than a decade of teaching high school history.

Praise for *Finding God Through Yoga*

"In fine style that makes this book fun to read, Neumann's much-needed study of Paramahansa Yogananda clarifies the relationship between Christianity and Yogananda's Hindu roots. Highlighting the development of an American Hinduism, Neumann reminds us that the great yogi died as an American citizen buried in the soil of his adopted country but also as a thoroughly global guru well before the term became widely adopted. I will use this book in my classes, too, as an insightful way to understand Yogananda's ever-popular classic, *Autobiography of a Yogi*."

—Joanne Punzo Waghorne, Syracuse University

"Uniformly perceptive and utterly convincing, Neumann reveals Paramahansa Yogananda's penchant for 'imaginative reconstruction' while preserving the guru's humanity through it all. At once fair, honest, and unflinching, this book will certainly be warmly welcomed and used widely as the standard scholarly source for the life and teachings of Paramahansa Yogananda, as well as for the understanding of Hinduism—and religious charisma—in America. There is nothing else like it."

—Jeffrey J. Kripal, J. Newton Rayzor Professor of Religion, Rice University

"An interesting study of the cultural phenomenology of a guru and his movement—its light and shadow, its success and contradictions."

—William Irwin Thompson, author of *The Time Falling Bodies Take to Light*

Finding God Through Yoga

PARAMAHANSA YOGANANDA
and the Making of a Global Religion

David J. Neumann

SPEAKING TIGER

SPEAKING TIGER BOOKS LLP
4381/4, Ansari Road, Daryaganj
New Delhi 110002

First published by The University of North Carolina Press
Published in India by Speaking Tiger Books 2019

ISBN: 978-93-89231-63-2

10 9 8 7 6 5 4 3 2 1

For sale in South Asia only

Printed at Sanat Printers, Kundli, Haryana

To

CHRISTA

for everything,

as always

Contents

Figures

Acknowledgments

Writing a book requires a paradoxical combination of solitary work and heavy dependence on others. I'm grateful for the friends and colleagues who helped me at various points along the path.

I owe a number of scholars at the University of Southern California my gratitude. I have to begin by offering a tribute to the memory of Kevin Starr, the don of California history, who took an early interest in my academic career and always urged me to think about the state's story in creative ways. Bill Deverell knows that I invented a game of reading the acknowledgments of monographs on California history looking for his name. He can add this book to a growing list that speaks volumes about the time he generously offers young scholars on their work. I appreciate the freedom he gave me to pursue a somewhat unconventional topic and for the support that enabled me to complete this project. Karen Halttunen always pressed me to refine my writing and hone my argument. She also assisted me in moving efficiently through graduate school and into a university career. Finding Diane Winston through the Southern California Religion Writing Group was truly providential. She introduced me to the world of American alternative religious traditions. More importantly, she quickly became a mentor, guiding me in thinking through the content, organization, and argument of the book from the beginning.

Several others helped me in vital ways. Jeffrey Kripal and Joanne Punzo Waghorne offered detailed, thoughtful, constructive feedback that helped me sharpen and clarify my argument at a number of points. Christina Copland, a good friend and colleague, offered intellectual companionship and incisive feedback on more drafts of this manuscript than either of us would probably care to count. John Parsons was a gracious host who generously set aside time in the middle of his workday for long discussions about Yogananda and Self-Realization Fellowship that helped deepen my understanding of the man and his organization. The treasure trove of materials he provided helped make this book much more robust. The online community Robert Ardito and Martine Vanderpoorten host provided many important documents as well. The Interlibrary Loan staffs at University of Southern California, California State University Long Beach, and, near the end, California Polytechnic State University Pomona patiently provided an endless stream of books and other materials. I'm very grateful to Elaine Maisner, who took an early and enthusiastic interest in this project and skillfully guided it to completion. Andrew Winters, Jay Mazzocchi, Laura Jones Dooley, and the rest of the staff of the University of North Carolina Press are outstanding professionals who have been delightful to work with.

Several others have helped out in less direct but still significant ways. Bob Bain taught me to think about world history conceptually and has been a persistent cheerleader through each stage of my career. Tim Keirn is largely responsible for responsible for my interest in India. Through a Freeman Foundation grant, he organized a trip several years ago that took me to India for the first time. That trip planted the seed that flowered as he and I ran Teach India workshops for secondary teachers for several years. A 2016 trip gave me the chance to visit a number of key locations in the story told in this book: Vivekananda's childhood home, the Dakshineswar Kali Temple, the Belur Math mission, the Dakshineswar ashram, Yogananda's childhood home in Calcutta, and Yukteswar's ashram in Puri.

My family has provided ongoing support. My mom and dad expressed enthusiasm and encouragement throughout the project, as they have with all my major life decisions. Christa, Anna, and Sarah listened without complaint to endless stories about Yogananda and with interest to new chapters in the ongoing saga of the book's development. They also agreed to be dragged along to various sites—though I'd like to believe they actually enjoyed the afternoons we spent together in Pacific Palisades and Encinitas and at the Biltmore Hotel. Christa has put up with more than anyone else. She always knew that this book would be dedicated to her as a very small token of my gratitude for the countless ways she has supported me. She made this book possible. More than that, she has always been the best thing in my life.

Note on Transliteration

I have been eclectic in my transliteration of terms from Sanskrit, Hindi, and Bengali. Metaphysical concepts, religious practices, social classes, and other technical terms have been printed in italics with diacritical marks. Words like swami, guru, yoga, and yogi, which occur repeatedly throughout the text and have roughly similar meanings to their English usage, appear without special marks. References to locations in India consistently follow conventions from Yogananda's lifetime, rather than contemporary usage.

Finding God
Through Yoga

Introduction

Paramahansa Yogananda, the Father of Yoga in the West

It is your greatest privilege to meditate. In one life you can find God if you put forth strength, energy, and determination. Without determination, He cannot be found. So remember, taking the Lessons only will not do, but if you practice them you will get results."

PARAMAHANSA YOGANANDA, *Your Praecepta: Step IV*, P92, 5

Devotees of the great Indian swami Paramahansa Yogananda placed two milestones in his honor in 2017. The first was the sixty-fifth anniversary of his departure from this world on March 5, 1952. And the second was the centennial of Yogoda Satsanga Society (YSS), the organization he founded before coming to the United States, where he lived most of his life. Prime Minister of India Narendra Modi used these twin anniversaries to celebrate Yogananda's life and work. Speaking at the parliament's conference center in New Delhi during an elaborate hour-long ceremony at which he unveiled a postage stamp in Yogananda's honor, Modi took the opportunity to remind audiences of Yogananda's Indian identity. Conceding that "the major part" of Yogananda's life was "spent outside India"—and ignoring altogether the inconvenient fact of Yogananda's American citizenship—he insisted that "Yogananda takes his place among our great saints." Yogananda was a guru, not just for India, but for the world, and "his work continues to grow and shine ever more brightly, drawing people everywhere on the path of the pilgrimage of Spirit."[1]

Growing Indian interest in Yogananda illustrates the so-called pizza effect, in which Indian teachers develop significant followings in their homeland only after they establish successful ministries overseas.[2] In recent years, a number of prominent Indians have claimed Yogananda as their guru. Indian cricket champion Virat Kohli, for example, revealed that Yogananda's *Autobiography*

The Indian government's stamp commemorating the centennial of Yogananda's organizational work, beginning with the Ranchi ashram (pictured).
Yogoda Satsanga Society is the India affiliate of the Self-Realization Fellowship, headquartered in Los Angeles. The stamp was unveiled by Prime Minister Narendra Modi during an hour-long ceremony on March 7, 2017.

of a Yogi was the secret of his success and could be for many others as well. "The understanding and implementation of the knowledge in this book," Kohli promised, "will change your whole perspective and life. Believe in the divine and keep marching on doing good deeds."[3] Once known largely as a spiritual guide to Americans, Yogananda has increasingly been claimed by Indians as one of their own.

Paradoxically, a part of Indians' attraction to Yogananda stems from his influence overseas, especially in the United States, as the herald of yoga. The United Nations' establishment of International Yoga Day in 2015, largely at Modi's urging, inspired a number of Indians to declare Yogananda's unrivaled importance in spreading yoga worldwide. One *Times of India* writer boldly claimed that if the United Nations had so easily welcomed International Yoga Day, "much of the credit must go to Paramhansa Yogananda, India's first guru in the U.S." Though he was not as well known among Indians as the ubiquitous Swami Vivekananda, Yogananda nevertheless "played a huge role in laying the foundation for yoga in the United States a century ago."[4] Another writer asserted that the advent of International Yoga Day was an opportune time to "tip our hats to the teacher who first introduced the modern world to the transformative power of yoga as a timeless inner discipline."[5] And a third declared, "We should pay homage to the enlightened mystic Paramhansa Yogananda who started it all," introducing yoga to Americans a century earlier.[6] Calling Yogananda America's first yogi may be an overstatement, but not by much. Given his imprint on the American spiritual landscape, it is appropriate to call him the Father of Yoga in the West, as followers of both Self-Realization Fellowship (SRF), his American organization, and YSS routinely do.[7]

Yogananda's followers have been making this claim in some fashion for decades, honoring him as the Indian founder of an international yoga organization headquartered in the United States. On March 7, 1977, forty years before Modi's commemoration, a similar—though much more subdued—ceremony took place in recognition of Yogananda's importance. On that occasion, a small group of SRF leaders, YSS members, and Indian dignitaries gathered at YSS's Dakshineswar ashram in Calcutta to honor Yogananda on the twenty-fifth anniversary of his death, likewise with the issuing of a postage stamp. Appropriately enough, former Indian ambassador to the United States Binay R. Sen led the commemoration: it was at a dinner in Sen's honor that Yogananda had departed this world in 1952.[8]

The location of the 1977 event was another reminder of Yogananda's Indian identity. The Dakshineswar property had been acquired as a result of Yogananda's return visit to India in 1935–36 after fifteen years of ministry in the United States. The site recalled the vital importance of that trip, when Yogananda's guru Sri Yukteswar bestowed the title Paramahansa on him. The Dakshineswar ashram abuts the Hooghly River half a mile upstream from the imposing Kali temple that Yogananda often visited as a young man in search of spiritual truth.

But the Dakshineswar ashram also hints at Yogananda's American identity. On the opposite bank of the Hooghly River sits the Ramakrishna Math and Mission headquarters, established by Swami Vivekananda. Yogananda chose the Dakshineswar location precisely because of this proximity. He wished to found an ashram within view of Ramakrishna Math as a reminder of Vivekananda, the first Hindu missionary to America and the inspiration of his own missionary endeavor.[9] Following in Vivekananda's footsteps, the young Bengali swami from an unremarkable middle-class Indian family had departed from this very city in 1920, arriving in a United States suspicious of Indians and Hindu beliefs. For more than thirty years, America was his home. He formed Self-Realization Fellowship shortly after his arrival, moved his headquarters to Los Angeles in 1925, acquired property throughout Southern California and elsewhere, and made disciples all over the country before expanding his

Yogoda Satsanga Ashram in Dakshineswar, Calcutta, looking across the Hooghly River toward Swami Vivekananda's Ramakrishna Math and Mission at Belur. Yogananda purposely chose this property for its proximity to sites associated with Vivekananda and his guru. The ashram is less than a mile from the Dakshineswar Kali Temple, where Sri Ramakrishna lived for many years.

mission overseas. He died an American citizen in Los Angeles and—after an abortive attempt was made to ship his body to India—was interred in a local cemetery.

If Yogananda's national identity is complex, his identity as a religious leader is even more so. The popular recent trend toward being "spiritual but not religious" has led several admirers to associate Yogananda with contemporary yoga as a popular postural health practice focused on mindfulness, which they explicitly distinguish from normative religious practice. One describes Yogananda as a "forerunner to a breed of twenty-first century psychologists, psychotherapists and neuroscientists who are generating powerful new insights on human nature—all aligned with Yogananda's how-to-live teaching." Although this author accurately identifies the "empirical, scientific nature" Yogananda claimed for his meditation technique, he completely ignores Yogananda's explicit central goal, the experience of God.[10] Popular speaker and author Deepak Chopra has expressed similar admiration for Yogananda as a forebear of New Age spirituality, the "most viable spiritual movement in place," rather than the "dogma" and "aggressive fundamentalism" of religion.[11] In his speech announcing the 2017 commemorative stamp, Prime Minister Modi, who practices yoga daily, engaged in similar feats of wishful thinking.[12] Lamenting that it is "unfortunate that some people link spirituality with religion, whereas the two are very different," Modi asserted that Yogananda had been interested in the former (*antaryatra*, "the inner journey," or self-realization), not the latter (*mukti*, liberation).[13]

These false dichotomies distort Yogananda's identity. He was a teacher *both* of the inner journey of self-realization *and* of religion. His first book was *The Science of Religion*; he first came to the United States to attend a gathering of religious leaders; he incorporated SRF as a "church" in 1935; and local branches have long hosted weekly Sunday services with devotional singing, prayer, and a sermon.[14] Self-Realization Fellowship, in other words, bears all the marks that advocates of spirituality attribute to religion. It is a hierarchical institution with formal membership that firmly regulates normative beliefs and practices focused on the transcendent reality of intimate communion with the divine. Self-Realization Fellowship conforms to the features of Modern Denominational Yoga, as stated in yoga scholar Elizabeth De Michelis's influential typology, in that it is collectivist, tightly structured, makes demands on members, has stable belief and organizational systems, and promotes adherence to its own beliefs, rules, and sources of authority.[15]

The leaders of the religious organizations Yogananda established remain the primary custodians of their master's legacy. When YSS-SRF representatives met with Prime Minister Modi at Parliament House in New Delhi in March 2016 to thank him for his efforts to establish International Yoga Day, they presented him with a letter from then-SRF president Sri Daya Mata expressing her "warm good wishes and prayers that God may guide and bless you in the work you are doing for the well-being and upliftment of India." Mata reminded the prime minister that Yogananda sought to disseminate yoga globally to promote unity through communion with the one God:

> Although he spent much of his time in the West disseminating India's ancient science of yoga meditation for attaining direct personal experience of God, Paramahansaji always cherished a deep love of India in his heart and left his physical form while speaking the words of his poem, "My India." One of his goals was to promote unity between East and West, and over the years seekers of many faiths and nationalities have been drawn to his universal message. He predicted that one day the message of yoga would encircle the globe aiding in

> the establishment of world peace on the basis of humanity's direct perception of the one God.[16]

Yogananda's global vision has been realized. Today, SRF has a truly worldwide presence with centers on six continents, in nearly sixty countries, including 170 in the United States and more than 300 in other countries.[17]

YOGANANDA AS A PIONEERING GLOBAL GURU

In this book, I explore Paramahansa Yogananda's ministry as an Indian, an American, and the founder of a global religious organization. Yogananda thus illuminates the role of religion in transnational history, a topic that has received scant attention from historians pursuing transnational themes in the modern era.[18] Investigating Yogananda opens a crucial window on the role of Hinduism in the development of early twentieth-century American religion. But Yogananda's hybridity extends beyond an Indian-American binary. Through overseas travel, participation in international religious gatherings, the creation of SRF branches around the world, and talks and articles addressing global issues, he became one of the earliest "global gurus," figures who "function as spokespersons, apologists, and unifiers of the Hindu religion" and "creators of newer and more universalized religious forms that break the bounds of territory, race, and ethnicity."[19] Yogananda exemplified "transnational transcendence," an attempt to reenchant the modern world with a universal message that intentionally rises above national borders.[20] More recent gurus have fueled the expansion of their global ministries by reaching out to growing diaspora Indian communities, taking advantage of inexpensive air travel to connect with followers, and, in the past few decades, using the Internet to establish a virtual presence.[21] Without the advantage of any of these later developments, Yogananda nurtured a fruitful transnational ministry. Yogananda illustrates, as religion scholar Amanda Lucia says regarding more recent global gurus, "an alternative narrative to globalization, which has often been imagined as a movement from center to periphery." Like later global gurus, Yogananda spread his message from peripheral India to the center of the modern world, the United States.[22]

The first Indian to establish a thriving American ministry, Yogananda played a significant role in popularizing yoga meditation and the Hindu cosmological tenets that have become increasingly prevalent in the United States. His American ministry, which spanned more than three decades, from 1920 to 1952, was established in the United States much earlier than organizations from the counterculture or hippie era, such as the International Society for Krishna Consciousness (popularly known as the Hare Krishna movement) and Transcendental Meditation. And unlike the founders of these two movements, Swami Prabhupada and Maharishi Mahesh Yogi, Yogananda chose to base his international headquarters in the United States. Yogananda's influence has proved at least as enduring as that of Prabhupada and the Maharishi. Self-Realization Fellowship remains a robust organization that boasts thousands of members and countless more casual followers around the world, due in large part to Yogananda's teachings and writings, particularly *Autobiography of a Yogi*, which is available in four dozen languages.

The ministry's success represents the emergence of a significant and distinctive phenomenon: a thriving, century-old form of modern American Hinduism. This new religious movement emerged not, like Theosophy, through the inventiveness of Americans discovering Asian traditions, nor as part of a larger Indian diaspora community transplanting its own practices, as began to happen in significant numbers after 1965, but through the intentional evangelism of one teacher whose practitioners were overwhelmingly white Americans. He was "a missionary," as SRF's current president, Brother Chidananda, once said, of an "ancient tradition of yoga meditation."[23]

Religious Nationalism and Missionary Hinduism

Five features of Yogananda's life and ministry shed crucial light on the modern global religious landscape. First, Yogananda's ministry was fueled by a religious nationalism that led him to conclude, with other leading Indians of his day, that Hinduism could uniquely fill the spiritual void in "the West." As an Indian nationalist residing overseas, he was monitored, as were other British subjects of the British Empire, by government officials for possible subversion. But they eventually concluded that his brand of nationalism was harmless. Though Yogananda was sympathetic to calls for Indian independence, he expressed his nationalism not primarily through politics but through culture. Throughout his life, Yogananda expressed ardent affection for his homeland and its traditions in prose and verse. But paradoxically, rather than rooting him in India, that affection drove him to the United States, where he sought to cultivate the same love among open-minded Americans. He abandoned the typical Indian pattern of monastic renunciation, wherein a handful of would-be disciples seek him out for face-to-face mentorship, and instead became an evangelist in reverse. As he traveled throughout a nation that routinely sent missionaries to his homeland, he spread the good news of Kriya Yoga. Few Americans had ever been instructed about yoga, since the Indian diaspora at the time was extremely small and consisted largely of Sikhs.[24] In short, Yogananda chose to proselytize Americans as a Hindu missionary.[25]

If conversion is, as historian Nicholas Dirks says, about "the project of translation, the shifting of one context to another,"[26] Yogananda shared the conviction of many later gurus that traditional Hindu beliefs and practices could be translated into a "language that resonates with modernity" and would be compelling to earnest seekers overseas, not just in India.[27] Yogananda's fundamental conviction that Hindu *dharma* was universal, transportable, and translatable—rather than being the preserve of India and its people—was of relatively recent vintage at the time he launched his mission. It was shaped by a view of world religions that, though complex, was ultimately *inclusivist*. Yogananda rejected an *exclusivist* interpretation of Hinduism, a view Anglican theologian Alan Race describes as treating one's own religion as "the sole criterion by which all religions . . . can be understood and evaluated." Indeed, Yogananda frequently criticized Christianity for such narrowness. And he often articulated an ostensibly *pluralistic* position, in which, according to Race, "religions must acknowledge their need of each other if the full truth about God is to be available to mankind."[28] But as with Vivekananda and other modern Hindu teachers, Yogananda's pluralism was subordinated to his conviction that Hinduism was the wellspring of truth. Religious scholar Joanne Punzo Waghorne's description, in reference to Vivekananda, of "the catholicity of his Hinduism, its inherent inclusion of all, [which] could serve as the very model for a rising new kind of universal religion," could equally be applied to Yogananda.[29] He claimed to offer a scientific religion, available to all, that transcended Hinduism and Christianity, but this universal religion was constructed mostly from Hindu materials.

Some of Yogananda's contemporaries recognized his inclusivism. Author Wendell Thomas observed in 1930, "The swami is seeking to explain Christianity in the light of the supposedly deeper knowledge of Hinduism. Like Ramakrishna and his followers he is using Hinduism as a basis for the reconciliation of all faiths. Like the Theosophical Society, he regards Hindu lore as the source of the esoteric, or essential, truths that underlie the exoteric, or literal, truths of Christianity."[30] Yogananda's deft, erudite integration of Christian teaching into a larger Hindu worldview was vital to his appeal to Americans who were more charitable toward his views than Thomas. For many American seekers, Yogananda's Hinduism fulfilled Christian aspirations in a way that American Christianity never could.

Yogananda was not the first missionary of universal Hinduism, as Thomas noted, but he was more successful than his predecessors. None of the prior Indian spiritual teachers established a movement of comparable size or duration. Swami Vivekananda, who came to the United States in 1893 to attend the World's Parliament of Religions held in conjunction with the World Columbian Exposition in Chicago, was the most influential forerunner of Yogananda, and he is sometimes characterized as an evangelist for Hinduism and yoga. But Yogananda, who consciously emulated Vivekananda, played a much more significant role in reshaping the American cultural and religious landscape. In part this is because Vivekananda only belatedly adopted the role of evangelist. He originally came to the United States seeking donations for social welfare projects in India and gradually adopted the role of religious teacher only after he recognized his audiences' interest in yoga and Indian philosophy. This lack of intentional, strategic evangelizing blunted his impact. Also, Vivekananda spent much less time in the United States than Yogananda; he toured the nation for three years after the World's Parliament and then paid a short second visit in 1899 just before his premature death at age thirty-nine. Finally, the modest infrastructure Vivekananda left behind through the Vedanta Society was not robust enough to survive his death. His successors were often less gregarious and more ambivalent about outreach than Vivekananda. A few Vedanta centers closed, while others limped along in the early decades of the twentieth century. Only after World War II did the Vedanta Society enjoy vibrancy in the United States. In contrast, Yogananda arrived in the United States poised to evangelize American audiences. His decades of ministry in the United States were interrupted only once, by an eighteen-month return journey to India. His long-term American presence significantly aided his reputation, his ministry's reach, and his financial resources.

Religious Entrepreneurialism in a Challenging Marketplace

The second feature of the global religious landscape Yogananda illuminates is the nature of religious entrepreneurialism. Several scholars of contemporary yoga have explored its connections with capitalist markets, and historians of religion have long done the same with American Christianity.[31] But in both cases, the religious tradition being studied was largely embraced by the dominant culture. Yogananda's entry into the American religious marketplace with a non-Christian product in the early twentieth century deepens our understanding of the relation between religion and the marketplace. Three years before Yogananda arrived, the United States passed the Immigration Act of 1917, which restricted many categories of immigrants, including most Asians. In a nation that was often hostile to Indians and Hinduism, his creativity was essential in finding an audience.[32] Popular stereotypes portrayed Hindus as charlatans and thieves. Swamis in particular were seen as lechers who used mind control to dupe followers. Shortly after his U.S. arrival, the Supreme Court, reflecting a trend toward xenophobia and isolationism, ruled that Indian immigrants were ineligible for citizenship.

In this setting, Yogananda became, quite literally, a religious entrepreneur. As an independent teacher, he was compelled to invent a variety of products to keep his ministry financially viable. He created a large-scale correspondence course to teach yoga, an innovation that transformed the nature of guru-discipleship instruction. Some scholarly declension narratives lament the supposed corruption of early pristine yoga through twenty-first-century commercialization, but Yogananda's example reveals how yoga entered American culture precisely as a commercial product.[33]

Yogananda's success depended on a number of key attributes. He understood the double-edged nature of Americans' Orientalist fascination with India and exploited it adroitly. He mastered advertising and appeals to popular culture. An authoritative presenter and genial conversationalist, he alternated between deep esoteric teachings and folksy anecdotes. His warm personality, sense of humor, and winning performance style aided his ministry. Embodying charisma in both the technical and popular senses, this creative entrepreneurial religious figure seemed made for the modern American age of consumption. Yogananda had a solid infrastructure in place by the time of his death—a radio program, a dozen books, a magazine, and SRF centers throughout the country—that ensured his ministry's continuity after his passing.

Hinduism in the Context of Christian America, Jesus in the Context of Yoga

Yogananda's ministry also reveal how missionary Hinduism's success hinged on a deep understanding of Christian belief and practice. Situating Yogananda merely in the small stream of American metaphysical tradition, as such scholars as Mark Singleton, Elizabeth De Michalis, and Catherine Albanese have done, is insufficient.[34] Yogananda can be properly understood only in the larger context of American Christianity. The scope of his ambitions far exceeded the small target audience of Theosophists and New Thought practitioners he effortlessly drew. Seeking to win over large numbers of Americans, he routinely appealed to the Christian mainstream. Centuries of European imperialism and Christian missionary work made Jesus the world's best-known religious figure. Yogananda was a young man when he encountered Jesus, and he was quickly drawn to him. In a strategic sense, comparing his own instruction to Jesus's made good evangelistic sense in a predominantly Christian culture. In personal terms, comparing himself to Jesus resonated deeply and provided a powerful sense of self-understanding that impelled his mission.

A careful examination of Yogananda's engagement with Christianity reveals his particular inclusivist techniques. He occasionally called his Los Angeles headquarters, a former resort hotel, "the only Hindu American Temple."[35] But he often went out of his way to emphasize the churchlike features of his organization, whose formal (if little used) title after 1935 was Self-Realization Fellowship *Church*. Before that, he experimented with different names, including "Christian Yogoda" and "Yogoda Fellowship of Religions," in reference to the name of his yoga brand. Local centers held weekly services on Sunday morning, the traditional day for Christian worship. Most sites offered Sunday school and hosted annual Christmas and Easter services.

If SRF centers imitated Christian churches, the instruction Yogananda provided echoed Christian themes. He always offered special season-themed talks about the birth of the Christ Child and the Resurrection, which were typically published in his magazine. And he routinely quoted the Bible and held up Jesus as an exemplary moral teacher. Using theological discourse familiar especially to American Protestants, he presented yoga as *the* essential practical tool that led to intimate communion with God. "Yogananda talked about Jesus," SRF president Brother Chidananda once explained, "as being a perfected exemplar of what the teachings of yoga were all about, which means one thing—union with God."[36]

But Yogananda's teaching was less an integration of the two religions than a reinterpretation of Christianity in light of Hinduism. As Chidananda suggests, Yogananda regularly explained how the New Testament, properly understood, spoke about yoga and revealed Jesus as the consummate yogi. He often expounded on the Bible as the partial revelation of a universal Indian *dharma* that elucidated and fulfilled all other religions. And in several ways, most notably in his famed *Autobiography*, he implicitly portrayed himself as a Christ figure. His Hinduism with a Christian "accent" selectively adopted loanwords from American Christianity while remaining largely an Indian language.[37]

Yogananda understood the broad context of American Christianity as Protestant. He had little interest in Catholicism, perhaps because it did not enjoy the cultural hegemony Protestantism did. And he was a frequent critic of conservative American evangelicalism and fundamentalism for what he perceived as theological stridency on such issues as the exclusivity of Jesus, the centrality of sin, and the reality of hell, which he thought unworthy of a loving divine Father. But paradoxically, while disagreeing with fundamentalists in substance, he often imitated their style of instruction. He resembled well-known evangelists in his personality-driven populist presentations that mixed entertainment and spiritual content, practical application and arcane doctrine.

Yogananda sought to reach a wide swath of the American public. His message, however, clearly resonated more with some audiences than others. He appealed most strongly to the restless souls in the liberal Christian tradition. Though these seekers are often associated with the baby boom generation and religious sociologists have created a vast literature describing contemporary seekers, some historians have applied this label to earlier eras.[38] Historian Leigh Eric Schmidt sees seekers as emerging around the turn of the twentieth century, just before Yogananda's arrival. Many of the features Schmidt applies to seekers fit Yogananda's followers: they longed for mystical experience or religious feeling, they valued meditation, they prized immanence in humans and nature, they expressed a cosmopolitan appreciation for religious diversity, and they emphasized self-expression.[39] Yogananda's following included Christians primarily from liberal Protestant traditions and those interested in spirituality outside the American religious mainstream — Christian Scientists, Theosophists, and Mormons. They were drawn to the authority of an Indian swami, to his focus on the experience of the divine, and to his integration of body, mind, and spirit in an era when there was deep interest in health and the body.

Religion, Region, and Sacred Space

The fourth way Yogananda deepens our understanding of the global religious landscape relates to the actual landscape. His life story, beginning with his childhood and continuing through his ministry, demonstrates the connectedness of spirituality and place. Visiting sacred Indian sites — Rishikesh in the Himalayas, Benares on the Ganges, Dakshineswar Kali Temple and Kalighat Kali Temple in Calcutta, among others — was central to his spiritual development, while coming of age in Calcutta and attending college nearby placed him in intellectual and spiritual networks that were equally formative. The very viability of an overseas mission as a vocation was a result of growing up in a particular milieu of a globalized Calcutta.

In the United States, not only did his message resonate with some audiences more than others, but it also found an easier foothold in particular regions while stumbling in others. True, any assessment of Yogananda must include the view at the national scale — he was undeniably an *American* religious figure who responded to national dynamics of culture, economy, and religion. But he must also be understood by zooming in the view to the scale of the local region. As a nonwhite purveyor of an unfamiliar religious tradition, he was rebuffed throughout the American South, and he fell flat on his face in Miami. In fact, he never seemed to recognize just how close he came to being lynched there.

More importantly, he began to gain traction in his ministry only after he found the Southern California landscape, with its hospitality to newer forms of spirituality. His experience suggests the importance of early twentieth-century Southern California as a unique spiritual frontier. Though historiographical trends tend to emphasize Southern California's relation to mainstream Protestantism, particularly the link between fundamentalism and the rise of the Religious Right,[40] a second — and in some cases, older — historiographic tradition paints a different portrait of the region as a magnet for religious diversity. Perhaps first articulated by California author Carey McWilliams, this alternative historiography depicts the region as home especially to aberrant religious traditions. Religious scholar Sandra Sizer Frankiel suggests that in the nineteenth century the California climate and landscape lured a disproportionate number of religious seekers, who perceived themselves as distinct from other Americans in their open embrace of nature, rejection of sectarianism, and reticence to build mainstream religious institutions. A distinctive religious climate resulted from this self-selecting migration pattern.[41] If that was a statewide pattern in the nineteenth century, early twentieth-century Southern California represented a stronger distillation of that larger brew. If the white Protestant establishment of Los Angeles found even the pluralism within Christianity "bewildering," historian Michael J. Engh observes, even more disconcerting was the large influx of Jews and the arrival of Asians who practiced Buddhist, Confucian, Taoist, and Shinto traditions.[42] But however grudging the cultural elite's tolerance may have been, it was sufficient to provide a stable foundation for an Indian swami's movement to flourish there in the early twentieth century.

In time, Yogananda transplanted the Hindu tradition of sacred spaces to the United States, establishing the properties his ministry purchased as new holy places. His Mount Washington headquarters in Los Angeles, the nearby Lake Shrine, which eventually housed some of Gandhi's ashes, and an ashram in Encinitas, near San Diego, all became key places for meditation and divine communion. In India, the same was true of the properties associated with his childhood and ministry there. For devoted followers around the world, these locations all became sites of pilgrimage. After his 1952 *mahasamādhi*, the Biltmore Hotel, where he died, and Forest Lawn, where he was buried, were added to the list.

A Divine Guru Reenchants the Modern World

The fifth and final point relates to the "reenchantment" that Yogananda effectively created through his instruction and his claims to divine authority. More than a century ago, the eminent German sociologist Max Weber argued that rational, bureaucratic, mechanized modernity had driven transcendence from the West, leaving it disenchanted. (Indulging in Orientalist prejudice, he contrasted this situation with Asia, where he thought spirits, idolatrous rituals, and magic continued to flourish).[43] Weber's argument was refined in subsequent decades, perhaps most compellingly by religious sociologist Peter Berger, who envisioned the inevitable collapse of a "sacred canopy" under the weight of modern, industrial life.[44] Although this argument in its extreme form has been largely repudiated — in part because Berger himself retracted elements of it — some recent scholars continue to assert it passionately.[45] The popularity of Yogananda's ministry and legacy certainly adds to the mounting evidence that science, technology, and the growing recognition of religious pluralism did not quash Americans' yearning for transcendence in the twentieth century. More importantly, modern audiences found his instruction attractive precisely because he seamlessly integrated scientific, positivistic, and pragmatic concerns with a robust affirmation of transcendence that allowed space for the miraculous.

One of the most striking features of Yogananda's transcendent worldview was his claim — and his disciples' acceptance — of divine status. Though a familiar pattern among Indian gurus, this declaration placed him within a very small group of American religious leaders. In India, a teacher's divine status is frequently anchored in hagiographic traditions that develop over decades or centuries. In contrast, Yogananda actively created his own hagiographical tradition, in large part through his autobiography, in which he hinted obliquely at his divine yogic powers. His reticence to claim divine status directly reflected his understanding of the humility a teacher was expected to display. It also stemmed from his ability to read his audience. He recognized that many Americans reared within a broadly Christian understanding of transcendent deity would find such claims difficult to embrace directly. In the wake of the counterculture, many Americans expressed concern with so-called cults led by gurus — whether homegrown, Indian, or from elsewhere — who claimed extraordinary authority, but Yogananda mostly escaped such controversies during his lifetime.

At least since Weber, scholars of religious movements have been interested in the transfer of power from a charismatic leader to a successor, as his or her death often spells doom for a new movement. The dynamics become more complex when the organization's founder has divine status. How could any successor hope to measure up? Self-Realization Fellowship successfully weathered the loss of Yogananda in 1952 in large part due to the way he deployed his divine claims to ensure the organization's resilience. His own proclamations helped devotees understand that no human need ever step into his shoes: his teachings and his continued postmortem presence would provide the necessary guidance. Yogananda's continued authority has relativized the significance of every SRF leader who has succeeded him. His proactive crafting of his legacy suggests one creative variant on Weber's model of the institutionalization of charismatic authority and the challenge of succession.

Outside of SRF, Yogananda's assertions of status and identity provided a template for his disciples who established their own independent communities during the counterculture era, gurus who claimed the same kind of authority and expected the same type of obedience. Thus, Yogananda does not simply provide insight into modern Hindu community formation in the United States. Because the imprint of his personal authority and unique views shaped his disciples in distinctive ways, he also provides a window into the development patterns of new religious movements.

RECAPTURING YOGANANDA'S IMPORTANCE

Yogananda's importance as a twentieth-century American religious figure makes his virtual neglect in the scholarly literature paradoxical. A few years ago, anthropologist Sarah Strauss observed that while dozens of yoga teachers and their organizations from the last century deserve their own "book-length treatments," one of the two figures "most conspicuous in their absence" was Yogananda and the Self-Realization Fellowship.[46] Mark Singleton, author of *Yoga Body*, acknowledges that Yogananda "inspire[d] several generations of Western spiritual seekers."[47] Professor of comparative religion David Gordon White argues that, along with a handful of other gurus, it is "the life and teachings of Yogananda that have had the greatest impact on modern-day conceptions of yoga as a marriage between the physical and the spiritual, the human and the superhuman."[48] Yet, despite this importance, few scholars—including Singleton and White—have studied Yogananda at length. In her influential

History of Modern Yoga, Elizabeth De Michelis reduces him to part of one sentence.[49] And in his discussion of "the most important modern gurus" in his book on Hinduism, David Smith ignores Yogananda altogether.[50]

Yogananda has appeared in some trade press books. Most recently, popular yoga author Philip Goldberg has offered a full-length biography in *The Life of Yogananda*. Goldberg provides a detailed chronology of Yogananda's life and tackles a number of controversies in his ministry, though the tone remains the same as his earlier *American Veda*, where he devotes a largely respectful chapter to Yogananda. In that earlier work, he highlights Yogananda's engaging personality and speaking style, the adaptations he made to appeal to an American audience, most notably his "enthusiastic embrace of Jesus," and devotees' attraction to being "in the presence of a genuine holy man."[51] Yogananda has typically made only cameo appearances in other trade press books. In *Transcendent in America*, an investigation of "Hindu-Inspired Meditation Movements," Lola Williamson gives due attention to SRF. But because her interest is more contemporary than historical, she deals with Yogananda himself fairly briefly and offers little in the way of broader context. In a remarkable oversight, Stefanie Syman, who claims to tell "the story of yoga in America" in her *Subtle Body*, devotes only a few terse, somewhat flippant pages to Yogananda and his movement.[52]

Until recently, the only sustained scholarly attention Yogananda received in the past two decades was through a handful of dissertations in which he figured merely as one of several figures. Polly Trout's 1998 "Hindu Gurus, American Disciples, and the Search for Modern Religion, 1900–1950," places Yogananda in the spotlight, but he has to share it with two other twentieth-century Hindu figures, Theosophical "World Teacher" Jiddhu Krishnamurti and Vedanta leader Swami Paramananda.[53] Theodore Anderson's 2008 "Re-imagining Religion: The Grounding of Spiritual Politics and Practice in Modern America, 1890–1940," likewise places Yogananda in the company of other figures, viewing him as one of five individuals who reinvented spirituality in early twentieth-century America.[54]

Anya Foxen's *Biography of a Yogi: Paramahansa Yogananda and the Origins of Modern Yoga* is the major exception to this pattern. As her title suggests, Foxen is interested in the emergence of contemporary yoga, particularly in the image of yogis in the West as purveyors of extraordinary powers, and Yogananda functions as a detailed case study. Foxen emphasizes from the outset that her book is "not actually a biography" but a study of his persona, largely as portrayed in the *Autobiography*.[55] *Biography of a Yogi* shares a few common themes with the present work: the Indian roots of Yogananda's teaching, his largely ignored contribution to the development of Western yoga, the centrality of the *Autobiography* to his reputation, and attention to the crafting of his persona in a culture that was often suspicious of yogis.

Despite some complementary perspectives, the two books differ significantly in emphasis. In *Finding God through Yoga,* I explore Yogananda's biography in substantial detail, in part because it seems to me that the best way to understand his persona creation is by teasing out the ways his life story diverged from the public image he so carefully cultivated. More importantly, although I portray Yogananda as a Kriya Yoga instructor, I see that as but one role he played. I emphasize his broader identity as a Hindu religious teacher who sought to connect disciples to God in various ways. The *Autobiography* is undoubtedly his most famous work, but Yogananda was a prolific author and poet, an entrepreneur who sold yoga lessons by correspondence, and a magazine editor. His labor on behalf of *East-West* magazine indicates both his leadership in the global interfaith movement and the deep and abiding interest in Jesus and Christianity that was a central feature of his identity. His commentary on the New Testament, more than a decade of work, easily rivals the *Autobiography* in scale and ambition. Given Yogananda's deep interest in Jesus, I place him in the broad context of American Christian culture. Yogananda was also the founder of a significant religious organization. And because that global organization continues to serve as custodian of his legacy, which includes maintaining his persona, any discussion of his significance should include investigation of this organization and its rivals.

Though recent scholarly work has begun to rectify the situation, Yogananda has long suffered neglect relative to his significance. There are two chief reasons for this state of affairs, one evidentiary and the other historiographical, both necessary to understand before proceeding. First, access to sources offers a genuine challenge to Yogananda scholars. Like many organizations, Self-Realization Fellowship takes great care to guard the reputation and legacy of its founder. It does occasionally cooperate in limited ways with those who request the use of archival materials.[56] More typical is the situation Polly Trout experienced a generation ago, when she noted that SRF's "historical archives are not open to the public."[57] My requests for access were declined due to SRF's lack of a research library and, after further inquiry, to the organization's many spiritual and humanitarian priorities, which make it impossible to help the scholars who request research assistance and archival access.[58]

Still, abundant Yogananda materials are available, and in more recent years, thanks in part to the Internet, the accessibility of some sources has increased significantly. *Finding God through Yoga* makes use of the extensive sources now available. Though few copies of early issues of Yogananda's magazine have made their way into libraries, I had access to the vast majority of issues from 1925 through 1960 for this project, which proved invaluable for understanding his views. Not only was he responsible for overall content and tone of the nearly two hundred issues that ran during his lifetime, but he also contributed more than eight hundred articles. Yogananda's yoga course was the instructional heart of his ministry. Early editions of the lessons are now available and provide essential insight into his teachings. Though SRF's editions remain private and secret, copies can be accessed in various ways and reveal changes that have been made over the years. And apart from the *Autobiography,* Yogananda wrote a number of other works that provide valuable understanding. Nearly one thousand newspaper advertisements and articles about Yogananda are extant. More than twenty books, memoirs, and reminiscences by friends and disciples—published both by SRF and independently, some quite recently—provide glimpses of the private Yogananda. Several of these texts reprint letters from the Master, and more than two hundred are extant. Scouring various online sources yielded additional letters, legal documents, videos, and other materials. Together, this substantial and varied evidence allows for a robust portrait of this important religious figure.

The other reason for Yogananda's scholarly neglect is historiographical. He has fallen between two scholarly stools, not really resting comfortably on either. As a teacher and practitioner of yoga, he would seem to belong in the burgeoning scholarship on yoga. But, as indicated above, few yoga scholars except for Foxen have seated him there. His affection for Jesus and the New Testament makes him an awkward fit for many yoga scholars, though this need not be the case, since his interest in Jesus and Christianity puts him in good company with many other contemporary yoga teachers and Hindu intellectuals.[59]

Also, he downplayed the *āsanas,* or postures, that have become a central feature—indeed, often the defining element—of most forms of contemporary yoga.[60] But his dislike for *āsanas* has sometimes been exaggerated. In *The Subtle Body,* for example, Syman overstates the case when she claims that Yogananda "publicly disdained" *haṭha yoga* and cites as evidence a footnote from the *Autobiography.* In fact, issues of his magazine near the end of his life include long articles by SRF's Reverend C. Bernard that provided detailed instruction on how to perform difficult *āsanas* (with accompanying photos) and discussed the health benefits of each position.[61] In the footnote Syman cites, Yogananda actually explained that *haṭha yoga,* "a specialized branch of bodily postures and techniques for health and longevity," was "useful and provides spectacular physical results." His only critique was that it was "little used by yogis bent on spiritual liberation." Though, as I will demonstrate, Yogananda never ignored health and well-being, he did think that the yoga practices that deserved most attention were those that led to God-realization.

Most importantly, the teleological interest within most yoga scholarship on the emergence of contemporary secular yoga, which focuses on postures, health, and mental well-being, has led to the neglect of individuals who do not fit that pattern. David Gordon White acknowledges that any element of yoga that falls outside the "modern-day sensus communis" of yoga scholarship, such as a focus on the supernatural, tends to be ignored.[62] Though Elizabeth De Michelis's influential taxonomy of yoga provides a place for "denominational movements," most scholars of modern yoga—including De Michelis herself—largely ignore yoga's religious dimensions. The influential work of De Michelis, Singleton, sociocultural anthropologist Joseph S. Alter, and others has concentrated on modern postural yoga, charting a transformation that another scholar, Sarah Strauss, describes in her own monograph as moving from "a regional, male-oriented religious activity to a globalized and *largely secular* phenomenon."[63] Yoga historian Andrea Jain offers a nuanced definition, acknowledging that yoga has always embraced varied practices and divergent aims, both physical and spiritual. Rather than treating postural yoga as the culmination of a secularizing trajectory, she views it as a "body of religious practice" with sacred behaviors, an ontology, and a set of values, all of which are maintained by ritual and story.[64] But many of the postural yoga practitioners engaged in the kinds of practices Jain has defined as religious would be quite uncomfortable with Yogananda's highly normative instruction on ontology, cosmology, supernatural achievements, and communion with the divine. If Yogananda does not fit easily into Jain's capacious definition of religious yoga, he is all the more out of place in the secular framework offered by most postural yoga scholars. But although Yogananda's emphasis on religious themes runs counter to the dominant scholarly trajectory, he was indisputably a teacher of yoga—and one of the most popular in the United States before the 1960s.

There is a second scholarly stool where Yogananda has failed to find the seat he deserves. Although many scholars have explored Hindu gurus as religious figures, both in India and in the United States, the homegrown gurus they profile typically postdate Yogananda. With the notable exception of Vivekananda, scholars tend to concentrate on individuals who established their own American ministries only in the past few decades.[65] This focus on the recent past stems in part from scholarly interest in baby boomers' attraction to Asian traditions and in the formation of diaspora Indian communities who transported their own traditions to the United States. With a few exceptions, the placement of Hindu leaders in the very recent past conforms to the dominant narrative arc of American religious history in which a pluralism broad enough to encompass Asian traditions is seen as largely a post-1965 phenomenon.[66] But the 1965 Hart-Celler Act's immigration liberalization did not yield a critical demographic mass of religious diversity, as some scholars assume.[67] The law did contribute modestly to the growth of non-Christian religions, but its primary effect was to diversify the Christian population, as the percentage of Asian and Latino Christians increased relative to Christians of European descent.[68] The Hart-Celler Act really functions as a *symbolic* watershed of Americans' growing *awareness* of other faiths, rather than as a marker of religious diversity per se.

Of course, many scholars recognize that Hindu traditions — and the interest of some white Americans in those traditions — have a much longer trajectory. In the wake of the counterculture era, scholars like Harold French and Carl Jackson explored the influence of Hindu religion and philosophy on early twentieth-century America. More recently, Catherine Albanese's masterly *Republic of Mind and Spirit* has provided a comprehensive survey of American metaphysical traditions, including influences from India and elsewhere in Asia.

These authors, however, tend to consider Hindu organizations either as independent stand-alone movements, like French and Jackson, or in the context of New Thought, like Albanese. Like the yoga scholars discussed above, Albanese frames her brief treatment of Yogananda by largely ignoring the role of Christianity, in effect walling off Hinduism and yoga from the nation's dominant religion. Yogananda, whose deep knowledge of Jesus and the New Testament is typical of many educated Indians of his generation, illustrates why the growth of modern Hinduism can be properly understood only in the context of Christianity.

THE PLAN OF THIS BOOK

Finding God through Yoga explores the life and ministry of Paramahansa Yogananda in five chapters that follow the chronology of his life, addressing key themes as they emerge. Chapter 1, "The Making of a Modern Religious Seeker: From Mukunda Lal Ghosh to Swami Yogananda, 1893–1920," places Yogananda's spiritual development in the context of Indian modernity, with rapid travel, exposure to diverse traditions, and awareness of the outside world — particularly the United States and the larger West. The chapter examines his childhood, adolescence, and young adulthood, focusing on the spiritual journey that culminated in his decision to become a swami under the leadership of a guru. His connection to modernity deepened with his college education and adoption of modern Hinduism, a framework that severed religious belief from its historic embeddedness in land, caste, life stage, and gender. This universalizing of Hinduism paved the way for Yogananda's American ministry as a Hindu missionary.

Chapter 2, "The Founding of a Home for Scientific Religion: Swami Yogananda and Southern California's Spiritual Frontier, 1920–1925," traces Yogananda's early years in the United States. The chapter begins by examining the conference that brought him to the United States and the presentation he gave there on "the Science of Religion." It places both in the context of an intramural Protestant debate that offered competing answers to the epistemological challenges modernity raised for the universalistic claims of Christianity. For the first few years after the conference, Yogananda struggled to establish a successful ministry. A cross-country road trip in 1924 took him to Los Angeles, which quickly became his national headquarters. This chapter explores the role Southern California played in fostering Yogananda's ministry at a time when many Americans were suspicious of so-called Orientals, their cultures, and their religions. The nation's new spiritual frontier, the Los Angeles region was an ideal space for a new religious movement, a relatively tolerant center that had already fostered Hindu movements by the time Yogananda arrived.

The third chapter, "The Creation of a Yogi Guru Persona: Marketing Swami Yogananda and His Yoga Instruction, 1925–1935," evaluates Yogananda's ministry through the lens of modern consumer religion, mass marketing, and religious branding. The early portion investigates the religious products he touted, most centrally his systematic, practical method for God-realization through yoga—in the innovative form of a correspondence course. Yogananda's instruction inculcated a larger Hindu worldview, not just a set of meditative techniques. His *East-West* magazine was a promotional tool designed to highlight his brand's distinctiveness. The chapter also explores the way the yogi, like evangelical preachers of the time, promoted his message to a modern American audience saturated with savvy advertising and modern products. The final section considers the hazards of the religious market, including negative press attention and several lawsuits that threatened his brand image as well as his solvency just as the Depression arrived.

"The Apotheosis of a Global Guru: Paramahansa Yogananda and His Autobiography, 1933–1946," the fourth chapter, explores Yogananda's growing status as a global spiritual authority and a divine figure. The chapter begins by placing Yogananda in the context of religious internationalism, a subset of interwar cultural internationalism driven by concerns for world peace.

It details his use of *East-West* as a vehicle for a cosmopolitan spiritual vision. An extravagant worldwide journey in 1935–36 from California to England, the Continent, the Middle East, and ultimately to his home city of Calcutta solidified his reputation as a "global guru." The chapter also explores his lengthy exegesis of two sacred texts. He provided extensive exegesis of the *Bhagavad Gītā* in the pages of *East-West,* presenting it as an allegory for personal struggle against evil temptations. In another long-running series in his magazine, he interpreted the New Testament gospel narratives, transforming the story of Jesus and his teachings into a revelation of yogic truth that hinted at Yogananda's own divine identity. But it was the 1946 *Autobiography of a Yogi* that firmly established Yogananda's reputation as a guru to the world. An analysis of this text's structural features reveals it to be a new scripture, designed to inculcate belief in the spiritual world Yogananda evoked and in the divine status of the yogi who wrote it.

Chapter 5, "The Death of an Immortal Guru: Charisma, Succession, and Paramahansa Yogananda's Legacy, 1946–1952," explores discipleship and conversion in Self-Realization Fellowship, Yogananda's dramatic death, and the transfer of authority that transpired afterward. The chapter profiles twenty Yogananda disciples, employing a model of conversion to offer insight into common patterns among those who chose to follow Yogananda and the challenges of spiritual apprenticeship they faced as Americans raised in an individualistic cultural ethos. The circumstances surrounding Yogananda's death and his followers' efforts to cope with the tragedy are considered next. Yogananda's death produced a crisis in leadership. Max Weber's model of the routinization of charisma, modified by subsequent scholars, offers insight into the common challenge faced by organizations led by charismatic individuals, particularly after their death. Yogananda spiritualized his own leadership by indicating that his writings were to become the "guru" after his departure, but this did not fully solve the problem of human leadership. After the short tenure of one leader, long-term female disciple Faye Wright was appointed president. Her half-century tenure at SRF stabilized the organization and routinized its publications by and about Yogananda.

A century after Yogananda came to the United States with the message of Kriya Yoga and three quarters of a century after *Autobiography of a Yogi* was released, yoga has become ubiquitous and Hindu beliefs have become an integral part of the spiritual landscape. Yogananda played a key role in this transformation. During his lifetime, he converted thousands of Americans. Since his death in 1952, he has influenced countless others around the world through SRF and independent organizations that trace their lineage to him, as well through *Autobiography of a Yogi* and his other teachings. The Father of Yoga in the West nurtured numerous religious offspring. Not simply a wise teacher, he came to be revered and worshipped—overwhelmingly by non-Indian Americans—as the very incarnation of deity. Yogananda's story is thus indispensable to understanding the emergence of contemporary yoga, modern American Hinduism, and modern global religion.

ONE

The Making of a Modern Religious Seeker

From Mukunda Lal Ghosh to Swami Yogananda, 1893–1920

Mukunda Lal Ghosh was deeply unhappy. The year was 1909, and the sixteen-year-old Bengali had been living in India's most sacred city of Benares for several months, seeking spiritual enlightenment. His stay at the Bharat Dharma Mahamandal ashram had been frustrating and disappointing. He did not get along with the other students and had not experienced the spiritual breakthrough he had been hoping for. But that was about to change. One morning, he was sent to the market to help with the community's grocery purchases. There he met Sri Yukteswar, the man who would become his guru and transform his life. Decades later Mukunda vividly recounted the marketplace meeting, presenting it as a miraculous encounter. Before leaving for the market, Mukunda received a heavenly proclamation delivered in King James English. "'Thy Master cometh today!' A divine womanly voice came from everywhere and nowhere." Near the end of the shopping trip, the prophecy was fulfilled:

> A Christlike man in the ocher robes of a swami stood motionless at the end of a lane. Instantly and anciently familiar he seemed; . . .
>
> Retracing my steps as though wing-shod, I reached the narrow lane. My quick glance revealed the quiet figure, steadily gazing in my direction. A few eager steps and I was at his feet.
>
> "Gurudeva!" The divine face was the one I had seen in a thousand visions. These halcyon eyes, in a leonine head with pointed beard and flowing locks, had often peered through the gloom of my nocturnal reveries, holding a promise I had not fully understood.
>
> "O my own, you have come to me!" My guru uttered the words again and again in Bengali, his voice tremulous with joy. "How many years I have waited for you!"[1]

The idealized nature of this retrospective account is evident. Yukteswar's effusive affection is sharply at odds with the stern taskmaster Mukunda consistently describes elsewhere. And the chance meeting four hundred miles from Mukunda's Calcutta home includes remarkable coincidences that suggest divine orchestration. Mukunda's own parents had been trained by Yukteswar's master, Lahiri Mahasaya, and Yukteswar's ashram just happened to be in Serampore, near Mukunda's family home in Calcutta.

There is, however, a more prosaic explanation of this meeting. Mukunda's father and older brother—his mother was dead—had expressed concern about Mukunda's excessive religious fervor to an uncle in Serampore. The uncle, a devotee of Yukteswar, suggested writing separately to Yukteswar and Mukunda, encouraging the two to meet, since they were both in Benares at the time.[2] It was precisely because Yukteswar lived near Calcutta much of the year that Mukunda's father and brother found this solution attractive. When Mukunda agreed to abandon the Bharat Dharma Mahamandal ashram and accompany Yukteswar home to Serampore, his family breathed a sigh of relief. The dreamer would be close enough to home for them keep an eye on him until he settled down to pursue a responsible career.

This anecdote hints at several important features of Mukunda's early life. He was a restless spiritual seeker, willing to travel hundreds of miles from home in search of truth. His quest led to frequent clashes with his family. Yogananda's father, Bhagabati Charan Ghosh, expected his son to follow in his successful footsteps, using modern India's civil service to carve out a comfortable middle-class life. A respectable spirituality, like Bhagabati's own, might aid that path, but extreme fervor bordering on recklessness would destroy his chances. Whether metaphysically orchestrated or arranged by his family, the meeting that brought Mukunda and Yukteswar together forever changed Mukunda's life. He became Yukteswar's disciple and eventually took his vows to become Swami Yogananda, a man who would ultimately interpret his life mission as being a Hindu evangelist to the United States.

The disparities between the account in the *Autobiography* and the less supernatural version found in other sources suggests Mukunda's penchant for spiritualized retellings of past events—and the challenges of using such sources to reconstruct historical events. Because the success of Yogananda's ministry depended in large measure on the persona he created, it is instructive to tease apart his biography and its hagiography to fully appreciate his labors of self-invention. It is also the best way to make sense of the context that gave rise to his successful outreach to Americans. Like many modern gurus, Yogananda created an aura of transcendence by mystifying the mundane events of his past, and his disciples have often emulated this practice.[3] A 2003 film about Yogananda's early years in the United States, produced by the organization he founded, Self-Realization Fellowship, plays on a well-worn trope about the spiritually adept but technologically backward guru overwhelmed by his first encounter with an American city: "He traveled via the novel Boston subway under a strange metropolis. Unfamiliar with Western customs, and away from the simple living in his guru's ashrams, the cautious visitor was entertained by many new sights," which apparently included tall buildings, busy streets, and electric streetcars. This anecdote depicts Yogananda as charmingly innocent and naive, adrift in the big city. And it is pure fantasy. Nothing would have been more familiar to the English-speaking son of a railroad bureaucrat who grew up in busy Calcutta—a city more populous than Boston—where electric streetcars had been introduced a decade before his birth.[4]

Accounts like this are inspired by Yogananda's own frequent dichotomy between a timeless, premodern, spiritual East and a soulless, modern, technological West. But such portrayals fundamentally misrepresent the context of his childhood by unwittingly recapitulating British Orientalist stereotypes about India. Orientalists began imagining India as part of a mystical, spiritual, timeless, and effeminate East in the late eighteenth century, a construct they routinely contrasted, explicitly or implicitly, with a modern West. This representation remains one of the most pervasive and pernicious legacies of the colonial encounter, often repeated in Western historiography.[5] For several decades, scholars of India have labored to disentangle the link between India and timeless tradition on one hand, and the West and modernity on the other. Members of the Bengali middle class, like the Ghosh family, had an "acute awareness," architectural historian Swati Chattopadhyay notes, "that they were living in a 'modern' age; they were becoming 'modern.'"[6]

But even as India took a distinctive path to modernity, it did so under the weight of British colonialism. Scholars of India have often felt caught between acknowledging the severity of colonial oppression, and thus risking diminishing Indian agency, or affirming Indian agency, and thereby potentially downplaying colonial domination. As Joseph S. Alter puts it, "Scholarship on colonial and postcolonial India has focused on the critical problem of identity, control over identity, and the articulation of a national identity which is neither anachronistically 'traditional' in an Orientalist sense nor derivatively Western—and thereby modern only by proxy—on account of colonialism and the colonial legacy."[7] The way forward, religious historian Richard King suggests, is by "dissolving the easy polarization of the two options" and instead viewing power relations as complex, multidimensional, and fluid, while still recognizing the very real disparities in power between colonizer and colonized.[8]

Yogananda's childhood and later ministry can be properly understood only in this complex matrix of late colonial Indian modernity that shaped his identity in distinctive ways. Bhagabati's secure civil service job freed Mukunda to explore his dream of spiritual enlightenment without pressure to contribute to his family's daily survival. Educational institutions (particularly higher education) deepened his knowledge considerably, while rapid modern rail transportation offered the physical mobility to travel widely in search of spiritual truth. And exposure to the dynamics of industrial capitalism, globalization, and science shaped Yogananda's worldview, enabling him to articulate a spirituality attuned to modern conditions.[9] At the same time, he developed a form of religious nationalism in response to the British colonial presence and its universalistic Christian traditions. Instructed by his guru, Swami Yukteswar, he immersed himself in the study of Sanskrit texts. He was also shaped by the intellectual milieu of the Bengali Renaissance, whose intellectuals reconsidered traditional Indian beliefs in light of evangelical Christian and utilitarian critiques to articulate an eternal moral, spiritual, devotional Hinduism that was both fundamentally Indian and universal.[10]

Yogananda assumed the identity of a modern yogi, rooted in ancient Sanskrit texts but also deeply conversant with Christianity, the modern world's most widespread religion. Learning about the New Testament as a young man, Yogananda eventually began subsumed Christian teachings within his own universalistic vision of spiritual transcendence. Choosing the unusual path of becoming an evangelist to the United States, Yogananda offered modern Hinduism to the decadent West. His message centered on yoga meditation as a practical tool for communing with God, situated within a larger body of Indian religious and philosophical teachings, articulated in modern categories of thought, and correlated with their ultimately inferior Western counterparts.

This chapter tells the story of the emergence of this yogi evangelist in four parts. It begins by placing Mukunda's upbringing in the context of Indian modernity, including the importance of his father's career in the British rail bureaucracy. The next part examines his adolescence through young adulthood, focusing on his spiritual pilgrimage, which culminated in his decision to become a swami under the leadership of Sri Yukteswar. The third deals with his education, both his training under Yukteswar and his reluctant completion of a college education. The final section considers how Mukunda, now Swami Yogananda, branched out on his own, engaging in activities that would eventually lead to his decision to come to the United States.

In attempting to reconstruct Yogananda's early life, the scholar is immediately confronted by the issue of sources. The obvious starting point might seem to be Yogananda's famous *Autobiography of a Yogi*, originally published in 1946. But this source is problematic for several reasons. Yogananda's interest in spiritual development — and frequent digressions and supernatural events — often led him to give short shrift to mundane chronological information. To take just one example, in an early chapter Yogananda tersely explains that the "family was now living in Calcutta, where Father had been permanently transferred." He provides no date or clear reason for the move, and he completely leaves out the family's sojourn in distant Chittagong that preceded the move to Calcutta.[11]

I draw on three sources beyond the *Autobiography*.[12] The first is a systematic 1980 account of Yogananda's life written by his younger brother, Sananda Lal Ghosh, who lived in India his entire life.[13] This account has problems of its own. Some of Sananda's anecdotes are suspect, in that he is always present when important events transpire in Yogananda's life, even though the *Autobiography* rarely mentions him. It seems unlikely that a sibling five years younger than Mukunda accompanied him everywhere he went. Also, Sananda's account shows clear awareness of the *Autobiography*, published more than three decades earlier. Ghosh's work is also a SRF-sanctioned text prone to hagiography. This comment from chapter 2 illustrates the book's tenor: "Those present at the time of Mejda's birth said Mother was having severe labor pains. She fervently cried out to Lahiri Mahasaya [her personal guru]. Suddenly a celestial light filled the room, and from the concentrated rays in the center emerged the form of Lahiri Mahasaya. Mother's pain vanished instantly. The divine light continued to illumine the room till Mejda was born."[14] Still, Sananda's embellishments do not challenge the basic veracity of the key events he describes with much more detail and precision than Yogananda himself. And it is possible that he was present during all of the events he describes. Even if not, he may still accurately recount incidents he heard secondhand from siblings or Mukunda's friends. Despite SRF's undoubtedly careful vetting of this account of their founder, discrepancies in detail between Sananda's and Yogananda's accounts remain, suggesting that Sananda penned an independent account. His occasional willingness to describe situations that paint Mukunda in a somewhat unattractive light confirms this text's usefulness as a source.

The next source is a recollection by Swami Satyananda Giri, a childhood friend of Mukunda from the time the Ghosh family moved to Calcutta.[15] Sananda confirms the close relationship between his brother and Satyananda (born Manomohan Mazumdar), including details about how and when the two met. Satyananda, who like Mukunda became a disciple of Sri Yukteswar, remained in India throughout his life. Late in life, he wrote an account of his childhood friend and Yukteswar's most famous disciple. Satyananda clearly had great respect for his childhood friend and reported a number of supernatural events the two experienced. Still, he also offered candid critical assessments and commented that "being in his company during childhood, adolescence, youth, and more advanced years, I have seen him actually as a human being. When I saw the usual weaknesses natural to human beings in the working world," rather than explaining them away as the "divine play" of a perfectly realized being, "I perceived them just as weaknesses."[16] An implicit jab at the *Autobiography*'s penchant for embellishment, this comment is also Satyananda's own pledge of accuracy.

The final source comes from Sailendra Bejoy Dasgupta, another devotee of Yukteswar, but one who met Yogananda only when he returned to India in 1935. Although Dasgupta had no firsthand experience of Mukunda's childhood, he served as Yogananda's personal secretary during Yogananda's return visit to India and was in his "constant company" for more than a year. The two felt a strong connection, and Yogananda, perhaps feeling nostalgic back in his homeland, recounted many childhood events to Dasgupta.[17]

I err on the side of caution in reconstructing the formative years of Yogananda's life, rarely extrapolating beyond what can be conclusively determined by the sources. But even a cautious approach yields a substantially fleshed out account of Mukunda's family, major events in his life—including key developments in his thinking and spirituality—and the fundamental ways that a turn-of-the-century Indian milieu shaped his development.[18]

MUKUNDA LAL GHOSH AND MODERN INDIA

Mukunda Lal Ghosh was born on January 5, 1893, the fourth of eight children of Gyana Prabha Ghosh, and her husband, Bhagabati Charan Ghosh, a career civil-service railroad employee.[19] Bhagabati's job had brought the family to Gorakhpur, a modest city of sixty-five thousand in northern India bordered by the Himalayas. Gorakhpur's key characteristics foreshadowed major spiritual, political, and nationalistic influences on Ghosh's life. The city was named for Gorakhnath, a famed twelfth-century yogi, and the Gorakhnath Temple drew pilgrims from all over India. Gorakhpur was also important to the British. After the East India Company conquered the city in 1801, it became a regional administrative headquarters and, later, a center for the region's rail system. It was a crucial staging area for Indian rebels in the 1857 Sepoy Rebellion against

The Ghosh family home, 4 Garpar Road, Calcutta, where Mukunda lived when he began his spiritual journey. The home remains in the Ghosh family, and the room where Mukunda meditated as a child has been converted into a shrine in his honor. Self-Realization Fellowship and Yogoda Satsanga Society commissioned a plaque outside indicating that the location was Yogananda's childhood home.

the company, a rebellion whose eventual defeat led to the transfer of India from company rule to direct British control. Indian nationalists came to view the rebellion as the first step in the bid for independence.

Bhagabati's fortunate position as an educated civil servant profoundly shaped Mukunda's development and eventual life course. By the time Mukunda was born, Bhagabati had been an employee of the British colonial government for twenty years. Bhagabati's completion of high school placed him in a select group of Indians.[20] Though he qualified for college admission based on his exam scores, he could not afford the tuition. After a few years spent struggling to find work after high school, Bhagabati had managed to win one of a small number of highly coveted positions working for the imperial authorities. One of the biggest complaints among well-off Indians at the time was the dearth of government jobs available for the glut of college-educated Indians, so Bhagabati's ability to secure government employment without a degree suggests his remarkable skill.[21]

Bhagabati became an assistant accountant for the Public Works Department of the Indian government in 1873 and was posted to Deoghar in Bihar, a province in eastern north India. A year and half later, he was sent to Rangoon, Burma, at that time a remote province of British India. Bhagabati's mother died in Calcutta while he was in Rangoon. He returned for her funeral and, while there, married Gyana. She was a good match for Bhagabati. The daughter of a deputy magistrate from Bengal, her family background in British government employment matched her husband's. The couple returned to Rangoon, and Bhagabati eventually worked there for ten years, serving his time in the distant outpost of the British Raj. While there, Bhagabati passed the government accounting examination, which paved the way for his advancement through the bureaucracy and an eventual return to north India.

For the remainder of his career, Bhagabati would work for various railway agencies, shuffling around the country as he ascended the career ladder. More than a quarter of a million Indians found employment in rail service, but the majority of these jobs involved hard physical labor. Only little more than 6 percent of this workforce dealt with general administration, like Bhagabati.[22] His job required the family to move several more times during Mukunda's early years, often for short periods and to locations scattered across fifteen hundred miles of British India.[23] Unlike the vast majority of the Indian population on the overwhelmingly rural subcontinent, Mukunda grew up in urban settings surrounded by British administrators, modern industrial technology and infrastructure, educational institutions, and links to the larger world.[24]

Railroads, along with steamships and telegraphs, were part of the technological apparatus that enabled a tiny number of British officials to control a subcontinent of nearly three hundred million subjects.[25] For this reason, the railroad has come to symbolize the pernicious effects of modernity in colonial India. But for Indian elites it also signaled opportunity. Employees like Bhagabati were "agents of modern transformation," their technical expertise indispensable for the ongoing supervision and maintenance of the railroad.[26] For these individuals, the railroad represented an opportunity to join the emerging Bengali middle class, the *bhadralok*. The term almost literally translates to "gentleman," connoting qualities of respectability, like "hard work, achievement, financial success, and social esteem *vis-à-vis* the Western world."[27] From the British perspective, this class provided ideal candidates for government positions.[28] The *bhadralok*'s characteristics prompted historian David Kopf, inspired by Max Weber, to describe them as Protestants. Though clearly problematic, this label does convey the ways *bhadralok* individuals exhibited characteristics associated with their middle-class counterparts in industrial Britain and America. Along with diligence and effort, Mukunda's family taught him a sense of optimism about the possibility of upward mobility that prepared him to understand the audiences he would eventually address. He was raised in a household with values strikingly similar to those of the striving American middle classes.

But occupational success in India depended on more than hard work. Late nineteenth-century Indian society was deeply shaped by the caste system, part of the identity that children were taught to internalize. As historian Tithi Bhattacharya explains, "One of the important things that a Hindu child learned even before he or she began school, were the names of his/her forefathers, including a detailed account of the subdivisions of his/her particular caste and clan. It was important for maintaining the intricacies of the kinship networks, in a familiar world which was at most times bound within the ancestral village."[29] Yogananda tells readers his parents' caste on the second page of his autobiography, and his brother does the same in his biography. Ghosh supplements this explanation in a genealogical appendix, which provides several detailed notes about the family's caste identity, describing with great pride relatives who were aristocrats, servants to kings, and those of "exalted social status."[30]

The caste system that helped shape the Ghosh children's identity was a dynamic political, social, and religious amalgamation of two taxonomies.[31] The first was the idealized fourfold *varṇa* system. In this taxonomy, the *brahmin,* or priestly class, was typically the most honored, followed by the *kshatriya,* or warrior class, and then the *vaishya,* or merchant class. Together, these three castes were *dvijas,* or twice-born, whose males were granted the privilege of learning the Vedas, the most sacred texts of orthodox religion, and performing the *saṃskāras,* or rites of passage prescribed in Vedic texts. *Dvijas* constituted a small elite presiding over a vast majority of *shudras,* or peasants.[32] In the second and more complex *jāti* taxonomy, there were thousands of occupational classes, some numbering no more than a few hundred members. Efforts to fit each *jāti* into one of the four *varṇas* led to a complex and fluid system full of exceptions. Historical anthropologist Susan Bayly notes that caste "is not and never has been a fixed fact of Indian life." Instead, both systems are "composites of ideals and practices that have been made and remade into varying codes of moral order over hundreds or even thousands of years."[33] Nevertheless, "certain basic ideas" were shared across the subcontinent, including the assumption that people were

> born into fixed social units with specific names or titles. Such a unit is one's caste or "community." And, insofar as individuals and kin groups

> recognize the claims of caste, these embody something broader than the notion of a common kin or blood tie. Indeed, caste is . . . a notion of attachment which bundles together a given set of kin groups or descent units . . . those born into a given caste would normally find marriage partners within these limits, and . . . regard those outside as of unlike kind, rank or substance. Furthermore, those sharing a common caste identity may subscribe to at least a notional tradition of common descent, as well as a claim of common geographical origin, and a particular occupational ideal.

Consequently, members of particular castes avoid sharing food "or other intimate social contacts" in a system of ranking viewed as "innate, universal and collective."[34]

The caste system of Bhagabati's time was in many ways a modern colonial creation. British officials, anxious to categorize the disparate peoples they ruled, reified caste identity as the sole, uniform, totalizing category of Indian social organization. Beyond ethnographic curiosity, a comprehensive ethnic taxonomy helped to facilitate governance. The first government study was conducted in 1871, but government efforts culminated in the 1881 census.[35] Because caste identity determined suitability for civil service employment, British categorization had very tangible consequences. An Anglo-Indian editorial from 1884, for example, recommended that "posts of trust and responsibility" be reserved for "those belonging to what are considered as respectable classes of the community from the native point of view."[36]

Bhagabati was a member of the Bengali *kayastha jāti,* by the nineteenth century a privileged group. Previously associated with *shudras, kayasthas* became widely recognized across northern India in the eighteenth century as they began to provide scribal services for princes. Through this association with royalty, *kayasthas* began to identify themselves with the *kshatriya varṇa. Kayasthas'* ability to upgrade their *jāti* status to conform to one of the twice-born *varṇa* paid rich dividends. Kopf notes, for example, that *kayasthas* were one of only three elite groups that constituted the intellectual class of late nineteenth century Bengal.[37] In the 1881 census, British officials upheld the high ranking of *kayasthas,* thus helping to secure access to civil service jobs.[38]

Once *kayasthas* had solidified their elite status, they relied on nepotism to pass the benefits on to their extended kin. Sanjay Joshi explains that "kin connections had played a very important part in getting jobs in the royal courts and bureaucracies . . . so much so that certain families and kin groups then came to monopolize particular kinds of jobs. . . . Such arrangements suited the administrative needs of the state, and also the families in question. Powers of patronage made kin or family connections of crucial importance, and put well-established kin elders in positions of great power."[39] Knowing how precarious civil service positions could be, Bhagabati was determined to use his connections to get Mukunda a railway job when he came of age.

Alongside *bhadralok* values, Mukunda's family imparted spiritual training. Bhagabati and Gyana reared their children in an observant manner, which included specific beliefs and practices. Then, as now, though Indian communities had many temples large and small, most Hindus participated in corporate worship only at large annual holidays; routine religious training and observances occured at home. As in many Indian households, Mukunda's mother assumed practical responsibility for religious devotion. She provided moral instruction from the great epics, the *Mahābhārata* and the *Rāmāyaṇa*.[40] She also maintained the family shrine. The Ghosh family were devotees of Narayan, another name for Vishnu, and the Mother Goddess.[41] The family paid a local priest to perform daily *puja*, the ritual sacrifice, commonly consisting of incense, sandalwood, and food (such as fruit or sweetmeats), to the family deities honored in a shrine in a dedicated alcove in the home. After the deity symbolically consumes the offering, the remainder becomes *prasada*, substantiated grace, sanctified by the deity and ingested by the devotee. The most important element of the worship service—whether at home or in the temple—is *darśana*, seeing and being seen by the deity, which confers a spiritual blessing.[42]

In 1890, three years before Mukunda's birth, a yoga master named Swami Lahiri Mahasaya joined the family pantheon. Bhagabati had been introduced to Mahasaya by one of the employees he supervised. Mahasaya trained disciples from all walks of life, but as a married pensioner who had worked for the British government for twenty-five years, he often attracted other civil servants like Bhagabati.[43] Together, Bhagabati and Gyana took yoga initiation from Mahasaya. Bhagabati would later initiate Mukunda into the first stage of this training.[44] Because a highly developed guru like Swami Mahasaya became a pure channel for the divine presence, his image could serve the purpose of *darśana* alongside the representation of a traditional deity. After Mahasaya's image was installed in the home shrine, Gyana performed daily *puja* to it.[45] When Mukunda was struck by cholera at age eight, she commanded him to bow to the image mentally, as he was too weak to move his arms. He did so and was enveloped in a brilliant light. He immediately felt his symptoms disappear.[46]

Through his parents' instruction, Mukunda learned the fundamental principles that shaped his worldview. He was taught that the human soul is a tangible, though subtle, material that outlives the individual life to be transplanted into another body after death in a nearly endless cycle of death and rebirth known as *saṃsāra*.[47] The nature of an individual's rebirth depends on the *karma*—the fruit of one's actions—acquired during the present life based on behavior, as well as the potential burden inherited from previous lives. Traditionally, *karma* was determined largely by *dharma,* or appropriate conduct, based on general principles and, in part, on one's sex, *varṇa,* and *āśrama,* or life stage.

The most crucial *saṃskāra* for members of the *dvija* was *upanayana,* or "taking near," in which a boy was presented before a guru to begin instruction in Vedic life. In this ceremony, the boy received the sacred thread consisting of three strands, each in turn composed of three threads. While members of the *kshatriya* were historically initiated at eleven years of age, there was flexibility in the practice. Over time, *upanayana* became increasingly restricted to *brahmins.* Since none of the sources indicate that Mukunda underwent this rite, perhaps Bengali *kshatriyas* were no longer practicing it by the late nineteenth century.

Dvija males passed through four somewhat idealized *āśramas* that embraced first the acceptance of worldly pleasure and later its rejection. Some Indian traditions celebrate married householders' enjoyment of material well-being and pleasure, including sexual pleasure. After raising children, a man eventually became a *saṃnyāsin,* or ascetic "renouncer," who had released himself from all worldly goods and attachments in pursuit of *mokṣa,* or release from the cycles of life and death.[48]

Mukunda's parents displayed particular dedication by embracing a modified form of *saṃnyāsin* while they remained in the household stage—well before the formal *saṃnyāsin* life stage. Through Mahasaya's inspiration, they had sexual intercourse only once a year, for the purpose of reproduction. Yogananda viewed this "remarkable admission" as an indicator of the way that his parents' devotion to Mahasaya "strengthened Father's naturally ascetical temperament."[49] Their devout conduct and sexual restraint provided a model for young Mukunda.

MUKUNDA LAL GHOSH'S SPIRITUAL PILGRIMAGE

Mukunda enjoyed a pleasant and unremarkable childhood. His family lived comfortably, if modestly, given Bhagabati's penchant for simplicity, and he attended elementary school. Mukunda's parents argued from time to time over Gyana's fondness for charity, which the parsimonious Bhagabati considered extravagant.[50] This unexceptional childhood was shattered when tragedy struck in 1904, the year the family moved to Bareilly, in central north India. Gyana was staying with her husband's extended family in Calcutta preparing for the wedding of Mukunda's older brother, Ananta. Gyana's nephew contracted cholera, and as she was nursing the sick child, she became infected. Cholera, endemic to India, is typically spread through contact with human waste and increased mobility in the modern era exacerbated its spread. Medical researchers were just beginning to understand the link between waste, bacteria, and disease in the late nineteenth century, so treatment was rarely effective. A British medical handbook published in 1861 still claimed uncertainty about whether "the disease spreads from direct contagion or atmospheric causes," while indicating that "there are abundant instances of its passing through a camp or city in such a manner as can only be accounted for by the almost demonstrated fact that a specific cholera-poison exists."[51] Victims often died rapidly from extreme diarrhea and vomiting, a fate that befell Gyana's nephew. Gyana sent a telegram to her husband notifying him of her illness. Bhagabati and the rest of the family rushed to Calcutta. But Gyana died before they arrived. "When we reached our Calcutta home," Mukunda later recalled, "it was only to confront the stunning mystery of death. I collapsed into an almost lifeless state."[52] Gyana was cremated according to custom.

This traumatizing experience shaped the course of Mukunda's life. His mother's tragic death, intensified by the shocking suddenness that prevented any farewells, was a devastating blow. Long after her death, he remained inconsolable, his grief a cause of great concern to his father.[53] "The rent left in the family fabric by Mother's death was irreparable," Mukunda later recalled.[54] Gyana's death caused a rift between him and his father. He later claimed that he had reported a premonition of her impending death to his father, who dismissed the vision and delayed departure for Calcutta by a few hours. Mukunda blamed his mother's death on Bhagabati's tardy response. This was a child's irrational response to trauma, as it is virtually certain that arriving earlier would not have changed Gyana's fate.[55] For his part, Bhagabati thought stoicism the proper response to suffering, which intensified his emotional coldness as a parent. But in private he clearly grieved the loss of his wife. Though he lived another thirty-eight years, he never remarried. A longtime family servant attempted to act as a surrogate mother, but Ananta generally assumed parental responsibilities in the home.

Mukunda's longing for maternal comfort encouraged a penchant for female representations of deity, prominent in Bengal, that both emulated his mother's religious practice and came to represent her. As an adult, he explicitly linked the loss of his earthly mother to his affection for the divine mother. His poem "The Lost Two Black Eyes" expresses how Gyana's death left the storm-tossed "Boat of my life" "Directionless." The "motherless sorrow" of "this orphan life of mine" was eased only when he found the love of "the Deathless Mother."[56] If his religious approach was shaped by affection for his absent mother, it was equally shaped in reaction to the emotional distance of his present father. His attitude to the divine—whether conceptualized as female or male—was consistently characterized by *bhakti*, or intense devotion. Such emotionalism was clearly at odds with his father's reserved demeanor and his austere religious practice.

In July 1906, not long after Gyana's death, Bhagabati was transferred to Calcutta. The city had been the center of British India since 1690, when East India Company agent Job Charnock chose a location on the east bank of the Hooghly River, an offshoot of the Ganges, as a protected port several miles inland from the Bay of Bengal. The East India Company consolidated its foothold in 1757, during the Battle of Plassey in the Seven Years' War. The Sepoy Rebellion, exactly a century later, led Parliament to replace the company's rule with direct Crown rule. Calcutta, however, remained the imperial administrative center. With a population of 1.1 million—roughly the size of Philadelphia, and double the size of Boston, Baltimore, or Saint Louis—Calcutta was a dynamic global city that provided a decisive cultural and intellectual influence on Mukunda as he moved from adolescence into adulthood.[57] Calcutta was one of a half-dozen global cities that had become deeply enmeshed in the industrial world by the late nineteenth century, and these cities' elites were, according to historian C. A. Bayly, "as much implicated in the industrial world system as those of the West."[58] The entire apparatus of British Indian government, including the viceroy's massive eighty-four-thousand-square-foot neoclassical mansion, was roughly three miles from the family home. Though the government determined in 1911 to relocate the capital to New Delhi, Calcutta continued to symbolize British colonialism.

In the late nineteenth century, India was central to the global economy, and Calcutta was the most important British port for exporting goods to England and continental Europe.[59] Humans were another export. The far-flung British Empire drew hundreds of thousands of poor, desperate South Asians into various forms of service in South Africa, Mauritius, and the Caribbean in what often turned out to be permanent resettlement. The vast majority of those migrant laborers embarked for overseas ports from Calcutta.[60] The same port that served as a transit station for goods was also a conduit for ideas. "Radical ideas that challenged the bases of the traditional world order in Europe and America were a form of intellectual cargo unloaded on the docks of the great metropolis, along with the other industrial and commercial products."[61] This dynamic metropolis confronted Mukunda with the reality of a globalized world and, perhaps, urged him to begin reflecting on his own place within it.

Brimming with curiosity, Mukunda had little interest in formal education. Perhaps the most important outcome of his high school years was beginning to learn English systematically. He was much more interested in physical activity. Despite his slight physique, he excelled in track, wrestling, and soccer. Almost immediately after moving to Calcutta, Mukunda met Manomohan Mazumdar. Mazumdar's father supervised the Calcutta Deaf and Dumb School across the street, and the family lived on the campus. Though Mazumdar was a couple years younger than Mukunda, the two clicked immediately.[62] Mazumdar later remembered his time with Mukunda as "one of inspiration which stirs the deepest part of my heart."[63]

It was during this period that Mukunda's deeply rooted interest in spirituality blossomed. His religious interests were both more earnest and more eclectic than those of his family members. In addition to Gyana's death, adolescence and the stimulating cultural environment of Calcutta formed a potent mix. Mukunda "left no stone unturned in his spiritual investigations," according to his younger brother.[64] Each morning on his way to school, he and Mazumdar would worship together at the Radha Krishna Temple on their way to school. The two frequently visited the Kalighat Kali Temple and meditated in Eden Gardens along the Hooghly River.[65] He also experimented with Tantrism, a tradition especially prominent in Bengal, where it may have originated in the seventh century as a movement outside of orthodox Vedic traditions. David Gordon White provides a helpful definition: "Tantra is that Asian body of beliefs and practices which, working from the principle that the universe we experience is nothing other than the concrete manifestation of the divine energy of the godhead that creates and maintains that universe, seeks to ritually appropriate and channel that energy, within the human microcosm, in creative and emancipatory ways."[66] Tantrism is a diverse, fluid movement that has often been misunderstood, in part because its traditions were usually kept secret. Knowledge about Tantra in the West was largely mediated through the British, whose zeal to describe the putative epitome of primitive religion often led to gross misrepresentations. Indians sometimes contributed to this exoticization.[67] Scandalous stereotypes notwithstanding, Tantrism *has* frequently included an erotic dimension. Some Tantric practitioners intentionally flouted orthodox Vedic religious conventions by engaging in taboo activities, including the use of five substances: wine, meat, fish, fermented grain, and sexual intercourse.[68] Employing a variety of texts, rituals, myths, art forms, *mantras*,

Mukunda as a teenager, far right. The adolescent Mukunda actively explored a variety of spiritual pathways in his search for the divine. His friend and spiritual companion, Mazumdar, is on the left. Also pictured are Mukunda's cousin Lalit-da and his Sanskrit tutor, Swami Kebalananda, who deepened his understanding of Kriya Yoga.

and *yantras*, or mystical designs, Tantra practitioners, according to Indologist Wendy Doniger, often engaged in "worship of the goddess, initiation, group worship, secrecy, and antinomian behavior, particularly sexual rituals and the ingesting of bodily fluids."[69]

As Mukunda and his friends explored Tantrism, they contemplated the meaning and power of death. They began visiting the Nimtala Ghat cremation grounds where his mother's final rites had been performed. There they followed the Tantra *sādāna* of sitting on corpses or piles of skulls. Violating the severe taboo of contact with dead humans, they confronted and thus overcame the power of death. At one point, Mukunda brought home a skull and crossbones, placing them on a wooden stand in his bedroom for meditation. He also routinely invited an ascetic home to help him navigate the labyrinth of Tantric arcana. The human remains and the ascetic, with matted hair and long vermilion stripe along his forehead, terrified Mukunda's brother, who reported Mukunda's conduct to their father. Bhagabati solemnly warned Mukunda of the danger of Tantrism's dark spiritual powers. Mukunda immediately ceased his most provocative activities.

But his devotion to the bloodthirsty warrior goddess Kali, often associated with death in Bengali Tantrism, continued. He was drawn to "her terrifying

Form, three-eyed and blazingly Radiant,"[70] and he often constructed his own images of her, building her body of straw and wood, and her hair of jute and then performing *puja*.[71] The *Autobiography* passes over Mukunda's dabbling in Tantrism in silence, a reflection of the tendency to minimize coverage of (literally) taboo activities. Still, crucial elements of Tantrism made their way into Yogananda's worldview. This includes his understanding of yoga as the stirring up of latent divine female power[72] and his lingering affection for Kali, though largely purged from the *Autobiography* and described there blandly in a footnote as "a symbol of God in the aspect of eternal Mother Nature."[73]

After abandoning Tantric practice, Mukunda explored any pathway that promised spiritual insight, including divination, hypnotism, and clairvoyance. He attempted to communicate with the dead—most notably, his mother.[74] Mazumdar, dragged along on many of Mukunda's spiritual adventures, recognized his friend's grab bag of Indian spirituality and Western metaphysical traditions. "Direct encounters with ascended beings, the radiant and divine appearances of supernatural power-endowed realized beings, the arrival of the spirit of a dead person in the midst of mesmerized people and speaking with that spirit, and ordinary sightings of ghosts and such were things that he believed in, and pursued with concentrated means in situations and occasions."[75] In the midst of these eclectic pursuits, Mukunda first began to proclaim his ability to perform miraculous feats. Transcending time and space through meditation, he began to make prophetic pronouncements about various individuals, using his younger brother as a medium for spiritual messages.[76] Mazumdar, something of a skeptic when it came to Mukunda's more fantastic claims, noted that not all of Mukunda's prophecies came to pass and that his skills in hypnotism were less effective on older subjects than younger ones—and even then did not always succeed.[77] Mazumdar's doubts were not lost on his more exuberant companion: "One day, because of some situation, he said to me, 'Oh! Of course, you don't believe all this?' I told him, 'I cannot say something so big and certain like, "I don't believe." My knowledge is limited. But I don't have much interest in these things—meaning these kinds of supernatural workings, and I have managed my own explanations for these things as well.' In any case, his belief in these remained firm and unshakable throughout his whole life."[78] However willing a companion Mazumdar may have been in their spiritual journey together, he remained grounded when Mukunda leapt into flights of fancy.

Mukunda began to fantasize about making a pilgrimage to Rishikesh, one of the few gateway towns to the Himalayas, considered sacred because the waters of the Ganges first reach the plains from the mountains at this spot.

Bathing in the Ganges at Rishikesh is believed to confer salvific benefits. Mukunda's father and older brother, spiritually devoted but also pragmatic, found this nearly thousand-mile journey extravagant. Mukunda, revealing both spiritual hunger and a willingness to defy parental authority, conspired to sneak away and travel there secretly with his friends. In 1906, the year the family moved to Calcutta, he executed his plan. Pretending to be ill, he stayed home from school and locked himself in his room; his escape through a window was not detected until much later. Two friends joined him in the flight, though one eventually turned back. Such a journey was only conceivable for a thirteen-year old boy deeply familiar with geography, railroads, and timetables. Still, it was a bold and risky undertaking. His defiant character was already well known to his family, as his older brother Ananta was on the lookout for just such a ploy. When Mukunda disappeared, Ananta immediately telegraphed the railway station with descriptions of Mukunda and his two friends. They eluded capture as far as Haridwar. Then, just fifteen miles from Rishikesh, a police officer detained them at the train station. They were held in a dismal police station for three days while they waited for Ananta to collect them.

The collapse of Mukunda's Himalaya plans did not dampen his spiritual fervor. Though Ananta expressed sympathy with Mukunda's disappointment with his Rishikesh capture, he nonetheless continued trying to dissuade his brother from his spiritual pursuits.[79] But Ananta's efforts to dampen his brother's ardor unwittingly fanned the flames instead. Ananta held Mukunda's Sanskrit tutor, who had engaged in philosophical and spiritual discussions with his eager pupil, responsible for planting the idea of a railway venture in Mukunda's head. So Ananta fired the tutor and replaced him with Sri Kabiraj Mahasaya. Unbeknownst to Ananta, Mahasaya was a dedicated yogi practitioner and an advanced disciple of Lahiri Mahasaya, Bhagabati's guru. While teaching his pupil Sanskrit, Mahasaya also introduced him to the stories of India's saints and the meditative practices of Mahasaya's yoga tradition. Together, tutor and disciple explored the meaning of the *Bhagavad Gītā*, the Purāṇas, and other religious texts.[80]

This personal mentoring was only one source of spiritual energy. Other nearby attractions also stoked Mukunda's spiritual fervor. He regularly visited the great Dakshineswar Kali Temple, which pulsated with massive crowds from all around the Calcutta metropolitan area. Several miles north of the Ghosh home, Dakshineswar was a large, sprawling complex, whose central shrine was devoted to the goddess Kali, while a dozen smaller shrines honoring Shiva surrounded the courtyard. Sri Ramakrishna, one of the most famous religious figures in nineteenth-century India, had resided at the temple for several years until his death in 1886. The alcove he inhabited within the temple complex became a shrine to his devotees. Directly across the Hooghly River from the Dakshineswar Kali Temple sat Belur Math monastery. Ramakrishna's most famous devotee, Swami Vivekananda, founded the monastery in his master's honor a decade after Ramakrishna's death. It became the headquarters of the Ramakrishna order, dedicated to expanding the reach of his teaching in India and abroad. Vivekananda had become a celebrated figure in liberal American religious circles when he visited the World's Parliament of Religions in 1893, the year Mukunda was born.

Mukunda never had a chance to meet Vivekananda, who died of a stroke at Belur Math at age thirty-nine in 1902, several years before the Ghosh family moved to Calcutta. A shrine containing Vivekananda's cremated remains was placed on the monastery grounds, on the banks of the Hooghly. But the Ramakrishna movement's influence in Bengal far outlasted Vivekananda's death, and Mukunda became an eager unofficial devotee. According to Mazumdar, during Mukunda's high school years, he "would become filled with the nectar of devotion whenever he would meditate on Sri Ramakrishna Paramhansa-deva, the divine worshiper of the Mother of the Universe." So he "would suffer the pains of going by foot to Dakshineswar," the temple where Ramakrishna had resided. He meditated there for long periods and conversed with Ramakrishna monks.[81] He also made frequent trips across the river to the Belur Math.[82] On several occasions, Mukunda met with Sri "M," an advanced disciple of Ramakrishna.[83] Mukunda requested both Sri "M" and Swami Prajnananda, the head of the Belur Math at the time, to make him their disciple, though both declined.[84]

Mukunda was nevertheless deeply influenced by Ramakrishna's teachings. As a college student, he carried a booklet of Ramakrishna's teachings in his pocket, meditated on them regularly, and offered to share them with interested acquaintances.[85] Yogananda's later penchant for lighthearted anecdotes, his sense of humor, and above all his passionate devotionalism — routinely expressed in poetic, emotional language — characterized Ramakrishna's informal style but were deeply at odds with both his father's stoicism and Yukteswar's austerity. Ramakrishna's writings likely provided the inspiration for Yogananda's infectious, deeply affectionate way of talking about communion with the divine.

Given Mukunda's apparently intense interest in his teachings, the depth of Ramakrishna's influence on the future Yogananda has too often gone unnoticed. This stems in part from the attention given to Mukunda's formal discipleship to Yukteswar and in part to the paucity of references Yogananda

The Dakshineswar Kali Temple in Calcutta, a massive nineteenth-century complex devoted to the goddess Kali and, in twelve smaller shrines surrounding the main temple, Shiva. The temple is a popular spot for devotees, and Mukunda visited it regularly as a young man, particularly the location in the complex where Sri Ramakrishna spent many years.

makes to Ramakrishna in his *Autobiography* or elsewhere. Given the significance of the guru-disciple relationship, he undoubtedly wished to give proper deference to his actual mentor. At the same time, his drive to emulate Vivekananda may have played a part. Fashioning himself in the mold of Vivekananda, he did not want to appear as a second-rate, knock-off version. To highlight the uniqueness of his own American ministry, he downplayed any sense that his teaching was derivative from Vivekananda. This included erasing most traces of his dependence on Vivekananda's mentor.

THE EDUCATION OF A SWAMI

In 1909, Mukunda continued his search for spiritual enlightenment by following his friend Jitendra to Benares, where he had gone to join the Bharat Dharma Mahamandal hermitage. One of India's most sacred sites, Benares had been a pilgrimage site for centuries. The Benares ghats on the edge of the Ganges always teemed with pilgrims waiting to cremate their departed loved ones, as this auspicious site was thought to automatically grant the deceased liberation from the cycles of *saṃsāra*. The Mahamandal, "perhaps the most successful orthodox organization on the subcontinent," according to Kenneth Jones, enjoyed the patronage of rajas, large landowners, and merchants.[86] A popular reform movement begun in late nineteenth-century Punjab, the organization grew dramatically after its relocation to Benares early in the new century. In 1915, it had six hundred branches spread throughout India, and another four hundred affiliated organizations. The Mahamandal was willing to make Vedic texts available to all people, regardless of sex or caste. Rather than assuming that Hinduism was the preserve of the Indian people, the organization also made the very modern claim that it "is the universal Dharma for all mankind." Still, its definition of *dharma* was extremely traditional, even occasionally reactionary, stressing the supreme importance of *varṇāśramadharma*, an individual's spiritual duties based on caste and life stage. Defending orthodoxy in the face of challenges by more radical reform groups such as the Arya Samaj, the Mahamandal's staff included missionaries who sought to convert Indians to the "one true faith." In addition to its emphasis on *varṇāśramadharma*, the Mahamandal stressed such traditional practices as child marriage and cow protection while opposing the construction of new mosques.[87] From his short stint with the Mahamandal, Mukunda would take several key ideas: the concept of a universal *dharma*, the vision of a unified Indian religion, and the novel concept (in an Indian religious context) of evangelization, though his target converts would be Americans rather than his fellow Indians.

Despite the crucial values the Mahamandal instilled in Mukunda, he was deeply unhappy there. Not long after arriving, he found himself at odds with his fellow ashram members. The "household was alienated, hurt by my determined aloofness. My strict adherence to meditation on the very Ideal for which I had left home and all the worldly ambitions called forth shallow criticism from all sides." They knew little about meditation, in his view, and "thought I should employ my whole time in organizational duties."[88] Satyananda offers a different account; he suggests that Mukunda's dreamy spirituality caused him to neglect mundane housekeeping routines, provoking resentment from his colleagues, who had to pick up the slack.[89] Either way, Mukunda was unable to get along with the other initiates and restless to leave the ashram. His rescue came through the fateful encounter with Swami Sri Yukteswar recounted above.

Yukteswar had been born in Serampore, near Calcutta, in 1855, the only child of wealthy, solidly middle-class parents. His father was a landowner and business owner, his mother a dutiful wife who taught her son Hindu traditions.

Yogananda's guru. Born Priya Nath Karar, he took the title Swami Yukteswar Giri when he entered the swami monastic order in 1884 to learn Kriya Yoga. He converted his family home in Serampore into an ashram and opened a second in Puri. His book *The Holy Science*, which sought to harmonize science, the Bible, and yoga, influenced Yogananda's later teaching.

He was a bright, curious person drawn to all kinds of knowledge and never one to suffer fools gladly. Even as a boy, he had a deeply analytical mind, resorting to scatological humor to ridicule teachers behind their backs when they failed to demonstrate consistent logic. As a young man, he was a strong student and gifted mathematician. His scientific curiosity later drew him to Calcutta Medical College, where he learned anatomy, physiology, and some medicine. He also became enamored of naturopathy, a German practice emerging in the nineteenth century.

His interests were broad and eclectic. He excelled in sports, horseback riding, and hunting. He was fond of music and learned to play the sitar. Through connections with a neighborhood noble family who took a liking to him, Yukteswar was introduced to a number of prominent Indians, including nationalist writer Bankim Chatterji. Chatterji's novel *Anandamath*, banned by the British as a symbol of colonial resistance, unveiled his song "Vande Mataram," destined to become an independent India's national anthem.[90]

A tragic family life freed him to pursue his spiritual interests more deeply. A few years after marrying, Yukteswar's wife died. Later, his only daughter also died. He viewed their deaths as having exhausted the *karma* he had carried into his present life. Now he was free to become a *saṃnyāsin* and travel widely, acquiring wisdom and knowledge. He displayed a spiritual thirst in many ways like his later pupil. He sought out a teacher of the Santal tribal people, learned Tantric and Vaishnavite traditions, and even became a member of the Theosophical Society. During this search, Yukteswar explored the Ramakrishna movement, headquartered ten miles from his family home, and eventually became friends with Vivekananda. Later, after founding his own community, Yukteswar sought to affiliate formally with the Ramakrishna Order. Although this did not transpire, Mukunda's future mentor clearly had some affinity for the movement.[91]

In 1884, Yukteswar found a focus for his peripatetic spiritual path. The noble family that had introduced him to Chatterji were devotees of Sri Lahiri Mahasaya. Yukteswar heard remarkable things from them about Mahasaya's wisdom and knowledge. He eventually departed for Benares, determined to track down the elusive swami. After finding Mahasaya's address, Yukteswar bathed in the Ganges, dressed in proper clothing, and presented himself before his would-be guru. Mahasaya agreed to give Yukteswar Kriya Yoga initiation. Yukteswar returned to Serampore and devoted himself to the guru's instruction. One of Yukteswar's disciples describes Kriya Yoga as "an esoteric doctrine of spiritual efforts practised in India from hoary ages by aspirants after Self Realisation and Emancipation from worldly bondage. It is a set of physical and mental techniques by following which consummation of Yoga can be achieved." Kriya "represents a specially designed mode of efforts, physical as well as mental, which is the secret technique of the Yogis," while yoga designates "the only process adopting which one can get over the disturbing factors, physical as well as mental, in attaining the quietude deemed essential for Self Realisation."[92]

As Yukteswar accepted the specific discipline of his guru and the Kriya Yoga path, he sought to integrate his broad knowledge of Hindu traditions and of other religions. He had spent some time learning about Islam, and at Serampore College he read the Bible and learned about the life of Christ. He was especially drawn to the book of Revelation, learning to interpret it as a prophetic confirmation of his own astrology-based Hindu eschatology.[93] At some point, Yukteswar shared with French missionaries his "new understanding and perspective of their religious scripture, the Bible, as it pertained to the arrival of Lord Jesus, His *sādāna*, education, the wondrous experiences of His companions etc." The missionary, anxious about the harm this perspective might cause to ordinary Christians, asked to borrow the book and later claimed to have lost it.[94]

In 1894, Yukteswar wrote a book in this same spirit, *The Holy Science*, a short work that presented yoga—though he avoided this word—as part of a coherent, systematic practice leading to the highest goal of religion, self-knowledge. His language reflected Christian terminology: the Gospel, God the Father, sin, and repentance. Employing this Christian vocabulary enabled him to translate Christian theology into the categories of Hindu thought. God the Father was really *sat*, the only reality in the universe. Repentance meant, not turning from sin, but abandoning *māyā*, or ignorance, and rediscovering one's participation in divinity and thus experiencing liberation. Practical methods to achieve liberation included vegetarianism, extended time in the open air, and spending time with those to whom one was "magnetically" drawn. Successful practice would lead to supernatural yogic powers:

> Life and death come under the control of the yogi who perseveres in the practice of Pranayama. In that way, he saves his body from the premature decay that overtakes most men, and can remain as long as he wishes in his present physical from; thus having time to work out his karma in one body; and to fulfil (and thus get rid of) all the various desires of his heart. Finally purified, he is no longer required to come again into this world under the influence of Maya, darkness, nor to suffer the "second death."[95]

The Holy Science also aligned modern science with ancient texts to fundamentally reconceptualize Indian cosmology. According to widely accepted calculations of astronomical treatises from the early centuries of the Common Era, all of history for the last several millennia—and for countless millennia to come—has fallen under the shadow of the Kali Yuga, a dark age in which knowledge of the Vedas progressively degenerates. Yukteswar carefully parsed the treatises that describe the sequence of the universe's great ages, proving the error in their calculation of the eras. Then, citing Kepler, Galileo, and Newton, Yukteswar correlated these Indian treatises with contemporary astronomical knowledge and concluded that the present age is Dwapara Yuga. Like arcane millennialist debates among Christians, Yukteswar's date-setting had important theological consequences. The upshot of his discovery was the recognition that, "the dark age of Kali having long passed away, the world is reaching out for spiritual knowledge, and men require loving help from one the other [*sic*]."[96] This fundamentally optimistic view of people's thirst for spiritual knowledge deeply shaped Yogananda's own upbeat expectation of a receptive audience for his message.

Yukteswar was also the first to introduce Yogananda to Jesus and the Bible, while reinforcing his pupil's incipient understanding that the Bible could only be understood in light of the greater truth of Hindu *dharma*. "Master expounded the Christian Bible with a beautiful clarity. It was from my Hindu guru, unknown to the roll call of Christian membership, that I learned to perceive the deathless essence of the Bible, and to understand the truth in Christ's assertion—surely the most thrillingly intransigent ever uttered: 'Heaven and earth shall pass away, but my words shall not pass away.'"[97]

Yukteswar embraced a view of other religions common among late nineteenth-century educated Indians. In the introduction to *The Holy Science,* Yukteswar explained that the "purpose of this book is to show as clearly as possible that there is an essential unity in all religions; there is no difference in the truths inculcated by the various faiths; that there is but one method by which the world, both external and internal, has evolved; and that there is but one Goal admitted by all scriptures." On one level, this pluralist view acknowledged the legitimacy of all religions. On another level, however, Yukteswar's inclusivism led him immediately to concede that "this basic truth" of unity "is one not easily comprehended," becoming clear only through an exposition that revealed the underlying dharmic understanding of reality.[98] Yukteswar shared the belief of other modern Indians that, as Hindu scholar Jeffery Long explains, "Hindu Dharma is an absolute, in terms of which all religions can be measured, sometimes being found praiseworthy, and at other times found wanting." Such an outlook "proceeds from a specific worldview that is held to be true and in terms of which the truth claims and the salvific efficacy of other religions may be evaluated." Indeed, leading Indian figures at the time, including Gandhi and Vivekananda, affirmed "religious pluralism while at the same time do so using unabashedly Hindu categories and extolling the distinctiveness of Hindu Dharma."[99] On one level, Vivekananda asserted that all religions were partial forms of God realization. But on a higher level, the eternal *Dharma*, derived exclusively from Indian sources, transcended all religions as the embodiment of the one eternal religion. Vivekananda ultimately resolved the tension between these two views by, as one scholar puts it, placing his view of "the absoluteness of Vedanta" above his competing view of the "harmony and unity of religions."[100] This outlook would prove deeply influential in shaping Mukunda's later theology.

The relationship between Mukunda and his mentor developed quickly. Though his father and older brother did not immediately allow Mukunda to take the swami vows that would make him a formal devotee, they were powerless to diminish the tremendous influence Yukteswar came to exert over him. Ironically, some of Yukteswar's directives were in line with Bhagabati's own desires for his son. The yogi convinced his academically indifferent protégé to attend college. Envisioning an international career for Mukunda early on, Yukteswar was convinced that his future success hinged on the credibility that came with a university degree, just as it had for Vivekananda.[101] Yukteswar had longed to travel to overseas himself, to "teach the universal methods by which the West will be able to base its religious beliefs on the unshakable foundations of yogic science." But by the time he took Mukunda as a student, he was in his mid-fifties and probably realized that the chance for his own overseas mission had passed. Instead, he would send his student as an "emissary to the West." Indeed, Mukunda made a much better candidate for this task than Yukteswar. The coldly analytical Yukteswar recognized that Mukunda's expressive devotional style and undisputed love for God would make him a "very effective tool to propagate his message in the Christian world."[102]

So Mukunda's spiritual father succeeded where his earthly father had failed. Bhagabati shared the sentiment of his *bhadralok* class that education was "the most important and marketable skill."[103] He had pressured Mukunda into completing some college coursework before he went to the Benares Mahamandal. His prodding had modest success, as Mukunda grudgingly enrolled briefly in both agricultural college and medical college in Calcutta.[104] Though he was undeniably bright, Mukunda found formal education extremely trying. But if his mentor now demanded it, he would comply.

The college system Mukunda entered in August 1910 was a relatively recent institution, a hybrid of Indian and Western traditions. Indian higher education had developed in a century-long process that culminated in the ostensible victory of a Western-based Anglicist approach over an earlier Orientalist approach that emphasized the study of Sanskrit and Sanskrit religious texts, though the earlier model had not been fully vanquished.[105] Efforts to Anglicize higher education began with Parliament's 1813 renewal of the East India Company charter, which required reauthorization every twenty years. Three distinct groups lobbied to enact a provision for higher education in the new charter.[106] First, the Bengali *bhadralok* viewed English-based higher education as a path to secure occupations for their offspring in commerce or government service that they themselves had enjoyed.[107]

The other two groups were non-Indians seeking to reform Indian society through enlightened higher education. Evangelical missionaries were eager to encourage reading of the Word among Indian elites. East India Company officials had fervently—and, until 1813, successfully—resisted missionary efforts, fearing that evangelical critiques of Indian beliefs and practices would be severely disruptive to trade. Their fears were not misplaced. Almost immediately, missionaries began to rail against polytheism and the so-called barbaric practices that went with it. Frenzied ceremonies, animal sacrifices, and hookswinging, where devotees hung suspended from a rope attached to a pole, became regular fodder for reports home soliciting funds for continued work. Indian social practices also came under attack, particularly those involving the treatment of women. Missionaries especially targeted *sati*, a widow's ceremonial self-immolation on her husband's funeral pyre as a display of marital devotion, and the marriage of young girls to adult men to ensure female sexual purity. Utilitarian thinkers easily rivaled evangelicals in their critique of traditional Indian society. According to historian Michael Curtis, prominent utilitarian James Mill "criticized Hindu manners and behavior, attributing to them many unpleasant characteristics such as indolence, avarice, lack of cleanliness, ignorance, absence of rational thought, insincerity, mendacity, perfidy, and indifference to the feelings of others."[108]

In 1835, lobbying by these three groups paid off when Governor-General of India William Bentinck began a halting effort to instruct "natives" in English and Western subjects, which would "teach the natives of India the marvelous results of the employment of labour and capital, rouse them to emulate us in the development of the vast resource of their country, . . . confer upon them all the advantages which accompany the healthy increase of wealth and commerce; and at the same time, secure to us a larger and more certain supply of many articles necessary for our manufactures and extensively consumed by all classes of our population."[109] Another half-century passed, however, before sustained efforts were made to create a functional system of higher education. In 1899, George Nathaniel Curzon, incoming viceroy to India, responded to nationalist agitation in India—which stemmed in part from dissatisfaction with the existing education system—by appointing a commission that ultimately announced reforms to move instruction away from preparation for civil service exams and toward a broader liberal arts education.[110]

Mukunda's college experience reflected a very recent model, conducted in English, that strove to move from rote memorization to a richer curriculum but retained vestiges of the older Orientalist tradition. Ample helpings of Western history, literature, science, philosophy, and theology were complemented by equally generous servings of the Vedas, Sanskrit, and "various works in Bengali and Hindustani."[111] This British education imparted as much knowledge about Indian religious texts as it did about Western humanities or the sciences.

Given the central role evangelicals played in higher education, it is not surprising that the two places Yogananda attended were both religious institutions. Indian higher education was a two-part system: two years of lower-division instruction, which culminated in an exam, and two years of upper-division instruction leading to the B.A. degree for those who passed the exam. First, Mukunda enrolled in Scottish Church College, an institution founded by evangelical Alexander Duff in 1830 that David Kopf describes as "a high-powered institution destined to play a critical role in the educational history of Bengal."[112] Mukunda completed his lower-division coursework in liberal arts, with areas of concentration in Sanskrit, philosophy, and chemistry. In 1912, he fell violently ill before matriculation exams, suffering severe dysentery.

When he passed the exam the following year, he hoped that he was done with higher education forever.[113] But Yukteswar, who brooked no disagreement, insisted that Mukunda complete his upper-division instruction and obtain his B.A. So Mukunda enrolled at Yukteswar's alma mater, Serampore College, founded by English evangelist William Carey in collaboration with Dutch missionaries. The curriculum largely mirrored Scottish Church College, with attention to Western learning and the Bible, alongside Sanskrit and Bengali texts.[114] Thus, Mukunda's college education deepened his understanding of Indian texts and traditions while providing extensive exposure to Western liberal arts, sciences, and religion. Awareness of a range of diverse intellectual and religious traditions, often seen as incompatible, prodded him to begin thinking about the importance of a single system of universal knowledge.

His education was not limited to the college campus. Mukunda and his friend Mazumdar also regularly attended a Calcutta branch of the Brahmo Samaj, the most influential reform organization of nineteenth-century Hinduism. The Brahmo Samaj spread from Calcutta, where it originated, throughout the major urban areas of India late in the century, but its presence remained strongest in Bengal.[115] Founded by reformer Rammohan Roy, the Samaj became the key organization in the Bengal Renaissance, an intellectual movement led by a group of Bengali political leaders, theologians, writers, and artists who produced what one scholar has called a "revolutionary awakening of the Indian mind."[116] These intellectuals conceded the outer domains of knowledge — science and technology — to European authorities, but asserted that in culture India remained superior and unconquered.[117] The Samaj was the lead organization in the emergence of a broader modern Hinduism. These intellectuals articulated a form of Hinduism as a universal religion, unmoored to the South Asian landscape and the Indian people, its eternal moral and spiritual truths transcending priestly rituals and divine images.[118] Vivekananda, whose views of Hinduism as an eternal religion were described above, derived this understanding from his own involvement in the Samaj. Samaj members also sought to reform Indian society, reducing or removing caste distinctions, outlawing child marriage, and reforming religious rituals that suggested polytheism and image worship.[119]

Some scholars have offered surprisingly harsh judgments against the innovations of the Brahmo Samaj and the larger Bengali Renaissance. German Indologist Paul Hacker popularized the pejorative term neo-Hinduism in the 1950s to identify Indian reformers' inauthentic brand of religion.[120] His disciple Wilhelm Halbfass softened his mentor's tone a bit, but retained the same basic judgment.[121] More recently, Gerald James Larson has said that "rather than being authentic products of India's ancient cultural heritage," modern Hinduism is "really much closer in spirit to traditions of late-nineteenth-century European notions of universal religion or liberal Protestant religion."[122] In viewing these intellectual changes as inauthentic, critics fail to recognize the organic nature of religion in general and the creativity of Indian responses to the challenges of modernity. It is true that Bengali Renaissance leaders developed their new understanding of Hinduism in the face of British and American Christianity and were inspired by Unitarian conceptions of divinity and spirituality. Still, it is better to see reformed Hinduism as a creative response to pluralism that maintained the centrality of Indian texts and spirituality. "The challenge of orthodox Christianity in India," as David Kopf explains, "stimulated the Hindu intelligentsia to rediscover the sources of their own religious tradition and to reform their religion according to their new image of the remote past."[123] Historian Kenneth N. Jones strikes the right balance on this question, describing Hindu reformers as drawing "symbol, concepts, and scriptural legitimization" from their "religious heritage as well as limited elements of western civilization."[124] Just as Christianity changed in response to modern challenges, some Indian leaders "produced a modernized religiosity in colonial India."[125]

The Brahmo Samaj shaped Mukunda in key ways. Though the emotional austerity of the Samaj's predominantly rationalistic theism left Mukunda cold, he fell in love with the poetry of Rabindranath Tagore, the most famous Brahmo Samaj figure in the early twentieth century. More importantly, Samaj leaders and other members of the Bengali Renaissance provided Mukunda guidance in his efforts to integrate Christianity into his worldview. As colonial subjects of a British Empire often associated with Christianity, nationalist leaders were virtually required to grapple with Christianity's central figure. Many Bengali intellectuals felt some ambivalence toward institutional Christianity, but they often had warmer feelings about Jesus himself. Rammohan Roy, the earliest Bengali Renaissance leader, assisted missionaries in translating the New Testament and then edited his own edition, *The Precepts of Jesus*, while Samaj leader Keshub Chandra Sen made a "careful distinction between 'Christ's message of universal harmony' and the institutional Christianity of the nineteenth century with its Europeanized, sectarian, and 'muscular' view of Christ."[126] Several other key Indian nationalist leaders wrote or spoke at length about Jesus, including P. C. Mozoomdar, Sri Ramakrishna, Swami Vivekananda, philosopher and Indian president Sarvepalli Radhakrishnan, and Gandhi.[127]

These individuals often found creative ways to make Jesus's instruction compatible with Indian teaching. The New Testament Gospels provide little information about Jesus before his ministry around the age of thirty, leaving the door ajar for any number of creative interventions. From the early Christian centuries, several apocryphal texts had already exploited this gap in the canonical Gospels to provide fantastic accounts of Jesus's childhood.[128] Giving Jesus an Indian childhood was, by comparison, a tame innovation. Ironically, this conviction probably sprang originally not from Indians but from Europeans fascinated, as religion scholar Simon Joseph explains, "with the 'mystic east' and the 'ancient wisdom' of India." An Indian childhood also helped explain the parallels many nineteenth-century Orientalists perceived between Christianity and Buddhism.[129] Following the lead of these Orientalists, several Indian intellectuals claimed that Jesus spent the Gospels' "missing years" in

India, absorbing the wisdom of the East.[130] Like Yukteswar's *Holy Science*, the treatment of Jesus and Christianity by Bengali Renaissance leaders and other Indian intellectuals reflected a form of modern "inclusivist appropriation of other traditions" that Richard King sees as "characteristic" of the movement.[131] Confronting a Christian tradition whose contemporary spokesmen often criticized Hinduism, Indian leaders refused to respond in kind. Instead, they subsumed Jesus and the religion he founded under Vedic truth. Properly understood, the teachings of Jesus dovetailed perfectly with the universal *dharma*.

SWAMI YOGANANDA'S INDEPENDENT PATH

Mukunda Lal Ghosh joined the elite ranks of Indian college graduates when he received his A.B. in the spring of 1915. Though his education had introduced him to science and Western liberalism, while deepening his knowledge of Sanskrit and Christianity, the grudging student had learned more from his guru than he had from formal coursework. Yukteswar's instruction went beyond intellectual knowledge to include the spiritual disciplines that aided Mukunda's personal development. Discipleship to Yukteswar was arduous. Mukunda's surrogate father, nearly forty years his senior, was no more affectionate than his biological one. By all accounts, Yukteswar was an emotionally distant instructor whose rebukes were severe and humiliating. Another disciple remembers Yukteswar's words as "harsh and incisive." "He would chastise any fault he would see of anyone who was somewhat close to him. Sometimes his reproof was deprecating. There is no point in not admitting that from time to time, even if his reprimand was not physically hard, the meaning of it would become unbearable to us."[132] But Mukunda remained convinced that spiritual renunciation was his path and Yukteswar his appointed guide.

Occasional moments of tenderness made Yukteswar's severity more bearable. Mukunda later described these moments in strikingly erotic terms. His recollection suggests the way that same-sex spiritual intimacy provided a celibate young man with some of the same kind of gratification that others found in heterosexual romantic relationships. In one incident, Yukteswar granted Mukunda the rare privilege of sharing a bed with him. "I am pleased over your cheerful labors today and during the past week of preparations," Yukteswar announced. "I want you with me; you may sleep in my bed tonight." Mukunda was thrilled by the offer. "This was a privilege I had never thought would fall to my lot. We sat awhile in a state of intense divine tranquility." The experience was akin to spiritual bliss. "I felt," he recalled, "a tinge of unreality in the unexpected joy of sleeping beside my guru."[133]

Mukunda's persistence in following Yukteswar's training kept him at odds with his father, who still hoped to win him over to more conventional forms of satisfaction. Until Mukunda's college graduation, Bhagabati had convinced himself that Mukunda's spiritual devotion was a childhood dalliance and not a lifelong path. He kept steering his son toward middle-class security and respectability. In the nepotistic tradition of the Indian civil service, Bhagabati planned to parlay his lifelong career into a comfortable railway service post for Mukunda. With his daughters' assistance, Bhagabati also played matchmaker, looking for a suitable mate for his son. Mukunda rejected two attempted matches before Bhagabati found the right woman. At this point, Mukunda lost patience with his father's refusal to accept the life course he had chosen. He exploded in rage. "What is the purpose of my marriage? To make *you* happy? If you think that *I* will be happy, you are mistaken. I will *never* be happy in marriage. No one knows this better than you."[134]

Though Mukunda's commitment to the spiritual path had long been clear, a vow of celibacy was not required. After all, Yukteswar, his guru Mahasaya, and his own father had all been householders who nevertheless pursued Kriya Yoga. But for Mukunda, rejecting marriage seems to have been an easy decision. No surviving evidence suggests that he experienced any romantic interest in his childhood—there is no hint of a crush, let alone a more serious relationship—apart from a few passing hints of deep intimacy between his two male childhood friends Basu Kumar Bagchi and Mazumdar. "The trio," as they were known by friends and family, were of "one body, one mind, and one soul."[135] Mukunda expressed a "deep affection" for Bagchi that often left him "entranced."[136] For his part, Mazumdar thought Mukunda quite handsome and felt an "attraction to him at first sight."[137] Sananda confirms this view, indicating that Mazumdar and his brother "were attracted instantly" and "felt the magnetic drawing of the heart's pure love."[138] The two eventually grew "so close and intimate" that they could not bear to be apart for long.[139]

Indeed, the intimate exploration of spiritual ecstasy with male companions, first his friend and later his mentor, proved undeniably blissful. *Ananda*, the "bliss" that devotees like Mukunda sought through meditation is etymologically related in Sanskrit to the sexual ecstasy of orgasm, suggesting that the two experiences are semantically linked. Mukunda's yogic practice might have functioned as an alternative to—or sublimation of—sexual desire.[140] Religion scholar Jeffrey Kripal made a case for Ramakrishna's homoerotic tendencies and suggested a link between the swami's sexual desire and his mystical experiences.[141] Whether the limited evidence reflects heterosexual discipline, repressed homoerotic desire, or asexuality on Mukunda's part is impossible to determine; what is certain is that he was determined to remain celibate in order to pursue spiritual bliss more wholeheartedly than he thought family life would allow. When Mukunda bluntly rejected the third prospective bride, Bhagabati reluctantly faced defeat, offering both the job and the bride to Mukunda's cousin. Mukunda had won a long and hard-fought victory in his quest to pursue his own spiritual path.

In July 1915, after his rejection of the third marriage proposal had forced his father to relent, Mukunda Lal Ghosh took his *saṃnyāsin* vows. He became an official member of the swami order, a monastic organization reputedly established in the eighth century by the great Advaita Vedānta teacher Śankara.[142] Taking vows necessitated assuming a new name, an apt symbol of this momentous step in his spiritual journey. Most swamis include the word *ananda* in their titles, as bliss is the highest plane of spiritual experience achieved through meditation. Given the centrality of yoga in his spiritual pathway to enlightenment, Mukunda wanted that word in his title as well. His full title indicated "the bliss that one achieves through yoga." Henceforth, he would be known as Swami Yogananda.

The following year, in August 1916, the young swami decided to test his newfound identity and independence by traveling to Japan. This was the first voyage outside India for a man who would ultimately spend more than half of his life abroad. The timing was not ideal. The Great War had been raging for two years. The Pacific was not a major theater of war, but both India (as a British colony) and Japan were belligerents, and there were some skirmishes over German possessions in the Pacific. The timing was awkward for more personal reasons as well. Yogananda's oldest brother and surrogate father, Ananta, was ill in Gorakhpur when Mukunda departed for Japan from Calcutta. Doctors wrongly diagnosed Ananta's malady as malaria. After Bhagabati transported Ananta to Calcutta for treatment by specialists, Ananta was seen by the principal of Calcutta Medical College, who became "furious" when he discovered that the Gorakhpur doctors had misdiagnosed what was actually a case of typhoid. By the time the illness was properly diagnosed, it was far advanced. Ananta soon died. Yogananda had insisted on traveling to Japan, despite knowing that his brother was ill and that he was ignoring his father's express wishes. As his normally admiring brother Sananda recalled, Yogananda "could not be deterred." Consequently, he was several thousand miles away when Ananta died.[143]

Given the opposition his travel aroused, Yogananda's reasons for insisting on the trip remain surprisingly murky. He offers the least compelling explanation in his *Autobiography*. Foreknowing his brother's eventual death, he fled to Japan out of despair. Given that his trip required cash, a passport, and travel to a belligerent nation in wartime, this account is not too plausible. Yogananda fashioned a melodramatic account of the event:

> "Ananta cannot live; the sands of karma for this life have run out."
>
> These inexorable words reached my inner consciousness as I sat one morning in deep meditation. Shortly after I had entered the Swami Order, I paid a visit to my birthplace, Gorakhpur, as a guest of my elder brother Ananta. A sudden illness confined him to his bed; I nursed him lovingly.
>
> The solemn inward pronouncement filled me with grief. I felt that I could not bear to remain longer in Gorakhpur, only to see my brother removed before my helpless gaze. Amidst uncomprehending criticism from my relatives, I left India on the first available boat. It cruised along Burma and the China Sea to Japan. I disembarked at Kobe, where I spent only a few days. My heart was too heavy for sightseeing.[144]

Although this account acknowledges his family's displeasure, it exonerates his character by suggesting that their dumbfounded reaction stemmed from their lack of appreciation for the depth of his grief. He transforms a presumably selfish act into a sympathetic one undertaken out of extreme emotional sensitivity. His claim that this was a spur-of-the-moment escape, however, is undermined by his having obtained a passport expressly for the Japan trip.[145]

If Mukunda's explanation of emotional strain is not convincing, the real reason remains unclear. Extant accounts offer varying explanations. Two sources see Japan itself as the destination. Satyananda claims that Yogananda had been selected to participate in a program whereby Bengalis learned about science and art in other countries. Apparently, he had been sent to Japan to learn about farming. Given Yogananda's lukewarm academic performance and, as a lifelong urban dweller and son of a professional civil servant, his utter ignorance of farming, this explanation is implausible. Still, it is possible that he may have taken advantage of a relatively obscure program, however ill-suited he was for it, as an opportunity to travel.[146]

More convincing is Dasgupta's explanation that Yogananda "wanted to follow in Vivekananda's footsteps," and at that time "Japan was sort of a place of pilgrimage for independence-hungry Indians." Along with Vivekananda's general example, Yogananda may have been inspired in his choice of Japan by Swami Rama Tirtha, who just a few years earlier had traveled to Japan to teach

Hinduism and had gone on from there to teach in the United States for two years. Yogananda admired Tirtha and later set many of his spiritual poems to music.[147]

Sananda suggests that Yogananda viewed Japan as a stepping-stone to the United States. Yogananda hoped to get a visa to the United States to study for a doctorate. Since direct access to the United States was closed during the war, he thought it would be easier to obtain the visa in Japan. Again, Yogananda's adversarial relationship with education, particularly higher education, makes it difficult to imagine that he ever intended to pursue a doctorate.[148]

Ignoring the element about higher education, it is very likely that Yogananda envisioned the United States as a long-term objective. After using Japan as an initial training ground, Yogananda may have intended to venture further afield to the United States, as Sananda indicates. After all, after coming to Japan from Calcutta, his unofficial role model Vivekananda had eventually made his way to the United States for his first visit in 1893. Whatever the case, it is clear that traveling to Japan was no act of spontaneous grief but a calculated step in his ministry plans. It is equally clear that the new swami was not yet ready for mission work. Shortly after arriving, "highly disillusioned by the societal behavior of the people," Yogananda became "mentally distressed." After only a few days in Japan, he boarded a ship to return home.[149]

By November, Yogananda was back in Calcutta, surprising his family and friends with his hasty return. Always one to keep his own counsel, he made no apology for a failed expedition—one undertaken in the face of family censure—that kept him from the bedside of his older brother and surrogate parent. Instead, he crafted a memory in which his excessive sorrow masked the apparent callousness of his behavior. His ex post facto prophecy of Ananta's death converted the event from a tragedy that caught him by surprise and revealed the foolishness of the entire trip into a foreknown eventuality that drove his departure. By invoking Ananta's *karma*, Yogananda shifted any question of blame from him to his dead brother. If Yogananda was now free to defy his father's wishes and travel where he chose, he was equally free to cast the resulting conflict in the manner he chose.

After his return from Japan, Sri Yukteswar—who is strangely absent from accounts of the debacle—encouraged Yogananda to devote himself fully to organizational work. His longtime friend Mazumdar, who also had taken vows and was now Swami Satyananda, would join him. Before departing for Japan, Yogananda had set up a modest ashram in Calcutta as an extension of Yukteswar's educational centers. Two boys resided at the ashram, while others came regularly for instruction. Inspired by the example of Rabindranath Tagore's

Shantiniketan Ashram, Yogananda, Satyananda, and their friend Bagchi envisioned launching a *brahmacharya vidyalaya*, a residential school that combined spiritual training and contemporary educational principles.

Lacking the funding to activate their vision, they began a pattern that Yogananda would follow successfully the rest of his career: they sought out prospective wealthy patrons and marketed their vision. Bagchi eventually found the ideal potential benefactor. The maharaja of Kasim Bazar, Manindra Chandra Nandi, had a reputation for supporting worthy causes.[150] In response to a petition that Satyananda drafted in English, Bagchi received a prompt, warm welcome from the maharaja. "You are God-sent," Nandi announced. "During the last few days, I had also been thinking about establishing just such an ashram-school." At the maharaja's request, the three young men (chiefly Satyananda) drafted a lengthy document outlining their vision for the school and the proposed curriculum. In March 1917, Brahmacharya Vidyalaya School was established in a house belonging to the maharaja in Dihika, roughly 150 miles west of Calcutta. The school quickly became successful and needed a new location within a year. Nandi offered some property near his palace in Kasim Bazar, north of Calcutta about the same distance as Dihika. After an outbreak of malaria, the school was relocated in 1918 to a twenty-five-acre property at the maharaja's summer palace in Ranchi, where it has remained ever since.[151]

Things seemed to be going well with the Ranchi school. But the restless Yogananda had not given up the idea of an American ministry—a ministry Yukteswar had also envisioned when he insisted on Yogananda's college education. In 1920, the young swami's opportunity to travel to the United States finally materialized. He was invited to be a delegate to an International Congress of Free Christians and Other Religious Liberals in Boston. This meeting, sponsored by a single Christian denomination, was no 1893 World's Parliament of Religions. Still, Yogananda saw it as an opportunity to emulate Vivekananda's earlier visit and chart his own course to fame as a spiritual leader. The *Autobiography* recounts the circumstances in typically dramatic, supernatural terms:

> "America! Surely these people are Americans!" This was my thought as a panorama of Western faces passed before my inward view.
>
> Immersed in meditation, I was sitting behind some dusty boxes in the storeroom of the Ranchi school. . . .
>
> The vision continued; a vast multitude, gazing at me intently, swept actorlike across the stage of consciousness.
>
> The storeroom door opened; as usual, one of the young lads had discovered my hiding place.

"Come here, Bimal," I cried gaily. "I have news for you: the Lord is calling me to America!"

"To America?" The boy echoed my words in a tone that implied I had said "to the moon."

"Yes! I am going forth to discover America, like Columbus. He thought he had found India; surely there is a karmic link between those two lands!"

The following day, out of the blue, Yogananda received an invitation to serve as the delegate from India.[152] Again, the circumstances of his invitation have a more prosaic explanation—one that reveals the characteristic way friends and colleagues were instrumental in advancing Yogananda's career. Heramba Chandra Maitra, who had been Satyananda's teacher at City College in Calcutta, was a leader of the Brahmo Samaj and an executive member of the International Congress of Free Christians and Other Religious Liberals. At Satyananda's urging, Maitra invited Yogananda to attend the conference.[153] Bagchi, now known as Swami Dhirananda, helped Yogananda edit a manuscript that would form the basis of his talk in Boston and his first book, *Science of Religion*.[154] Beyond the conference, Yogananda had no concrete plans. But he was confident that if he made it to the United States, he could find some way to stay and begin a teaching ministry there.

There remained the obstacle of money. When Bhagabati, still unresigned to his son's spiritual passions, asked Yogananda how he would fund his expedition, Yogananda assured him that "God will surely provide it." "Let's see which god gets you the money!" Bhagabati cynically grumbled.[155] God works in mysterious ways. Ultimately, Yogananda persuaded his skeptical father to fund the trip. The independent-minded Yogananda undoubtedly hated to ask his father for funds, and the request could not have been any more pleasant for Bhagabati. His son could have had a comfortable career by now, rather than begging him to fund an expedition with a very uncertain prospect of success. The funding issue resolved, however unpleasantly, in August 1920, Yogananda set sail for the United States, traveling first class on the S.S. *City of Sparta*. He would not see Calcutta—or his family—for fifteen years. This would be the most momentous step in his life's journey. The renunciant would not retire to solitary meditation as swamis traditionally did, gathering a small group of Indian disciples. Instead, he would take the message of yoga to the heart of the Western world.

Although the relationship Mukunda Lal Ghosh shared with Sri Yukteswar rarely matched the *Autobiography*'s idyllic depiction of their first encounter, it was profoundly transformative. Yukteswar embodied the fulfilment of Mukunda's childhood search for spiritual enlightenment, mentoring his protégé in the mysteries of Kriya Yoga and many other metaphysical truths. But significant as Yukteswar's guidance was, he was not the sole influence on Yogananda's spiritual and intellectual development.

Life in metropolitan Calcutta offered the young swami the chance to swim within the larger currents of Indian modernity. The explosion in print culture facilitated access to a wide variety of texts on sacred subjects. The cheap paperback copy of the *Gospel of Ramakrishna* that Yogananda carried around as a young man would not have been available to a previous generation. His mobility, particularly through his father's contacts in the railroad, enabled him to visit various sacred sites and experiment with different organizations — such as the Bharat Dharma Mahamandal, the Ramakrishna Mission, and the Brahmo Samaj — firsthand. His college education, a function of British colonial modernity, aided his development of Sanskrit, which enabled him to formally study a range of Vedic texts. And the *bhadralok* public sphere, formed through newspapers, other periodicals, and informal discussions with college classmates and in coffeehouses, reinforced a nationalist understanding of Indian traditions that had developed in response to Western critiques.

As a result of this widespread exposure, Yogananda developed a worldview that reflected the influence of several distinct Hindu intellectual traditions with competing ontologies.[156] Yukteswar taught him Kriya Yoga and he clearly read Patañjali's *Yoga Sūtras*, the most influential treatise on classical yoga. Yoga promotes a *dualist* ontology, where through meditation the self comes to experience pure, inactive consciousness, a separation from changeable material reality. *Saṃkhya*, closely related to yoga, also embraces a dualist ontology of consciousness and matter, asserting that the material universe was created through a nonsentient process: a disturbance of the perfect balance between the *guṇas*, the three elements of all reality.

As a swami in the order of Śankara, Yogananda was also rooted in the *monistic* cosmology of Advaita Vedānta, which emphasizes that all reality is ultimately one, *Brahman*. The perception of duality is real only on the empirical level. Ultimately, however, this perception is *māyā*, or cosmic delusion. On the absolute level, the individual is not different from *Brahman*, the one eternal, universal, and formless reality.

Alongside the dualistic and monistic traditions, Yogananda also learned a *theistic* tradition from his exposure to the *Bhagavad Gītā*, the Purāṇas, and goddess worship. Theistic traditions often envision a divinity who creates the world as a conscious, intentional act. This personal savior god or goddess offers devotees protection out of sheer grace and is thus worthy of *bhakti*, or devotion, sometimes expressed with great emotion.

Yogananda forged these disparate monist, dualist, and theistic traditions into a serviceable if fluid worldview. Hinduism has generally tolerated a high level of flexibility, and Yogananda never felt compelled to express his views in a rigidly systematic way. Some have assumed that modern Hindu teachers inevitably reconciled divergent beliefs by privileging Advaita's monism. But the picture is not so clear. Even Ramakrishna, the quintessential modern monist, frequently talked about God in theistic ways.[157] Richard King warns that accepting modern Advaitans' claims "to represent all Hindus *in toto* is to fail to grasp the heterogeneous nature of Indian (and indeed human) religiosity in general."[158]

A number of recent scholars have challenged the notion that Advaita was the predominant view throughout Indian history, pointing out much prominent theistic teaching throughout India's past. Andrew Nicholson suggests that Advaita, far from being the sole authentic voice of Hindu philosophy, is a relative newcomer in the larger sweep of Indian intellectual history.[159] Jeffery Long likewise argues that Advaita Vedānta "does not reflect the dominant historical consensus, or even the contemporary consensus, of the Hindu tradition with regard to the ultimate nature of reality."[160] Instead, as David Ray Griffin concludes, "most Hindu piety is theistic, being *bhatkti* (devotion) to a personal deity."[161] The dualism of yoga makes Advaita's absolute monism particularly problematic.[162]

Among the various strands of tradition that formed Yogananda's worldview, he seemed most at home with the theistic cosmology expressed in *bhakti* and the empirical level of Advaita. He encouraged a devotional relationship with a personal creator God while affirming that in some way the individual actually shared the divine nature.[163] He captured this oneness in difference through metaphors relating the ocean to the wave, the flame to the spark, and the flower to the fragrance and through more personal examples. "Thou art the Father to the child," he reflected, "and I am Thy Child; We are One."[164] Satyananda clearly distinguished his childhood friend's devotion to a personal deity from his own absolute monism.[165] Yukteswar thought Yogananda's devotionalism made him especially suited to an American ministry, as U.S. audiences largely hailed from Christian backgrounds and typically thought of God in transcendent terms.[166]

The most significant innovation of modern Hinduism that shaped Yogananda's worldview was the radical reassessment of the faith's possible adherents. Indians had traditionally neither sought nor accepted converts, viewing their traditions as inherent to South Asia and its people. Torkel Brekke identifies three stages in the nineteenth-century transformation of Indian traditions that led to an embrace of audiences outside the subcontinent: the objectification of religion as a separate element of social organization; the individualization of religion that severed people from caste, life stage, and pilgrimages and regional festivals; and the universalization of Hinduism that "now was linked to human nature and could be applied to anyone, anywhere, any time." Universalizing Hinduism as eternal truth for all people abstracted Indian belief from the land, culture, and people of the subcontinent and made them transportable to new lands. As a result, in the late nineteenth century, "Hinduism became a missionary religion." This was a dramatic development. "The thought that a Hindu should travel abroad in order to preach Hinduism simply makes no sense before the transformation in religious perception that took place in the nineteenth century."[167] This radical development in modern Hinduism was the sine qua non of Yogananda's evangelistic efforts.

As a missionary Hindu, Yogananda jettisoned the celebration of seasonal festivals, eschewed building Indian-style temples, downplayed physical depictions of deities, and rejected the notion of caste as a hereditary social system. He was also indebted to modern Hinduism's inclusivism. He selectively incorporated elements of Christianity, New Thought, and physical culture while insisting on unique transcendence of the eternal *dharma*. His mission to the United States sprang from the conviction that India possessed a uniquely rich spiritual tradition that was lacking in the West.

His evangelistic career reflected a form of religious and cultural nationalism especially prominent in Bengal. In embracing the Orientalist dichotomy between a technologically advanced West and a spiritual East, he followed the path charted by such Indian predecessors as Vivekananda, who engaged in "judo" by taking tropes about the spiritual East and adopting them as weapons to celebrate the superiority of Indian culture.[168] In response to attacks on Hindu traditions and caricatures of India as a passive recipient of superior Western knowledge, Yogananda offered India as the ultimate source of spiritual truth, an eternal wisdom desperately needed in the decadent United States. This truth transcended human knowledge, remaining pure even as it absorbed and reinterpreted Western categories of thought and Christian doctrine.

By the time twenty-seven-year-old Swami Yogananda prepared to set sail for the United States, he had explored the rich diversity of Indian spiritual traditions and formed his own distinctive understanding. In 1920, the young yogi prepared to begin his true vocation, offering Americans a spirituality of mental discipline, bodily control, and ecstatic spiritual experiences rooted in ancient beliefs and practices, but in tune with the fast-paced, urban pragmatism of middle-class business people. The first stage in his life journey had ended, and a much longer one was about to begin.

TWO

The Founding of a Home for Scientific Religion

Swami Yogananda and Southern California's Spiritual Frontier, 1920–1925

The young turbaned swami embarked for the United States in August 1920, a visual paragon to Western audiences of the exotic spirituality of the East.[1] His physical journey from Calcutta to Boston—via the Suez Canal and then from Liverpool to the United States—also constituted a symbolic journey, a decisive "crossing" from the only spiritual and physical home he had known.[2] Before embarking, his friends had suggested that, in deference to American audiences, he cut off the beard he wore in keeping with *saṃnyāsin* practice. On board ship, he concluded that the unspoken hostility he sensed from fellow passengers stemmed from his appearance. So he decided to shave his beard.[3] But he kept his hair long and donned a turban for the first time, to gratify American expectations and likely in imitation of Vivekananda's earlier practice.[4] He also continued to wear his ocher robes. Later, when he discovered that his cotton robes would make Americans think him "poverty-stricken" and thus reluctant to follow him, he traded cotton for silk.[5]

Yogananda's sartorial compromise captures his nascent efforts to craft a persona for American audiences. Traveling from one world to another offered unparalleled freedom to invent an image of himself. Understanding both the peril and the promise of his exotic identity, he avoided extremes: he rejected the appearance of a severe ascetic, which would have played into American fears of the Oriental primitive, but he also avoided Western suits and American barbers, judiciously protecting the cachet of his Indian identity. Yogananda's management of his appearance reflected a larger effort to calibrate his message to his audience's frame of reference. His initial audience was a gathering of religious leaders, but he hoped to find a national audience for his Hindu message. A missionary aims, as religious sociologist Lewis R. Rambo explains, "to communicate the new religious message in a manner that is understandable," which typically involves "the creativity of missionaries in finding comparisons and analogies with indigenous culture and customs that will familiarize the message, clothe the new story in recognizable garb."[6] Humanities scholar Srinivas Aravamudan posits a uniquely Indian version of cross-cultural self-presentation called "Guru English," an intentionally ambiguous transnational discourse of translating "South Asian spiritual superiority in search of hegemony." Aravamudan includes Yogananda in his retinue of global gurus, arguing that Yogananda counseled audiences to "abandon the bullock cart vehicle of Western theological paths to God for the Hindu equivalent of the aeroplane—surely a fitting ironic reversal of the perception of India as a technically backward and historical underdeveloped culture."[7]

So where does a Hindu swami fit into a narrative of 1920s America? In this period, Protestants "still thought of themselves largely as guardians of the moral and spiritual treasure carefully cached away by ancestors centuries before," as religious historian Edwin Gaustad puts it,[8] and major American periodicals like *Harper's, Scribner's,* and the *Atlantic Monthly* reflected Protestant establishment views not only in their editorials but often in their articles as well.[9] Public and press attention to religion focused on the fundamentalist-modernist debate within Protestantism, the growing ethnoreligious diversity that prompted nativism, and, to a lesser extent, the growth of Pentecostalism. Given the continued hegemony of Protestantism in American culture, it is no surprise that Hinduism and yoga were not incorporated into older narratives of this period in surveys of American religion.[10] Yet newer surveys, written decades after the first calls to recast the dominant narrative of mainstream Protestant unity as a story of religious pluralism, continue to ignore South Asian spirituality before the 1960s.[11] In contrast, scholars who discuss metaphysical traditions and Eastern religious imports tend to treat these faiths in isolation from the dominant Protestant religion, perhaps in an effort to redress the neglect of nonmainstream traditions. In her magnum opus on American metaphysical traditions, *Republic of Mind and Spirit,* Catherine Albanese places Yogananda in the context of New Thought and other metaphysical movements of the late nineteenth century, without considering his relationship to hegemonic Protestantism.[12]

Yogananda's efforts to reach American audiences with the message of yoga can be properly understood only through an examination of the *intersection* of hegemonic Protestantism and modern Hinduism. Viewed in this context, Yogananda's use of Christian terms and categories reflected an effort to articulate the superiority of Hinduism as a universal religion, using his audience's own universalistic discourse. Yogananda turned the conventional evangelism nar-

Swami Yogananda as he looked at the time of his departure for the United States in 1920.
This is one of the few extant photographs of Yogananda as a young swami before the start of his American ministry. He had donned a turban to look more exotic and had not yet shaved the beard that made Europeans aboard ship with him think he looked sinister.

rative on its head: a subject who hailed from a region long targeted by American missionaries, he had become an evangelist to America. Having come of age in an India deeply enmeshed in modern conditions, he was well prepared to present scientific religion to interested audiences. But such audiences were unevenly spread throughout an isolationist and xenophobic nation often deeply suspicious of Asians and Asian religious practices. Finding a suitable base of operations in Southern California proved a crucial step in his missionary endeavors.

This chapter traces Yogananda's early years in the United States in the context of Protestant upheavals in the modern era. The first section examines his years in Boston, beginning with the religious conference that brought him to the United States and his relatively modest role in the proceedings. The intramural Protestant debate of this period featured opponents who offered competing answers to the epistemological challenges that modernity raised for Christianity's universalistic claims. This section also explores his relationship with the Lewis family, his earliest devotees, who established the template for all his later relationships. Given how challenging and exotic his gospel was, he tended to draw spiritual seekers who found him personally compelling as an authentic and authoritative teacher. This section concludes with the cross-country road trip that took Yogananda to Los Angeles, which quickly became his national headquarters.

The second section shifts the focus of religious ferment to Los Angeles, unfolding in some detail the religious context of the city that became a much more congenial home base for Yogananda's ministry than Boston. The nation's spiritual frontier in the early twentieth century, Los Angeles lured a critical mass of spiritual seekers. As religious diversity increased, Protestant elites extended a grudging tolerance toward nonmainstream movements that provided sufficient space for Yogananda to set up shop. Southern California offered another kind of openness. Boston's landscape had been claimed as sacred space by Christian groups for centuries — by seventeenth-century Puritans, then Transcendentalists, and, more recently, the Christian Science movement. Southern California's landscape, in contrast, was still largely unmarked by religious symbols and available for Yogananda to claim as sacred space.

Finally, to account for the welcome Yogananda received in Los Angeles, the chapter draws on notions of Orientalism to explore the ambivalent position of Indians in Southern California. Indians, in the eyes of many Americans, were both a pagan people with a predilection for lawlessness and simultaneously the embodiment of the exotic East's opulence, mystery, and ancient traditions. Yogananda capitalized on the latter, building on the belief held by some cosmopolitan Angelenos that India possessed unique spiritual wisdom. The chapter ends with Yogananda's purchase of a hotel and property in Mount Washington as his movement's permanent home. In these crucial early years, Yogananda experimented with the persona he presented to audiences, challenged his first disciples to find their own true selves through his teachings and relationship with him, and found a headquarters in the nation's new spiritual epicenter—a quintessentially American place where seekers could encounter God through yoga.

YOGANANDA'S SCIENCE OF RELIGION AND PROTESTANT MODERNISM

The 1920s, contrary to stereotypes that emphasize the era's secularity, were a boom decade for American religion.[13] When Yogananda arrived in Boston in September 1920, his Unitarian hosts and their fellow liberals were enmeshed in a long-running debate with conservative Protestant opponents about the fate of Christian universalism in a modern world—a world in which science provided a comprehensive worldview, "an account of the mysteries of the world" that rivaled Christianity.[14] Many Protestant leaders attempted to steer a middle course, but the intensely polarized debate left the less militant without a voice. Both camps were responding to the challenges of modernity, including "positivistic science, corporate and government bureaucracy, the research university, Darwinism, historical-critical study of the Bible, consumerism, [and] urbanization."[15] The fundamentalist-modernist debate represented competing answers to three major epistemological questions with far-reaching implications: supernaturalism, including the divinity of Christ; the relation between contemporary science and religion, which held implications for views of nature and human ontology; and the rise of higher criticism, which called into question the Bible's unique authority as divine revelation by subjecting it to the same critical judgments as any other text.

Leaders of the conservative faction called themselves fundamentalists for the first time in 1920, the year Yogananda arrived in Boston. Though often attacked by modernist critics as anti-intellectual, fundamentalism was an "intellectual movement" committed to Scottish Common Sense Realism and Baconian inductive empiricism. In fundamentalists' minds, the emergence of "speculative" evolutionary theory had disrupted the earlier harmony between science and religion.[16] Their self-designation reflected the significance of *The Fundamentals*, a set of pamphlets with contributions from scholars around the world, sponsored by oil baron Lyman Stewart, who also got the fledging

Bible Institute of Los Angeles off the ground.[17] The editors aimed to send the pamphlets to "every pastor, evangelist, missionary, theological professor, theological student, Sunday school superintendent, Y.M.C.A. and Y.W.C.A. secretary in the English speaking world" because the "time has come when a new statement of the fundamentals of Christianity should be made."[18] Unsystematic and redundant, the articles in *The Fundamentals* circled back repeatedly to several cardinal supernatural tenets, most notably the divinity of Jesus, the reality of a transcendent God who had intervened in human affairs in miraculous ways, the immortality of the soul, and life after death. They also affirmed the need for conversion, evangelism, and global missions.[19]

Unitarians and other religious liberals, typically labeled modernists, found common ground in their willingness to reconsider traditional tenets in light of scholarly and scientific discoveries. Preeminent modernist Reverend Harry Fosdick argued that while fundamentalists were "driving in their stakes to mark out the deadline of doctrine around the church, across which no one is to pass except on terms of agreement," Christian liberals refused to abandon intellect. Rather, to "really love the Lord their God, not only with all their heart and soul and strength but with all their mind, they have been trying to see this new knowledge in terms of the Christian faith and to see the Christian faith in terms of this new knowledge."[20] Liberals accepted a partly disenchanted world and, consequently, a shrunken role for the church in public life, particularly in the academic realm.[21] They began to think more in terms of divine immanence and this-worldly goals. They also rethought the nature of missions, often concluding that serving the poor remained a legitimate goal but that calls for conversion smacked of cultural arrogance. Instead, Christians should be willing to learn from other religions.[22]

Boston Unitarians were the advance guard of liberal Christianity. They signaled their repudiation of evangelism and openness to other religions by inviting non-Christians like Yogananda to the 1920 International Congress of Free Christians and Other Religious Liberals. The congress commemorated the four-hundredth anniversary of the Pilgrims' landing at Plymouth Rock, eloquently attesting to liberal Protestantism's trajectory from Anglo-Puritan sectarianism in the seventeenth century to broad religious pluralism in the early twentieth. Since the late eighteenth century, Boston had been the hub of Unitarianism, an Enlightenment-inspired movement in Congregationalism that renounced the narrowness of its Puritan heritage. The invitation to the conference expressed its conveners' temperament: "All religious liberals of constructive temper and disinterested purpose share the rich inheritance of the Pilgrim spirit. All are endeavoring to express in the terms that befit the twentieth century the principles and hopes that animated the Pilgrims at Plymouth. We believe, as they did, in liberty under law, in religious toleration, in popular government, in industrial cooperation, and we seek to make these principles vital in the life of modern commonwealths."[23] By the time of the conference, Unitarians had enjoyed a century-long relationship with Indian intellectuals. They had been especially influential in supporting the Brahmo Samaj, the flagship Hindu Renaissance organization described in chapter 1. As the functional headquarters of Unitarianism, Boston was home to many of the Unitarians who established warm friendships with Samaj members in the nineteenth century.[24] Yogananda's modern Hinduism was quite congenial with early twentieth-century Unitarianism, and with American religious liberalism more generally, and throughout his career he would find allies among its ranks.

The International Congress of Free Christians and Other Religious Liberals ran from October 3 through 7 and offered a relatively modest slate of presentations. And despite the hosts' avowed commitment to inclusiveness, the conference remained a largely Christian affair. The keynote speakers were all Christian clergy, including one of the few nonwhites, Professor S. Uchigasaki, leader of a Unitarian church in Tokyo. Along with Uchigasaki and the Buddhist J. Rikumani, Yogananda was relegated to a special session on the relation between "Oriental" religions and liberal Christianity.[25] Still, Yogananda viewed the gathering as an august body, and his own participation as an honor and, in retrospect, a significant milestone in his career. In a commemorative program photograph of several delegates, Yogananda stands conspicuously front and center in turban and flowing robes, surrounded by pale, stern Anglo-Americans in suits; Uchigasaki, with short hair and a suit, peeks out from behind the group. Yogananda serves as an eloquent prop for the organizers' message of broad-minded tolerance, as well as their implicit paternalism.[26] The official program described Yogananda as the "delegate from the Brahmacharya Sanghasran of Ranchi, India," and praised his "fluent English" and "forcible delivery."[27] As a foreshadow of many future occurrences, the local press presented a garbled description of Yogananda. A Boston news article described him, not inaccurately, as "principal of the Residential School of Religion for boys," but added the odd description that he was a representative of "an organization in India which is endeavoring to end religious strife and bigotry and develop broadmindedness."[28]

The organizers' summary of his talk expressed their evident approval of his views. "Religion, he maintained, is universal and it is one. We cannot possibly universalize particular customs and convictions, but the common element in religion can be universalized, and we can ask all alike to follow and obey it. As God is one, necessary for all, so religion is one, necessary and universal. It is only the limited human point of view that overlooks the underlying and universal element in the so-called different religions of the world."[29] Indeed, Yogananda's presentation on rational universal religion, which reflected the language of modern Indian elites, was perfectly calibrated to appeal to the conference's liberal audience.

The title of his talk, "Science of Religion," was a catchphrase among the Brahmo Samaj based on well-established Samaj ideas regarding the "discovery of natural laws about religion" discerned through nonsectarian comparative religious study.[30] Joseph S. Alter argues that modern Indian yoga literature frequently refers to yoga as a science, in the somewhat idiosyncratic sense of a "precise and special way of knowing" whose ultimate goal is "to transcend knowledge and realize absolute truth through direct experience."[31]

Yogananda echoed this language of scientific religious truth. He explicated the "one truth" underlying all religions, "that unless you know yourself as spirit, as the fountain-head of Bliss—separate from Body and mind—your existence is devoid of meaning, your life is akin to that of a brute. We can know God only by knowing ourselves, for our natures are similar to His. Man has been created after the image of God. If the methods suggested are practised in right earnest you will know yourself to be Blissful spirit and in it you will feel God." Yogananda offered a certain means for "the control, regulation and turning back of the *life-force* to transcend the body and mind and know the 'Self' in its native State."[32] God, he said, can be experienced through "four fundamental methods": intellect, devotion, meditation, and science.

Yogananda's erudite presentation, which fit squarely within the liberal camp, provided eloquent testimony to the wisdom of non-Christian religion, challenging the fundamentalist call to evangelize heathen India. He also emphasized the this-worldly benefits of spiritual practice, spoke of the divine as immanent, and embraced a pragmatic, experiential approach to religion. In line with the language of Advaita Vedānta monism, he suggested that God was equivalent to Bliss. "God may be or become anything—Personal, Impersonal, All-merciful, Omnipotent, etc., etc. But what I say is that we do not require to take note of these. *What conception we have put forth is just according to our purpose, our hopes, aspirations and our perfection.*"[33] Indeed, it is his lack of dogmatism about the conceptualization of God that harmonized best with liberal Christianity at this point in his career.

Still, certain elements of Yogananda's presentation seemed more in line with the fundamentalist-evangelical camp, in tone and even in content. The narrative trajectory of his written text, *The Science of Religion*, echoed evangelical Christianity. The book's arc imitated a revival sermon or a gospel tract that moves from despair to hope. It began with the universal desire of humanity to know God, unveiled the false and idolatrous substitutes humans find, and concluded with the liberating transformation that comes when people discover the truth. In matters of content, too, the text had affinities with fundamentalist principles. Religious liberals had retracted the sacred canopy, granting religious truth a narrower authority than in the previous century. Yogananda, however, like fundamentalists, viewed his truth claims as applicable to all areas of life, having direct implications for health, psychology, business, physics, and chemistry.[34] And despite his protests of agnosticism or indifference to depictions of God, he nevertheless simultaneously advanced a view of God as transcendent and personal. Acknowledging that "our spiritual hopes and aspirations . . . require the conception of God as a Personal Being," Yogananda assured listeners that "He is a Person in the transcendental sense. Our being, consciousness, feeling are limited, and empirical, those aspects of His are unlimited and transcendental. Nor should He be thought as an Abstract, Impersonal Being full of His own power and glory, beyond the reach of all experience—even our internal one. He, as we remarked, comes within the calm experience of men."[35] Though instruction on the absolute monism of Advaita continued throughout his career, this devotional view of a personal deity—a deity on whose loving concern humans depend and in whose nature they partake—remained a characteristic feature of Yogananda's teaching.

Paradoxically, it was in his very claim of broad-mindedness that he was most like fundamentalists. *The Science of Religion* assured readers that "*as God is One, necessary, so religion is one, necessary and universal*," and Yogananda downplayed the "question of the variety of religions—that of Christ, of Mahomet, or of the Hindus." But he presented "universal religion" from within a distinctly Indian cosmology.[36] Though he used the English word *Bliss* instead of the Sanskrit word *ananda*, he relied on Vedānta theology throughout. He argued that Bliss was the goal of life (identical to the experience of God), that the search for Bliss was stifled by the "delusion" of confusing the Self with the body, that Bliss could be achieved only by destroying desire and attachment, that a "life current" animates humans physically and spiritually, and that behavior is shaped by innate tendencies known as *saṃskāras*. Rather than celebrating the diversity of various world religions, Yogananda used scientific and Christian language to present an inclusivist vision of Hinduism through which all other religions found their true meaning—a faith that in his view provided uniquely satisfying answers to the anomie of a modern materialistic society.

One central theme of Yogananda's later writing is visible in nascent form in *The Science of Religion*. Though Yogananda discusses Christ only once in the text, his outlook is already evident as he reinterprets Christian understanding of the Crucifixion in light of Hinduism. He begins by dismissing the Gospels' explanation of Jesus's words that the Son of Man will be delivered to Gentiles to be crucified. It is "absurd" to think, Yogananda scoffed, that "Christ, the Eternal Spirit was to be crucified by material nails and His Spirit destroyed." But an alternative explanation made considerable sense: "unless we can *transcend* the body and realise ourselves as spirit we can not enter into the kingdom or state of that Universal Spirit." Not surprisingly, Yogananda found "an echo of this in a Sanskrit couplet of the oriental scriptures. 'If thou canst transcend the body and perceive thyself as spirit thou shalt be eternally blissful and free from all pain.'"[37]

The five-day congress, despite its grand rhetoric about the nation's Pilgrim heritage, remained a modest affair. By contrast, the World's Parliament of Religions in 1893, the model for this gathering in Yogananda's mind, had included more than two hundred formal addresses, drew several thousand participants a day, and lasted more than two weeks.[38] Consequently, Yogananda did not become an immediate sensation like Vivekananda. Instead, when the meeting ended, he was cast adrift in an unfamiliar country. The next few years after the conference proved challenging. In his later *Autobiography*, he glossed over this period from the winter of 1920 through the summer of 1924 with two short, upbeat sentences: "Four happy years were spent in humble circumstances in Boston. I gave public lectures, taught classes, and wrote a book of poems, *Songs of the Soul*, with a preface by Dr. Frederick B. Robinson, president of the College of the City of New York."[39] But at the time, he viewed this period as one of "lean months," "difficulties," and "trials."[40] For two years, Yogananda could not meet his basic needs and leaned heavily on his father, who sent him 250 rupees a month (roughly $100), and continued to support him financially in some fashion for a decade.[41] British government officials, who were quite literally reading his mail, as they did for colonial expatriates with the potential to foment nationalist rebellion, concluded that the swami's American sojourn was temporary. Based on a letter to Bhagabati, they concluded that Yogananda was in the United States "to make a fortune" before returning to India for good.[42]

In November 1920, four weeks after the conference ended, Yogananda attended a talk on Rosicrucianism, a late nineteenth-century esoteric spirituality that, in its Christian form, emphasized secret inner teachings of Jesus. After the talk, one of the meeting's organizers introduced Yogananda to Mildred Lewis, a blue-blooded Bostonian. She was captivated by his exotic appearance: "a dark-skinned, Indian Swami whose long black hair flowed over his shoulders. He was wearing an orange turban, orange coat, puttees, and sort of orange-colored, high-laced shoes. I was not accustomed to seeing anyone dressed this way; I must have been a strange-looking person to this Hindu Swami, as he was for me." She described her meeting with Yogananda to her husband, Minott Lewis. He was not initially interested in the exotic religious teacher. A graduate of Tufts' school of dentistry and an occasional instructor of clinical dentistry there, he had been reared to be wary of "charlatans in the name of religion."[43] A short time later, Yogananda met Alice Hasey at West Somerville Unitarian Church, who invited him to her home to meet several women friends and discuss metaphysics. Ironically, she also contacted her good friend Dr. Lewis and encouraged him to meet Yogananda. After prodding from his wife and Hasey, Lewis finally agreed to meet Yogananda.

Yogananda's first interaction with Minott Lewis illustrates the approach that won over many Americans, a facility with Christian teachings combined with instruction in meditation based on an authoritative guru-disciple relationship. Despite his reluctant agreement to meet Yogananda, Lewis remained on guard. He decided to test Yogananda's theological acumen by challenging him to explain a cryptic apothegm from Jesus's Sermon on the Mount: "It says in the Bible, 'If thine eye be single, thy whole body shall be full of Light.' Can you tell me anything about this? . . . I have asked many, but no one seems to know about it." Without missing a beat, Yogananda answered Lewis's query with another New Testament apothegm, "'Can the blind lead the blind? They both fall into the same ditch.'" This sage reply prompted the doctor to exclaim, "For heaven 's sake, please show me." Yogananda immediately looked into Lewis's eyes and asked, "Will you always love me as I love you?" Though Lewis had never received such an audacious demand from a virtual stranger, he looked at Yogananda and "saw something that I had not seen before in anyone." So he quickly responded, "Yes, I will." Yogananda then proclaimed, "That's fine. I take charge of your life." He introduced Lewis to meditation, as both men sat cross-legged on a tiger skin. Yogananda showed Lewis the Light, "the star in the spiritual eye and the thousand-petaled lotus."[44] With this remarkable exchange, Yogananda's first American guru-disciple relationship commenced. Mildred's own much less dramatic conversion followed, but she always struggled to submit to Yogananda as her guru with the same abandon as her husband.

Given Protestant American aversion to clerical authority and attraction to individual autonomy in spiritual matters, the Lewises' submission to the bold demand of total allegiance from a new acquaintance is surprising.[45] Throughout his career, disciples routinely attested to Yogananda's magnetism. He personified Max Weber's as yet unpublished notion of charisma: "A certain quality of an individual personality, by virtue of which he is set apart from ordinary men and treated as endowed with supernatural, superhuman, or at least specifically exceptional powers or qualities. These are such as are not accessible to the ordinary person, but are regarded as of divine origin or as exemplary, and on the basis of them the individual concerned is treated as a 'leader.'"[46] Minott, and to a lesser extent Mildred, were spiritual seekers when Yogananda appeared in their lives. He offered himself to them completely as the answer to their search, and he demanded unqualified devotion in return. Seeking required openness to the possibility that spiritual truth would manifest in unexpected, even uncomfortable, ways. The very confidence of Yogananda's invitation to discipleship conveyed a self-authenticating spiritual authority. And it promised profound spiritual revelations the Lewises could only imagine.

For Yogananda, this new relationship brought practical benefits. The dentist was no maharaja, but he was as lavish in his financial support as his means allowed. From the outset, Dr. Lewis—who had been taken financial advantage of by an earlier acquaintance—pressed for assurances that Yogananda would not fleece him. Yogananda replied that "with a truly religious man, that is not possible."[47] Still, Yogananda stretched the Lewises' faith. He regularly challenged them to give more—sometimes substantially more—and insisted that his spiritual work could not carry on without them. While Mildred and Minott both continued to wrestle with these demands, Mildred was by far the more reluctant. On one occasion, Yogananda abruptly announced, "Doctor, I will have to have a thousand dollars." The Lewises had two young children, a mortgage, and a new automobile. Mildred balked at this extraordinary entreaty but was overruled by her husband. "I was completely upset by this, but that was the way it went. Master got it; and so he went off to New York with [Alice Hasey] and two or three other students who had been attending lectures in Boston," while the Lewises stayed home.[48] Frustrated by Yogananda's demands, she was occasionally aloof.

Never entertaining the possibility that he had contributed to relational tensions, Yogananda deemed Mildred's conduct a form of spiritual weakness. As the essential mediator of the Lewises' spiritual journey, he viewed any lack of trust in him as tantamount to a lack of faith in God's provision. He rebuked Mildred directly, or in letters jointly written to the couple, or, more manipulatively, as asides in letters written to Minott but sure to be read by Mildred. "Please remember one thing," he wrote to Mildred in 1923, "Sat-Sanga does not depend on anyone's mistakes, it is grounded in truth and its doctrines should be received as such. I invite constructive criticism, but ruthless public criticism simply for the love of it is against the laws of even simple friendship." He quoted Jesus to her, "Judge ye not others that ye be [not] [*sic*] judged." Then he promised to visit her in Boston, commanding, "Let the virus, the inharmonious spirit that disturbs your own peace be removed, and let Sat-Sanga be made alive with your newer expressions during my absence."[49] The following year, in a letter addressed to both Lewises, he expressed the tough love that motivated his reproof. "It sometimes becomes very hard for me to rebuke Mildred, knowing what she feels within. I know and you know, how dearly God has grown our friendship."[50]

Despite the rough patches in their relationship, the Lewises became the swami's closest friends, most admiring followers, and most generous early donors. Yogananda always expressed effusive gratitude for their support. "Words fail to express," he wrote in one 1923 letter, "what you have done for Sat-Sanga. . . . You have been the golden instrument of God's Touch—to manifest His Work. You have shown to me again that God helps when everybody fails." He also assured them of the spiritual—and perhaps material—benefits they would accrue as the ministry matured. "May He give you unceasing faith and fulfill your desires and make you prosperous in every way."[51]

Their trust in his authenticity and authority deepened as they witnessed him heal Minott, the couple's son, and their daughter. In 1921, Yogananda's naturopathic remedy rid their son, Bradford, of a persistent stomachache that never returned. Mildred viewed this as a "miracle of healing," and "from this time on, my faith was established in Master's spiritual powers." This incident was her "first realization of the supernatural powers of Swami Yogananda."[52] He interceded for their daughter, healing her permanently from routine convulsions.[53] Yogananda also healed the elder Minott from a "very depressing, serious condition with the body, which caused me great pain and made the practice of my profession very difficult." Though Minott withheld details, he offered the tantalizing comment that Yogananda had applied a "very peculiar, drastic remedy." Again, the illness left never to return.[54]

Through the Lewises' generosity, Yogananda founded his first "Sat-Sanga," or spiritual community of truth, in Boston and an ashram at Hardy's Pond in Waltham. Ten miles from Concord, birthplace of Transcendentalism, the modest cottage in Waltham was a tribute to Henry David Thoreau's experiment there seventy-five years earlier. Yogananda also visited Ralph Waldo Emerson's Concord home in 1921.[55] He had an affinity for the Transcendentalists and their celebration of feeling, intuition, and self-discovery. The core faithful Yogananda disciples in the Boston area amounted to about a dozen apart from the Lewises, Alice Hasey, and Minott's sister, Laura Elliott. Yogananda's reassurances to Dr. Lewis that the movement would become nationwide must have sounded hollow.[56] Yogananda was right that the number of followers would grow dramatically, but their demographic pattern would change very little. For starters, "His clients appear to be mostly women," the British officials keeping tabs on Yogananda accurately concluded.[57] Educated, middle-class women were generally most responsive to his message, a gender pattern that characterized Christian churches but was more pronounced among non-mainstream spiritual movements.[58] Also, Yogananda generally drew individuals from liberal Protestant denominations or new religious movements, such as Theosophy and Rosicrucianism. His followers were in the forefront of the seekers who have been a prominent feature of American spirituality since the 1960s—individuals engaged in the "universal search for human meaning" outside the constraints of traditional church structures.[59]

The Boston community of seekers struggled to survive. Yogananda tried to increase membership by pitching his talks to a popular audience: "The Inner Life," "Quickening the Right Prosperity," and "Concentration." The absence of religious language was a prominent element of his broadened appeal, especially notable given that "Science of Religion" was the talk that brought him to Boston. He experimented with different ways of presenting himself, often sacrificing accuracy for the sake of presumed appeal. One newspaper advertisement—which appeared in the Amusements section sandwiched between announcements for vaudeville productions, casinos, Charlie Chaplin films, and an Al Jolson blackface performance—displayed a picture of the turbaned "psychologist" and his "sensational discovery of everlasting youth," a topic outside the purview of most psychologists.[60] Despite having no formal training in psychology, Yogananda often labeled himself a "famous psychologist and educator of Calcutta."[61] His self-appointed title may stem from the fact that he viewed his meditation training and its attendant benefits as at least partly psychological. The revised and enlarged 1925 edition of *The Science of Religion* was advertised as a "true psychological account of inner culture, concentration and religion."[62]

Taking inspiration from the developing fields of psychology and personality profiling, Yogananda offered his *Psychological Chart* in 1925 as a tool to "greatly help all individuals, men, women and children . . . especially . . . my students in America." He recommended that they "keep a record or at least a mental diary of their changing tendencies, marking out their progress in the development of any good qualities which they may lack and which they are trying to cultivate." French psychologists Alfred Binet and Thomas Simon had introduced a standardized intelligence test in 1905 and refined it in 1908 and 1911. Meanwhile, Carl Jung's *Personality Types*, which appeared in English in 1923, offered an eightfold typology based on combinations of sensation or intuition, thinking or feeling, and extraversion or introversion.[63] Yogananda claimed that his own test was superior, because "methods like the Binet-Simons Intelligence Test [*sic*] emphasize the analysis and development of the human intellect only, leaving the other faculties of man's nature, such as feeling, moral consciousness, and will, out of consideration."[64] Yogananda's "very comprehensive" inventory also assumed that personality was dynamic, where his contemporaries viewed individual personality as essentially fixed. His understanding was based directly on the faculty psychology of ancient Saṃkhya, which interpreted human personality as resulting from fluctuating combinations of the three *guṇas*, or primordial evolutes. As Yogananda explained: "Sattwa, Raja and Tama are Sanskrit words denoting the three causative principles behind all creation. In human nature, Sattwa manifests as good and noble qualities; Raja produces the active, energetic and worldly qualities; Tama is evil and hateful, obstructing both the light of Sattwa and the activity of Raja."[65]

After an individual conducted an inventory that detailed general background, health, handwriting, attention, memory, reason, imagination, obedience, and "general nature," Yogananda offered six overarching personality types—with corresponding English translations—based on combinations of the three *guṇas*: Sattwa (Elevating), Sattwa-Raja (Elevating-Activating), Sattwa-Tama (Elevating-Obstructing), Raja (Activating), Rajas-Tama (Activating-Obstructing), and Tama (Obstructing). Each type included a list of qualities that individuals could use to measure themselves or their children. Rather than constituting an intellectual hierarchy or a neutral description of personality types, Yogananda's taxonomy was largely moral. For example, Sattwa was characterized by love toward neighbors, animals, and good qualities, while Tama included "attachment to objects of senses," "hypocritical sympathy," and people who were "stupid," "morose," and "lustful." But where intelligence and personality were basically fixed qualities in the better-known systems, Yogananda's psychological chart featured personality profiles that could improve. He counseled readers that their chart, "if read and studied daily or even weekly, will serve as a reminding mirror for detecting and removing your psychological and material shortcomings. By self-analysis and constant watching of all your actions and moods, you will gradually learn your true nature and how to express it flawlessly."[66]

Yogananda's sluggish ministry acquired some vigor with a multicity tour financially backed by the Lewises and promoted by Mohammad Rashid, usually referred to as M. Rashid, a "scion of a distinguished Mohammedan family" whom Yogananda had met on his voyage to the United States. After joining Yogananda's staff, Rashid rented Carnegie Hall, charged a modest but respectable entrance fee, advertised aggressively, and made sure the press showed up to provide more free publicity.[67] Recounting this event to his friend Dasgupta years later, Yogananda confessed that Rashid's resourcefulness initially unnerved him. "Rashid! What have you done?" he asked. "There's not enough money in the bank account to rent Carnegie Hall!" Then Yogananda reflected, "It seemed that Rashid believed in the efforts to cause a stir to bring people to Yogoda Satsanga even more than I did." Rashid's faith proved well-founded, and the talks drew large crowds and plenty of press.[68]

Yogananda did his own part to promote his speaking tour. The novelty of his dress provided free publicity from the press; the New York *Tribune* printed a large photo of Yogananda strolling the streets of Manhattan, with a caption announcing, "A famous Swami comes to town." The content of his New York talk, which eschewed overt religious language, also stirred up interest. The "East Indian mystic"—"wrapped in a salmon-pink robe, draped with sashes, well brushed black locks cascading over his broad shoulders"—"assured his hearers they need never grow old." The article, more cheeky than respectful, informed readers that Yogananda "will establish his fountain of youth at a popular hotel."[69] But even derisive commentary was free press. Suddenly, a moribund ministry had been jolted to life.

Yogananda's successes in New York, followed by visits to other eastern cities, spurred him to more ambitious plans. He decided to take a cross-country automobile tour that would terminate in California. In the late nineteenth century, Southern California became, as historian Lawrence Culver terms it, a "frontier of leisure." While other locations offered temporary escape, Southern California promised "leisure as a permanent way of life."[70] By the early twentieth century, California had become a popular culture synecdoche for adventure and open-mindedness. In *Main Street,* Sinclair Lewis's extremely popular 1920 novel about the provincialism of small midwestern towns, the narrator informs readers that the most intelligent and resourceful small-town residents "leave them in old age, if they can afford it, and go to live in California or in the cities," refuges for the forward-thinking. Anthony and Gloria Patch, the glamorous protagonists of F. Scott Fitzgerald's 1922 novel *The Beautiful and Damned,* honeymoon in California as well. Yogananda had a similar restlessness to travel to California, though for avowedly nobler reasons. Prompted by "an inner call to further extend the work," he "saw in his mind's eye the West of America and especially Los Angeles, swept by his teachings." On his way to the West Coast, he hoped to find new audiences and gain additional financial support for his ministry. He also wanted to learn more about his mission field by touring the nation from one end of the continent to the other.[71]

A cross-country road trip in the 1920s was a significant undertaking, only beginning to be eased by a national highway-building boom that was bringing a "slow, uneven, but steady improvement in roads and technology."[72] The Lewises enabled the five-thousand-mile trip by loaning Yogananda their car. In a letter he sent en route, he referred to "our car" as he told its owners back home, I "wish you both saw this wonderful place."[73] He occasionally wrote to them during the journey, in part to thank them for their generosity. "God has been very kind to me," he wrote, "so he will be kind to you. Never did you bring so much goodness out of me as you have done. What spiritual help you want, that is yours."[74]

Yogananda combined lectures and sightseeing as he toured the country. He spoke on concentration to a "cultured audience" of three thousand at Denver Auditorium. "Bedecked in a dazzling orange turban and golden gown," Yogananda met the mayor. Coloradans betrayed some ignorance about Indian customs, assuming that his first name was Swami or that he was a prince. Yogananda contributed to the confusion by unaccountably claiming that as "the owner of two large schools in India" he was in the United States to study its school system.[75]

As he explored the United States, Yogananda frequently expressed admiration for the nation's landscape. South of Denver, he drove to the fourteen-thousand-foot summit of Pike's Peak, a journey that inspired one of many rhyming rhapsodies: "Ne'er did I expect to roam, On wheels four, Where thousand clouds do soar." But his poetic praise of American beauty typically spurred a comparison with the landscape of his beloved India. "Enthralled" by the beauty of Yellowstone's natural wonders, he was "reminded of our Indian forests." Later, on board a ship along the Alaskan coast, he reflected, "If it were possible to hold a beauty contest of all Nature's grandeurs and scenes of loveliness, it would be difficult to choose between Alaska and her Hindu sister Kashmere for the Queen's throne."[76] In drawing parallels to the sublime landscape of his homeland, Yogananda imbued the scenery of his adopted land with a sense of sacredness. Photos from the trip reinforce this link between the United States and India, juxtaposing the turban-clad Indian swami with quintessentially American images, such as feeding a black bear from his car in Yellowstone. Returning to the continental United States from his Alaska trip, he spoke in Seattle, Portland, and San Francisco with financial and logistical support from local organizers. Finally, he set his sights on Los Angeles.

SOUTHERN CALIFORNIA—MODERN AMERICA'S SPIRITUAL FRONTIER

When Yogananda arrived in Los Angeles in January 1925, he caught a glimpse of the nation's future, a "metropolis in the making" that would offer the most conducive environment for his message of any place he had experienced throughout the nation.[77] Not just a frontier of leisure, California had long been a spiritual frontier for liberal Protestants as well; more recently it had become a haven for various non-Christian traditions, including a few Hindu teachers. Los Angeles grew from a small village of 11,000 in 1880 to a metropolis of 1.2 million by 1930 and the nation's fifth largest city.[78] In a region where municipal boundaries often blur, the county is a more helpful indicator of growth. During the 1920s Los Angeles County added "an average of 350 newcomers a day for ten years."[79]

A vibrant and diversified economy stimulated this urban growth, foreshortening into a half-century developments that typically accompany urbanization: geographic expansion through municipal growth and annexation of surrounding communities, massive investment in infrastructure, real estate speculation, and thriving centers of finance and industry—including oil, airplanes and automobiles, film, and tourism. Though its tourism and entertainment economies dominate popular perceptions of early twentieth-century Los Angeles, the city was also the nation's second largest tire manufacturer and the center of oil production after "spectacular oil discoveries" in nearby Huntington Beach, Long Beach, and Santa Fe Springs turned the Port of Los Angeles into the second busiest port in the world behind New York.[80] The *Los Angeles Times*, the Los Angeles Chamber of Commerce, the Los Angeles Realty Board, and the Automobile Club of Southern California tirelessly promoted the region to a national audience.[81] Real estate boomed and tourism flourished: a million and a half visitors came in 1923, and by the end of the decade, tourism accounted for 10 percent of the city's economy. The nascent Automobile Club of Southern California promoted road trips as the "vanguard of an era of mass leisure and recreation" and claimed that 125,000 cars visited the region in 1926.[82] Decaying Spanish missions, the U.S. equivalent to ancient Mediterranean ruins, became popular tourist destinations for motor enthusiasts.[83] No other region embraced automobile culture—and mobility—like Southern California.[84] Los Angeles was a city on the move, and this restlessness carried into the spiritual realm.

Anglo Protestantism enjoyed unquestioned cultural hegemony in 1925.[85] At the beginning of the century, Los Angeles was one of the "most homogeneous cities West of the Mississippi," whose white midwestern transplants had introduced a "staunch mainline Protestantism" that fashioned a pious, abstemious culture.[86] Protestant ministers spoke at all high school commencements, while Protestant lay people dominated the local press, city government, school boards, and community organizations, including the YMCA, Woman's Club, and Chamber of Commerce.[87] The scathing evaluation of former resident Willard Huntington Wright reflected the views of many critics: "These good folks brought with them a complete stock of rural beliefs, pieties, superstitions and habits" that explained the "Quakerish regulation of public dance halls" and the "stupid censorship of the theaters."[88]

Despite Protestant hegemony, migration was beginning to change the city's religious profile. "Religiously, something distinct from the rest of the nation was happening in the City of Angels in the first decades" of the twentieth century, says Michael J. Engh. "During the 1920s in particular, the multiplicity of faiths and the variety of forms of worship aggravated the apprehension of many outside observers and the skepticism of many residents."[89] By 1941, the Works Progress Administration city guide to Los Angeles could comment, only a bit hyperbolically, that the "multiplicity and diversity of faiths that flourish in the aptly named City of the Angels probably cannot be duplicated in any other city on earth." The section on religion concluded with an attempt to keep marginal sects from tarring the city's reputation. "In Los Angeles today," mainstream religious organizations, "together with the less eccentric unorthodox groups, form a dignified background against which the fantastic stands out in garish high lights."[90] Catholicism grew in part from Mexican immigration into the state following the Mexican Revolution of 1910–11. While some were converts to evangelicalism as a result of American missionary work in Mexico, the majority remained faithful to Rome.

By the 1920s, the Great Migration of black southerners had expanded beyond northern industrial cities like New York, Chicago, and Detroit to western cities like Los Angeles. African American visitors described Southern California as a new Eden, convincing many southern blacks that the region was a haven from the South's violence and discrimination.[91] These mythic evocations overstated the case, as opportunity and prejudice expanded side by side. Still, the city afforded its black residents space to create a public sphere.[92] The black community quickly realized the limits of toleration when Hollywood's first blockbuster film, D. W. Griffith's *Birth of a Nation*, celebrating masculine white Protestant resistance to black rights, was screened in 1915. The film helped relaunch the Ku Klux Klan, this time as a national organization devoted as much to nativism as to antiblack racism. Los Angeles's fledging National

Association for the Advancement of Colored People chapter was one of the first organizations to protest the film nationwide.[93]

Innovative movements flourished in this dynamic global metropolis as well. New Protestant sects with biblicist theologies established deep roots in the Southland. These movements' conservative theological beliefs should not obscure their spirit of innovation. Los Angeles was one key center of the national fundamentalist movement, and the region's leaders "were obsessed with modernism," using "every available modern means—magazines and radio, especially—to voice their response to the transforming metropolis."[94] The early Bible Institute of Los Angeles was a quintessentially L.A. institution. Begun in 1909 with funding from Unocal founder Lyman Stewart, the Bible Institute became a key fundamentalist institution nationwide. Bible institutes served as new educational institutions, unaccredited alternatives to theological seminaries and liberal arts colleges—and upstart challenges to them.[95]

Pentecostalism, currently the fastest-growing religious tradition worldwide, had crucial Los Angeles roots. The Azusa Street Revival, often celebrated as the birth of Pentecostalism, broke out in 1906 with an interracial group of Holiness Wesleyans who experienced the supernatural gift of speaking in tongues.[96] On January 1, 1923, Aimee Semple McPherson, a Canadian convert to Pentecostalism, officially opened the doors of Angelus Temple in Echo Park, the headquarters of her nascent Foursquare Church, eventually an international denomination. Though she upheld a literal interpretation of the Bible, McPherson was an innovator in both theology and presentation. She proclaimed a brand of Christianity that integrated the physical, emotional, and spiritual. A dramatic performer who used radio effectively, she had many friends in journalism and Hollywood. Even as she criticized modernism in religion, her own ministry was indisputably a modern product. Ministers and evangelists from established denominations certainly recognized the innovative qualities of her theology, as their frequent criticisms reveal.[97]

More importantly for Yogananda's ministry, the region also drew spiritual seekers from metaphysical movements outside the Christian mainstream, disproportionate to their size in most of the rest of the country. The absolute numbers of Christian Scientists and Theosophists remained small, though their presence fostered a sense of openness that provided a gateway to Yogananda's teaching on yoga and Hinduism.[98]

Christian Science founder Mary Baker Eddy, who came from pious New England Congregational stock, sought a harmony between science and religion, mind and spirit—a message broadly congruent with Yogananda's. Christian Science speakers in Los Angeles earnestly promoted their movement's

Christian identity in response to criticisms of heresy and dissociated themselves from suspect practices like mesmerism, hypnotism, and mind cure. Church apologists explained that Eddy's teachings aimed to restore primitive Christianity and closely followed the teachings of Jesus, who conquered sin, banished evil, and healed the sick.[99] Despite its claims to biblical fidelity, core Christian Science tenets were at odds with traditional Christian cosmology and ontology. Christian Scientists viewed God as the only reality and God's fundamental identity as Mind. Humans were a product of God's thought and thus truly themselves only in exercising thought. Matter was illusory, which meant that evil—including sin and especially sickness—did not really exist and that sensory perception was delusive. Salvation came from coming to understand the truth and being liberated from the shackles of the body. Though many of these tenets align with Advaita Vedānta, the similarities were likely coincidental, since Eddy knew little about South Asian spiritual traditions or their texts. Eddy generally distanced herself from Hinduism and Buddhism, emphatically rejected Theosophy, and insisted on her movement's Christian identity.[100]

For a small new sect, Christian Science enjoyed a robust presence in early twentieth-century Los Angeles, receiving frequent and generally positive coverage in the press. Speakers from around the country, certified through the Mother Church's Board of Lectureship, routinely filled public spaces like the Philharmonic Auditorium. Reaching out to audiences using evangelical-style rhetoric, they pointed out the elusiveness of the quest for liberty, comfort, contentment, and peace. They then explained how Christian Science could meet their audience's deepest needs.[101] Despite these efforts to connect with audiences, their outreach was not particularly engaging, and their talks never moved beyond rehearsing staple doctrines. Though Yogananda took pains to highlight the differences between his movement and Christian Science, some seekers were undoubtedly drawn to him by the similarities between the two.

Theosophy also had a minor but important presence in Southern California, and like Christian Science it could function as a gateway to Yogoda. But unlike both Yogoda and Christian Science, Theosophy was overtly hostile to Christianity, which considerably limited its mainstream appeal. In 1875, two elites, Henry Steel Olcott, attorney, Civil War veteran, and member of New York's "metropolitan gentry," and Russian émigré aristocrat Helena Blavatsky met and formed an esoteric movement that aimed to reform popular spiritualism.[102] Its most important early work, *Isis Revealed*, revealed the rediscovery of an ancient tradition rooted in Egypt. One could contact ancient Masters and access their power for one's own growth and healing. Within a few years, Olcott and Blavatsky had explicitly embraced Indian ideas, including reincarnation, though they drew more from Buddhism than Hinduism.[103] In 1880, they relocated to India.

A split in the movement left Katherine Tingley, a Massachusetts woman of old Congregational stock, head of the American branch. She eventually relocated the national headquarters to Point Loma, a San Diego bluff overlooking the Pacific Ocean. "Lomaland" became a utopian community that experimented with equal gender roles and communal childrearing.[104] It also created a Raja Yoga boarding school that occasionally came under suspicion for allegedly mistreating children.[105] Los Angeles benefited from the proximity of the national headquarters, with Tingley herself regularly providing talks. But turning such a religion into a popular movement for evangelistic purposes was no easy matter. Even more than Christian Science, Theosophy earned criticism from Christian ministers. One Presbyterian minister in L.A., for example, Dr. Herbert Booth Smith of Immanuel Presbyterian, complained that while the movement claimed to embrace universal truth, it actually showed "strong preferences for Hindu belief" while showing "scant appreciation for Christianity." The result was to "make Jesus a debtor to Eastern wisdom."[106]

Tingley and others tried to strike a balance between highlighting the uniqueness of Theosophy's arcane tenets and their compatibility with the mass culture of the 1920s. Leaders rooted the movement's authority in the ancient past. "Theosophy is not modern," Tingley claimed, "it is a restatement of the ancient wisdom—that religion adapted to recent conditions. It is as old as the ages, and if one will study it he will find that it was lived and practiced very beautifully and altruistically centuries before time of Jesus."[107] Tingley's assertions notwithstanding, Theosophy was fundamentally a modern project of self-liberation, a syncretic product of a globalized world. Though Theosophy drew more from Buddhism than Hinduism, people in the market for Eastern spirituality could easily have been drawn to both Theosophy and Yogoda. And some undoubtedly preferred the authority of an Indian-born teacher to the eclecticism of Theosophy.

Two other communities with spiritual connections flourished in Southern California in this period; both contributed to making the region hospitable to Yogananda. First, from the late nineteenth century, Southern California's climate lured health seekers, who often linked spirituality and physical well-being.[108] Though the first wave peaked by 1900, a second wave was cresting at the time Yogananda settled in the region.[109] The quest for health often produced unorthodox medical approaches that gave Los Angeles a bad reputation. Writer Louis Adamic found "no end of chiropractors, osteopaths, 'drugless physicians,' faith healers, health lecturers, manufacturers and salesmen of all sorts of health 'stabilizers' and 'normalizers,' psychoanalysts, phynotists, mesmerists, the flow-of-life mystics, astro-therapeutists, miracle men and women." With more technical expertise, the *Journal of the American Medical Association*'s editor claimed that the city was known "throughout the medical world as one of the richest stomping grounds in the country for medical quackery and 'cultism.'"[110] Yogananda would capitalize on this interest in the spirituality of health, presenting a coherent interpretation of the relation between physical, mental, and spiritual well-being.

Second, utopian communities began to flourish in Southern California's open spaces and mild climate in the late nineteenth century. As historian Donald E. Pitzer concludes, "The focus of much of America's communal utopian experimentation shifted" to the West Coast, "where all manner of religious and social causes found a sympathetic hearing" around the turn of the century.[111] These communities were by no means all religious, but "perfectionism lay at the heart of California utopianism," according to historian Robert Hine. This spiritual ethos encouraged members to agree that humans "can achieve in this life not only freedom from sin, but the highest of the virtues, truth, beauty, goodness. And society itself, like man, can be perfectly remolded. In this sense, utopians were also millenarians looking for the coming of the ideal commonwealth and eternal happiness on this earth."[112] Elements of Yogananda's teaching, including the idealized harmonious community he envisioned, resonated with these utopian traditions.

There was something in the soil — or maybe the air — of Southern California. From the Gold Rush era, the opportunities and hazards of America's furthest western frontier drew adventurers and nonconformists of all types. By the late nineteenth century, attention was beginning to shift from the San Francisco Bay area to Southern California. The region's real estate booms may not have been gold rushes, but they drew some of the same types of risk-takers.[113] Where social geographers argue that high urban density intensifies the sense of intrusion felt by long-term residents, forcing them to confront difference — including religious difference — the opposite dynamic was at work in Southern California.[114] The lack of a single population center and the geographic openness of the Los Angeles Basin, hundreds of square miles in area, allowed diversity to flourish in spite of Protestant institutional hegemony. Groups had space to invent their own eclectic traditions, as open space fostered a live-and-let-live ethos.[115] The landscape lured many who found the divine in nature and converted many who came for other reasons. Sublime encounters with blue skies, golden sunlight, and the vast Pacific inspired evocations of Eden or the exotic Orient at the ocean's far shore: "California is a gilded state," proclaimed poet Vachel Lindsay. "The gold of California is the color of the orange, the glitter of dawn in the Yosemite, the hue of the golden gate that opens the sunset way to mystic and terrible Cathay and Hindustan."[116]

Yogananda would not be the first to make explicit the attractions of landscape and climate in supporting a spiritual quest. "In order to make our philosophy of life and health of practical value in the world," the founders of the Rosicrucian Fellowship bought forty acres in Oceanside, about ninety miles south of Los Angeles, on "one of the sightliest spots in sunny Southern California." Mount Ecclesia, as they named the headquarters, offered "an unobstructed view of the beautiful blue Pacific Ocean. Directly west lies the island of San Clemente, 75 miles out, and ships are often silhouetted upon the skyline as they sail by." Looking eastward, "we may behold a landscape equally glorious, varied, and wide": "Immediately below Mount Ecclesia lies the smiling San Luis Rey valley with its fertile green fields and its historic old mission; a little further away are the rounded foothills with their wonderful play of light and shade, then the mountains with their rugged contours, and farthest to the east we see . . . snowcapped peaks." Continuing with its boosterist tone, the fellowship touted Southern California's climate, "as wonderful as the view, and as incomprehensible to all who have not lived here. One may wear a white shirtwaist outdoors on every day in the winter," and "we do not perspire on the warmest day in summer on account of the sea breeze," which fills "our lungs with invigorating ozone fresh from the heaving bosom of the great Pacific Ocean." This salubrious climate was a remedy for physical as well as spiritual well-being, "a veritable elixir of Life" that "offers such rare physical conditions for the attainment of health that it is probably without a peer."[117]

For various reasons then, Southern California provided soil for new religious movements by the early twentieth century. One journalist called the region "the most celebrated incubator of new creeds, codes of ethics, philosophies and near philosophies and schools of thought, occult, new and old."[118] Los Angeles–area residents observed the bewildering diversity of the region's spiritual landscape with a mixture of anxiety, bemusement, and an odd sense of local pride. A columnist proclaimed in 1900, "Los Angeles is the headquarters for scientific, socialistic, humanitarian, occult and other societies dealing with matters—or rather with ideas—that are more or less beyond the ken of the average every-day mortal," including "Harmonial Spiritualists, the Universal Brotherhood, the Cooperative Spiritual Workers, the Theosophists, a School of Metaphysics, a school of 'sciento-philosophy and psycho-pneumic culture' (God save us!) and a 'home of truth.'"[119] In 1908, an editorial described the city's ethnoreligious diversity, where the "Swiss man and maid in costume

. . . jostle the turbaned, swart Hindu from Calcutta or Benares. . . . The Brahmin from Bombay talks to the sun-worshiping Parsee from Teheran." He encouraged readers to welcome all newcomers and avoid the inconveniences of travel. "We can have the world in a nutshell, so to speak, in this cosmopolitan city."[120] Paging through the weekend paper, Aldous Huxley witnessed the remarkable diversity of the city's spiritual marketplace, where "a whole page was filled with the announcements of rival religious sects, advertising the spiritual wares that they would give away, or sell on the Sabbath."[121] More than a decade later, Huxley would be drawn deeply into the Vedānta movement. Willard Huntington Wright noted the city's taste for "spiritualists, mediums, astrologists, phrenologists, palmists and all other breeds of esoteric windjammers."[122] This journalistic trend reached its apogee in the 1940s with Carey McWilliams's assessment of L.A. as home to "the world's prize collection of cranks, semi-cranks, placid creatures whose bovine expression shows that each of them is studying, without much hope of success, to be a high-grade moron, angry or ecstatic exponents of food fads, sun-bathing, ancient Greek costumes, diaphragm breathing and the imminent second coming of Christ."[123]

Early twentieth-century Southern California epitomized the spiritual options available in the modern world. If Boston had historically served the nation's spiritual anchor, a point the organizers of the International Congress of Free Christians and Other Religious Liberals tried to remind delegates with a visit to Plymouth Rock, the city no longer played that role. By the early twentieth century, the focus of spiritual energy had shifted to Southern California, the nation's "spiritual frontier."[124] Yogananda could not have found a better place to call home.

YOGANANDA, ORIENTALISM, AND HINDU SPIRITUAL LEADERS IN SOUTHERN CALIFORNIA

Observers of the religious landscape of Los Angeles often gestured to the presence of Indians and Hindus, which they viewed interchangeably as a key indicator of the region's spiritual diversity.[125] As "America now looked at India through British eyes,"[126] white Angelenos' views of "Hindoos" mirrored British concerns about infanticide, child marriage, and widow suicide and the need to evangelize India to usher in civilizational—not just religious—transformation. Though the few Indians in the United States rarely registered on the national nativist radar, whites in Southern California expressed occasional anxiety about a heathen Hindu invasion. In stoking their own racialized fears, whites drew on the region's robust nativist tradition. Nativism included a history of ethnic violence against Mexicans and Chinese. In the 1920s, the region hosted a vibrant Ku Klux Klan, which focused on immigration restriction and often received strong support from conservative Protestant churches.[127] A mutation of nineteenth-century Western fears of a yellow menace, white panic about Indians was an amalgam of racial, cultural, and religious elements. In the early twentieth century, Los Angeles residents became concerned that Indians in Vancouver might begin migrating to the city, particularly after a white mob's attack on Indians in Bellingham, Washington, in 1907 prompted many Indians to leave the state.[128]

Anticipation of Indian immigrants proved more terrifying than their actual arrival. When the "first of their race to be employed so near here" began work on the Los Angeles–Pacific trolley in 1908, the event was greeted with remarkable equanimity. "They are a picturesque lot in their turbans," a distinctive form of dress responsible for much of the hostility they faced. Because local law "protects all who behave themselves whatever their race," these hardworking laborers who are content with low wages "may be but the advance guard of many who will come this way when they find that there they will be given a chance to labor peacefully without molestation."[129]

Still, many whites assumed a link between racial and civic identities, and they doubted that Indians could make good citizens. The Reverend Dana Bartlett, a Congregationalist minister who operated a settlement house in Los Angeles, warned local citizens that ten thousand Hindus—a great exaggeration of the actual total, which probably numbered a few hundred—were already in the city, and "this army is constantly being augmented." Bartlett contended that Indians were even more problematic than Mexicans, Chinese, and Japanese, who had all failed to assimilate.[130] Indians insisted on maintaining caste and traditional food customs, refusing to "develop into good citizens."[131] Other critics thought Indians' unwillingness to doff their turbans in a courtroom symbolized their broader inability to assimilate. This issue popped up intermittently for a decade, when Indians finally won the right to wear their turbans in court, to the dismay of many white citizens. Ironically, the turban-wearing Indians were almost certainly Sikhs, a religious tradition that began in northern India in the late fifteenth century and is often considered distinct from Hinduism, though this distinction was clearly lost on white observers.[132] The civic critique of Indians intensified during the Great War, as Indians agitating for home rule made their headquarters on the Pacific coast. Conservative middle-class Americans trained to fear political radicalism were horrified by the self-rule movement in India, especially when armed rebellion broke out.[133]

The landmark 1923 Supreme Court case *United States v. Bhagat Singh Thind* epitomized the intersection of racial identity, citizenship, and religion that Hindu teachers in Los Angeles and elsewhere were forced to combat. Thind, an American World War I veteran, was denied the right to naturalize by the Immigration and Naturalization Service. The Immigration Act of 1917, the first of several nativist federal immigration laws, broke with previous legislation by restricting rather than regulating immigration. Among other provisions, it created an Asiatic Barred Zone, preventing immigration from most of that region. Immigration officials asserted that immigrants from the restricted zone who arrived prior to the law's enactment were disqualified from naturalizing. Because the Naturalization Act extended naturalization rights to "free white persons," Thind based his right to citizenship on his identity as an Aryan and thus a white man. Thind's argument reflected the prevalent theory that northern Indians descended from Caucasus migrants in the ancient period, based on the linguistic scholarship of prominent Orientalist scholars William Jones and Max Mueller. The U.S. District Court ruled that Thind qualified for citizenship as a white man, based on the majority of lower court rulings that Indians were white. The Supreme Court itself had recently affirmed two lower court rulings that high-caste whites were eligible for naturalization, only to reverse course three months later and overrule the lower court rulings.[134] In appealing the district court's ruling, the federal government argued that a vast cultural and civilizational chasm separated Indians and whites—irrespective of racial origins—and cited Rudyard Kipling's "White Man's Burden" to buttress this claim. Persuaded by such compelling scholarly evidence, a unanimous Supreme Court dismissed Thind's claim in favor of a definition of whiteness understood by the average American on the street. As some critics immediately pointed out, there was evidence that during the era of both the original naturalization law and its 1875 revision, popular American texts included Indians as part of the white population.[135] In response to news of the case, Yogananda urged his followers to support a bill by New York senator Royal S. Copeland that would define Indians as whites eligible for naturalization. He prodded "truth-loving, Christian Americans" to recognize that "their high and sacred duty is to uphold the beautiful standards of Christianity, whose Founder said, 'All ye are brethren' (Matthew 23:8). If Christianity is to remain a vital and redeeming faith in the world, it must inspire its followers with courage to maintain its principles. Mental sloth is spiritual stagnation. We must fight for the right, and be willing to actively bestir ourselves in a spiritual cause against injustice."[136]

The *Thind* ruling, a disaster for the region's Indians, caused elation among white Angelenos. The *Times* thought that the Court had displayed "considerable enlightenment" in reinforcing the boundary of white identity against Thind's cunning legal argument. The author expressed approval of the Court's argument that recent congressional legislation barring admission to "all natives of Asia . . . including the whole of India, constituted conclusive evidence . . . of the 'Congressional attitude of opposition to Asiatic immigration generally.'"[137] Apart from jurisprudential considerations, Singh's agitation on behalf of Indian self-rule played a role in the Court's final decision. As a founding member of the Ghadr Party, a radical nationalist group that advocated violence in the pursuit of self-rule for India (and instigated the violent 1916 uprising against British troops in India), Singh was ineligible for citizenship, U.S. government officials argued.[138] While whites celebrated, California attorneys sued unsuccessfully to allow their Indian clients to retain citizenship papers granted by state officials before *Thind*. And because California's 1913 Alien Land Law—which primarily targeted Japanese immigrants—prevented noncitizens from owning land or negotiating long-term leases, Indians' landholding claims were annulled.[139] Reaction to the *Thind* decision highlighted white stereotypes about Indians. Critics often insinuated that Hindus displayed a general disposition toward crime, violence, and immorality. Many lumped together various activities like hypnotism, superstition, astrology, and palm reading, often popularly linked to crimes of passion and sexual degeneracy.[140] State and municipal government officials took the threat of psychics and palm readers seriously enough to launch a major campaign in late 1924, aiming to "seriously cripple, if not eliminate, purported psychic and pseudospiritualist activities on the Pacific Coast."[141] Press coverage of a famous 1905 case highlighted this amalgamation of racial, cultural, and religious perceptions. A "Hindu fake palmist" named F. Rubel shot a white competitor during an altercation. On trial, "whatever powers of occultism" he possessed, "he utterly failed to hypnotize the jury," which found the "long-haired Hindu with sensuous eyes" guilty of assault with a deadly weapon. In announcing his sentence Judge Smith betrayed his own prejudices, commenting that the altercation had resulted from competition between a Yankee faker and the defendant "with the flowing locks and robe, and with the melodious voice."[142]

Whites' denunciations of Indian belief and practice often revealed their own ignorance. William T. Ellis thought Hinduism "foolish and futile" in teaching that a practitioner could "sit and look at the end of one's nose and think of nothing" as a method for "escaping from sin and entering into bliss."[143] Another observer, adopting a more tongue-in-cheek tone, described an open-air meditation meeting led by Swami Touryanda where the white devotees made clear that "the attempt to sit cross-legged, with hands clasped, spine on a perpendicular line, and eyes inclined toward the nose, is an accomplishment not yet within the grasp of the western barbarism [*sic*]." They made a great effort "to pay no attention to things ordinarily called dangerous, such as chill winds, poison oak, and things that crawl." During meditation, the swami occasionally "uttered a long, weird chant in Sans Krit, entirely unintelligible." Despite the lighter tone, the author still concluded that the "entire trend of the teaching is diametrically opposed to the Christian philosophy of thought—no sin, no hell, no devil, but bliss absolute within the grasp of all."[144]

On their own, Indian practices might simply remain misguided heathen efforts to achieve salvation. But the greater concern was that Indian religious teachings were spreading beyond their own communities and into the living rooms of gullible white women. Los Angeles swami Baba Bharati, discussed below, became a national symbol of these fears through Mabel Potter Daggett's "Heathen Invasion," which placed photos of swamis alongside images of American women in Victorian dress, suggesting the inappropriate domestic intimacy that yoga training fostered, where "dusky-hued Orientals sat on drawing-room sofas, the center of admiring attention, while fair hands passed them cakes and served them tea in Sevres china." Viewing religious allegiance in military terms, Daggett warned that while churches were busy sending out missionaries, the "pagans have executed an amazing flank movement; they have sent their emissaries to us."[145] Though yoga ostensibly meant the path that leads to wisdom, "it is proving the way that leads to domestic infelicity and insanity and death." She excoriated the shallowness of women and the showmanship of gurus who come "silken clad and sandal shod" with their "gorgeous robes," outcompeting plainly dressed American ministers. Yoga's "promise of eternal youth" assures American women "health and long life and the power to stay the ravages of time."[146] These xenophobic warnings were not confined to the pages of middle-brow magazines. Elizabeth Reed, a reputable scholar of Hinduism and Buddhism and member of the Royal Asiatic Society, offered a more academic version of this argument. She warned about the dangers of modern moneymaking gurus, who hypnotized hapless women and exploited them sexually.[147] Popular religious survey texts assumed that the Hindu worldview was intrinsically problematic or associated Hinduism with the growth of cults.[148]

The occasional if malicious critiques of Indians and their spirituality do not tell the full story, however. American Orientalist tropes—like their English counterparts—provided an alternative view of Hinduism. Though undeniably patronizing, Orientalist discourse did reflect an open, affirming attitude toward "Hindus" and "Hinduism." As a result, *Hindu* became a polyvalent reference to people and culture, sharing positive connotations related to fashion and culture, as well as negative connotations associated with dubious spiritual practices. Americans tended to collapse high-caste Indian people, their culture, and their fashion items into a single exotic subcontinent of luxurious princedoms. When members of a "Hindu royal family" from Bombay visited Los Angeles, the wife "created quite a sensation." Reflecting the vague geography that amalgamated North Africa and Southwest Asia into a single "Orient," the article explained, "She is traveling in the native Hindu sari, which resembles the gowns worn by Egyptians and residents of Palestine. . . . Another feature of her dress that attracted considerable attention . . . was that she wore a large diamond set on her right nostril."[149] Oriental culture inspired fashions that prompted one author to proclaim that Kipling needed to recant his assertion that East and West would never meet. "The orient, alluring, beautiful and with a mysterious charm, contributes a fashion."[150] In addition to the turban as a women's fashion accessory, desirable fabrics included dresses in "Hindu crepe" and autumn frocks in "Hindoo brown."[151]

The visual appeal of Indian dress carried over to the arts, which were likewise captivated by an exotic and undifferentiated Orient that represented fantasies of lush scenery and erotic titillation.[152] Los Angeles residents encountered depictions of Indians through drama, dance, and poetry. *The Hindu*, an extremely popular Broadway play starring Maud Allan, showcased one rendering of Hindu culture.[153] Ruth St. Denis, who had a background in Theosophy and Christian Science, founded the Los Angeles Denishawn School in 1915, providing interpretations of Eastern dance. The "Kama Dance," inspired by Laurence Hope's poems of the Orient, ultimately derived from an Indian legend.[154] Romantic poems and florid prose pieces by Calcutta-raised film director Surendra Guha were occasionally reprinted in the newspaper as well.[155] The famous Bengali poet Rabindranath Tagore, gushingly branded the "Shakespeare of India" by affectionate Angelenos, drew large audiences during visits in 1916 and 1923. For one Angeleno, the opportunity to meet India's famous poet was just one of the "many glories of California," which included ethnic diversity, natural scenery, and the film industry.[156]

Film provided a particularly attractive medium for depictions of Orientalist fantasy. Especially in the era before sound, film relied on spectacle, making an idealized India the perfect subject. Though negative stereotypes of lower-caste Indians occasionally appeared, they were overshadowed by admiring portraits of wealthy elites.[157] Sid Grauman staged an elaborate production called *City of Dreams*—which included nautch girls (royal courtesan dancers) and a Hindu conjurer—as an introduction to screenings of *The Thief of Bagh-*

dad at the Egyptian Theater in Hollywood.[158] Films like 1922's *The Young Rajah* invited audiences to sympathize with the protagonist, silent screen heartthrob Rudolph Valentino, a likable character raised in the American South who discovers that he is really an Indian prince robbed of his kingdom. *The Young Rajah*'s director, Phil Rosen, became "thoroughly familiar with Hindu lore" through making the film and decided to incorporate a "Rajah Dance" into the annual Hollywood directors' ball the year after the film premiered.[159]

The region's widespread interest in health and nontraditional medicine also created some respect for Indian traditions. Los Angeles doctor Philip Lovell became a sort of 1920s public intellectual for health issues with his regular *Los Angeles Times* column, "Care of the Body."[160] Lovell was a naturopath deeply interested in all dimensions of well-being—environment, diet, mind, and exercise—and a cosmopolitan with at least limited knowledge of many foreign traditions. His column frequently noted beliefs held by "Hindoos," including the importance of breath control and an Ayurvedic diet. His tone could be patronizing, but his openness to Indian traditions contributed a sense of tolerance to public discourse about Indians.[161] Similarly, Barclay L. Severns ran a weekly column beginning in November 1922 related to health and fitness that particularly emphasized diet, exercise, posture, and breathing. He showcased an example of an Indian whose mental control contributed to his overall health: "Ram Murth Naider lives in India. He has proven his almost superhuman strength before huge Hindu and European audiences." Though short and stocky, "he can swim for two hours continuously and run twelve miles at a stretch." Incredibly strong, Naider broke heavy iron chains placed around his shoulders in a test of strength. "Naider's control of breath and power of concentration helped him to localize his energies in that part of his body where they are most needed."[162] Other cosmopolitan whites found Indians and their culture intriguing. Like Severns and Lovell, these individuals largely hailed from middle-class educated backgrounds.

Part of Angelenos' interest stemmed from the fact that as residents of a diverse metropolis, they had the opportunity to encounter Hindus in person. As early as 1901, one observer noted, "Hinduism has a no [*sic*] considerable following in Los Angeles."[163] Swami Vivekananda was one of the first Hindu teachers to gain notoriety in the city, though it proved fleeting. Touring widely after the World's Parliament of Religions, Vivekananda took "this country by storm," and his six-week visit to Los Angeles in 1900 during a second U.S. visit made a splash there.[164] But local enthusiasm soon waned, and his death two years later merited only a terse obituary in the *Los Angeles Times*.[165] Nationwide, Vedanta groups struggled to survive for several decades after Vivekananda's death.

There were only four organized Vedanta centers in the early 1920s—in New York, Boston, San Francisco, and Los Angeles—claiming a total of roughly two hundred members altogether.[166] In the decade before Yogananda's arrival in the United States, two teachers, Swami Abhedananda and Swami Paramananda, attempted to reinvigorate the Vedanta movement. Both were Bengalis and direct disciples of Swami Ramakrishna and Vivekananda. Abhedananda originally came to New York in 1897. Tensions grew as Paramananda, Abhedananda's more charismatic young assistant, became a more popular speaker. In 1910, after a number of difficulties with the New York leadership, Abhedananda was suspended from the organization and began touring the country independently before departing the United States for good in 1921.[167]

Abhedananda spoke regularly in Los Angeles between 1917 and 1921. He addressed various topics aimed at modern Western audiences: "The Secret of Success," "Evolution and Religion," "How to Gain Self-Mastery," "What Is Perfection?" and "The Spiritual Needs of Today."[168] He also wrote a slew of publications emphasizing meditation and self-discovery. "Man's greatest achievement," Abhedananda explained, is to understand the mysteries of his own being to know himself. No sage, whether a Buddha or a Christ, no saint, whether of the past or of the present, has ever found peace without practising meditation." Like Yogananda he embraced inclusivism, using Western language and quoting the Bible in the service of Hindu ideas. He incorporated frequent references to Jesus Christ and explicated the way Christianity was based on Jesus's recognition of his "divine nature," that is his "God-consciousness." By attaining the "state of God-consciousness . . . the soul has now become a Christ, or a Buddha. Both these words signify the highest spiritual state of God-consciousness and not any particular person."[169]

Abhedananda also defended Hindu ontology against its Christian counterpart. He challenged the common assumption that reincarnation was a purely Eastern tenet, adducing support from Greek, Muslim, and Jewish mystical traditions, as well as the New Testament. "John the Baptist was according to the Jews a second Elijah; Jesus was believed by many to be the re-appearance of some other prophet."[170] He contended that this ancient belief held obvious appeal in the modern age of Darwin: "Vedanta accepts evolution and admits the laws of variation and natural selection, but goes a step beyond modern science by explaining the cause of that 'tendency to vary.' It says, 'there is nothing in the end which was not also in the beginning.'"[171] Contrasting the scientific evidence for reincarnation with the "mythical" nature of Christian belief in resurrection, he traced the historical development of resurrection belief, which, unlike reincarnation, must be a human invention. He concluded that resurrection could not be believed today because "modern science denies miracles."[172]

He also expressed passionate cultural nationalism. His polemical account of India's ancient and noble history provided a defense against common Western misunderstandings. He explained that India's religion was not polytheistic and that the modern caste system was a corruption of an original flexible system based on aptitudes. He showed how, since the ancient period, the West had continually benefited from Indian wisdom. Ancient Western authors respected Indian math, science, and medicine. John the Baptist and Jesus had been trained by Buddhist missionaries from India. More recent philosophers like Arthur Schopenhauer and Transcendentalist authors Emerson and Thoreau had also received inspiration from India.[173] Then he turned his attention to influences that flowed the other direction during the modern period of Western dominance: "European civilization . . . has left moral and spiritual standards in the background, and made material prosperity and intellectual culture the chief factors of civilization."[174] Crass materialism for spiritual enlightenment was hardly an equal exchange.

In 1916, Swami Paramananda opened a Vedanta Center in Los Angeles, joining his former colleague and now rival in the city.[175] Angelenos were struck by his "jet black hair and eyes," "rich brown" skin," "mellow and resonant" voice, and "irreproachable" command of English.[176] His teaching was virtually indistinguishable from Abhedananda's—he sounded the same themes of personal growth, scientific meditation, and Vedanta philosophy—and he enjoyed greater popularity as a result of his charismatic personality.[177] But his plan to build a retreat center for the national Vedanta movement in the warm Santa Clarita hills, rather than frigid Boston, stoked fears that "a full-fledged colony of devotees" would be established just a few miles from the city.[178]

Paramananda's devotees included a number of women who fit a remarkably similar pattern, one not unlike Yogananda's disciples. They were typically well off, from prominent families in major cities like Boston, well educated, and often single. Many had some background in Theosophy, New Thought, or other nonmainstream religious traditions. Katherine Sherwood descended from the Saltonstalls, a first family of Boston. Growing up Unitarian, she had drifted toward Christian Science before exploring a number of other philosophies. Eliza Kissim, a member of an old New York Dutch family, became Sister Saya Prana. The unmarried Mary Lacy Staib, later Sister Shanta, grew up in an aristocratic southern family and had attended New Thought lectures. May Gladwell, raised a Mormon, became a psychic before she heard Paramananda in Los Angeles and eventually became Sister Seva. Georgina Jones Walton, daughter of a U.S. senator and millionaire miner father and a cosmopolitan mother reared in France, married a Theosophist and moved to Krotona, the Theosophy commune in Los Angeles. She eventually became Paramananda's disciple, Sister Daya.[179] Vassar graduate Laura Franklin Glenn took vows to became Sister Devamata, Paramananda's first female devotee. Remarkably, she came to view herself as her guru's partner and equal. She became a prominent Vedanta speaker in her own right and produced several books and booklets, including *Days in an Indian Monastery*, an account of her experiences in India; *Sri Ramakrishna and His Disciples; Building of Character*; *What Is Death?*; *Health and Healing; Practice of Devotion; Development of the Will*; and *Sleep and Super-Consciousness*.[180]

Though Paramananda possessed the charisma that Abhedananda evidently lacked, as well as an ability to make Vedanta philosophy intelligible to an American audience, his movement ultimately failed to take deep root in Los Angeles or anywhere else. Like traditional gurus, he preferred a small group of devoted disciples to large public presentations. As a strong critic of a materialistic society, he "recoiled from the carnival atmosphere of mass movements," refusing to engage in the "Madison Avenue techniques" other swamis employed to spread their message.[131] Both his refusal to adapt to the large American audiences and his principled rejection of advertising kept his movement from expanding beyond a small circle of devoted followers.

The Hindu sage whose ministry in early twentieth-century Los Angeles most effectively paved the way for Yogananda's own work, however, was not associated with the Vedanta movement. Like Yogananda, Baba Bharati forged his own independent movement. His biography remarkably paralleled Yogananda's in many ways. Bharati was born into a well-off Calcutta family and received a college education that included English.[182] Sponsored by Indian elites, Bharati came to the United States as a Hindu evangelist. One advertisement called him the "Henry Ward Beecher of India," comparing him to one of the late nineteenth century's most famous evangelical preachers,[183] while a reviewer of one of his books labeled him a "self-identified missionary," a "chosen instrument of God to carry the religion of the sages of India to western lands."[184] As with Paramananda, audiences viewed Bharati through an Orientalist lens, noting his piercing eyes, flowing locks, and command of English.[185] He spent a few years in Boston and New York before settling in Los Angeles, since he felt most at home in the nation's spiritual frontier. As he put it, "Of all spots of Columbia, the most blessed is Southern California: more warm-hearted than any other part of the Union; in her center here in Los

Angeles, I have met the warmest American hearts."[186] After returning to India for a few years, he planned to build a large temple in Los Angeles, the city with "the Greatest number of Brahmin Hindoos in America."[187] His plans, however, never materialized. With no institutional infrastructure, he lacked the ability to raise sufficient funds to make his dreams reality.

Bharati's inclusivist message was strikingly similar to Abhedananda's and Paramananda's, while strongly anticipating Yogananda's, suggesting that educated Bengali missionaries' talking points rode a well-worn groove. Bharati routinely asserted the superiority of Hindu spirituality over competing religious traditions. And he regularly contrasted ancient Hindu spirituality with the emptiness of Western material progress and technology. Still, he explained that his views did not conflict with Christianity. He insisted that "if I have talked of Krishna and exposed you to the Hindoo Bible, it was only to illumine the teachings of your own Christ; to present him before you in the limelight of the Vedas, with the X-Ray of our scientific philosophies."[188] With titles like "The Coming Christ" and "Christ: Proofs of His Divinity," Bharati's talks might be confused with those of a fundamentalist minister. The substance of his teaching, however, offered little to comfort orthodox Christians. For Bharati, Jesus was a "god-man" who fully embraced the divinity within, just as previous religious prophets had done—Zoroaster, Buddha, Confucius, and sixteenth-century Vaishnavite *bhakti* teacher Caitanya.[189]

In addition to weekly sermons, Bharati conveyed his ideas through a regular magazine, the *Light of India*, which mixed spiritual articles with devotional poetry and commentary on current events. His most notable text was *Sree Krishna: Lord of Love*, a five-hundred-page exposition of Indian belief detailing the laws of *karma* and *saṃsāra*, the necessity of the four *varṇas*, and the role of *dharma*. Following Caitanya's lead, he revealed a vision of personal deity that contrasted starkly with the abstractness of Advaita Vedānta's monistic vision of *Brahman* as ultimate reality. Bharati talked about the gracious love Krishna—a popular *āvatara* of Vishnu whom Bharati presented as the one God—had for his whole creation. Humans owed him loving devotion in response. In contrast to popular American understandings of Indian religion as inherently monistic, Bharati cast an essentially monotheistic vision.

Bharati found support among many Christian liberals, including several broad-minded Protestant clergy. B. Fay Mills is typical of this group. Mills "threaded his way in and out of Congregational, Unitarian, Presbyterian, and Free Religious Association folds. He was successively an advocate of revivalism, the social gospel, Unitarianism, and free religion."[190] Mills brought Bharati to Los Angeles from Boston, and Bharati came to think of him as a brother.[191] As with Paramananda, a number of educated, cosmopolitan, upper-middle-class women also backed Bharati. Three female supporters were particularly prominent, writing about Indian spiritual traditions in his magazine and in other venues. Rose Anton, a professional Broadway actress, became a passionate devotee and moved from New York to Los Angeles in 1906 to be near her guru. She regularly provided poems for Bharati's magazine and wrote a collection of folk stories called *Tales of India*. Like many other native-born Americans, she made a point of rejecting any contradiction between her Vedic learning and Christian tradition.[192] Similarly, Christina Albers wrote poems about Hindu and Buddhist traditions, as well as stories about India. Her books include *Palms and Temple Bells* (1915), *Himalayan Whispers* (1923), and *Ancient Tales of Hindustan* (1923). Elizabeth Delvine King was the most deeply influenced by Bharati. After his departure from Los Angeles, she forged her own eclectic metaphysical tradition, publishing a number of works on spirituality. More boldly than Anton, she also integrated Christian theology with Indian cosmology. In such works as *The Lotus Path, Sayings of Jehovah,* and *The Higher Metaphysics,* she cited the Bible and talked regularly about Christ, Christ Consciousness, and the spiritual process of being "Christed."[193]

Bharati got a mixed reception from Angelenos. Not surprisingly, evangelicals attacked him for his unorthodox views of Jesus. In one case, defending himself against an evangelist who called him "an audacious pagan" and "an ass," Bharati denounced the man for "speaking from his holy place in the pulpit, in the holy Church of Christ, the Preacher of Meekness, calling the preacher of another religion who is perhaps a more enthusiastic preacher of Christ than he . . . language fit for the lips of a swaggering saloon rough."[194] More remarkably, he gained the respect of L.A.'s Protestant civic leadership. The *Los Angeles Times* granted him lengthy space on several occasions to explain important geopolitical issues, including the Treaty of Portsmouth, which ended the Russo-Japanese War; the disastrous effects of Lord Curzon's viceroyalty of India; and the emergence of the *swadeshi,* or self-rule, movement in India. Most intriguingly, Bharati was called as an expert on Eastern languages to unmask the claims of prominent area doctor Henry S. Keyes, an Azusa Street convert to Pentecostalism. Keyes claimed that when he spoke in tongues, he was speaking a north Indian language. After examining text that Keyes wrote under the Spirit's influence, Bharati testified that the words were "neither Hindoo or Persian or Arabic or Chinese or Japanese or Sanskrit. Neither do they look like the characters of any Asiastic Language I know of."[195] The credibility of Bharati's conclusion hinged on both his linguistic expertise and his veracity, qualities whites were often unwilling to grant to any Indian. Despite his remarkable cachet, Bharati was ultimately unable to sustain his momentum, and his movement expired with him when he died in Calcutta in 1914.[196]

Diverse Indian teachers and their followers in early twentieth-century Los Angeles shared a number of common features that facilitated Yogananda's own evangelistic efforts. These teachers understood their audience well and couched their message in the language of modernity, emphasizing realization of the self, the integration of science and religion, and an optimistic portrayal of reincarnation. They promoted the attractiveness—indeed, the superiority—of their spiritual product while attempting to maintain the equanimity appropriate to a pluralistic setting. They recognized that they were addressing culturally Christian audiences and routinely quoted the New Testament and lauded the example of Jesus. They all faced mixed responses to their racial identity: interest, prejudice, condescension, and some affection. And they disproportionately drew well-educated women from wealthy families, who had some experience in metaphysical or nonmainstream religious traditions. Despite these teachers' prospects, each leader had significant liabilities, whether personal, organizational, or promotional. Their movements were declining or dead by the time Yogananda arrived in Los Angeles. Yogananda would succeed where they failed by cultivating their individual strengths—deep learning, charisma, warm spiritual devotionalism—and adding savvy marketing and an institutional structure to sustain his movement.

When Yogananda arrived in Los Angeles in early 1925, he received an enthusiastic welcome. "The Great Divine Power seemed to have roused the whole city to receive the message of Yogoda. . . . Clubs, colleges, societies, educational centers, churches and newspapers extended him every courtesy and Swami's days were filled to overflowing with engagements to speak write and be interviewed everywhere."[197] The *Los Angeles Times* reported that Yogananda drew "immense crowds" to his free talks at the Philharmonic Auditorium.[198] He filled the three-thousand-seat venue to capacity, and thousands more were turned away. One observer commented on the seeming incongruity of a "Hindu invading the United States to bring God in the midst of a Christian community. A so-called heathen from a so-called heathen land preaching the essence of Christian doctrine to the millions who contribute to foreign-mission boards in order to enlighten the benighted Asiatics!" Despite the sardonic tone, the author noted the "absorbing attention and acclamation" of the audience, "which is the highest tribute to the eager reception of his message." Yogananda's Yogoda teaching, he thought, "is a practical message which Christian preachers might well adopt to teach self-made happiness."[199]

Key local figures became admirers and supporters. They included former naval captain Richmond Pearson, the Anti-Saloon League's most prominent speaker; Elisabeth von Kleinsmid, wife of the University of Southern California's president; Isidore Dockweiler, a member of the Democratic National Committee; Harry Haldeman, business leader and president of the probusiness Better America Federation, headquartered in Los Angeles; and Church of Divine Science minister Walter W. Raymond.

Inspired in part by the favorable response he had received from Los Angeles audiences, Yogananda made the momentous decision to establish the headquarters of his ministry in the city. Shortly thereafter, he explained how he found the appropriate site:

> One day during his Los Angeles stay, one of his students casually mentioned Mount Washington. Swami's soul was strangely stirred at the mention of this place and suggested that they drive up there on the following day. When he entered the grounds of the Mount Washington Hotel site, he strolled about, and then touching the bars surrounding the tennis court, he exclaimed to his companions, This place feels like *ours*! Today it is "ours," for thru the kind and willing cooperation and donations of his thousands of students throughout America, this property was purchased for the American Headquarters of Sat-Sanga and Yogoda.[200]

The Mount Washington property was less than four miles from the home where Vivekananda had lived for six weeks in 1899 during his second visit to the United States. It strains credulity to imagine that with hundreds of square miles from which to choose, by mere coincidence he established his headquarters a short walk from the former home of the man he most sought to emulate.

Whatever the reason for his decision, divine providence worked through hardheaded legal maneuvering to secure the property. The site on Mount Washington had been a resort hotel of eighteen guest rooms between 1910 and 1922. An incline rail system carried visitors and hotel guests up the steep hillside, though a road quickly supplemented the incline.[201] By the early 1920s, improved cars with stronger engines could more easily navigate the steep road. After some financial struggle, the hotel closed and vagrants began to occupy the grounds. The swami was blessed with legal agents with shrewd skills. Operating separately, they surreptitiously bought up nine separate parcels in quick succession so as not to arouse suspicion.[202] The opening of the Mount Washington Educational Center in late October 1925 was, Yogananda insisted, a "memorable day for Los Angeles."[203]

Despite the site's inaccessibility, the 940-foot-high crest was hardly a

Self-Realization Fellowship's Mount Washington Center in Los Angeles. Formerly a resort in the northeastern part of the city reached only by incline rail, it became Yogananda's international headquarters in the metropolis that was then emerging as the nation's spiritual frontier. This beautiful spot in a prime location became sacred space for Yogananda and his disciples.

mountain. But Yogananda was eager to dramatize the site for two reasons. First, its aesthetic virtues made it a potential tourist destination. Early promotional literature made the location sound as if it were still a luxury resort. "The grounds are seven and half acres in extent, and are planted with camphor, date, palm, pepper and other beautiful trees, as well as plants, shrubs and wonderful flower-beds, making it one of the most beautiful spots in Southern California." The site offered great scenery. "The Center commands an unsurpassed view of the city below, as well as of other nearby cities, including Pasadena, the 'City of Roses.' The Pacific Ocean sparkles in the distance, and at night the million twinkling lights of Los Angeles and distant cities may be seen below, a veritable fairyland."[204]

More important than attracting tourism, however, Yogananda sensed that Mount Washington had the potential to convey a sense of sacred space for his spiritual movement's headquarters. Most white Americans were not accustomed to imbuing their country's landscape with sacred meaning, though for some the nation's capital or historic battlefields might be hallowed ground.

The emergence of tourism in the late nineteenth century had also introduced sightseers to Yellowstone, Yosemite, and the Grand Canyon, often stimulating sublime experiences in more naturalistic settings.[205] Yogananda hoped to capitalize on such sentiments as he sought to turn Mount Washington into a holy pilgrimage site that reflected both the American landscape and sacred sites in India. Invoking one of the holiest pilgrimage sites in India, he later said, "I have always considered Los Angeles to be the Benares of America."[206] In 1925, he composed a poem called "Life's Dream" that celebrated the place—named for the nation's first president—that he saw as the embodiment of his longing to draw the spiritual East and freedom-loving West together:

> The summer-East
> And the wintry West
> They say—but Mount Washington
> Named rightly after that pioneer
> Of Freedom's great career,
> Thou dost stand, the snowless guardian Himalaya
> Of the angel land in perpetual green regalia.
>
> Nippon's camphor trees and perfumed wisteria and smiling roses
> Palm, date and well-beloved spicy bay leaves of Hind stand close,
> With endless scenic beauties
> Of ocean, canyon, setting sun, moon-studded sky
> And nightly twinkling cities
> To declare
> Thy ever-changing beauty.
>
> On thy crown thou shalt newly wear
> A priceless starry-school which in all future near
> Shall draw the lost travelers of the East and West.
> To find their goal and one place of rest.
>
> Here one path
> Shall merge with all other paths.
> Here the love of earthly Freedom's paradise, America,
> Shall blend forever with spiritual Freedom's paradise, India.
> Here church in deepest friendliness shall all other churches meet,
> Here the temple the mosque shall greet.
> Here the long-divorced matter-laws
> Will wed again in peace the spirit laws.
> Here all minds will learn that true Art

> Of living life and the way to start
> Straight to the One great place
> Where all must meet at last.
>
> Jehovah! This is the land of solace
> Where my life's dream in truth reappears![207]

In Yogananda's vision, Mount Washington's sacredness ultimately stemmed less from the inherent beauty of the location or the symbolism of the name than from anticipation of the spiritual work that would be done there through the advancement of Yogoda. On a later occasion, he linked the humble L.A. peak to the great Himalayas, explicitly evoking a sense of Mount Washington's sacredness. In his autobiography, he recounted a prophecy he was given during a pilgrimage with Sri Yukteswar to a temple devoted to Śankara, the founder of the swami order. When they arrived, Yogananda had a profound experience.

> As I gazed upon the mountain-peak hermitage, bold against the sky, I fell into an ecstatic trance. A vision appeared of a hilltop mansion in a distant land; the lofty Śankara temple in Srinagar became transformed into the edifice where, years later, I established Self-Realization Fellowship headquarters in America. When I first visited Los Angeles, and saw the large building on the crest of Mount Washington, I recognized it at once from my long-past visions in Kashmir and elsewhere.[208]

In comparing Mount Washington to Srinagar, Yogananda also implicitly compared himself to the great Śankara, whose presence made the hermitage holy. Mount Washington was sacred because the swami who had settled there had consecrated it as a base to promulgate the divine Yogoda message to countless thousands of Americans.

SCIENTIFIC RELIGION ON THE NATION'S SPIRITUAL FRONTIER

By 1925, more than four eventful years had passed since the young swami arrived in the United States on the S.S. *City of Sparta*. His understanding of the challenge of self-invention had matured considerably since he had shaved off his beard aboard the ship in an effort to present himself appropriately to American audiences. This was no mean feat in a postwar nation where many were deeply suspicious of foreigners, heathens, and the darker races. After stumbling a bit following the International Conference of Free Christians and

Other Religious Liberals, Yogananda had found his stride. Southern California, the nation's spiritual frontier, proved essential to his success. Home to nonmainstream religions of various kinds, it boasted a long history of Indian religious teachers who paved the way for his own ministry. The Mount Washington Educational Center, perched on a prominent hill overlooking Los Angeles, became the practical and symbolic center of his ministry, a sacred Hindu site in a booming American metropolis. Yogananda proved himself skilled in translating his yoga message to middle-class white Americans as he established a firm foundation for scientific religion in a nation that was deeply shaped by Protestant beliefs, ethics, and practices. Building on his own Indian training—through his mentorship under Yukteswar, his college education, and his exposure to broader Bengali ideas—Yogananda had constructed a sophisticated understanding of modernity, its challenges, and the way his spiritual message could resonate with the transcendent longings of modern Americans. He had established a loyal if modest base of followers and financial supporters among spiritual seekers and key civic leaders. Now he could settle down to the task of refining and communicating his message of self-realization in powerful, engaging ways—and honing his unique product to compete in the marketplace of American religion. Meditation promised a practical, systematic, guaranteed method for God-contact, a deeply profound, devotional experience of the divine.

THREE

The Creation of a Yogi Guru Persona

Marketing Swami Yogananda and His Yoga Instruction, 1925–1935

> The business man hurries to his office, rushes in, sits in his chair, and begins to concentrate upon some difficult problem. The din of his secretary's typewriter annoys him. He shouts at her to stop. A moment later, he realizes there is need for hurry on the letter she is typing, so he shouts at her to go on again. Then he begins smoking his after-breakfast cigar. Every day he resolves to quit smoking some time, as he knows that it is a useless, expensive, and unnecessary habit, but he never does quit. After a little more deep thought on the problem, ragged nerves tug at the shirts of his concentration, and finally, hardly able to bear himself any longer, he madly dashes the cigar into the cuspidor, stops the typewriter, and dismisses his secretary because she brought him some bills that needed to be paid. He shouts at the inwardly-laughing, outwardly-respectful secretary, and pleads: "Have pity on me. Be considerate. Don't you see that I am trying to put over a big deal?" He decides to try to concentrate once more, and dozes off in disgust at his inability to work out his problem, and he quietly drifts into deeper slumber, while his secretaries happily and quietly steal off to lunch. He wakes up to find that he has missed his train, lost his appointment, and with it his big deal falls through. This business man does not know the real art of concentration.[1]

It was this kind of harried businessman who most needed Yogananda's teachings. Had that businessman stopped at a corner newsstand on his way to the train, he might have been drawn to the exotic-looking cover of *East-West* magazine. Opening the front cover, he would have found an advertisement promising to solve a problem he didn't know he had. Large, bold letters announced a "Yogoda Correspondence Course," providing instruction in a technique to "recharge the body batteries with fresh life current by increasing dynamic power of will." Improved "beauty of form," "grace of expression," and "power of mental receptivity" were just a few of the benefits he would receive. The technique also guaranteed him all-around health, the ability to take off (or put on!) fat "as desired," and power over his spiritual destiny. All of this was available through a correspondence course for a nominal fee.[2] Staring back from the page was Swami Yogananda, clad in a silk robe, long hair flowing over his shoulders, his confident expression assuring readers of the message's authenticity. Couched in modern scientific language, the advertisement largely eschewed religious terminology as it offered techniques perfected by an "eminent Hindu master of metaphysics and psychology." Yogananda began his ministry at the height of an early twentieth-century boom in consumer capitalism aided by a revolution in manufacturing, mass communication, increased disposable income, and easy credit.[3] Advertisements became more pervasive and more persuasive. Besides newspapers and magazines, people encountered ads on roadside billboards, at bus stops, and on the radio. Relying heavily on the new field of psychology, ads guaranteed the fulfillment of desires and self-transformation. For some, consumption's promise of transcendence threatened to displace religion. Spiritual leaders like Yogananda had to assure audiences that their product was uniquely able to deliver happiness and personal development in ways that consumer goods never could.

Scholars have long investigated intersections between American religion and the market.[4] The nation's early religious disestablishment has long provided a religious marketplace that allows for a wide range of religions to compete. Though this analytical framework has typically been applied to competition among Protestant denominations, the market context is essential for making sense of Yogananda's efforts to expand his ministry. Although Yogananda's frequent references to Christianity and metaphysical movements expressed ecumenical concern, they simultaneously and paradoxically reflected an effort to draw comparisons to inferior products in a competitive religious market. American religious leaders have often disregarded Jesus's warning that the faithful cannot serve both God and mammon, demonstrating great skill in marketing both literal and metaphorical spiritual products.[5]

A growing body of scholarship applies this type of capitalist analysis to Indian yogis, such as Mumbai-area guru Muktananda, who launched Siddha Yoga in 1956, and Bhagwan Shree Rajneesh, who started teaching in India in the 1960s before becoming infamous in the United States as sex-guru Osho in the 1980s. Yogananda was never as blunt or provocative as Osho, who acknowledged that he was part of a "marketplace" and claimed to "sell enlightenment."

But Yogananda was a significant forerunner of many later figures, successfully commodifying Indian spirituality in early twentieth-century America—and, from there, around the world—charting a path for entrepreneurial spirituality in which "every form of exotic cultural knowledge, every yogic posture, and every spiritual technique has become a commodity."[6] If there was irony in a yogi—whose ascetic tradition represented a fundamental rejection of "materialistic religiosity," in Edwin Bryant's words—peddling a line of spiritual products that he promised would liberate Americans from the deception that happiness could be achieved through the "acquisition of an infinite number of material things," Yogananda failed to see it.[7]

The three sections that comprise this chapter explore Yogananda's early ministry in a marketplace context. The first section addresses the way the yogi promoted his message to modern Americans steeped in a culture of consumption. In the 1920s, advertisers "relentlessly tried to persuade Americans to buy a particular manufacturer's brands and, above all, to accept no substitutes."[8] Ads used authority and expertise to gain the audience's trust. Ironically, evangelical preachers, whose theology differed from Yogananda more than any other Christian group, offer the closest parallel to his own personality-based style of religious branding. Like them, Yogananda embodied sacred authority through his image—both his literal appearance and his persona—and his religious expertise. He evoked and subverted Orientalist tropes to manage his message and his image as an exotic, authoritative, sacred teacher.

The second section investigates the religious products he touted, most centrally the course he created to teach yoga, a systematic, practical method for God-realization, through the thoroughly modern medium of a correspondence course. His *East-West* magazine helped to reestablish the personal link between guru and disciple severed by his distance-learning strategy while highlighting Yogoda's distinctiveness as a religious brand. His magazine was also a vehicle for Indian cultural and religious nationalism, reflecting his desire to protect the reputation of his homeland and its treasured teachings. His final product was a community, both real and virtual, of shared values and practices.

The final section considers the risks of the religious market. Staying solvent in a competitive market presented numerous challenges. In the decade between establishing the center at Mount Washington in 1925 and departing for India in 1935, Yogananda rode a wild financial roller coaster. Though savvy in some ways, Yogananda was surprisingly naive in others, unaware of how different the southern market was until he riled white southern men who drove him out of town. He faced several lawsuits that threatened his brand image and his bank account. And, like many churches during the Depression, his center suffered financially. But just when things looked bleakest, he was rescued from his distress by his biggest customer of all.

MARKETING YOGODA RELIGION

Paging through any Southern California newspaper's religious advertisement section in the 1920s would illustrate the region's vibrant spiritual marketplace. Announcements for dozens of established denominations, newer movements like Theosophy and Christian Science, and permutations within each group all jostled for space. Canny religious leaders like Yogananda used advertising, an intrinsic element of the nation's new consumer economy, to sell religion, from literal newspaper advertisements to personal testimonials from respected figures in science, the arts, and Hollywood. Ultimately, a religious figure's persona—personality, appearance, and delivery style—was both a product and a sales tool. Yogananda bore many similarities to the flamboyant evangelists of the era, though his product and audience differed from theirs in crucial ways.

As advertising executives came to understand how needs, desires, and insecurities shaped behavior, their techniques became modern. According to historian of advertising Roland Marchand, "As it came to accept the paradox of its role as both apostle of modernity and buffer against the effects of modern impersonalities of scale, and as it developed strategies for accommodating the public to modern complexities, American advertising in the 1920s and 1930s took on what we now recognize as a distinctly modern cast."[9] "Just as the manufacturing world has been compelled to turn its attention to physics and chemistry and as the manufacturer's vocabulary is composed of many terms which were but recently technical terms used only by scientists," explained Walter Dill Scott in his 1908 book *The Psychology of Advertising*, "so the advertising world has turned its attention to the subject of psychology, and many words formerly used only by professional psychologists are to-day commonplaces with advertisers."[10] Advertisers seeking to elevate the desirability of their products often subtly evoked familiar sacred imagery to convey the transcendent possibilities of consumption.[11] Modern advertising increasingly blurred consumer goods and the sacred in the early twentieth century.

Some observers in the 1920s characterized advertising itself as a kind of religion. Advertisers, who were often former ministers or their offspring, aspired to evoke the sublime. The "attention engineers" of mass culture, they were seen as "spiritual and cultural redeemers." President Calvin Coolidge congratulated advertisers for their work in "the regeneration and redemption of mankind," through "inspiring and ennobling the commercial world."[12] A contemporary proclaimed that "advertising probably is our greatest agency for spreading an understanding and love of beauty in all things," praising its "peculiar power as an educative force."[13]

Even within the religious fold, some embraced the creative possibilities of the new consumer culture. Advertising executive Bruce Barton, the son of a Congregational minister, penned *The Man Nobody Knows*, an immediate best seller that revealed Jesus as a worldly man who displayed remarkable commercial acumen. "The founder of modern business," "Jesus picked up twelve men from the bottom ranks of business and forged them into an organization that conquered the world." Barton sketched a portrait of Jesus as an executive and advertiser with a clear method. Barton appreciated that Jesus was "successful in mastering public attention," "because he recognized the basic principle that all good advertising is news. . . . Reporters would have followed him every single hour, for it was impossible to predict what he would say or do; every action and word were news.[14] Barton's interpretation of Jesus healing "shattered nerves," "divided minds," and "complexes" reflected a modern fusion of religion and psychology.[15] As religious historian Matthew Hedstrom comments, *The Man Nobody Knows* "perfectly encapsulated the confluence of consumer cult, religious publishing, theological liberalism, and gender anxiety in the 1920s. Barton's book received intense scorn from both conserve and liberal critics, mostly for its indisputable theological shallowness and naked celebration of American capitalism."[16]

Yogananda was much more sanguine about *The Man Nobody Knows*. He favorably reviewed Barton's book in 1926, proclaiming it "original, gripping, alive! It succeeds in actually conveying the personality of Jesus. It takes a great historical figure, somewhat vague from the mist of centuries, and sharpens His outline . . . until the reader can see, feel and understand His compelling charm and power. Jesus as an executive, and the founder of modern business! His methods and advertising! These chapter headings hint at the contents. Every Yogoda student should read it!"[17] In his admiration for Barton's effort to link pragmatism, advertising, and business organization with the West's greatest spiritual figure, Yogananda discloses his own assessment of the relation between spirituality and commerce.

Yogananda's newspaper advertisements for the benefits of Yogoda illustrate his marketing acumen. The ads benefited early on from his promoter, Mohammad Rashid, who recognized that deep spiritual matters and amusement were not inherent antagonists. Yogananda decided to advertise in both the religion and entertainment sections of local newspapers. This strategy embraced common American perceptions of Hindu-speakers as novelty acts rather than as spiritual leaders. At the same time, the uniqueness of a Yogananda ad sandwiched between promotions for vaudeville productions, casinos, and Al Jolson blackface performances gave him an advantage over his competitors who advertised only in the religion section.[18] The ads themselves, while terse, arrested readers' attention with a headshot of Yogananda wearing a turban. He adopted the turban almost as a prop in conformity with American expectations. Judging by extant photos, he never wore one in India and donned one for the first time in 1920 when he attended the Boston conference. In the religious advertisement section, his portrait was often the only image on the page. He also relied heavily on volume. He barraged audiences with ads, offering readers multiple opportunities to learn about his talks. This was a risky calculation, a gamble that his extensive up-front advertising costs would pay for themselves with a larger volume of audience donations.

In various ways, Yogananda sought to convey a sense of personal authority that made his message compelling and trustworthy. From the time of his arrival in the United States, he had experimented with different ways of presenting himself. The frontispiece to his 1923 work *Songs of the Soul* showcased one approach. In it, he established his bona fides with a cascade of titles: founder of "Ranchi and Puri Brahmacharya Residential Schools in India, Sat Sanga (Fellowship with Truth), Boston; Sat Sanga Summer School, Waltham; Vice-President: SADHU SABHA, India; Delegate from India to International Congress of Religions, Boston 1920."[19] "India's foremost educator" often embellished his credentials.[20] He called himself a "distinguished Hindu psychologist," though he had not studied psychology.[21] He donned the title "Swami from University of Calcutta," implying that he was formally associated with that institution, though his sole connection there was the bachelor's degree he received years earlier from Serampore College, which was affiliated with the university.[22] He claimed that as "the owner of two large schools in India" he was in the United States to study the school system. The Denver press understood him to be a prince.[23] He described himself as the personal representative of the maharaja of Kasim Bazar, a "powerful reigning prince of India,"[24] though the prince—who did finance Yogananda's schools in India—neither underwrote Yogananda's American ministry nor saw Yogananda as his agent. Exploiting the glamour of Oriental rulers and Americans' ignorance of Indian governance structure—India had several hundred princely states, each with its own maharaja—Yogananda suggested a prestigious, formally sponsored mission.

Endorsements by famous Americans also provided significant cachet for Yogananda and his work. Renowned horticulturalist and liberal Christian

Luther Burbank invoked his own scientific authority to provide a vigorous testimonial about Yogananda and his teaching:

> I have examined the Yogoda system of Swami Yogananda and in my opinion it is ideal for training and harmonizing man's physical, mental and spiritual natures. . . . Through the Yogoda system of physical, mental and spiritual unfoldment by simple and scientific methods of concentration and meditation, most of the complex problems of life may be solved, and peace and good-will come upon earth.
>
> The Swami's idea of right education is plain common-sense, free from all mysticism or non-practicality, otherwise it would not have my approval. . . . I am glad to have this opportunity of heartily joining with the Swami in his appeal for international schools on the art of living, which, if established, will come as near to bringing the millennium as anything with which I am acquainted.[25]

Burbank contributed an article to the first issue of Yogananda's magazine, discussing science and civilization. Yogananda expressed his admiration for "Beatific Burbank" in verse a few pages later in the same issue, calling him "the great reformer Luther . . . of living plants and flowers." His admiration for Burbank extended beyond his scientific expertise to his reverence for "the Mighty Invisible Sun . . . that lights little plants, distant stars, the bursting bubble, thee and me and man." Burbank, whose experiments with plant hybrids made him a perfect example of the practical application of science that Yogananda prized, authoritatively confirmed the harmony between science and religion.

Opera singer Madame Amelita Galli-Curci's endorsement won Yogananda his first reference in a national publication, when *Time* described their relationship in 1928.

> Amelita Galli-Curci (coloratura soprano) gave her name for advertising purposes to Swami Yogananda of India and Los Angeles, Calif., a man who looks like a plump woman. She was quoted in copy in Manhattan theatre programs as saying: "YOGODA gives Health, Strength, Power to Accomplish, Peace and Poise." Among other things, YOGODA claims to teach people "to Recharge their body, mind and soul Batteries from Inner Cosmic Energy . . . to meditate, to know Divine truths."[26]

Time's snide tone notwithstanding, the article provided free advertising on a national scale. Galli-Curci later wrote the dedication to Yogananda's *Whispers*

In this 1925 advertisement for a talk in Los Angeles, Yogananda highlights India's ancient wisdom as a source of revolutionary change. He hints at yoga's transcendent possibilities with religious language of revelation, inspiration, miracles, and "a higher destiny." Though the teaching is free, the salesmanship—with testimonials, evidence of Yogananda's expertise, and the promise of attaining every desire—is hard to miss.

from Eternity, celebrating a scientific approach to a relationship with God that would reap great rewards:

> The prayers in this book serve to bring God closer, by describing the feelings which directly arise from actual God-contact. God is expressed here as something definite and tangible. The Cosmic Idol is the grand conception of the Infinite and Invisible made finite and visible. Nature, man, mind, and every visible object are all taken as materials to build a colossal Divine Idol, on which we can easily concentrate.
>
> Followers of all religions may drink from this fountain of universal prayers. These prayers are an answer to the modern scientific mind, seeking God intelligently. This book gives us a great variety of prayers, which enables one to choose that prayer most suited and helpful to his particular need.
>
> My humble request to the reader, I express in the following lines:
>
> Pass not by, with hurried intellectual reading, the mines of realization hidden beneath the soil of words in this sacred book. But, as the Swami says, daily and repeatedly dig deep into them with the pickax of your attentive, reverential and meditative study, when you will find the priceless gem of self-realization.[27]

Yogananda forged relationships with other entertainers, taking advantage of his proximity to Hollywood to cultivate friendships with key figures in the film industry. In 1928, Sid Grauman invited Yogananda to a Hollywood Association of Foreign Correspondents dinner in honor of filmmaker Carl Laemmle. Samuel Goldwyn, D. W. Griffith, William C. DeMille (the older brother of Cecil B. DeMille), actress Delores Del Rio, and "dozens of other screen luminaries" were in attendance.[28] Yogananda delivered a talk on India to these guests who frequently purveyed images of the exotic East on the screen.

Orientalism became a "staple of American popular culture during the 1920s" through film, books, and magazines.[29] This was particularly true of film, which was born at the height of European imperialism.[30] Clearly smitten by the film industry, Yogananda began to describe life as a "Paramount picture, shown in serials and by installments, infinitely interesting, ever-fresh, ever-stirring, ever-complex." Everyone could play his part but need not fear that the movie plot would end in tragedy, since the "great Director of the Motion Picture Company of Life is made of Joy."[31] Yogananda could be quite voluble with his life-as-film metaphor. In the "cosmic cinema," "the box office is open; the house is full, and we are on the screen and have shown some of our work. The climax has to be reached, and then the audience will be thrilled with our everlasting picture. Then we will disappear during the intermission of earthly departure. But even though we would be gone, our work will be repeated; in the continuous film we will work for all time to come."[32]

His infatuation with filmmaking also played a part in his theatricality. He displayed an intuitive understanding of the principle that "religions that lend themselves to visual intensity and symbolism have greater appeal in consumer culture."[33] Besides playing up his visual appearance—his long hair, turban, and robes—he developed the aural impact of his dramatic performance, controlling the tone, volume, and pitch of his voice, as he undulated dramatically. Audiences noted how his resonant "God power-driven voice" complemented his eyes, face, and gestures.[34] As one disciple appreciatively explained, "Master's voice—well modulated—rose and fell in pitch and decibels to express the internal feelings he projected. To capture the full attention of his listeners, his voice ranged from whispered phrases to a great booming volume. It always commanded attention and, no doubt, kept the listeners interested."[35] Even his Indian accent—which occasionally made him difficult for Americans to understand—conveyed a charming, exotic wisdom. In effect, he presented himself as if constantly aware that he was on screen, or at least in front of the camera.

As all of these advertising techniques suggest, Yogananda intuitively understood that marketing his message was indissolubly linked to marketing himself. The centrality of self-promotion reflected a key transformation in the individual's identity in the modern era: the development of what cultural historian Warren Susman has called personality. The nineteenth-century vision of a person committed to duty, work, honor, and reputation began to give way to an ideology that stressed the attractive, magnetic, forceful, and creative qualities of each individual. By the early twentieth century, "the development of consciousness of self" emerged in conjunction with a consumer economy, mass culture, and the expansion of leisure time, emphasizing "individual idiosyncrasies, personal needs and interests."[36] According to Susman, the new technologies of radio and film gave birth to celebrity culture, in which audiences paid attention to athletes, performers, and film actors at all times, not just when they performed. "Stars" were famous simply for being themselves or at least the selves projected in their personas.

Yogananda found himself in a crowded field of religious stars promoting their own personality-driven brands in the 1920s. Given evangelical preachers' long tradition of theatrical performance, from George Whitefield, "the divine dramatist" and "pedlar in divinity" in the eighteenth century, through Charles Finney and Lorenzo Dow in the nineteenth, their adept marketing is no surprise.[37] It was often the evangelists' personas, including their endearing personal idiosyncrasies, that enabled them to entertain large audiences through public addresses, modern print, and radio ministries. Their flamboyance, self-promotion, and attention to rhetorical flourish over oratorical substance inspired Sinclair Lewis's novel *Elmer Gantry* in 1927.[38] However fervently these preachers may have railed against materialism, their approach inevitably turned them into purveyors of a commodified religion.[39] Evangelist Billy Sunday is a prime example of this phenomenon. An Iowa native and former professional baseball player, Sunday possessed more passion than intellect, along with a canny knack for drawing large audiences. While not all Americans loved this flashy showman, he became a household name in the 1910s and 1920s and gained a number of friends in Hollywood.[40] He marketed everything he could think of: his biography, his sermons, hymn books, and postcards of himself, his family, and his evangelical team.[41] "Fighting Bob" Shuler was one of several fundamentalist preachers whose nickname hinted at his unwillingness to compromise theologically, as well as his pugnacious style of communication. A Tennessee native, Shuler relocated to Los Angeles in 1920, where he continued to pastor until his retirement in 1953, though a once robust radio ministry had been dead since the FCC revoked his license in 1931 for libel. He directed his militancy as much toward internal enemies like Aimee Semple McPherson as he did toward political targets he accused of misdeeds.[42] Sister Aimee, whose ministry was described briefly in chapter 2, claims pride of place as a Southern California personality-driven minister. In her 1927 autobiography, she explained, "Religion, to thrive in the present day, must utilize present-day methods." Sister Aimee, who became friends with Hollywood celebrities like Charlie Chaplin, was an extremely innovative presenter who appeared on stage on a motorcycle for one sermon, staged theatrical productions, and dramatically displayed the crutches of those physically healed through her ministry.[43]

Yogananda shared much in common with these popular evangelists. He could hold his own with the best of them as an entertainer. He offered a compelling message of sublime encounter with the divine. Most importantly, like these evangelists, he recognized that his persona was his most potent weapon and labored to develop a distinctive cult of personality. As one researcher of the movement perceptively noted at the time:

> Swami Yogananda himself is the biggest advertisement for the Society, in spite of a newspaper announcement that "Swami Yogananda keeps himself in the background." His face appears in newspapers and on

> billboards, in some of his books, and several times in his magazine. Every Yogoda class has its photograph; the class-members are seated while the swami stands well in the foreground. On one Fourth of July a large notice board at the entrance of the Mount Washington grounds displayed a life sized picture of the swami beside his message to America. The organization arranges for photographs of the swami playing one of his four musical instruments or conversing with some American notable such as Governor Fuller of Massachusetts or President Coolidge.[44]

Understanding that he was part of a crowded marketplace, the yogi shouted to make himself heard over the din of competitors.

The competition between rival religious stars was sometimes quite apparent. In one case, an ad for Sister Aimee appeared directly above one for Yogananda. Other than his foreign-sounding name and exotic image, Yogananda's ad was scarcely distinguishable from one she might have placed: the ad described a Sunday devotional service and Sunday school, announced the upcoming talk, "Healing by Christ Power," and explained how the previous week's "Healing Prayer" service had led to a woman being healed and throwing away her crutch.[45] He even stole a page from Sister Aimee's playbook. A report in 1926 announced that a "Los Angeles student, Mrs. Otto Crimman," had thrown away her crutch "in the presence of a large number of students." Her name and address were offered as verifiable proof of the effectiveness of his cures.[46]

But he differed from these evangelists in equally crucial ways apart from theology. First, for many evangelists, their lack of formal education underscored the divine nature of their calling: God chose to work through weak instruments to increase his glory. At best, these preachers were ambivalent toward intellect and education, and at worst they were overtly hostile. Yogananda had been reluctant to attend college. Yukteswar, however, had been prescient in his conviction that a college degree would be an asset in Yogananda's self-promotion as an authoritative religious personality. His advertisements always mentioned his bachelor's degree. A number of his publications included technical illustrations and official-sounding jargon, from medical terms to anatomical labels and to health and exercise techniques. In all of these ways, Yogananda demonstrated his expertise in addressing health issues through scientific religion.

Second and related, Yogananda targeted a very different audience—both in religious identity and in class. He calculated that he would never win doctrinaire Christians, so he never really tried. Neither was he a populist. Though the masses often crowded to his meetings seeking entertainment, few would become faithful disciples of his esoteric message. Yogananda's typical target audience was liberal Christians and followers of metaphysical traditions who disdained evangelists' brand of showmanship and preferred a dignified intellectual approach more suitable to a club meeting or lyceum.

Yogananda particularly reached out to this striving professional middle class, open to his self-improvement message as a path toward advancement. The 1920s consumer and service revolution catalyzed the emergence of a new "white collar" middle class composed of civil servants, salesmen, managers, and advertising agents.[47] In Los Angeles, the booming economy in the manufacturing, real estate, film production, and leisure industries increased the region's white-collar pool.[48] Yogananda appealed to such workers, assuming that they felt a spiritual void in striving only after earthly reward. He routinely used businessmen as examples in his illustrations. The "ordinary successful business man uses his powers of concentration only about twenty-five per cent," while "the student of Self-Realization can develop his power of concentration one hundred per cent and can use it scientifically to bring him success."[49] In one provocative essay, "Who Is a Yogi?" Yogananda confronted stereotypes of the yogi as "a sword-swallower, crystal gazer or snake charmer" and reappropriated the label as a dignified term that applied to his followers. In contrast to popular misconceptions, real yogis—or at least aspiring ones—hailed from respectable middle-class backgrounds. Though anyone could follow yoga, the nation's "business man, literary man, artist, musician" were particularly drawn to the path. These kinds of seekers understood "the scientific psycho-physical technique of uniting the matter-bound body and soul with their source of origin, the Blessed Spirit."[50]

Given how inseparable Yogananda's personality was from Yogoda's authenticity, there was no better way to promote his ministry than to travel the country and present himself to live audiences. In 1925, Yogananda took to the road—and the rails. A large photo in the *Los Angeles Times* that year announcing "Swami Buys Swanky Car" showed Yogananda, who apparently needed to replace the Lewis's worn-out roadster, posing next to a new automobile. Rehashing hackneyed clichés about ancient India, the paper commented that the modern Packard was "a far cry from the crude transportation of India."[51] Though the *Times* thought the incongruity of the enrobed swami standing next to an automobile amusing, the photo captured the indispensable role modern transportation played in the success of Yogananda's ministry.

For the next decade he was an indefatigable traveler, rarely spending more than a few nights at a time at Mount Washington, and not more than a few weeks altogether. It was fortunate that he had learned to charge his body battery, because he kept up a grueling pace that would have exhausted anyone relying on his or her own strength. He racked up thousands of miles and hundreds of speaking presentations in cities big and small across the United States. Yogananda's childhood in India, particularly his regular use of trains, served him in good stead in his U.S. ministry. From the beginning of 1926 through the end of 1928, for example, Yogananda traveled to the following locations in order, staying anywhere from a few days to several months: Cleveland, Los Angeles, Pittsburgh, New York, Detroit, Pittsburgh, New York, Los Angeles, Cincinnati, Cleveland, Washington, D.C., Pittsburgh, Detroit, Buffalo, Washington, D.C., Cleveland, Cincinnati, Pittsburgh, Minneapolis–Saint Paul, Cleveland, Washington, D.C., Detroit, Ann Arbor, Battle Creek, Miami, Philadelphia, Buffalo, Pittsburgh, Cincinnati, Detroit, Philadelphia, Buffalo, Los Angeles, Boston, Washington, D.C., New York, and Philadelphia.

This relentless travel spawned the growth of new Yogoda centers around the country. Though a few, such as Philadelphia, failed to thrive, the network generally grew in this period. By mid-1932, the Boston and Los Angeles centers had been joined by centers in Oakland, Salt Lake City, Denver, Minneapolis, Saint Louis, Milwaukee, Cincinnati, Cleveland, Buffalo, Pittsburgh, and Washington, D.C. Organizations were heavily concentrated in the urban, diverse, and densely populated Northeast. There were also notable gaps. The lack of any significant presence in the Pacific Northwest is surprising, since Yogananda made many trips early on to Seattle, Tacoma, and Portland. Perhaps he could not get local support, the sine qua non for getting a center established. Yogoda centers were absent from the South, from Texas to Florida and Georgia to Virginia. Protestant hegemony in the Bible Belt culture encouraged deep suspicion of Eastern traditions, and he never penetrated further south than Saint Louis and Washington, D.C., relatively atypical Southern cities. The nation's cultural boundaries limited the expansion of even the most innovative spiritual entrepreneur. Around this time, the Vedanta Society began to make a comeback, from four societies to more than a dozen by the late 1930s, in Hollywood, San Francisco, Portland, Seattle, Chicago, New York, Washington, D.C., Providence, and Boston. Still, even with its weak points, the dramatic overall growth of his ministry in little more than a decade eclipsed what the Vedanta Society had been able to accomplish in the same timeframe a few decades earlier.[52]

YOGANANDA'S RELIGIOUS PRODUCTS

Like more recent popular Christian leaders, Yogananda succeeded in a competitive religious marketplace by being "quick, decisive, and flexible in reacting to changing conditions, savvy at packaging and marketing" his ministry, and "resourceful at offering spiritual rewards that resonate with the existential needs and cultural tastes of the public."[53] He offered three types of religious products. First, he promised the *personal* goods of spiritual liberation and physical and emotional well-being through yoga, a set of scientific disciplines that allowed God-contact. Second, he offered *communal* goods through Yogoda Sat-Sanga groups. Founded throughout the country, these local centers created communities of like-minded individuals who shared the same rituals and values. Finally, he offered *consumer* goods that linked disciples to their religious tradition.[54] His bimonthly magazine, *East-West*, and a flood of books helped to sustain a sense of community through Yogananda's spiritual teachings and news about sister groups around the country. As material objects, books and especially the subscription-based magazine were literal products that provided a tangible reminder of community identity.

As with every product associated with the restless ad man, Yogananda gave various names to his yoga method, hoping to achieve the proper resonance. In the early years, he commonly labeled it *Yogoda*, a neologism designed to differentiate his product from the other forms of yoga practice customers might have learned about from the Vedanta Society or elsewhere. According to Satyeswarananda, a disciple of Yogananda's former colleague and childhood friend Satyananda, Yogananda coined the word *Yogoda* while still in India. Inspired by Satyananda's Yogad Sat Sanga Sova meetings in India, Yogananda apparently planned to create his own Yogoda Sat-Sanga, or Yogoda Community, in the United States. When informed that *Yogoda* was a grammatically incorrect rendition of the Sanskrit—and inappropriate because it sounded too much like Yogananda's own name, and would thus confuse a large organization of many teachers with one representative—Yogananda reputedly brushed off the objections: "Oh! For us it is okay."[55] For his first fifteen years in the United States, his organization was officially labeled Yogoda Sat-Sanga until he renamed it Self-Realization Fellowship in 1935.

He published his first teachings in the 1923 *Yogoda or Muscle-Will System of Physical Perfection*, a series of physical and breathing exercises designed to provide healing and wholeness through *prāṇāyāma*, control of the life force, or *prāṇa*. At the beginning of *Yogoda*, Yogananda directs the practitioner to invoke the Eternal Energy, introducing a larger discourse about the body as a mechanism that needs electricity to run. Yogananda may have borrowed his terminology from metaphysical thinkers, who were often fascinated by the relation between spirituality and electricity, but it would have also sparked interest broadly among audience members.[56] Electricity fascinated modern Americans, who viewed it as "an energy flowing between mind and body," which "merged with new therapeutic conceptions of the psyche and the self. . . . Americans made electricity a metaphor for mental power, psychological energy, and sexual attraction." By the late nineteenth century, a number of commercial devices promised to restore health, strength, or sexual potency through electricity.[57] Beyond its spiritual and psychological implications, electricity captivated early twentieth-century Americans in more material ways. Electricity generated new forms of transportation, amusement parks, labor-saving appliances, and artificial lighting that turned nighttime cities into day.[58]

Yogananda seized on this fascination with electricity, energy, and spirituality and developed it into a coherent explanation of his program's efficacy. He compared the conventional yogic notion of *prāṇāyāma* to the most powerful source of energy the modern world knew. And he regularly employed the trope of the body as an engine. "An automobile battery needs to be recharged once in a while when run down. So the battery of the body parts, exhausted by physical work and brain labor, requires to be recharged by fresh nerve current sent down by Will."[59]

To attract modern audiences who might be more concerned with health and energy than with spiritual benefits, Yogananda emphasized the temporal benefits of Yogoda. Beginning with proper posture, Yogananda guided practitioners through a set of exercises to concentrate on muscles and then systematically tense and relax them. Like a physician, he provided a prescription, a frequency, and expected outcomes of Yogoda exercises: fifteen minutes of practice a day would lead to remarkable results. These brief routines appealed to busy working people who might only have pockets of free time throughout the day. Yogananda seems to have borrowed the exercises in large part from a nineteenth-century Danish physical culturalist named J. P. Muller, who made a similar pitch about the ability to practice these exercises in the midst of a hectic life in the modern world.[60] Satyeswarananda, often critical of Yogananda, saw the energization techniques as a concession designed to "inspire and motivate his Western devotees who love exercises."[61]

But the physical exercises were only the entrée to the more important goal of God-contact, which required a specific set of more rigorous meditational techniques. A small booklet that employed relatively little Sanskrit terminology, *Yogoda* eschewed detailed discussion of metaphysics, cosmology, or theology. It was essentially a teaser for those interested in more comprehensive instruction. Yogananda soon launched a yoga correspondence course, an elaboration of the *Yogoda* outline that delved more deeply into yoga proper. Over a ten-year period, the lessons developed into increasingly advanced techniques:

1923: *Yogoda or Muscle-Will System of Physical Perfection* (three lessons)
1924: *Highest Technique of Concentration* (two lessons)
1925: *Yogoda System of Physical, Mental and Spiritual Perfection*—the first five lessons from 1923 and 1924, and seven new lessons (twelve lessons)
1926: *Advanced Course on Practical Metaphysics* (twelve lessons)
1930: *Super-Advanced Course Number 1* (twelve lessons) and *The Art of Super Realization* (one lesson introducing Kriya, Maha Mudra, and Yoti Mudra)
1934: *Advanced Super Cosmic Science Course* (six lessons) and *New Super Cosmic Science Course* (seven lessons)[62]

As Yogananda revised the materials in the early 1930s, the correspondence course grew to include 182 lessons consisting of seven "Steps" of 26 lessons each. Each 26-lesson Step ended with an "intermediate exam"; a successful exam score enabled the disciple to receive the next set of lessons. If lessons were completed at the prescribed "fortnightly" rate, the entire sequence would take seven years, though some eager aspirants undoubtedly completed them more quickly.

The course began with the Yogoda energization exercises, enhanced with additional practices. Yogananda then introduced two additional stages, concentration and meditation. Reflecting a division in Patañjali's *Yoga Sūtras* between *dhyāna* and *dhāraṇā*, Yogananda distinguished between concentration techniques that taught disciplined focus on any subject and meditation proper, which allowed one to engage in single-minded contemplation of God. Instruction in practical techniques included improving memory, curing nervousness—which included the suggestion to "avoid jazz and loud music for some time at least" and instead listen to violin music—and learning to heal oneself. Cross-promotion was imbedded in Yogananda's instruction. To deepen one's skills, he recommended buying his writings, such as *Songs of the Soul, Scientific Healing Affirmations,* and articles in back issues of *East-West.*

The original lessons began without much preamble, often ran no more than a page and a half or two, and included syntax errors common to nonnative English speakers. By the early 1930s, the format had become more elaborate. The lessons followed a consistent sequence that Yogananda explained as "the Scientific Theory to a Technique, the concise Technique itself, invigorating health recipes, a highly enlightening Apologue for you and your family, a vibrant affirmation, and an inspirational poem."[63] The lesson began with an inspirational poem, or an affirmation, and a prayer. The bulk of the lesson consisted of detailed instruction on one technique of concentration or meditation, which included a philosophical introduction and practical implementation, often with sequential steps. The lesson concluded with an "apologue"—a fable or allegory that provided some moral truth about yoga—and another affirmation.

Despite Yogananda's routine insistence on the importance of practical religion, his lessons contained more than techniques for concentration and meditation. Yoga practice made sense only within a larger cosmology, and he used the lessons to provide this instruction. He taught that the universe is a vibration caused by the primordial sound "Om," and meditating on this sound allows a practitioner to "develop Soul and Spiritual vibratory magnetism."[64] All material reality consists of five *koshas,* or sheaths, "stages of evolution through which all matter has to pass in order to become spiritualized and emancipated."[65] Creation, while real, is also in a profound sense *māyā,* or delusion, "which makes the Indivisible spirit seem finite and divisible to all appearances. Matter has existence in the same delusive way as the mirage in the desert."[66] Human experience is fundamentally shaped by the endless cycles of reincarnation that result from one's *karma,* the "natural law of cause and effect and law of action."[67] Only the teachings of the ancient yogis can liberate humans from the limitations and confusions of human existence, providing both guidance for living successfully on earth—health, prosperity, work success, and happy relationships—and ultimate wisdom and spiritual liberation.

After completing the first two Steps (the first fifty-two lessons), the devotee was invited to apply for Kriya Yoga, "a special technique for quickening your evolution."[68] But only the patient practitioner was rewarded, persevering through one hundred additional lessons as the course meandered, ambled, and wandered through anecdotes and advice before finally introducing "the Higher Initiation" in Praeceptum 150 with the announcement that "Words are inadequate to express to you the Self-Realization-producing vitality of this Kriya (Kree-ya) Instruction."[69] But the technique of "Kriya Proper" actually began another four lessons later in Praeceptum 154. And it was anticlimactic after all the buildup. First, in one page of instruction, disciples were taught *prāṇāyāma,* how to move the breath and life current through a hollow spinal canal from the coccyx to the Spiritual Eye.[70] The other two Kriya techniques, "Maha Mudra" and "Yoti Mudra," were taught in Praeceptum 157. The former

YOGODA

THE HIGHEST TECHNIQUE OF

CONCENTRATION

MEDITATION

AND

SPIRITUALIZATION of the BODY

SWAMI YOGANANDA

YOGODA is a scientific system for conscious control of involuntary life forces, perfected by the eminent Hindu master of metaphysics and psychology, SWAMI YOGANANDA, A.B.

YOGODA can be practiced anywhere, anytime, in public or private, sitting or reclining, walking or standing, unobserved by others, and without apparatus or expense of any kind. Ten minutes by this system exceeds in benefit hours of ordinary exercise.

This marvelous science of applied life vibration, technically known as YOGODA, endorsed by foremost scientists and educators, draws thru concentrated absorption from cosmic energy a recharge of life-giving elements into the physical and spiritual system. This principle can be put into CONSTANT operation within your being, proceeding without interruption in its constructive processes even while your physical body is in repose.

EVERY MUSCLE, ORGAN AND FUNCTION OF BODY STRENGTHENED

Parts unaffected by any other system of development are brought to their maximum powers by this miracle-working science.

WHAT "Y O G O D A" DOES

Teaches how to literally RECHARGE body-batteries with fresh life-current by increasing dynamic power of will.

Improves (a) Beauty of Form; (b) Grace of expression; (c) Centre of Consciousness; (d) Power of mental receptivity; (e) Contact with the Infinite Reservoir of Power.

YOGODA prevents hardening of arteries and insures lasting youth by stimulating even circulation and helping to eject foreign matter from the system. Drives away headaches instantly. Harmonizes all muscle actions. Makes colds impossible.

It exercises those parts which you think you cannot exercise.
PUTS ON or TAKES OFF FAT, as desired.
Teaches you to control your material and spiritual destiny.

This YOGODA system has accomplished wonderful results in several residential schools for boys in India, established by Swami Yogananda, and has brought lasting health and happiness to thousands of American students.

F A M O U S   S T U D E N T S   O F   Y O G O D A

Amelita Galli-Curci—Luther Burbank—Luigi von Kunits, Conductor of the New Symphony Orchestra of Toronto, Canada—Huston Ray, brilliant pianist—Countess Ilya Tolstoy—Homer Samuels, distinguished pianist—Judge T. J. Hewitt of Oregon—Vladimir Rosing, eminent tenor and director of the Rochester American Opera Co.—Clara Clemens Gabrilowitsch—Maria Carreras, famous pianiste.

A descriptive pamphlet, "Yogoda," simple, illuminating and intensely interesting, will be mailed you for 15c. It will prepare you for priceless benefits in health, success and radiant happiness. Send 15c in stamps or coin to

YOGODA CORRESPONDENCE SCHOOL

Dept. J-F   3880 San Rafael Avenue   Los Angeles, Calif.

An early advertisement for Yogoda, the proprietary name for Yogananda's yoga correspondence course, which teaches "spiritualization of the body" by "literally" recharging the "body battery" to ensure everlasting youth. A number of famous Yogoda students, many professional musicians, testify to its practical results. But beyond its physical health benefits, this course also offers control over "spiritual destiny."

is a standard *haṭha yoga* technique that adds specific leg positions to the *prāṇāyāma* described in Kriya Proper, and the latter, Yogananda's idiosyncratic label for *yoni mudra*, involves using the hands to seal the eyes, ears, mouth, and nose so that, as he explained, "the Third Eye reveals God and Spirit."[71]

Despite the promise that initiates would learn proprietary techniques reintroduced to Lahiri Mahasaya by special revelation after having disappeared millennia ago, Yogananda's yoga instruction basically reflected classical yoga as exposited in Patañjali's *Yoga Sūtras*. Yogananda echoed Patañjali's guidance on breath control, concentration, meditation, and the repetition of mantras to realize that the true self must not be confused with the individual body. He also included Tantra-inspired *haṭha yoga* elements, teaching, for example that *kuṇḍalinī* was a "creative nerve force which flows through a coiled passage in the coccyx."[72] "It takes very high development," the initiate was assured, "to see the ray-petaled lotus stars or chakras," and that began in the coccyx and continued upward to the "Spiritual Eye or Christ Center."[73] Eventually, the practitioner could reach *samādhi* at will, the state "in which the devotee, meditation, and God become one."[74] Yogananda obliquely acknowledged the availability of similar teachings, commenting that "any Yoga book or Scripture, or the Christian Bible, can be bought for a few cents and intellectually swallowed."[75] Proper spiritual digestion, however, required the aid of a guru.

If these techniques all replicated stock yoga instruction, what *was* remarkable was the affectionate devotional language Yogananda used to present *samādhi*. His lessons defined *samādhi* as "when the student becomes one with God," and defined Self-Realization, a common way of describing the outcome of *samādhi*, in terms of divine intimacy: "Self-Realization is the KNOWING, in all parts of the body, mind, and Soul, that we are now in possession of the Omnipresence of God; that we do not have to pray that it come to us; that we are not merely near It at all times, but that God's Omnipresence is our Omnipresence; that He is just as much a part of us now as He will ever be, and that all we have to do is to improve our KNOWING."[76] His language routinely encouraged a devotional understanding of divine reality. When he explained that "God loves to drink devotion from the secret wine-press of the devotee's heart," he sounded like many a medieval *bhakti* poet.[77] Yogananda's thousands of references to God—buttressed by routine quotations from the Bible, whose God has traditionally been understood as emphatically transcendent—portray a personal deity with consciousness and volition. This is a God who thinks, creates, reveals himself, sends gurus, responds to prayer, gives direction, loves, and offers strength and energy. In turn, humans should love God, be devoted to Him, and be intoxicated by Him. In Advaita nondualism, "devotion must occupy a lower position than pure knowledge," and the advanced devotee abandons notions of a personal deity after achieving the realization of *Brahman* as ultimately "devoid of qualities."[78] But though Yogananda regularly used the language of absolute monism, he never abandoned his affection for depictions of a personal deity. In the very last correspondence lesson for his most advanced disciples, he was still counseling disciples to ask God, "May Thy love shine forever on the sanctuary of devotion, and may I be able to awaken Thy love in Truth-thirsty hearts."[79]

Though Yogananda's theistic impulse stemmed from a number of sources, his reading of yoga texts may have encouraged him to express a more theistic outlook. Indic religion scholar Stuart Sarbacker argues that alongside the familiar "cessative" yoga tradition emphasizing the goal of *kaivalya*, or pure consciousness, resides a second "numinous" strand that celebrates supernatural powers the devotee enjoys when through mastery of practice he or she "becomes like a deity."[80] David Gordon White describes historical yoga as a "soteriological system that culminates in union or identity with a supreme being."[81] Indologist Edwin Bryant argues that the *Yoga Sūtras*, often considered the foundational text for yoga practice, can only be understood in the "greater theistic landscape of Patañjali's day." Parts of his yoga system "requir[e] a theistic practice." Significantly, it is precisely in the section on "*kriyā yoga*"—the name Yogananda gave his own practice—that Patañjali's theism is most direct and insistent. *Kriyā yoga*, in Bryant's translation, "consists of self-discipline, study, and dedication to the Lord." "Surrender to God," Bryant concludes, "is a mandatory part of this practice."[82] Andrew Nicholson argues that following Patañjali, "belief in God was widespread" among authors of Saṃkhya, the philosophical tradition closely associated with yoga, "throughout most of the history of Indian philosophy."[83] Whether such an approach to reading yoga texts informed Yogananda's understanding, his theistic tendencies were deeply rooted.

But it was the format of Yogananda's yoga instruction that was most notable. Yoga by distance learning was a radical invention—and viable only in the context of modern mass marketing and a vibrant consumer culture. Correspondence courses fit with the United States' spirit of self-improvement, its belief in equality of opportunity, the growing importance of education in an industrialized society, and a pragmatic business model of efficiency and profit maximizing. As the consumer economy blossomed in the early twentieth century, correspondence courses flourished.[84] Although offerings included cultural and liberal arts courses, 80 percent of correspondence courses provided training in technical, vocational, and business fields. Lack of accreditation or accountability led to wildly varying levels of quality, but despite shortcomings, distance learning offered a practical instrument for meeting demonstrable educational needs.

While practical courses predominated, many religious courses were also available. A religious reference book from the time explained the "great value" correspondence courses provided: an educational opportunity that was otherwise unavailable, an incentive to study that an individual usually could not muster on his or her own, training by a specialist, and the suitability of a particular course to the individual's needs. There was a biblical precedent for such learning: the text argued that the "first correspondence school was conducted by the Apostle Paul, and his pupils included private individuals and whole churches." Moody Bible Institute, the premier turn-of-the-century fundamentalist Bible school, began correspondence courses in 1901. And William Rainey Harper, often credited with launching university-based correspondence courses as president of the University of Chicago in 1891, began a course in biblical Hebrew that had expanded by the early twentieth century to more than thirty advanced courses in Hebrew, Greek, theology, and church history.[85]

Yogananda's yoga course did have precedents in biblical instruction, but the closest parallels were courses offered by two New Thought leaders. Born in Baltimore in 1862, William Walker Atkinson converted to New Thought after a physical and mental breakdown in the 1880s. Thereafter, the sometime businessman and lawyer moved to Chicago, a major center for the movement. By 1900, he began editing a New Thought journal and, as Carl Jackson puts it, "churning out a seemingly endless series of volumes" under his own name and several pseudonyms, including Theron Q. Dumont, Swami Panchadasi, and Yogi Ramacharaka. In his Ramacharaka persona, he commented, "For anyone to write intelligently upon the subject of Hindu Philosophy or Religion, it is necessary that he must be in sympathy with the Hindu mind and soul—not necessarily a believer in their religions, or a follower of their philosophy, but most certainly possessed of a mind in sympathy with the fundamental conceptions."[86] His knowledge of Hinduism and yoga was sufficient to deceive many in the New Thought movement, who remained convinced that Atkinson and Ramacharaka were two different people.

In late 1903, Ramacharaka began to offer lessons by correspondence course through the Yogi Publication Society, endorsing himself in an anonymous third-person advertisement as "a student and writer who is renowned for the profundity of his thought, the clearness of his mental vision, the depth of his spiritual knowledge and his remarkable simplicity and plainness of style." Originally four monthly lessons, the series quickly grew to fourteen, each providing philosophical instruction, a topic for meditation, a *mantra,* and "Class

Notes," which provided an opportunity to connect subscribers to a larger community—and to advertise more books. Despite the "deep Indian influence on his thinking," which fooled many colleagues in the New Thought movement, his instruction represented a synthesis of Theosophy and New Thought occult teachings on mesmerism, magnetism, auras, and ether.[87] The lessons offered very little instruction in practical meditation techniques. Whether Yogananda knew of Ramacharaka's courses is uncertain, but given the abundance of Ramacharaka's writings it is certainly possible.

Another predecessor to Yogananda's correspondence course was created by fellow Southern Californian Max Heindel. In 1910, he converted his twenty "Rosicrucian Christian Lectures" into talks available by mail. The following year, as letters were "coming in from students all over the world asking for a deeper and more explicit teaching on certain points of the Higher Life," Heindel "decided that in order to meet such a demand it would be necessary to start a Correspondence School." So he abandoned the lecture circuit and established his international headquarters in Oceanside, California, offering "the fruitage of true esoteric research" through a series of nearly one hundred monthly lessons on topics that included "Spiritual Research," "Etheric Sight," "The Dangers of Excessive Bathing," and "The Color Effects of Emotion in Assemblages of People."[88] The first service held in Mount Ecclesia's newly dedicated temple took place on Christmas Day, 1920, at precisely the time Yogananda was beginning his ministry in Boston. Some of Yogananda's earliest Boston followers had Rosicrucian connections, so it is possible that they suggested the correspondence course model to Yogananda.

If there were antecedents to Yogananda's correspondence course, there would also be successors. In the 1930s, Los Angeles resident Ivah Bergh Whitten launched what author Kurt Leland calls "an esoteric correspondence school with study groups and privately published lessons" explicating an esoteric Western elaboration of the *cakra* system.[89] It is difficult to determine whether Whitten's instructional format was inspired by her Los Angeles neighbor Yogananda. In the 1950s Indian Swami Sivananda also used coursework, but only in response to his inability to keep up with actual correspondence from devotees and not as a primary strategy, as with Yogananda. Sivananda's biographer Sarah Strauss explains that the "ideal situation was for them to visit the ashram at some point," so "books, tapes, and photographs remain only supplements."[90]

Yogananda's correspondence course shared some broad similarities with his two predecessors. The courses all taught metaphysical knowledge about unseen realms, spiritual truth, and health that their guides claimed revealed "true" Christianity. As esoteric knowledge, both proceeded though a sequence of instruction in which mastery of lower mysteries was a prerequisite for advanced understanding. And they had a similar fee structure; as autonomous ministries outside the framework of an existing church or other institution, these self-published efforts relied on initiates' donations, as the founders felt ambivalent about charging for spiritual instruction. Ramacharaka emphasized disciples' freedom to pay when they were able. "Do not trouble yourselves, dear students, about the small sum you owe us, and do not send us money which is really needed for other purposes. But when the sum comes into your hand in an unexpected manner, in such a way that it seems to have been sent you for just this purpose, then send it to us, and it will be used in paying the cost of printing and mailing these lessons. And don't feel uneasy about the indebtedness, for we are not afraid to 'trust' those who feel hungry for that which we have to offer."[91]

Despite these similarities, one difference was crucial. Heindel's and Ramacharaka's courses were designed largely to teach intellectual content, which was quite different from offering to mentor devotees in a complex sequence of physical, mental, and spiritual practices. This was an extremely novel approach within the Hindu tradition as well, a dramatic departure from the face-to-face model of transmission from guru to disciple that swamis considered indispensable. Yogananda's approach was extremely controversial among swamis trained by his mentor Sri Yukteswar. Decades after Yogananda established his American practice, his spiritual siblings continued to grouse that "the learning of any spiritual discipline through easily available materials, such as, lessons, books, literature, lectures, seminars, and through organizations, is not the righteous way. Learning through these means could never solve the subtle problems of the seeker."[92] Throughout the lessons, Yogananda continued to emphasize that advancement was possible only through his guidance as "Guru-Preceptor."[93] But Yogananda's mentorship was at best virtual, not the flesh-and-blood presence he had received from his own guru. Yogananda showed flexibility in other matters that he deemed unessential to the core of yoga practice. He allowed practitioners to sit in chairs while meditating rather than sitting in the lotus position, cross-legged on the ground. A fellow disciple in India called accommodation to Americans unused to sitting on the ground a "fundamental modification and deviation from the original" tradition, while another doubted that yoga could be "taught properly by letters and circulars."[94]

Yogananda's adaptability had several beneficial consequences. Distance-education yoga allowed Yogananda to enroll a much larger number of followers than he could ever have trained personally, and thus also provided a steady source of income. The restriction of the lessons for "private and personal use only" also served a number of purposes. "This pledge is necessary, to prevent misunderstanding and incorrect teaching of the Yogoda exercises."[95] Every lesson began with the reminder that it was "To be Confidentially Reserved for MEMBER'S USE ONLY." This echoed the traditional stricture that disciples not reveal their guru's training to anyone except their own future disciples. As one lesson warned, "Any violation will disturb the inner harmony of your Spiritual life due to casting Spiritual pearls before unappreciative eyes."[96] Pragmatically, secrecy affirmed the value of the lessons, creating a mystique about instruction that, as discussed above, was often available in some form from other sources. And secrecy protected an important proprietary source of revenue.[97]

The lessons played a crucial role in Yogananda's developing programmatic vision. Enrollment in the lessons essentially constituted membership in Yogoda Satsanga. As explained by a later disciple: "Yogananda saw the individual students first receiving the [Yogoda] lessons, and practicing Kriya Yoga in their own homes; then, in time, forming spiritual centers where they could meet once or twice weekly for group study and meditation. In areas where there was enough interest to warrant it, he wanted . . . churches, perhaps with full- or part-time ministers."[98] Those who expressed interest in beginning the course but did not follow through received aggressive follow-up messages. "Delay in taking up this valuable course of study . . . may lead to serious losses in your all-round material and spiritual development and your life's happiness." They also received an offer of discounted prices on the lessons and free copies of the magazine.[99]

After the Yogoda lessons, the bimonthly *East-West* magazine was Yogananda's most important published religious product. Launched at the end of 1925, the magazine's terse hyphenated title elegantly captured both the distinction between the two regions, the spiritual East and the technologically advanced, materialistic West, and the potential to build a bridge between them. *East-West* was "devoted to Spiritual Realization, Development of Body, Mind and Soul; Practical Metaphysics, and Hindu Psychology" and aimed "to inspire, to enlighten, and to encourage all to live the Practical Spiritual Life."[100] The magazine supplemented the yoga lessons by providing instruction in Hinduism. It also gave readers a sense of personal connection with their guru-from-a-distance, as Yogananda was executive editor and the magazine's most prolific contributor. In providing regular news about Yogoda centers nationwide, *East-West* fostered a sense that readers belonged to a larger spiritual community.

From the beginning, the magazine signaled a commitment to ecumenical spirituality by including contributions from a variety of religious traditions. Stories, images, poetic tributes, and texts by and about Buddha were prolific, including an early poem by Buddhist leader Dharmapala. Yogananda also featured Sufism, a popular, nondoctrinaire form of Islam prominent in parts of India, which shared *bhakti*'s devotional impulse. An early *East-West* issue included a story about Guru Nanak, founder of Sikhism, a monotheistic northern Indian movement with roots in devotional *bhakti* Hinduism and Sufism. Yogananda even expressed his concern for fellow performer-evangelist Aimee Semple McPherson. He defended her after the press widely reported that her brief disappearance—which she claimed resulted from being kidnapped—stemmed from a romantic rendezvous in Mexico. "If Mrs. McPherson has done no wrong, then what untold injustice and persecution is being heaped upon her! And if she has committed any error then that error should be balanced against the great works she has done by inspiring thousands of people."[101] McPherson might have been less than enthused by such a cautious defense, but Yogananda was more gracious to her than most Christian leaders.

A closer look at Yogananda's references to other religions reveals the limits of his ecumenical generosity. He essentially ignored his fellow Vedanta and yoga teachers, whether authentic gurus from India such as Swami Paramananda and Bhagwan Bissessar or American-born pretenders such as William Walker Atkinson and Perry Baker, aka Pierre Bernard, dubbed "the Omnipotent Oom" by the era's press.[102] This was true even if Yogananda was teaching in the same city at the same time as the teachers, which suggests that he saw them more as rivals than as fellow envoys of a common spiritual message.[103] And his inclusivism extended beyond Christianity (addressed at length in the following chapter) to include various other groups. Yogananda likely developed elements of his teachings about mind, energy, and magnetism from metaphysical traditions, and he showed some openness to prominent New Thought figure Ralph Waldo Trine. He even invited Trine to be a special guest of honor at the fourth anniversary celebration of Mount Washington in 1929. But conclusions about Yogananda's borrowing from New Thought are less clear-cut than scholars sometimes assume.[104] His overt interest in New Thought never developed from a respectful cordiality into a deeper exchange of views. More often, he placed metaphysical traditions on the scale of his own universalistic Hinduism and found them wanting. He acknowledged Theosophy's contributions to the West's understanding of reincarnation but criticized its confused and misleading teaching. Theosophist Charles Leadbetter's 1927 introductory text, *The Chakras*, had offered a stern warning about the dangers of arousing *kuṇḍalinī* prematurely: "I should like most solemnly to warn all students against making any effort whatever in the direction of awakening these tremendous forces, except under such qualified tuition, for I have myself seen many cases of the terrible effects which follow from ignorant and ill-advised meddling with these very serious matters."[105] Yogananda complained that Theosophical teaching had made American audiences unnecessarily anxious about the potential dangers of *kuṇḍalinī*. Conceding that "our Theosophical brothers have done a great deal of good in the world," he grumbled that some "thru their utter ignorance or very partial knowledge of Sanskrit, have created much panic and wrong ideas in the minds of Westerners by giving the impression, through their entirely wrong translations of certain Sanskrit passages, that danger results from such practices as rousing of the kuṇḍalinī, meditation and other forms of inner development." These ideas, which have "spread like wild-fire," "mislead them and hamper their evolutionary progress." Frightening people out of the path to salvation was nothing less than a "spiritual crime."[106]

A piece comparing Christian Science and Hinduism was equally critical. Yogananda began on a positive note, praising the "great triumphant power of Christian Science over disease and distress." He acknowledged that both traditions were based on "the same universal truths" and claimed that the first edition of Mary Baker Eddy's *Science and Health* included quotations from the *Bhagavad Gītā*, though he was quick to point out that Eddy's doctrine "had been worked out by the Hindus prior to the birth of Christian Science." As with Theosophy, he denounced wrongheaded Christian Science teaching. Christian Science unwisely rejected medicine and fasting and attempted to heal the body through imagination rather than will, "the great inner generator of energy." Though the movement "intellectually grasped" the impermanence of the material world, it failed to perceive that this truth "cannot be *realized* until one has learned the conscious method of converting matter into conscious energy and conscious energy into Cosmic Consciousness." In short, those who embraced the tenets of Christian Science were "still under the delusion of the dream-world."[107] Yogananda's approach toward other religions was consistent: he began with broad-minded commendation and ended with harsh critique. In a crowded religious market, he remained convinced of the superior value of his own brand.

One place this superior Hindu wisdom was most evident was in his teaching on mind, body, and spirit and the relation between them. Yogananda discussed the body's importance in the early pages of *East-West*. A column called "Health Hints," which appeared in the magazine's second issue, recommended pineapple, raisins, and carrots ground in a meat chopper ("good for teeth and bones"), mixed with pistachios and cream, and served on lettuce. The column also suggested that "business men and women" fast on Sunday to "eliminate unwelcome meals" and clean their teeth after lunch—rinsing ten times is "what the Hindu pundits prescribe."[108] Two issues later, a column on healthy recipes began to evolve into a more coherent recommendation for self-improvement based on an integrated view of mind, body, and spirit. Entitled "Three Recipes," the column offered helpful tips on "Spiritual," "Intellectual," and "Health" issues. By labeling all three sets of suggestions "recipes," Yogananda conveyed a cozy domestic tenor while nodding to the burgeoning home economics movement's notion of applied science: if the reader followed the steps carefully, the desired outcome was assured.[109]

In a magazine devoted primarily to religious issues, "Spiritual Recipes" represented the most conventional component of the "Three Recipes" column. In the first column, Yogananda offered this rather bland exhortation: "Try to consciously contact God. Will to know Him, persevere in the effort to know Him, and be dissatisfied until you do know him."[110] Other early issues urged regular meditation, concentration and effort on the spiritual path, finding times to pray whenever possible in the midst of a busy day, and the value of meditation on Scripture like the *Bhagavad Gītā*. For reading, he recommended "only spiritual books which contain self-realization."[111] The staleness of the "Spiritual Recipes," which initially seems counterintuitive, reflects Yogananda's effort to avoid detracting from the yoga lessons.

"Intellectual Recipes" was also a half-baked feature, essentially amounting to short book recommendations. Occasionally, he endorsed new spiritual works. Bruce Barton's *The Man Nobody Knows* earned his praise as "the best modern book on Jesus."[112] Yogananda also praised contemporary devotional books by Sister Nivedita, praising her reputation while remaining strangely silent about the fact that her fame derived from being Swami Vivekananda's disciple. His suggestions were often vague or redundant, and some months absent altogether. These defects likely reflect his own inability to keep up with reading new material amid an unrelenting work schedule. His recommendations often returned to established texts like Shakespeare and Thomas à Kempis's spiritual classic, *Imitation of Christ*. He also suggested reading texts that were not explicitly spiritual, such as science books and magazines. More often, he simply commended "great books" because "books are your best friends." Still, his regular exhortation to read broadly implied that deepening one's knowledge was an inherently spiritual task.

For a short time, Yogananda inserted "Prosperity Recipes" into the column. This topic proved an awkward fourth guest at the "Three Recipes" table.

Unlike the other components, which were all dimensions of the self, "prosperity" was instead a goal or attitude. Yogananda's advice in this section consisted of bromides such as these:

> The one who creates does not wait for opportunity, blaming the fates, circumstances and the gods. He seizes opportunities or creates them with the magic wand of his will, effort and searching discrimination.[113]
>
> Never turn back. . . . Make up your mind you *will* succeed.[114]
>
> Money-making is the next greatest art after the art of realizing God.[115]

This trite feature suggests the pressure Yogananda routinely felt to offer practical hints to businesspeople and other middle-class professionals. But offering new tips in each issue apparently proved even more challenging for "Prosperity Recipes" than for "Intellectual Recipes," and the column departed as abruptly as it had arrived.

By far the longest and most consistent member of the "Three Recipes" concerned physical well-being. Variously entitled "Health," "Food," and "Health and Food," this topic preceded the formal launch of the "Three Recipes," and lingered on into the 1930s as the "Prosperity," "Intellectual," and even "Spiritual Recipes" trailed off. Topics in this category included a variety of tips on physical health. The column cautioned against overeating and exhorted fasting regularly to give "needed rest to the body-machine which overworks incessantly thru over-eating or wrong eating." Chewing food thoroughly was necessary for proper digestion. In warning against alcohol, Yogananda matched the fervor of contemporary temperance advocates: "Awake! Young men and women! Fight the liquor habit!"[116]

But physical health required more than proper food and drink. "Over-sex" and gluttony were both dangers to avoid. Daily bathing "cleans the body pores and keeps the sweat glands working properly, eliminating impurities." This spiritual practice was recommended by "the Hindu savants," who taught that "the person who bathes daily and keeps the pores of his body open, helps his increased body heat to escape through these pores."[117] Adequate exercise, including routine walking, maintained health. And Yogananda repeatedly recommended bathing daily in the sunshine, "God's Ocean of X-Ray," which had proven scientific benefits:

> Sunlight and ultra violet ray baths are also necessary to fill the tissues and pores with life-giving energy from without. They redden the

> hemoglobin of the blood, recharging it and making it richer and healthier. As an ordinary bath washes away and clears the bacteria and dirt from the human body, so also the ultra violet rays in the sunlight not only cleanse the body of bacteria but also destroy them. The ultra violet rays are the death rays which penetrate the homes of enemy bacteria hiding in the finger nails and body pores, and scorch them out.

Yogananda acknowledged that a walk outdoors might not always be practical. In that case, "open your glass windows and let your life-giving, soliciting friend, Sunlight, fall on you and bathe you all over. Keep on jumping up and down, if you are afraid of catching cold, but each morning do bathe in the ocean of X-Ray which God has created for you. Without a daily bath in God's sea of X-Ray, you cannot be healthy. And remember, only healthy persons are happy."[118]

Most of the column space in the "Food and Health Recipes" was given over to literal recipes. Though the recipes ran the gamut from snacks to main courses, side dishes to desserts, they all reflected Yogananda's commitment to vegetarianism. Ideas relied heavily on the use of fruit, nuts, and a surprising fondness for Thousand Island dressing, a relatively new condiment at the time. A number of recipes offered meat substitutes, including curd curry, nut steak, mock lamb, and vegetable hamburger. Yogananda also emphasized the value of whole raw foods, particularly fresh fruits and vegetables. He warned about the dangers of white flour and advocated consuming brown rice ("the Father of all Cereals"), green-leaf vegetables, and almond milk. Occasionally, he attempted to glorify basic recipes with spiritual-sounding names — Swami Salad and Swami Pudding, Yogoda Curry Sauce and Yogoda Strawberry Ice Cream, and Hermitage Avocado. Apart from their health benefits, several of Yogananda's recipes served a cultural purpose, introducing South Asian foods like "Hindu curry" to a white American audience largely unfamiliar with such delicacies.

As often happened, Yogananda eventually found a way to commodify his instruction about a healthful diet. He developed a small line of vegetarian health foods that could be purchased from his Mount Washington headquarters in Southern California and shipped across the country. Advertisements for these products began to appear in *East-West* in 1934 — sometimes immediately adjacent to the "Health Recipes" — and continued in some fashion for the next half dozen years. Beginning a new product line during the Great Depression is a surprising strategy. This timing may reflect a desperation born of the organization's dire financial straits, as well as an effort to capitalize on families' need to economize at a time when meat was often the meal's central and most expensive portion. The six-year duration of the product line suggests that it met with some success. The timing of its departure — the end of the Depression with the onset of America's role as "the arsenal of democracy" — reinforces the contention that product appeal was tied to tightened Depression era food budgets.

In touting these products, Yogananda characteristically reinforced the link between mind, body, and spirit. He employed medical-sounding language to explain their physical and mental effects and sprinkled in a few spiritual words as well. "This food is good," proclaimed one ad, "not only from the chemical standpoint, but from the intuitive standpoint as well." "Intuitive analysis" conducted by "India's Masters," "finds the effect of food on the constitution of the cells, and on the entire Spiritual life, which chemical analysis reveals only superficial results of food on the human system. This intuitive food builds brain, muscle, and mind. It is also a Soul Food. It will help to invigorate the body, make youth lasting, increase the beauty of body and skin, and create a serene mind and temper."[119] Clearly, it was difficult to overestimate the value of these products.

Self-Realization Fellowship's first food product and the one that enjoyed the greatest longevity was a mysterious one. Nutritive nuggets were "pleasant and nourishing" for breakfast, lunch, or dinner. The ingredients were never disclosed, but because nutritive nuggets were rich in oil, they benefited "the digestive tract, liver, and gall bladder." And "although mildly laxative," ads reassured readers, they "are not habit-forming." And for good measure, "children love them."[120]

"India nut steak," another popular long-term product, was "undoubtedly the most perfect meat substitute ever offered to the public," an ideal product for "spiritually minded people." "Just as nourishing as a large steak, but . . . free from meat poisons," nut steak allowed vegetarians to "have the same enjoyment as they would eating steak." In fact, it was "more delicious that real meat loaf." Because nut steak was made from "choice, carefully selected nuts," it contained "the high nutritional value found in such great abundance in nuts." Prepared "under the most exacting conditions, in clean, spotless kitchens," nut steak was "unsurpassed in purity." Why not "order a few cans and surprise the family"? After all, nut steak "will be enjoyed by the entire family," and was "especially good for growing boys and girls, as it gives them the proper nourishment so essential to growth in childhood."[121]

A few other products were offered from time to time, but with much less fanfare. Many were advertised as both tasty and beneficial, like the "delightfully different" cactus candy, which possessed "a medicinal and spiritual value."[122]

Yogananda often described the health virtues of his products using scientific terminology. Organic, mint-flavored alfalfa tea, for example, was "recommended by authorities everywhere on account of its high alkalinity, vitamins, and rich organic content." It was made from "young alfalfa leaves only harvested at bud to insure maximum chlorophyll content and aromatized with the lasting fragrance of orange blossoms and mint." Since only the moisture was removed, "maximum food values" were maintained. The tea was "produced from seeds and packaged under scientifically controlled" conditions. But not every product received a rousing endorsement for its scientifically verifiable health benefits. Some products were attractive because they tasted good. Though "nutritious and healthful" honey-dipped Mount Washington prunes should be consumed for "your health's sake," their primary benefit seemed to be their "delightful flavor."[123]

Yogananda's dietary advice and food products point to the role a vegetarian diet played in his form of Hinduism. Though the majority of Hindus are not vegetarian, vegetarianism has been an important tradition among some castes and religious traditions for millennia. For devotees of yoga, the clearest directive comes from the *yamas* in Patañjali's *Yoga Sūtras*. The first of Patañjali's eight "limbs," the *yamas* are "great vows" that constrain the ethical behavior of a yogi aspirant. *Ahimsa*—or nonharm—is especially weighty, as it is the first *yama*, and traditional exegesis grants extra interpretive authority to introductory statements. Nonharm to other living things has often been understood to include not killing animals for food. More than an ethical imperative, this restriction safeguards the purity of the yogi's body. In the Saṃkhya philosophy undergirding yoga practice, the balance between the three *guṇas* that constitute all matter should be tipped against *rajasic* foods that make one both physically and spiritually dull. Consumption of pollutants—coffee, tea, alcohol, and especially meat—should be avoided altogether.[124] Thus, Yogananda's recommendations for healthy food extended beyond a practical concern for health, physical comfort, and happiness. The body was ultimately a divinely ordained spiritual vessel. "Remember," he counseled, "that this bodily machinery has been given to you to enable you to accomplish certain works on this material plane, and that you should guard it and take care of it as your most precious possession."[125] In his attention to the body's indispensable spiritual function, Yogananda underscored the crucial integration between spirit and matter.

Yogananda was not alone as a spiritual teacher touting the benefits of vegetarianism in early twentieth-century America. Some Protestant movements had begun to devote more attention to the body and its spiritual role around the turn of the century. Muscular Christianity focused on physical strength and masculinity.[126] Pentecostals embraced physical healing as central to promise of the gospel. In fact, divine healing was one of the core tenets of Aimee Semple McPherson's Foursquare Gospel.[127] And as the title of Mary Baker Eddy's essential work, *Science and Health with Key to the Scriptures*, indicates, Christian Scientists were deeply concerned about the relation between health, body, and spirituality. And though vegetarianism had been comparatively rare in American Christianity, a vegetarian thread running along the edge of the Protestant tradition had formed a more pronounced pattern by 1900. Seventh-Day Adventists embraced diet reformer Sylvester Graham's aversion to stimulants such as coffee, tea, alcohol, and tobacco; after visions from God, cofounder Ellen White began encouraging followers to avoid meat as well. John Kellogg's Adventist-inspired water cure sanitarium in Battle Creek, Michigan, represented the culmination of nineteenth-century Christian vegetarianism. Kellogg's experiments with flaked cereals stemmed from a desire to find a "satisfactory substitute" for breakfasts that "had been built and around meats," since "to most people a meal without meat as its center was unthinkable."[128] Outside of the Christian tradition, the Vegetarian Society of America was founded in 1886.[129] Consequently, by the time Yogananda began his series, vegetarianism had become a hot topic in the United States. Beginning around the turn of the century, periodicals including *Good Housekeeping, American Literary Digest, Harper's Bazaar*, the *New York Times*, and many other large-circulation publications began to run articles on vegetarianism.[130] Yogananda's attention to the integration of mind, body, and spirit—particularly his affirmation of physical health's spiritual value—offered a compelling vision based in ancient yoga wisdom but attuned to the concerns of modern Americans.

Apart from mail-order health foods, the magazine offered a variety of objects for sale. Mount Washington sold mounted photographs of Yogananda, which helped disciples maintain connection with their guru from a distance and create a sense of sacred space within their homes. Leather binders, stamped "EAST-WEST" in gold on the cover, allowed readers to preserve magazines. Though of clearly lower status than the yoga lessons, the magazines were repositories of wisdom worth preserving and consulting in the future. Other items were of more symbolic value. "Gold-plated, in orange and blue enamel," Yogoda pins and lapel buttons "proclaim to the world your adherence to Yogoda principles" while deepening their wearers' sense of identity with the organization at the same time. Christmas proved an especially fruitful opportunity for sales: *Whispers from Eternity*, "his first new book in years," was available in cloth binding "exquisitely gotten up"; a "special Christmas offer" of "a set of Swami's 6 books," and "beautiful Christmas greeting cards with Yogoda sentiments and designs" could be purchased "at the various Yogoda centers throughout the country." And no list of products was complete without the correspondence course.[131] Taking a cue from the widespread sales of Christian trinkets—from candles and decorative Bibles to rosary beads and artwork—Yogananda used material goods to deepen his followers' daily connection to their spiritual leader.

East-West supported the ministry financially in other ways as well. It sold advertising space to third parties, mostly promoting books on healthy diets and the occult. Key sections of the magazine also served as advertorials for Yogoda, where practical information was wholly entangled with boosterist reports of large audiences, impressive venues, and new converts. Yogoda advertisements and news updates frequently profiled professionals—business people, artists, and performers—whose occupations made them especially concerned about physical health and energy. Yogananda coveted the testimony of such upwardly mobile individuals for the prestige they brought to his organization and work. He also took a page from the playbook of Protestant churches that followed the business-savvy ethos of a consumer age in their approach to finance. As historian of American religion James Hudnut-Beumler indicates, "Ritualizing a definite pledge for the coming year was becoming increasingly prevalent in Protestant churches that were embracing business methods such as annual budgeting, accounting for gift receipts to donors quarterly, and urging weekly gifts on the analogy of an installment plan of credit."[132] Yogananda emulated this model well:

> MONTHLY DONATION PLEDGES. We hope that every Yogoda student will see his way clear to donate a regular monthly sum to the upkeep of the Mount Washington Educational Center, so that its energies may be free to devote to educational activities of a world-wide nature. We want to feel that every Yogoda student is taking an active interest in our work, and is willing to do his share in maintaining it and helping to spread its message of peace and a fuller understanding of life.[133]

Finally, *East-West* functioned as a commercial product itself. Current subscribers were urged to renew their subscriptions, and casual readers were routinely encouraged to subscribe so that they could reread important articles. Magazine subscriptions provided consistent, reliable revenue for the ministry. Yogananda even got swept up momentarily in the fervor for corporations that typified the era. He made plans to form the Yogoda Publishing Company to sell all of his texts and gave SRF members exclusive right to his initial stock offering. But his timing — five months before the Black Tuesday stock market crash of 1929 — proved inauspicious.[134]

WEATHERING THE RISKS OF THE SPIRITUAL MARKETPLACE

All of these efforts to find predictable streams of revenue reflected the reality that religious markets could be as risky as traditional consumer markets. Competition creates opportunities, but it also creates uncertainty. Ventures into new regional markets can be flops, negative publicity can damage the brand, and economic downturns can harm religious organizations as much as corporations. The first decade at Mount Washington brought great successes, as well as some serious difficulties.

As Yogananda's movement spread across the country, so did his fame. In 1927, Yogananda was President Calvin Coolidge's guest at the White House. While lecturing in D.C., Yogananda had offered advice on the president's diet in the *Washington Post*, including suggestions for "meatless Mondays," a ban on drinking ice water, and a regimen of fasting, exercise, and meditation.[135] Though a *Post* columnist pronounced that "as a dietitian Swami Yogananda doesn't know beans," Coolidge was more impressed with the swami and his novel vegetarian recipes.[136] Brokering a meeting through British ambassador Sir John Balfour, Coolidge invited a Hindu to the White House for the first time. The two met for a few minutes, as Yogananda informed the president that it was only "spiritual understanding between all nations that can bring lasting peace." Even international disarmament, he said, likely referring to the 1922 Washington Naval Treaty, would make no difference, "for the people still would fight if their weapons were but stones." The president agreed with Yogananda's sentiment and the brief meeting was over, since Coolidge declined to pose for a photo.[137] However lackluster, Yogananda played up this private meeting with the president as a sign that his renown was catching up with his spiritual stature.[138]

His growing fame was also evident in coverage in surveys of contemporary American religion. Charles Ferguson devoted a few pages to the "ineffable" swami who sold "Hindu philosophy to Americans by American methods and upon the basis of Yankee desire and ambition."[139] Much more thorough — and generally positive — was the profile offered in Wendell Thomas's 1930 book *Hinduism Invades America*.[140] Despite its alarmist title, Thomas claimed to strive for neutrality, as he explained in the foreword. "This work is not an attack on Hinduism. It is not meant to inflame American citizens by pointing to a foreign menace. Nor is it a defense of Hinduism. Nor is it a defense of Christianity or anything else. It is simply a study of the amazing adventure of an Eastern faith in a Western land." He included "Hindu friends" in his acknowledgments.[141] After historical chapters devoted to Vedanta, Ramakrishna, and Vivekananda, Thomas turned to contemporary American movements. The Vedanta Society and Yogoda Sat-Sanga were the only two organizations to which he devoted individual chapters; he lumped individual speakers, smaller movements, and hybrid groups like Theosophy into one chapter. Thomas devoted more than forty pages to Yogananda's biography, a synopsis of his writings and teachings, and a profile of members based on fifty surveys. He exaggerated the yoga evangelist's willingness to adapt the content of his message to his audience's interests, and he erroneously attributed Yogananda's emphasis on "healing" to the influence of Christian Science and New Thought. He also raised philosophical objections to the conception of Bliss. But all in all, though probing, Thomas was hardly hostile. He generally viewed Yogananda, not as a charlatan, but as a fundamentally sincere leader. Thomas reported a membership of "twenty-five thousand Yogodans scattered over the United States in groups and as individuals." This number, which may have been supplied by the organization itself, suggests a vibrant, if modest, national movement.[142]

Even as astute an observer as Thomas viewed the ministry as a one-man show, which is not a surprise, given how hard Yogananda worked to cultivate his persona as a wise, omnicompetent spiritual leader. In reality, he could not manage the ministry workload on his own. He tapped three gifted friends from India to be his associates. Basu Kumar Bagchi was Yogananda's colleague from Ranchi who was initiated into the swami order in Ranchi, taking the title Swami Dhirananda. Yogananda eventually invited Dhirananda to join him in the United States, confessing that although he was good at publicity and attracting followers, "I cannot manage things properly and I cannot write systematically."[143] Dhirananda accepted the call and came to Boston in 1922. In 1925, Yogananda appointed him head of the Mount Washington Educational Center, overseeing operations there while Yogananda traveled.

In 1928, Yogananda sent for Brahmachari Jotin, a friend of the Ghosh family whom Yogananda had ordained before he left India in 1920. On his way to the train station, Jotin visited Yogananda's father, to offer his "reverential salutation at his hallowed feet." Bhagabati blessed him, saying, "Jotin, now go to America and spread my Guru's (Lahiri's) message." Jotin "promised him with my soul that I would do my very best to fulfill his wish."[144] Jotin took over the challenging task of running the Washington, D.C., center, located in a poor section of the city, an assignment that caused him physical and emotional suffering. He persevered with the thought that one day India would be an independent nation, and his ministry in the nation's capital—indeed, the world's capital—would uniquely position him to offer the world "something of the best, the highest and the noblest that India has to offer."[145]

Nirod R. Choudhuri, who came to be known as Brahmachari Nerode, was a young Bengali whose family was friendly with both Mohandas Gandhi and Rabindranath Tagore. He graduated from the University of Calcutta with a degree in Sanskrit and traveled throughout India, Burma, and China before coming to the United States to attend graduate school at Harvard University. In 1927, Yogananda appointed him to take charge of the Detroit Yogoda Center.[146]

These bright, knowledgeable friends contributed to Yogananda's success in significant ways. Dhirananda helped edit *Science of Religion* and was listed on the title page as its "publisher." Yogananda's friend Satyananda, who remained in India, was also "able to help somewhat in the publication of the book."[147] In a brief preface, Yogananda offered his thanks to Dhirananda, Satyananda, and others "for the help I received from them in various ways."[148] Satyeswarananda claims that Dhirananda was substantially responsible for rewriting and editing the revised edition of *The Science of Religion* in Boston as well.[149] Dhirananda became indispensable in preparing Yogananda's course materials and books, beginning with the first Yogoda correspondence course booklet. The *Yogoda* title page credits the techniques to "SWAMI YOGANANDA, A.B. OF INDIA." In much smaller font, after a list of Yogananda's titles, the title page lists "Swami Dhirananda, M.A., *Associate*." In later editions, after a falling out between Dhirananda and Yogananda, Dhirananda's name was dropped from the title page and replaced with "Brahmachari Nerode, A.B., Honorary Associate."

An advanced yoga teacher, Nerode also provided substantial support to Yogananda's work. However, Yogananda and Nerode later also had a falling out. Both Dhirananda and Nerode published works—most, though not all, after breaking with Yogananda—on topics such as the *Bhagavad Gītā*, Patañjali's *Yoga Sūtras*, the unity of world religions, symbolism in religious texts, and "divine power science" that bear a strong resemblance to Yogananda's publications. Nerode's son, Anil Nerode, says that the teachings of his father and Dhirananda represent the "genesis of the Kriya Movement in America," as "each played an essential role in the development of Kriya."[150] It is difficult to determine the scope and form of Dhirananda's and Nerode's contributions to Yogananda's teaching and writing. Yogananda's general pattern with his publications, Satyeswarananda argues, was "to make the first rough draft of the manuscript," and "the rest would be taken care of by his trusted editors."[151] In any case, it is clear that Yogananda was not the sole, undisputed authority of Kriya Yoga he sought to project.

Even with the support of gifted colleagues, Yogananda faced a number of daunting challenges. The first was the harsh stereotypes about India, Indians, and Hinduism that implicitly impugned his ministry's integrity. Yogananda went to great lengths to defend India, its people, and its spiritual traditions through articles in *East-West*. At times, he endorsed Indian political nationalism. Gandhi was a favorite magazine subject, and Yogananda's adulatory articles often compared him to Jesus. "Gandhi! Politically crucified, Thou art not only the saviour of a race, of India, but also of all the selfish, hatred-stricken races of the world." But this Jesus promised not spiritual but political salvation. "Gandhi! Thy saintliness, and the fragrance of the unfading flower of Thy determination, will charm the menacing fire of cannon, until they sing instead the Freedom of India through Peace."[152] The magazine also expressed support for Indian self-rule with a tribute to Sarojini Naidu, president of the Indian National Congress, calling her an "eminent daughter of India" and urging Yogodans to hear her speak during an upcoming U.S. visit.[153]

Yogananda, a British subject by virtue of his Indian birth, came to the attention of British officials from Los Angeles to New York, San Francisco to Washington, D.C. British officials were concerned about radical political activities, having already concluded that "the majority of the Indian lecturers now in the United States would seem to be of doubtful tendencies."[154] In several cases, they secretly tracked and reported on Yogananda's activities. Yogananda's May 1926 passport renewal request received extra scrutiny, even though he had not "openly preached any revolutionary doctrines, his notoriety being mainly due to the way in which he obtains money from audiences attracted by his mysticism.[155] The British ambassador sent underlings to attend Yogananda's talks in New York and Washington, who determined that "it did not appear that he touched upon any political subjects,"[156] but instead "the usual type of psychological platitudes that emanate from the Hindu apostles of new religious who derive lucrative incomes by imposing upon certain elements of the American public."[157]

British officials may not have accurately captured Yogananda's message, but it is true that he was not fundamentally political. Indian cultural nationalism was more germane to his organizational concerns. Displays of the richness of Indian provided incontrovertible evidence that India was a great civilization, a logical prerequisite to Americans' acceptance of Indian beliefs and their messenger. *East-West* articles about Indian pageants, folk tales, dance, and the sacred nature of Indian music complemented frequent discussions of sacred Indian texts. When the 1932 summer Olympics were held in Los Angeles, the Mount Washington Educational Center hosted a celebration for the Indian competitors.[158] Yogananda often expressed his love for India in verse. "My Native Land," for example, celebrates the natural landscape, the "inviting shades of banian [*sic*] tree" and "the holy Ganges flowing by," before turning to its spiritual gift: India taught him "first to love . . . the God above." He concluded with the maternal personification familiar to Indian nationalists: "I bow to thee, my native land / The Mother of my love so grand."[159]

Defense of Indian culture became pressing after publication of Katherine Mayo's *Mother India* in 1927, a scathing indictment of India's animal sacrifices, gender relations, sexual practices, and hygiene.[160] Designed for a popular audience, published by a reputable press, and filled with superficially plausible documentary evidence, the book clearly presented an existential challenge to Indian civilization—and to anyone whose ministry hinged on the legitimacy of that heritage. A number of Indians and Indophiles took up the gauntlet. The editor of the *Indian Social Reformer*, K. Natarajan, offered a point-by-point rebuttal of Mayo by challenging her evidentiary base (particularly her use of a century-old French Christian source), critiquing the distortions she produced through selective citing of the worst examples, and pointing out the ongoing efforts of reformers such as his own organization to root out Indian social evils.[161] Journalist C. S. Ranga Iyer concentrated on Mayo's charges of sexual misbehavior and turned the tables by systematically highlighting the sexual depravity of American society.[162] Englishman Ernest Wood, former principal of Sind National College in Hyderabad, offered a defense of Indian culture even longer than Mayo's original.[163]

East-West joined this chorus of rebuttals in early 1928. One article explained how Mayo's book had unleashed an Indian backlash against Americans, warning about harm to the delicate relations between East and West. The magazine included a reprint of a reply by one Professor Cornelius, former professor of philosophy at Lucknow, who said that criticisms were welcome as long as they were fair but that Mayo "packs her book full of half-truths and no-truths. She overstates, suppresses, misinterprets facts and distorts evidence to support her prejudices; she uncompromisingly condemns the moral and religious life of a whole people."[164] *East-West* provided evidence that India's rich spiritual character had long influenced American culture. Arthur Christy contributed an article based on his doctoral dissertation demonstrating that Ralph Waldo Emerson borrowed from the Hindu scriptures, particularly in his "Song of the Soul (Brahma)" and in the notion of the Over-Soul. More provocatively, he argued that the quintessentially American ideal of Self-Reliance derived, at least in part, from Indian sources.[165] *East-West* also published an on-the-nose rebuttal that displayed more sympathy than skill:

Oh India! Country of Divine discontent,
Grieve thou not, at the cruel comment
In a recent book;
Having eyes the author seeth not at all.
Having ears she heareth not the call
Of thy soul. She's swayed by things external,
As most of us are.
She hitched not her vehicle to a star—
She loveth "brass tacks."
She heweth down here and scattereth there
She forgetteth her anscestors [*sic*] bowed in prayer
For the truths which she lacks.[166]

Vicious anti-Indian and anti-Hindu stereotypes were sometimes aimed directly at Yogananda and his ministry. An anticult hysteria reached a peak in the 1920s, with fears that secretive groups, particularly those led by mediums, and esoteric groups like Theosophy engaged in deceptive practices that lured people into sexual misdeeds and eventual insanity.[167] Echoing previous warnings about inappropriate domestic intimacy between swarthy swamis and delicate white women, in January 1928 the Los Angeles district attorney's office investigated accusations that Mount Washington was maintaining a "love-cult" "under the cloak of the Vedantic religion of India."[168] The investigation was driven by a review of Yogananda's "various books and pamphlets in which an unusual philosophy of love and sex control" were expounded. The British consul in Los Angeles was alerted to the controversy by a visit from Dhirananda, who was anxious about immigration officials' efforts to expel him and Yogananda as a result of the rumors. The consul privately concluded that since no woman came forward, that "probably confirms the suggestion already made that the sole basis for the accusation consists of vague unfounded statements."[169] Investigators reached the same conclusion, and the inquiry fizzled. In another case that came to the consul's attention, a married couple who worked at Mount Washington for a time—the wife as a secretary who saw a lot of Yogananda's correspondence—quit when they concluded that Yogananda was "a swindler" who misled women. They did not know what he did with his money, but they were concerned enough to bring the matter to the British consulate in Los Angeles.[170]

The month following the Mount Washington investigation, a similar accusation was hurled at Yogananda during one of his few trips to the American South. In Miami, outraged husbands threatened to lynch Yogananda when they heard about instruction taking place inside women's homes without men present. Breathless newspaper accounts included salacious reports: "The Hindu, it was alleged by indignant husbands, charged $35 a head for approximately 200 Women to hear his private lectures entitled 'Sex Consciousness.' He said the money was going to be used to start a love cult school over which he would preside."[171] City Manager Welton A. Snow and Chief of Police Leslie Quigg approached the British vice consul in Miami for advice on how to handle the situation without stirring up trouble unnecessarily. Presenting themselves as voices of moderation, they insisted that although they recognized that Yogananda was "an educated man," given the "strong public commitment against a coloured person acting in the capacity of teacher to white women," he was "in great danger of suffering bodily harm from the populace" if he insisted on lecturing.[172] Snow issued an injunction preventing Yogananda from speaking, while Quigg pressured the yogi to leave the city "for his own good."[173] Police wielding tear gas surrounded the hall where Yogananda had been slated to speak to quell the anger that remained even after his lecture had been canceled.[174]

Despite routine brushes with American prejudice, Yogananda underestimated the South's deep racial divide and penchant for mob violence. The British vice consul paid Yogananda a visit, explaining that "his colour, while not negro, was such as might cause high feeling in the community," and urged him not to try speaking again. Yogananda agreed not to lecture further but refused to leave without fighting the injunction to clear his name.[175] In court, witnesses against Yogananda claimed that two followers had gone insane from his teaching, one of whom was at that moment in an asylum refusing to eat until reassured that Yogananda had "contacted" her food.[176] The flood of outrage that ensued drowned out Yogananda's defense.[177] He claimed that the mentally ill woman had suffered from her condition for twenty years, that he had received her husband's permission to treat her, and that the husband was not angry with him. Former U.S. district attorney James McLachlan in L.A. testified by telegram that he had known Yogananda well for four years and found him one of the godliest men he had ever met.[178] This testimony—absent from many press reports of the case—failed to persuade the Miami circuit to lift the injunction.

Because wire news stories were syndicated, Yogananda's ouster from Florida was recounted in papers across the nation, often preserving intact the presumption of guilt offered by southern reporters who covered the story directly. The following year, a book on American religious cults made two gleeful references to Yogananda's ignominious treatment in Miami.[179] Yogananda had a few defenders. One man wrote a lengthy letter to the editor of the *Washington Post* describing his experiences with the Yogoda center in D.C. and attempting to clarify misunderstandings about Yogananda's teachings.[180] In another letter, a woman echoed this sentiment with her own positive story about her experiences with Yogananda.[181] But these few voices could not be heard over the din of denunciation.

Clearly shaken by the incident, Yogananda wrote in *East-West* about the press's ability to destroy a person's reputation through slanderous accusations. While granting the importance of ethical reportage, he excoriated "yellow journalism" for catering "to a depraved public taste that lacks sufficient moral and intellectual background to enable it to detect truth from falsehood;" its "only aim was sensationalism and 'thrills.'"[182] To avoid giving the accusations raised against him more notoriety, he only alluded obliquely to the specific situation that prompted his article. The magazine also noted when, a few months later, Quigg was charged with first-degree murder for the death of a black prisoner in his custody. Without mentioning the incident with Yogananda, the article explained how Quigg was known "throughout America thru his race and color prejudice against non-whites and his high-handed methods of dealing with them." It might have seemed that his crimes would go unpunished. "However, the day of reckoning comes in its own good time."[183]

Yogananda also attracted, whether from duplicity or naïveté, a number of lawsuits that militated against his efforts to craft an impressive persona. The first occurred in 1925, within months of establishing his Mount Washington headquarters. Emma S. Mitchell sued Yogananda for the return of a piece of property in Mar Vista, an upscale L.A. neighborhood near the coast, estimated to be worth thirteen thousand dollars. She claimed that she had donated the land to his organization on the understanding that he would be opening a school for children. Feeling deceived that the land was not to be used for this purpose, she wanted it back. Yogananda addressed the charges head on, both through his attorney and in person after one of his talks at the Philharmonic Auditorium. He told the audience that he possessed title to the property free and clear and that he had never deceived anyone. Still, he magnanimously offered to return the property. In an aside, he lamented that he understood how Jesus felt being persecuted, offering an early glimpse of his penchant for seeing himself as a latter-day Christ. The case was shortly settled out of court. In the meantime, Walter Carr, a local immigration official, promised to look into Yogananda's immigration status. This question had no direct bearing on the case, which suggests a presumption of Yogananda's guilt and a desire to rid the city of a stereotypical Hindu fraud.[184]

About the same time, Yogananda's partner Mohammad Rashid, who had masterminded his successful advertising campaign, sued for 25 percent of the "net proceeds of all lectures, fees, contributions or other monies received" by Yogananda. Rashid obtained a writ of attachment on two of Yogananda's bank accounts, effectively freezing the funds. The two ultimately settled out of court, and the controversy stayed out of the press.[185]

The lawsuit that most threatened Yogananda's image and the organization's finances was filed by his longtime friend and associate Swami Dhirananda. In April 1929, Dhirananda suddenly traveled from Los Angeles to New York to meet Yogananda on tour. The two, who had clashed as far back as their Dihika ashram days, had a heated exchange.[186] Yogananda signed a promissory note for the sizable sum of eight thousand dollars, to be paid in monthly installments, for Dhirananda's seven years of unpaid service to the organization. Returning to Mount Washington, Dhirananda unceremoniously packed his bags and departed, leaving the national headquarters rudderless.[187]

Yogananda was so depressed by the bitter rupture with his longtime friend that he departed for Mexico in late May to recover. The day he sailed from New York, he wrote to Minott Lewis, "With a heavy heart I am starting for Mexico. When the sword of so many responsibilities hangs on my head, Dear Doctor we must fight the battle to the end. . . . We all have to bear our crosses, the few who love to live for God and God's work." Lewis's cross continued to be financing the ministry. "I would never have taxed you further," Yogananda continued, "if God did not already respond. Without your cooperation we will be soon in the same trial we were before. So please do not fail God at this hour. It may be very hard but please do it. Without your help great danger is in sight. We will fight our way to freedom."[188]

In Mexico, Yogananda was able to lay down his own cross for a time. Guadalajara especially captivated him.

> From the balcony, I gazed westward. On wings of fancy I was carried far. I stood on the shores of the horizon. To the left and right were two mountain ranges which turned mystic violet. When I looked again some fairy hand had already dressed them in intense blue. Behind me lay the twilight-bathed man-made mystic city of Guadalajara. . . . This

> sunset city of dream-isles is the long-past, hidden dream of my fairy fancy come true to-day. I beheld the long-buried treasure of my Soul brought out to dazzle my longing gaze.[189]

While in Mexico, he also founded a Yogoda center and was received at the presidential palace by President Emilio Portes Gil. He returned home in the late summer. On September 1, he gave a talk at Mount Washington on "The Spiritual Vibrations of Unique Mexican Sceneries" and showed film he had taken in Mexico.[190]

Dhirananda was gone but not forgotten. Nearly six years later, he sued Yogananda for failure to pay the promissory note. Privately, Yogananda fumed about his former colleague, calling him a renegade, deserter, liar, fiend, and Judas.[191] Yogananda had paid one hundred-dollar installment in late 1929 and then reneged on his legal responsibility. Yogananda countersued, claiming that Dhirananda had agreed to waive any right to remuneration after being named a swami. He also asserted that Dhirananda had blackmailed him into signing the promissory note, threatening to destroy Yogananda's reputation through slanderous accusations if Yogananda failed to pay.[192] The judge ruled against Yogananda on all counts. Having failed to pay the promissory note, he owed the original balance (minus the hundred-dollar payment) plus 7 percent interest per year on all payments in arrears. The judge further found that Yogananda's countersuit had no merit and that his accusations against Dhirananda had no basis in fact.[193] This unseemly legal squabble and the judge's ruling fed into the stereotype of the untrustworthy trickster yogi, implying that Yogananda had lied in his countersuit and was motivated by base pecuniary motives.

The final challenge of this period came from the financial juggernaut of the Great Depression. From the maharaja of Kasim Bazar to the Lewises, Yogananda had always proved effective at finding financial backers for his ministry. At some point in 1925, Yogananda had met Mary E. Foster and quickly charmed her into supporting his new magazine venture. Foster had a storied life. The offspring of a white shipwrecked captain and a Hawaiian princess, she had established a Theosophical branch in Hawaii before converting to Buddhism and becoming a generous patron of Dharmapala, a Buddhist Indian who had attended the World's Parliament of Religions in 1893.[194] In fact, Yogananda and Dharmapala apparently met at Dharmapala's recently founded Mahabodhi College Bhavan in 1913, when Yogananda, Satyananda, and two other companions journeyed across south India and over to the island of Ceylon, now Sri Lanka.[195] Despite such supporters, the ministry's finances were always tenuous. The magazine had already missed one issue in September–October 1928. The following year, only half of the year's issues would be published, and in 1930 the number dropped to two.

As the Depression set in, things got worse. After July 1930, the magazine ceased publication altogether for nearly two years as financial support dried up. Yogananda fell behind on Mount Washington's mortgage payment and had to beg for an extension.[196] Yogoda Sat-Sanga was not the only religious organization in this situation. Mainline churches particularly "experienced an institutional 'religious depression' to match the nation's economic depression."[197] Church leaders made special pleas for continued giving. As one minister explained, "If the person gives cheerfully; . . . if his gift really represents his ability to support the Kingdom and is consequently sacrificial; if he really feels that his is giving unto the Lord"; then the gift would inevitably result in spiritual growth.[198] Yogananda made similar entreaties, but still came up short.

His desperation for funds overrode concern for his reputation. In 1930, he decided to tour with his friend Hamid Bey. A vaudeville performer who said that he had originally traveled from Egypt to the United States to compete with Harry Houdini before the magician's unexpected death, Bey—who was really the Italian-born Naldino Bombacci—masterfully exploited American Orientalist tropes.[199] Claiming to be a Coptic Christian, he nevertheless introduced himself as a Hindu yogi and "the youngest of the Egyptian *fakirs*," or Muslim ascetics.[200] Yogananda helped Bey burnish his mysterious identity, describing him as an Egyptian from the Sudan, "famous land of sheiks," "reared under an austere mystical training, and the feats he performs are a part of the religious rites of his sect."[201] In their tag team act, Yogananda lectured on superconsciousness and breath control before introducing "Master Teacher of Yoga" Bey's "astounding demonstrations of the art of MENTAL TELEPATHY (mind reading), COMPLETE CONTROL OVER CIRCULATION, and the PAINLESSNESS OF THE FLESH," which culminated in a stock routine of his being buried alive.[202]

Fortunately, Yogananda did not have to keep up this act for long. In January 1932, near the Depression's nadir, a providential encounter proved his ability to direct God's will to his own ends. During a rare tour in Kansas City—he traveled to the midwestern plains states only infrequently—he met James Lynn, a businessman with a restless heart and an astounding fortune. Lynn had a remarkable rags-to-riches tale. The child of sharecroppers, his intuitive business acumen, hard work, and good luck allowed him to acquire a range of companies that included a citrus farm, an insurance firm, railroads, and oil businesses. But by his own reckoning, when he met Yogananda, "my soul was sick and my body was decaying and my mind was disturbed." In short, "I was a totally frustrated man."[203]

The two met each other's needs perfectly. Lynn found salvation in Yogananda, who immediately became the millionaire's guru. Yogananda offered him a sense of purpose and routinely affirmed his rapid spiritual development, calling him Saint Lynn. Yogananda, in turn, found financial salvation in Lynn. He could not have found a more loyal customer, deeply committed to the ministry and with boundless buying power. Lynn quickly got Mount Washington's finances in order and underwrote *East-West*. Within a few weeks of their initial meeting, Yogananda thanked Lynn for "saving the work at a very critical period of its existence."[204] In April 1932, publication of *East-West* resumed, "under Divine guidance." Yogananda had "refused to burden the National Yogoda Organization with debts by publishing the magazine during depression-tortured times, so he waited until the-great Power destroyed difficulties which stood in the way of publishing the magazine regularly." Now it would be published "through the great spiritual cooperation of a very dear Yogoda student, who has undertaken to have it printed every month. May God bless him in every way. We rejoice that God and the great Masters of India have chosen this very noble spiritual instrument to spread the message of Yogoda."[205]

The two immediately formed an intimate bond. Yogananda told Lynn, "You are the Hindu yogi of Himalayan hermitages of the past who was sent in this life as an American prince, a Western maharaja-yogi, to light the lamp of Yogoda in many groping hearts."[206] In one case, Yogananda converted a letter explaining his delay in communication into an erotically tinged affirmation of their friendship. "I have been so intoxicated with the God in you, and with the remembrance of the pillar of light that we saw enveloping us during the meditation in Chicago, that I did not realize I have been so long in writing you. You have never before been so strongly present in me. (You are always with me now, so I can't miss you). So vividly have I seen your soul, like a glimmering jewel and an ornament in God's omnipresence."[207] His bond with Lynn quickly supplanted the relationship he had enjoyed with the Lewises for more than a decade.

Circumstances had taken an unexpected turn for the better. Even the Dhirananda trial had a silver lining, despite the bruising Yogananda suffered. Yogananda's attorneys assisted him in turning Yogoda Sat-Sanga into a nonprofit corporation to protect Mount Washington and any other assets from seizure in the case of a legal defeat.[208] Beyond this pragmatic legal aim, incorporation compelled Yogananda to articulate clearly his organization's purpose and iden-

James Lynn was a retired Kansas City millionaire looking for greater life purpose when he met Yogananda in January 1932. The two quickly became intimate friends. Lynn's generous donations assured the financial survival of Self-Realization Fellowship. Yogananda nicknamed him Saint Lynn and, when Lynn took monastic orders, bestowed the title Rajarsi Janakananda on him. He became SRF's first president after Yogananda's *mahasamādhi*.

tity. He had experimented with a number of names in the years leading up to the incorporation, such as Christian Yogoda in the early 1930s. But he had also used "self-realization" language for some time, both in *East-West* and in the Yogoda lessons. The 1935 articles of incorporation listed the official name as Self-Realization Fellowship Church.

The redundant use of both fellowship and church emphatically underscored that the organization was a religious body just like other American (Christian) bodies. There was certainly nothing innovative about the use of the label "self-realization," which was in widespread usage as an English translation for the salvific goal articulated in various Hindu traditions.[209] But bestowing the title on his organization captured the essence of the ministry, an essence very much in tune with modern audiences' interests in their own self-realization.[210] The statement of the organization's purpose was a verbatim reprint of the "Aims and Purposes of the Movement" first published in *East-West* in March–April 1928, which outlined the "development of men's physical, mental and spiritual natures" by "Contacting Cosmic Consciousness, the ever-new, ever-existing, ever-conscious Bliss-God" through scientific concentration and meditation. But the new statement added two ambitious points: "Temples of Self Realization Fellowship for collective worship" and "development of a world spiritual University . . . where an universal technique of salvation, art of self-realization, art of super-living and super-technique of body, mind and soul perfection would be taught."[211] He envisaged all of these aims as literally global in scale. Though his reach well exceeded his grasp, even while under assault by multiple lawsuits and the world's worst recession he continued ambitiously to envision new products.

SUCCESSFUL YOGA SALESMAN

Many harried businessmen such as the fictitious one Yogananda depicted in the correspondence course anecdote did find relaxation, energy, and enlightenment from his teachings. And some were content with that benefit. But others pressed on to pursue the deeper promises of yoga, a profound understanding of one's self and a transcendent encounter with God. They found that even without a direct personal relationship with their guru, they could still make some progress in the spiritual path—yoga distance learning worked. In fact, Yogananda could well have been describing himself in the anecdote, a successful and often beleaguered businessman who needed to make a conscious effort to relax. With shrewd marketing and a clear understanding that his brand appeal hinged on his own persona, Yogananda convinced thousands of Americans to consider his spiritual product. And he created a number of tangible material products that assisted disciples along the spiritual path while helping to fill the organization's coffers. He deftly navigated the religious marketplace's tricky waters, first during a raging economic boom and later as a treacherous financial storm threatened to engulf him. Along the way, he had to steer clear of opponents who sought to damage his reputation or sink his ministry. But his ministry survived, even thrived, as his own prominence grew. In 1935, his prestige would become global. Through Lynn's generous financial support, Yogananda undertook an extensive tour of England, continental Europe, and his own beloved Indian homeland in the comfort of a brand-new luxury car. When he returned to Calcutta for the first time since departing on the S.S. *City of Sparta* fifteen years earlier, he was not the same young man. After a triumphant tour in India, he would return to the United States as a "global guru," a spiritual leader of international stature and with increasing hints of divine power.

FOUR

The Apotheosis of a Global Guru

Paramahansa Yogananda and His Autobiography, 1933–1946

Near the end of *Autobiography of a Yogi*, the five-hundred-page epic that established Yogananda's global spiritual reputation, he includes a seemingly minor event from late 1936. Playing Santa Claus at Mount Washington's Christmas party, Yogananda handed Self-Realization Fellowship member E. E. Dickinson a box containing a silver cup he had bought in Calcutta during his recent return trip to his homeland. According to Yogananda, Dickinson opened the box and exclaimed, "For forty-three years I have been waiting for that silver cup! It is a long story, one I have kept hidden within me." Dickinson proceeded to relate that as a five-year-old, he had almost drowned in a Nebraska pond. Just before he sank to his death, he had a vision of a man in a "dazzling flash of light." He was rescued immediately thereafter. Twelve years later, he was in Chicago during the World's Parliament of Religions when he spotted Swami Vivekananda and recognized him immediately as the man who had appeared when he was drowning. After Vivekananda's lecture, Dickinson approached the Hindu master.

> He smiled on me graciously, as though we were old friends. I was so young that I did not know how to give expression to my feelings, but in my heart I was hoping that he would offer to be my teacher. He read my thought.
>
> "No, my son, I am not your guru." Vivekananda gazed with his beautiful, piercing eyes deep into my own. "Your teacher will come later. He will give you a silver cup." After a little pause, he added, smiling, "He will pour out to you more blessings than you are now able to hold."

When Yogananda gave Dickinson the silver cup that Christmas, Dickinson saw the same flash of light he had seen at moment of his rescue nearly a half-century earlier.[1]

At first glance, Yogananda's inclusion of this anecdote about an otherwise insignificant SRF member is puzzling. The mystery deepens when the reader recognizes that this story, placed in the *Autobiography*'s penultimate chapter, is the only event he chose to recount from the entire decade between his return from India and the time he began writing his life story. This apparent postscript was in fact a carefully crafted finale that placed Yogananda in the company of Swami Vivekananda, the great teacher of Hindu truth to American seekers a generation earlier. The resolution to Dickinson's story revealed that the torch—or the silver cup—had been passed from Vivekananda to his spiritual heir. Passionate seekers like Dickinson had yearned for their guru, a uniquely venerable personal spiritual instructor, and he had finally appeared. The swami from India had become a guru to Americans, and to seekers further afield.

By the mid-1930s, Yogananda was emerging as a global guru, a transnational figure with a following in the United States, India, and, increasingly, around the world. Gurus with international followings have typically been distinguished by their tremendous personal charisma and often have reputations as divine *avatāras* with supernatural powers. Global gurus have generally emerged in the later twentieth century. Bolstered by Indian audiences, diaspora communities, and other supporters, they have availed themselves of modern transportation and communication to sustain their communities. But long before a vibrant Indian diaspora had formed in the United States, Yogananda achieved the same status with largely white followers. From his American base of operations, he began his outreach to the rest of the world.

This chapter explores Yogananda's apotheosis in three parts. The first part places Yogananda in the context of religious internationalism, a subset of the cultural internationalism that emerged in the interwar period driven by the quest for global peace. He participated in international religious conferences. He also made an extravagant worldwide journey from California to England, the Continent, the Middle East, and across India. The young man who left for the United States in 1920 with slight prospects of success returned triumphantly, a mature spiritual leader who spent time with Mahatma Gandhi and drew crowds wherever he went. He arrived back in the United States both a world figure and a *paramahansa*, having been granted this exalted title by his guru, Sri Yukteswar.

The second part explores how he solidified his reputation as a global guru in the pages of *East-West*. He used the magazine as a vehicle for cosmopolitan sentiments, commenting on international trends from a religious perspective. More significantly, he introduced long-running columns that offered his authoritative interpretations of the sacred texts of Hinduism and Christianity, the two great world religions he sought to bring together. This chapter part examines his lengthy exegesis of both the *Bhagavad Gītā* and the New Testament Gospels, both of which he viewed as revelations of yogic truth. As he explicated both texts, he hinted at his own exalted identity as a yogi guru.

The third section analyzes the 1946 *Autobiography of a Yogi*, which firmly established Yogananda's reputation as a guru to the world. While following many tropes of Indian hagiography, the *Autobiography* also diverged from tradition in important ways. Most hagiographic accounts of supernatural feats gradually accrete over centuries, as later disciples embellish their master's feats. But Yogananda took charge of fashioning his own dramatic life story, masterfully presenting a fully formed narrative of his spiritual journey in an enchanted world. As a rhetorical analysis of this text's structural features reveals, the *Autobiography* functioned as a new scripture. Designed to inculcate belief in a world of supernatural possibilities, the *Autobiography* simultaneously sought to reveal its author, the narrative's protagonist, as a self-realized yogi, the embodiment of divinity in human form.

YOGANANDA AND RELIGIOUS INTERNATIONALISM

Since the 1960s, Indian gurus have often achieved global status by acquiring large numbers of followers in multiple international locations, a consequence of clever advertising, widespread international travel and, more recently, the use of modern media like video to close the distance between teacher and disciple.[2] Much of the technology that has facilitated such an international presence was not available to Yogananda in the 1930s, but he resourcefully used the means available to him to address international concerns.

Internationalism enjoyed a vogue in the decades following World War I, as various groups forged "world citizenship" identities based on political, cultural, scientific, or gender ideals, spurred by both the hopes and disappointments of the Treaty of Versailles' "Wilsonian Moment."[3] Aided by advances in transportation and communication, many forms of internationalism sprang up in the early twentieth-century world. "Cultural internationalism," according to historian of diplomacy Akira Iriye, sprang up alongside political and economic internationalism.[4] The Great War's devastation led many to conclude that more meaningful connections could prevent future large-scale tragedies, a conviction that drove efforts to ensure world peace through global community. By 1932, the League of Nations counted well over five hundred international organizations, more than 90 percent of which were private or nongovernmental.[5] Many organizations sought to promote global peace.[6] While many forms of cultural internationalism went into decline as the global depression worsened in the 1930s, religious dialogue remained one hope for peace through internationalism.[7] Yogananda made a presentation at the Fellowship of Faiths' Inter-Religious Symposium in Washington, D.C., in 1929, attended a world religion gathering in London in 1936, and spoke at a local branch meeting in Los Angeles the following year, but his participation in the 1933 event was the most high-profile and significant.[8]

That year, the worst year of the Great Depression, Yogananda joined two hundred other invited speakers to the World Fellowship of Faiths, an interfaith conference held in Chicago to coincide with the fortieth anniversary of the 1893 World's Parliament of Religions. Yogananda's invitation to address this gathering cemented his reputation as a guru on the world religion scene. The meeting took seriously a vision of religion as a worldwide force for peace. Bishop Francis J. McConnell, national chairman of the World Fellowship of Faiths, parsed the organization's name as a way of explaining the purpose of the gathering. The meeting was "world-wide in its scope," as "no part of the world is outside its reach." It promoted genuine communion because, despite the many differences of the various faiths, "fellowship between these religions as they are and as they aspire to be, in the common attempt to solves man's deepest problems, is the very heart of the movement." Finally, rather than use the restrictive word *religion*, the organization invited into its fold people, wherever they "are to be found dominated by a great faith or conviction by which they are impelled to seek a more abundant life for men individually or socially."[9] In his aptly titled "Fellowship with the Universe," conference coorganizer Francis Younghusband endorsed McConnell's outlook, stressing that a spiritual worldview facilitated genuine human connection. "The really significant thing about the universe," he explained, "is its coherence. It is a real whole in which all parts are interrelated, interconnected and united together."[10]

In the wake of Japan's invasion of China and Adolf Hitler's rise to power, a number of speakers addressed religion as a significant tool for the prevention of war. Nepalese prince Rajah Jai Prithvi Bahadur Singh called the World Fellowship meeting "the most outstanding event of the century," noting that never "before have the representatives of all faiths, races and countries come together to seek for spiritual solutions to the urgent present problems which impede human progress."[11] Former secretary of state Frank B. Kellogg—coauthor of a 1928 international treaty binding signatories to "condemn recourse to war for the solution of international controversies"—telegraphed that there "never was a time when the peoples of the world needed to exercise their influence on governments for world peace."[12] Gandhi, social reformer Jane Addams, and other disarmament advocates echoed Kellogg's sentiments.

Yogananda's conference address, "What Nineteen Faiths Contribute to Spiritual Technique," was very much in this pacific vein. He ultimately envisioned a spirituality that promoted unity by transcending specific religious doctrines. He called on all religious groups—"Protestants, Catholics, Christian Scientists, Jews, Quakers, followers of Unity, Rosicrucians, Theosophists, Buddhists, Shintoists, Mohammadens, Jains, Mormons, Zoroastrians and Hindus"—to end their conflicts over the "infallibility of their individual dogmas" and instead to cooperate in finding "the real meaning of life." Having defined religion's essence as practical, experiential "spiritual technique," he undertook an evaluation of each tradition's strengths and weaknesses. He commended Catholic devotion to God, Jewish "hygienic teachings," and the Islamic "spirit of resignation." Then he turned to the flaw of each tradition, which invariably led back to some form of exclusivism, whether "sect exclusiveness," "clannishness," or a "clannish spirit."

But Yogananda's talk reflected his own inclusivism. While placing himself on the high road of tolerance, he dismissed religious paths he deemed unacceptable while commending only religions very much like his own. His "Nineteen Faiths" reflected his core assumption that all pure religion derived from India, as fourteen of the groups had roots there. His list began with Hinduism and Buddhism and moved from there to several numerically small and relatively insignificant groups, including the Brahmo Samaj, Arya Samaj, and Bharat Dharma. Gandhi merited his own "faith" since he has "outdone all the saints and prophets who preceded him."[13] Rather immodestly, Yogananda counted "The Self-Realization Fellowship (Yogoda Sat-Sanga)" as one of the faiths as well. Apart from Gandhi, the only organization that escaped criticism of any kind was the Self-Realization Fellowship, a group that, he assured listeners, "is not a sect." Even in the august interfaith gathering, the entrepreneurial yogi could not stop promoting his brand.

His participation in world religion conferences helped to establish an international reputation, but a major return voyage to India in 1935 was ultimately much more significant in this regard. He envisioned the trip as a reverse pilgrimage to his spiritual and physical home that would allow him to revisit the formative places of his childhood and enjoy tearful reunions with family members both literal and spiritual—his brother disciples and his yoga father, Sri Yukteswar. A decade earlier, Yogananda had driven west to California from New York in a car belonging to well-off supporters. Now, amid the nation's worst recession, he began a mirror-image road trip from California to New York in a car donated by a devotee. But unlike 1925, this trip did not end in North America. Lynn financed the purchase of an elegant touring car, as well as the costs to fuel and maintain it and to ship it all over the world. As Dasgupta, Yogananda's personal secretary in India, put it, "Thus Swamiji's return trip to home was arranged to be in royal fashion."[14]

On June 9, 1935, he and his retinue boarded the S.S. *Europa* in New York bound for London. Yogananda toured England and Scotland by car during the second half of June. Departing England, he took a ferry to Calais to journey throughout France, Belgium, the Netherlands, Switzerland, Italy, and Greece. The highlight of his European trip was his visit to Nazi Germany. There he met Catholic sister Therese Neumann, who experienced ecstatic states, visions, clairvoyance, and stigmatization — which he took to be a true indication of the Holy Spirit's presence. He also confirmed that all of the carefully accumulated evidence pointed to the reality that she had neither eaten nor drunk anything since September 1927, save the Eucharist, which was the only nourishment that stirred hunger pangs in her. After departing Germany, he lectured in Rome and toured Egypt and the Holy Land, rhapsodizing over the opportunity to walk where Jesus lived and taught. Finally, he boarded the S.S. *Rajputana* to cross the Indian Ocean, landing at Mumbai (then Bombay) on India's northwest coast in mid-September 1935.

For fifteen years, Yogananda had carefully packaged his Indian background for American consumption. Now back in India, he employed this strategy in reverse as he treated Indian audiences to an inflated account of his activities in the United States. Yogananda described the modest, aging guesthouse on Mount Washington as an "immense" and "enormous" hotel, and the "magnificent" Self-Realization Fellowship center there as one of the three main tourist attractions in Los Angeles, the other two being Hollywood and Griffith Observatory.[15] He told his childhood friend Satyananda that Mount Washington had become "one of the sights to see in America."[16] Though Mount Washington was the organization's only developed property at the time, advertisements for Yogananda's Indian talks also announced that he had "established Hindu Temples in America." In 1930, Yogananda had reported twenty-five thousand Yogoda students, but an Indian advertisement five years later bragged that he had "initiated more than One Hundred Fifty Thousand AMERICANS."[17] Yogananda inexplicably claimed official status for Self-Realization Fellowship, presenting it as "the only institution of its kind recognised by the American Government."[18] Reversing Western missionary tropes about the challenges of working in heathen India, he reassured listeners that the dangers he faced as an evangelist in the American missionary field were overblown — "despite all that one hears of gangsters and kidnapping, the country has a big quota of spiritual men."[19]

Yogananda also reimagined his disastrous 1928 Miami trip. Rather than an ignominious ejection by police over rumors of inappropriate contact with women, the visit became a triumphant vindication. Instead of Yogananda's attorney appearing in court on his behalf, Yogananda himself arrived "radiant, magnetically attractive in form, with beautiful yet incisive eyes brimming with virtue. When those eyes cast their gaze on the judge, the magistrate could not withstand its power. . . . Swamiji was cleared of all charges and walked away in dignity with the highest respect of the court. The next day, most newspapers and journals had their headlines boldly announcing the verdict, and Swamiji's message of practical spirituality went on to gain even more fame." In Satyananda words, Yogananda's attackers "failed because of Swamiji's firmness of strength."[20]

En route to his Ranchi ashram, Yogananda stopped at Wardha and met privately with Gandhi, which helped legitimate his standing as an American representative of Indian nationalism and as a world leader. Yogananda's account of his meeting with one of the twentieth century's greatest leaders portrays an encounter in which Gandhi submitted to Yogananda's superior wisdom. The only extant account of dialogue between the two actually suggests Gandhi as the sage and Yogananda his conversation partner. Yogananda offered few independent thoughts, and Gandhi either rejected or reframed those he did propose:

GANDHIJI Why is there evil in the world, is a difficult question to answer. I can only give what I may call a villager's answer. If there is good there must also be evil, just as where there is light there is also darkness, but it is true only so far as we human mortals are concerned. Before God there is nothing good, nothing evil. . . . I therefore say that I am not going to bother my head about it. Even if I was allowed to peep into the innermost recess of God's chamber I should not care to do it. For I should not know what to do there. It is enough for our spiritual growth to know that God is always with the doer of good. . . .

YOGANANDA But if He is All-mighty, as unquestionably He is, why does he not free us from evil?

GANDHIJI I would rule out this question, too. God and we are not equals. Equals may put such questions to one another, but not unequals. Villagers do not ask why town-dwellers do things which if they did would mean certain destruction.

YOGANANDA I quite see what you mean. It is a strong point you have made. But who made God?

GANDHIJI If He is All-powerful, He must have made Himself.

YOGANANDA Do you think He is an autocrat or a democrat?

GANDHIJI I do not think these things at all. I do not want to want to divide power with Him and hence I am absolved from having to consider these questions. I am content with the doing of the task in front of me. I do not worry about the why and wherefore of things.[21]

Shortly after the visit, Yogananda reported to James Lynn that Gandhi had received Kriya Yoga instruction from him.[22] This claim raises questions. The earliest reference to the meeting between Yogananda and Gandhi in *Inner Culture* (as *East-West* was renamed in 1934) makes no mention of this yoga training, and major biographies of Gandhi do not report it.[23] If the induction took place as Yogananda described, it apparently did not have a significant impact on Gandhi. Whatever transpired between the two, Yogananda thought it crucial to present the encounter as Gandhi submitting himself to Yogananda's authority in a "childlike" manner.[24]

In late September, Yogananda arrived at the Calcutta train station to a fantastic welcome reception whose hosts included the current maharaja of Kasim Bazar, successor of his longtime Ranchi supporter who had died several years earlier. The young man who had departed Calcutta for an uncertain fate in the United States was returning in triumph, a hero to his physical father and his spiritual one. His reunion with Yukteswar was much more important to Yogananda than his encounter with his own father. Yogananda recounted that when he and Yukteswar saw each other, "We flew into each other's arms and remained there in sobs for long." He mentioned his own father quite literally as a parenthetical afterthought.[25] Yogananda's American companion, Richard Wright, offered a dramatic rendition of Yogananda's momentous meeting with Yukteswar:

> Before us, near the head of the stairs, quietly appeared the Great One, Swami Sri Yukteswarji, standing in the noble pose of a sage.
>
> My heart heaved and swelled as I felt myself blessed by the privilege of being in his sublime presence. Tears blurred my eager sight when Yoganandaji dropped to his knees, and with bowed head offered his soul's gratitude and greeting, touching with his hand his guru's feet and then, in humble obeisance, his own head. He rose then and was embraced on both sides of the bosom by Sri Yukteswarji.
>
> No words passed at the beginning, but the most intense feeling was expressed in the mute phrases of the soul. How their eyes sparkled and

were fired with the warmth of renewed soul-union! A tender vibration surged through the quiet patio, and even the sun eluded the clouds to add a sudden blaze of glory.[26]

Yogananda's most important interaction with Yukteswar occurred when his mentor formally initiated him as a *paramahansa*. This took place on Christmas Day, auspicious timing for a yogi with Christ Consciousness. Yogananda initially made little of the event. In a letter to Lynn shortly after the bestowal, he briefly shared news of the title almost offhandedly after a discussion of prosaic administrative duties.[27] The account in *Autobiography* is likewise terse, especially given the immense later significance of this designation: "The next afternoon, with a few simple words of blessing, Sri Yukteswar bestowed on me the further monastic title of *Paramhansa*. 'It now formally supersedes your former title of *swami*,' he said as I knelt before him. With a silent chuckle I thought of the struggle which my American students would undergo over the pronunciation of *Paramhansaji*."[28] Dasgupta, Yogananda's personal secretary, who was present at the event and generally spoke of Yogananda with great deference, reported that he and others close to him were unaware of any bestowal of title. Instead, he offered an earthy account of how Yukteswar (referred to here as "Gurudev") jokingly conferred the title.

> It was almost nightfall. Maharajaji was standing on the upstairs veranda and someone was standing next to him. Ananda-da and the writer were downstairs. Before going upstairs, Yoganandaji went to a drainage spot, a bit apart from the area, and began to urinate into the drainage passage. This caught Gurudev's attention and he cryptically joked, "Yogananda has become a 'paramhansa' [great swan or great soul]!" After urinating, Yoganandaji saw Ananda-da standing at the front door and quietly said, "Ananda-da! Did you hear? Swamiji [Sriyukteshvarji] called me a 'paramhansa!'" Later, Ananda-da laughed and said to the writer, "You'll see. Yogananda will one day use this title!"[29]

If accurate, this account would explain why Yogananda did not immediately share the news of the new title with American devotees. But however Yogananda acquired the honorific from his guru, he came to embrace it as a mark of his own exalted guru status.

The bliss Yogananda shared with his guru was short-lived, as his desire to acquire property in India led to a clash between them. Yogananda was particularly interested in establishing a presence near the famous Dakshineswar Kali Temple, Ramakrishna's former longtime residence, and Vivekananda's Belur

Math. His childhood friend Satyananda remembers Yogananda standing "on the bank of Ganges, at Dakshineswar, pointing to the Belur Math, . . . he said to me, 'Bama! I will make mine bigger than theirs.' It seemed to me as if Swamiji was caught up with some kind of competetion [*sic*] game with Swami Vivekananda." Satyananda thought that Yukteswar saw Yogananda as "envious of the image of Swami Vivekananda, because of Yogananda's ambition of wanting to be great."[30] Yogananda and Yukteswar met with an attorney so that Yukteswar could will all his property to Yogananda at his death. The attorney drew up a legal deed describing Yukteswar as founder of "Yogoda Sat Sanga Society of India and America" and Yogananda as president. When it came time to sign, Yogananda, unable to contain his resentment at these labels, burst out, "I was really the one who did everything." Yukteswar stared at Yogananda momentarily before collecting his walking stick and stalking out, leaving everyone in the attorney's office "absolutely dumbstruck." In the car, an enraged Yukteswar exploded, "That is not self will; that is unlawful conduct."[31] Yogananda's brother Sananda, witness to Yukteswar's outburst in the car, quietly passed over any conflict between the two in his terse account of their time together.[32]

Still smarting from their argument, Yogananda decided to attend the Allahabad *kumbha mela*, the great religious pilgrimage that drew millions from all over India. Yogananda persisted with his plans, even when Yukteswar ridiculed him by asking what he would gain by witnessing a throng of naked *sadhus*.[33] As a result, Yogananda was hundreds of miles from Yukteswar's Puri ashram when his mentor fell gravely ill. Receiving the urgent telegram, "Come to Puri at once," Yogananda chose not to leave on the night train. Instead, he waited until the next day to depart, a delay his brother Sananda found inexplicable.[34] Yogananda later explained that he stayed away because he had a presentiment of Yukteswar's impending death, and had he been present, "there would have been a great battle" as he sought to keep his master from giving up his body.[35] Whatever the reason, having traveled halfway around the world at Yukteswar's behest for one last visit, Yogananda missed his guru's final moments on earth.

Yogananda found Yukteswar's death "unbearable." "If I could weep, I would feel relieved. If I would cry, the gods would cry with me. If I had a thousand mouths, I would say India lost one of the greatest in wisdom." Though absent from the physical plane, however, Yukteswar "is divinely haunting me day and night. I see him in every direction I turn my eyes."[36]

He soon experienced a supernatural vision of Yukteswar "resurrected in a strange new way" that provided great comfort. Yukteswar unfolded cosmological mysteries about the astral world and more mundane instructions about Yogananda's authority to inherit and administer his master's property.[37] Like the earlier premonitions of his mother's and brother's deaths, his vision of Yukteswar provided reassurance that seemingly tragic events fit within a larger cosmic scheme. "He answered all my questions," Yogananda reflected simply.[38] A hint of eroticism accompanied their reunion. Yogananda "advanced to gather him hungrily in my arms." Embracing his master, he "could detect the same faint, fragrant, natural odor which had been characteristic of his body before. The thrilling touch of his divine flesh still persists around the inner sides of my arms and in my palms whenever I recall those glorious hours." The resurrected Yukteswar promised his ongoing presence and expressed his unconditional love as he never had in his earthly form. He had waited sixteen years for his pupil's return, "but no more—I love thee—I will ever be with thee."[39]

The resurrection appearance also functioned as a transfer of power. Yukteswar's death created a leadership vacuum in the swami lineage, a vacuum naturally filled by his handpicked successor, their previous disagreements notwithstanding. Yogananda became an important channel for Yukteswar's messages. "Henceforth, my Master shall speak through me," he declared.[40] Yogananda passed one such message to Lewis in Yukteswar's voice. "Beloved son, your life and actions have glorified us. You are a celestial instrument. Expand fearlessly in the realm of renunciation for the cause of Self-Realization, India, and humanity. India's spiritual habits mark your forehead. Your actions are joyfully recognized and witnessed by the All-Supreme and by the Gurus."[41]

Throughout the trip, Yogananda never lost sight of James Lynn's resources as the indispensable foundation for his growing role as an international guru. He wrote Lynn several dozen letters during the trip. Typically much longer than the terse notes he dashed off to others, they were also effusively affectionate and, like his reminiscences of Yukteswar, tinged with eroticism:

> I am with you always, ever going deeper, ever feeling deeper bliss in you and in your devoted group and in me and all.
>
> You have satisfied all my desires for an ideal beloved one who has carried out all the demands of divine discipline. What more could I want?
>
> Dreams about our divine communion often flit by my mind, and I have caught one of those dreams of happiness and painted it in words as it comes straight from the chamber of my heart.[42]

He signed off with some variation of "With deepest love and blessings to you, my beloved one of many lives. Ever yours."[43] As with Yogananda's relationship with his own mentor, divine communion and homosocial intimacy were closely entwined in his relationship with his most cherished disciple.

Along with these reassurances of affection, Yogananda boldly pressed Lynn for more funds, assuring him that he wanted nothing for himself and thought only about SRF's well-being. He warned Lynn "not to give Satan opportunity to cause us and our work trouble." He flattered and pressured Lynn simultaneously while describing Mount Washington as the childless millionaire's true offspring.[44] Lynn's reluctance to provide the required funding stemmed partly from concern that his financial resources were being used to commercialize religious work. In countering this concern, Yogananda offered rare insight into his thinking about the role of religious promotion:

> About commercializing our work, I really do hate to see anyone commercializing religion. By commercializing it means "using religion for individual benefit or benefit of the business." Are we doing that? No. Then what are we doing? We are not using religion for business, but we are using business methods in religion, which we must do. Sincere seekers won't be found in a hundred years unless they know our work and me. The quicker they know through advertisements, the better it is. Some may turn away because of advertisements, but careful wording would not turn sincere seekers away; they would be increasingly found. Aren't Bibles sold? Somebody has to pay for them. What sin in selling to-the-point benefitting instructions and using the money to print more of such. You must know of hundreds of others who hungrily wait for the weekly Lessons. Sincere seekers are satisfied with truth, and they never mind helping the cause of spreading same by paying.[45]

In asking for greater financial support, Yogananda appealed to Lynn's altruism and self-interest, reminding him of "my spontaneous gift of my deepest love to you." He had given Lynn half of his spiritual realization. "I have taken almost all of your karma on myself—and I will work the sufferance out in this body—that you may be free from the subtle traps of desires and attachments and have a clear sailing, like a shooting star in the distant heavens."[46] Lynn's spiritual credit was reserved for him "manifold in heaven, to be used in any incarnation you want."[47]

Yogananda's lobbying eventually paid off, as Lynn agreed to retire Mount Washington's mortgage. "What freedom," he told Lynn, "you have given to the institution; may that freedom be yours in spirit and in material things."[48] Lynn topped off his generosity by paying for the Ranchi ashram as well.[49]

On his return voyage to the United States, Yogananda stopped in London to attend the 1936 World Congress of Faiths. Yogananda had decided to attend while in Ranchi in February, too late to be a presenter as he had hoped.[50] But he took advantage of the large gathering of religious seekers to host a number of Yogoda classes, which proved a big success.[51] En route home from England, Yogananda was detained briefly at Ellis Island for a board of special inquiry hearing, a process that flagged passengers whose answers to detailed questions posed by immigration officials either did not align with information on the ship manifest or was questionable in some other way.[52] Given previous scrutiny of Yogananda as a possible nationalist, perhaps his visit to Gandhi had raised a flag that British officials passed on to American immigration agents. Whatever the reason, Yogananda would not have been subject to this treatment—a closed hearing conducted without counsel—had he been an American citizen. But more than fifteen years after settling in the United States, he remained a resident alien, prevented by federal law from naturalizing. This humiliating detention was undoubtedly especially embittering on the heels of his celebratory global trip. When at long last he arrived at Mount Washington in December 1936, eighteen months after his departure, he received a more fitting welcome from his own community.

He was greeted with a huge celebration banquet filled with adoring speeches. Nerode characterized Yogananda as the one who had "washed away" the "many sorrows" in his life, and a "great flame" from which he had "tried to gather light." Jotin compared Yogananda's physical presence to the sacredness of pilgrimage places. "Being here at my Master's feet, I have visited all the holy places on earth." Sri Ranendra Kumar Das offered the boldest tribute: "There is only one parallel that can be given to the life of Swami Yogananda. As nineteen hundred years ago in the streets of Galilee Jesus used to walk, his long robe flowing, his benign countenance lightened with the consciousness and realization of God, his mouth uttering the divine message to bring the wayward souls back to God, so similarly Swamiji goes on unselfishly, pursuing the ideal of service to all the children of God." Lynn's speech, though less stirring, was equally reverential. Reflecting on common stereotypes about India, he noted, "What a blessing it has been for us that India, a country that many people think of as a land of snake-charmers, did send one to our shores who could bring us God consciousness that our souls might be revealed and bring us Divine Joy and Divine Happiness."[53]

While his close disciples offered proper adulation of Yogananda, rank-and-file SRF members needed training to understand the grandeur of their teacher as a *paramahansa*. Yogananda exacerbated this confusion by continuing to use the swami title for himself for at least a year after his return from

India.[54] Richard Wright launched a campaign to educate SRF members about the significance of the new title, so that Yogananda would not have to trumpet his own swan title directly:

> During Swami Yogananda's visit to India in 1936, after fifteen years' spiritual work in America at the command of his great master, Swami Sri Yukteswarji of Puri, the latter honored him with the title of *Paramhansa*. *Param* means "supreme" and *hamsa* means "soul." It is the highest spiritual title which a divine guru-preceptor can bestow on his disciple. It is never merely a title, given without reason or just in recognition of material service to others. The guru only bestows it on his disciple when the latter has reached a very high state of Cosmic Consciousness, Divine Joy, Wisdom-Bliss, and God-contact in Self-Realization.
>
> *The Divine Swan*
>
> Another meaning of *hams* in the word Paramhansa, is "swan." The ancient scriptures speak of a fabled swan which when drinking can separate the milk from the water if the two are mixed. In this sense, the title Paramhansa means the divine swan or he who is able to extract the milk of spiritual bliss from the waters of material life. The swan also floats in water without drowning or getting its feathers wet. So the royal divine swan or Paramhansa is he who can float on the waters of material life without getting attached to it or drowned in it.[55]

This message was slow to catch on. Five years later, *Inner Culture* was still posting announcements in each issue explaining the term.[56] Disciples eventually took to calling Yogananda "Master," an English substitute for the tongue-twisting *paramahansa*.

The December banquet also included a major announcement. Lynn had purchased land for an ashram on a beautiful bluff in Encinitas, near San Diego. Yogananda reacted with "astonishment" and "delight" to this surprise welcome home gift. "Not a word of the hermitage construction had been allowed to reach me during my stay in India and Europe."[57] The real surprise was that Lynn had finally purchased this tract of land, which Yogananda had been urging him to acquire for two years. In 1934, he had written, "Some day I know God will free you from your business life and then you could come there, free from the entanglements of an organization, and meditate on that sacred hill in complete ecstasy with God."[58] During the trip, Yogananda directed SRF staff member Merna Brown, “Positively show Mr. Lynn the place on the beach hill in Encinitas. When he acquires that land, my last wish will be fulfilled. There is no place like it. Try your utmost.”[59]

This breathtaking spot overlooking the Pacific Ocean was prime Southern California real estate. Self-Realization Fellowship described the Encinitas site as “one of the garden spots of the world,” providing “the finest beauty of sky, mountain, ocean, trees and caves offered by Nature.”[60] The four-hundred-thousand-dollar project on seventeen acres, “conspicuous by its oriental design and striking decorative features,” as the *Los Angeles Times* described it, soon became a landmark for drivers along Pacific Coast Highway.[61] Prominent Los Angeles architect Charles C. Frye, first Civil Works Administration director in Los Angeles County and creator of the San Francisco Palace Hotel, designed the buildings.[62] Encinitas quickly became the soul of SRF. Southern California had been SRF's headquarters for a decade, and Yogananda viewed it as the part of the United States most like India—a uniquely sacred place.[63] Encinitas became the center of that sacred space, surpassing Mount Washington as SRF's most crucial location and the place where Yogananda spent most of his remaining years.

When he was there, Yogananda was often in the company of his benefactor and intimate friend, James Lynn. Their overt displays of same-sex affection would not have been easily tolerated in mainstream American religious organizations of the time. Every evening, Master and his “most blessed beloved little one” “could be seen walking hand in hand like two small children, up and down the flagstone path on the lawn in front of the Hermitage. Their eyes would be shining with the love and friendship they shared with God and with each other.” Yogananda reportedly claimed regularly that Lynn “fulfilled one-hundred percent the wishes of his heart.” They kissed each other multiple times on the forehead and cheek as a greeting. Disciples thought their behavior epitomized spiritual companionship. “I'd never seen such affection,” devotee Leo Cocks commented, “such unconditional love in my life.” Daya Mata thought their relationship was “the perfect divine friendship.” Brother Premomoy viewed the bond as more like a father-son relationship, with Yogananda, almost the same age as his disciple, playing the paternal role.[64]

INTERPRETER OF THE SACRED TEXTS OF HINDUISM AND CHRISTIANITY

Apart from his international travels, Yogananda promoted his religiously based vision of peace through the pages of *East-West* and then *Inner Culture*.

He held Self-Realization Fellowship out as an organization capable of tangibly advancing global peace efforts. A 1937 article entitled "The Spread of Self-Realization Fellowship . . . over the Earth" narrated Yogananda's ministry as the creation of a global fellowship. The article then shared his vision for the formation of a "World Brotherhood City" that aimed to "make each man an ideal world-citizen" by speaking one universal language, adhering to universal laws of hygiene and diet, recognizing the unity of all races, and teaching "one religion of Self-Realization."[65] Although this plan never moved off the drafting table, it conveyed his hope for peace grounded in Hindu unity and his understanding of himself as a central agent in this reconciliation.

From the first rumblings of renewed war to its cataclysmic nuclear end, Yogananda spoke repeatedly on themes of world peace and cooperation, presenting spiritual unity as the solution to global turmoil.[66] As the threat of war intensified in the 1930s, he advocated "success through unity." "It seems as if God is trying to evolve the art of right living by expressing His Truth through a combination of particular civilizations, mentalities, and nationalities. No nation is complete in itself."[67] He warned that the Spanish Civil War and Italy's invasion of Ethiopia, both wars of aggression, had created "vibrations of injustice . . . moving through the ether waves" that were "causing floods in America, storms in England and Portugal, and earthquakes in India."[68] And on the eve of armed conflict in Europe, he proclaimed, "Amidst the prevailing confusion of so many ideas and ideologies, here and abroad, what we need most is the materialization of that for which Jesus lived and died, peace on earth and good will to mankind."[69] Later, while war raged across the globe, *Inner Culture* bucked the nationalist trend with a poem invoking global community. Entitled "The United States of the World," it began

> Oh, poets and singers,
> Oh, preachers, statesmen, teachers and seers,
> In Asia, Africa, North America, South America
> Europe and Australia
> Take up this chant and sing a song of songs:
> The Song of the United States of the World.[70]

As the war wound down in 1945, Yogananda published a poem entitled "Wreath of Unity," which envisioned the motherly image of deity as the healer of the world.[71] The same year, a local minister predicting the world's impending end earned a rebuke from Yogananda for his "hallucinary vision": "When the Creator of the Universe does destroy this little earth it will be millions of years hence—after all His children have learned to use His gift of free choice wisely and have evolved beyond this earth."[72] Initially an admirer of atomic power—his cosmological emphasis on energy made fission alluring—he was horrified by the unleashing of atomic weapons on Japan.[73] As World War II gave way to the Cold War, Yogananda spoke on issues like "Averting the Coming Atomic War."[74] One article argued that lack of understanding, literal and metaphorical, was the root of global conflict and advocated "Mondi Linguo," a new global language on the model of Esperanto.[75]

Yogananda also attempted to present *Inner Culture* as a cosmopolitan periodical, a forum for universalism built on pluralism, curiosity, engagement, and conversation.[76] Though cosmopolitanism and religion are not often linked, they belonged together intuitively in Yogananda's thinking. The predominant image of cosmopolitanism derives from Enlightenment visions that take for granted "the privatization of religion, and indeed, disenchantment with the world." But, as Srivinas Aravamudan argues, the transnational language of Hindu spirituality has provided one "amongst several alternative and popular forms of cosmopolitanism."[77] Some magazine articles were essentially travel writing pieces that gave audiences a window into exotic places they might never visit themselves, such as a Cleveland Yogoda member's detailed Holy Land travelogue. But from its first issue in 1925, the magazine had aspired to unite Orient and Occident. Yogananda hoped that the magazine would appeal to discerning upper-middle-class readers who could appreciate both broad global trends and spirituality. Defining "spirituality" broadly, Yogananda made generous space in the magazine's pages over the years for an assortment of discussions—diet and health, landscape and beauty, mind and spirit.

When the magazine ventured beyond international cultural trends into the realm of politics, it often revealed the ignorance and political naïveté of its authors, particularly Yogananda, its executive editor and most prolific contributor. Some articles, like his assessment of the League of Nations' prospects for achieving world peace, were thoughtful and informed. But others were more troubling. Long before Italy's invasion of Ethiopia caused him to reconsider his views, Yogananda showed great admiration for Italy's fascist leader, Benito Mussolini. Yogananda reprinted a 1927 Mussolini speech, lauded Mussolini's plans for a brown rice–based diet, his reintroduction of brown bread, and "other sensible and health-giving ideas on diet," and proclaimed that a "master brain like that of Mussolini does more good than millions of social organizations of group intelligence. . . . Great individuals are sent on earth as a pattern after which ordinary members of society must model themselves."[78] He also praised Hitler and his policies. The year Hitler came to power, Yogananda offered his sanguine assessment that

> Hitler is to be admired for leaving the League of Nations because peace can never be attained by the victor and vanquished attitude, but only on a basis of equality and brotherhood. Instead of preventing Hitler from having equal armament with other nations, the other nations should reduce armaments to the level of Germany, then the millions of dollars that are thrown away on idle battleships could be used for national or international prosperity. . . . An insulted, snubbed Germany, if it gets away from the uplifting guidance of Hitler, may join Russia and make her a more powerful enemy of France, and so on. The Allies must reduce their own armaments first, and then they will find out that example speaks louder than words.[79]

The month after the Nazi government announced the Nuremberg Laws, which stripped Jews of citizenship and prevented them from marrying ethnic Germans, Yogananda expressed enthusiasm for "the German awakening—a new Germany."[80] Yogananda's colleague Dasgupta recalled that Yogananda admired the "new state of uniformity and rules" Hitler enacted. "He used to say that the entire German nation was alive, and that it was absolutely mesmerizing to see groups of young men marching together with the 'clack, clack' sounds of their boots resonating in unison."[81]

THE *BHAGAVAD GĪTĀ* AS A METAPHOR FOR SPIRITUAL STRUGGLE

Yogananda's contributions to *Inner Culture* were much more compelling when he stayed within his métier as an expositor of religious truth. In the 1930s he demonstrated his interpretive skills through an exposition of the *Bhagavad Gītā*. Given the *Gītā*'s elevated status in modern Hinduism, especially its role in interfaith dialogue with Christianity, Yogananda's attention to this text was no surprise. The model had already been provided by his de facto mentor, Swami Vivekananda, who called the *Gītā* the "only commentary, the authoritative commentary on the Vedas" and routinely taught on it at home as well as during his American visits. Just as Vivekananda's universalizing of the *Gītā*'s Hinduism "authenticated his own deep missionary imperative,"[82] Yogananda's commentary in *Inner Culture* conveyed his message of modern Hinduism to American devotees.

He identified the *Gītā* as "the Hindu Bible," employing a familiar term among educated Indians of the time.[83] The *Gītā*'s biblical status was of relatively recent vintage, due in part to the nineteenth-century encounter between

Hinduism and Christianity.[84] From the perspective of traditional orthodox teaching, the *Gītā* fell into the lower-ranking category of *Smṛti,* or "remembered," texts. The higher-status sacred texts, *Śruti,* that which is "heard" or divinely revealed and thus eternal, consisted solely of the four Vedas and the Upaniṣads.[85] Access to *Śruti* texts was traditionally reserved for male members of the three twice-born castes, who learned them secretly through oral transmission from a guru. Ironically, the very secondary status of the *Gītā* among Brahmins made it an ideal candidate to become Hinduism's Bible. Because its access was not restricted as the Vedas and Upaniṣads were, the *Gītā* was more widely known. Its greater popularity aided its accession to prominence as a spiritual text for Hindus.

By the time Yogananda came of age, the *Gītā*'s position was firmly fixed, and his own views reflected its status. "The Bhagavad Gita," Yogananda pronounced, "is the greatest metaphysical, psychological treatise that was ever given to the world. It describes definitely, in detail, all the experiences of the Spiritual traveller in the path of emancipation." This trail, as always for Yogananda, led to communion with God. "The true devotee not only trusts in God, but worships Him through understanding and wisdom. Blind worship may be meagerly accepted by God, but we, being gifted with the greatest Divine gift of human intelligence, that of reason and free choice, must worship God in Truth and Understanding. It pleases God to see His human children, who are made in His image, employ His highest gift, the searchlight of Intelligence, in quest of Him."[86]

Composed a century or so before the Common Era,[87] the *Bhagavad Gītā* functions as a stand-alone narrative within the much larger epic, the *Mahābhārata.*[88] The main character, Arjuna, is a warrior on a great battlefield who carries on an extensive dialogue with his charioteer, Krishna, later revealed to be the great god Vishnu in disguise. As recent translator and interpreter Laurie L. Patton explains, essentially the *Gītā* "is about a decision":[89] should Arjuna fulfill his duty to slaughter his foes, who are also his kin? Krishna urges him to do so. In the extensive philosophical and metaphysical discussion dialogue that ensues, the *Gītā* addresses the key ideas in Hinduism as it emerged in the Common Era, including *karma, saṃsāra, dharma,* yoga, the nature of divinity, and *bhakti,* or proper devotion to God.

The *Gītā* has long been read allegorically. Its battlefield setting has sometimes proved a challenge for readers. The narrative also reveals Vishnu as a fearsome divine warrior, not a gentle master.[90] And the *Gītā*'s conceptually dense, tersely worded sutras are capable of bearing many meanings. Gandhi, who adopted it as his central devotional text, is one of the *Gītā*'s most famous allegorical interpreters.[91] He viewed the military setting as an extended metaphor for mental and spiritual struggle against evil.[92] Yogananda likewise sought to interpret the *Gītā* nonviolently and to unfold the full meaning of the densely packed text for lay audiences.

Premiering in 1932 under the banner of "Spiritual Interpretation of Scripture," Yogananda's *Gītā* commentary series went through several modifications in structure before taking stable form nearly a year later. Some features proved short-lived. In January 1933, Yogananda began introducing each article with a selection from the Sanskrit text transliterated from Brahmi script into Roman letters. The result was a sequence of seeming gibberish to a readership who knew no Sanskrit:

> Dristawa tu Pandavaneekam Budham
> Durjodhana Acharyam upusangmya
> Raja Bachanamabaraheet, stada.[93]

Yogananda's transliteration conveyed his skill as a translator of India's ancient sacred text, reminding readers of his formal swami training in India and of his spiritual and intellectual authority to mediate the text to students. Transliteration may have also offered readers direct exposure to the pronunciation of Sanskrit words, whose very sound was often thought to be spiritually efficacious. Whatever the case, this feature was more confusing than helpful, and he dropped it after mid-1934 in favor of simply providing the English translation.

Irrespective of adjustments to the exegetical structure, his interpretive approach remained fundamentally allegorical. Despite the familiarity of this interpretive strategy, he claimed that this interpretation of the text "as received from within" was being offered "for the first time."[94] Allegory allowed him wide latitude to talk about spiritual and philosophical issues. A passage describing how one warrior "roared aloud like a lion and blew his conchshell," for example, was glossed as "King Material Desire had called upon the Preceptor Past Habit to protect General Ego with all the soldiers of the senses, but when the Preceptor Habit did not give inner support, General Ego himself roared with the vibration of pride."[95] Like Gandhi, he used allegory to portray spirituality as a vital internal fight against evil thoughts and behaviors. "Every night," Yogananda counseled, "the student of the Bhagavad Gita should . . . ask King Soul and his children what they accomplished as they gathered together, eager for battle of proper management against untoward circumstances which affect the body."[96]

Allegory often shaded into metaphor, allowing Yogananda to indulge his penchant for poetry. "Desires," he reflected, "are silken threads of material pleasures which the spider of habit continuously spins around the Soul, to form the shrouding cocoon of ignorance."[97] These metaphors sometimes became more elaborate, taking on local color. In explaining how control of desire might lead to anger, Yogananda relied on popular Southern California stereotypes about the automobile and the beach. "If the average man, who is not free from anger, is driving a car joyfully from Los Angeles to Santa Monica for a picnic, and then is forcefully asked by his wife to stop at her relatives' place against his will, he may suddenly be blinded by wrath," which might in turn lead to a car wreck. The story illustrated how "the car of one's life may be smashed by insurmountable difficulties or run into the ditch of failure."[98]

The flexibility afforded by allegorizing led to a potentially limitless commentary. He lingered on the first of the *Gītā*'s eighteen chapters for two years. By the time of his death, twenty years after he began the series, *Inner Culture* had only reached the middle of chapter 5. His productivity dramatically outpaced available magazine space, however, and the series continued under his name posthumously for nearly two decades.

Yogananda's allegorizing analysis of the *Gītā* underscored self-mastery, bolstering the contrast he had drawn since his 1920 *Science of Religion* between useless theological doctrine and pragmatic spirituality. An early subtitle of the *Gītā* series made this point clear, as it promised "practical application of the teaching" of the text. He elucidated five related and overlapping points about practical religion. The first and most foundational was the commonplace notion shared by many spiritual traditions that the physical body was the locus of a spiritual battle. In his first article on the *Gītā*, Yogananda quoted, "Fight the battle of life, or you will acquire sin," which he glossed as "unless the soul battles continuously to overcome the consciousness of the flesh by experiencing soul-consciousness in meditation, that soul acquires sin."[99] Yogananda explicated the notion that the human body recapitulates the universe in microcosm, a common tenet in yoga traditions.[100] Spiritual battles taking place between divine entities in the unseen realm paralleled dramatic struggles occurring within the self: "Life is a series of battles between spirit and matter, knowledge and ignorance, soul and body, life and death" and "the scene of battle is the body."[101]

Yogananda's second point was that bodily desires were temptations that must be mastered for growth in divine communion. Every physical longing threatened a perilous debilitation of both body and soul. "Over-indulgence in sex, over-eating, lack of exercise, lack of fresh air, and lack of sunshine, all destroy the red blood corpuscles and especially affect the fighting power of the white corpuscles."[102] Sexual desire topped Yogananda's list of dangers. While his admonition was common among celibate renunciants, his call to sexual restraint even within marriage presented a daunting challenge to his many "householder" followers, particularly given the increasing cultural emphasis on marital sexual satisfaction in twentieth-century America. He unapologetically warned against the danger a modern "young person" faced in pursuing a family first, "thinking he will seek God afterwards." "Husbands and wives who think that the 'holy bonds of matrimony' permit them to indulge in over-sexuality, greed, anger, or displays of 'temperament' are ignorant of the true laws of life."[103] His uncompromising stance stemmed from a desire to provide everyday Americans with practical tools to overcome the forceful tug of natural human cravings that could not be controlled by mere will.

Sexual desire was not the only powerful temptation. The businessman who is striving to be honest and observes his dishonest peers growing wealthy "is often so strongly tempted to partake of gain attained by graft that he says he is 'forced' to do so."[104] The spiritual stakes were high, and spiritual victory was by no means assured—it required a genuine subjugation of evil. Yogananda warned that "when one begins to be restless, the Spiritual bow of spinal energy and perception, which can kill sense attachments with arrows of super-happiness, is destroyed and the Ego's surrounding thoughts begin to be scorched with restlessness, even as the skin is scorched with over-heated rays."[105]

Third, to master desires effectively, a devotee had to recognize the power of *māyā*, the spiritual delusion that life and the desires that came with earthly existence were real. Human existence is merely a motion picture, and a yogi, like the "operator in the booth, knows that talking pictures are unreal, combinations of light and sound."[106] There was an effective weapon against bodily temptation and *māyā*. "Meditation," Yogananda explained, "is the inner war-drum which rouses the good and bad habits from the slumber of indifference and makes them willing to increase their forces in order to attain victory over the consciousness of the devotee."[107] As elsewhere, Yogananda offered extensive guidance on technique, often with accompanying illustrations. A proper understanding of the body's microcosmic composition was essential to self-mastery. Yogananda explained how the body's six *cakra* centers were associated with the four elements, ether, and the combination of the five.[108] One article provided diagrams contrasting views of the human body and its *cakras* under the rule of "the Soul" and in bondage to "Rebel, King Delusive Desire."[109]

In the battle against spiritual weakness, novice devotees were not alone. Yogananda's fourth theme was the example of successful yogis who had conquered these struggles already. The yogi, "awake in spiritual pursuits and asleep in the bazaar of worldly desires," provided an instructive model to "the worldly man."[110] Among other achievements, advanced yogis overcame physical bodily decay; Yogananda's "Supreme Master, Babaji, has a young body, preserved for several centuries."[111] He routinely insisted that all disciples needed a master who would train them to contemplate "the soul as a wonder."[112] While most yogis avoided entanglement with the world and were therefore unavailable to assist wayward seekers, a few "live and teach in the world" "to show mortals the way to free their souls from this prison of flesh."[113] Their stern guidance was essential. Unlike American ministers, who "spoil their church members by too much coaxing and by lack of administering discipline," Indian masters who "admonish" their disciples achieve far greater spiritual results.[114]

Fifth, Yogananda used the *Gītā* commentary to uphold himself as the kind of guru disciples needed, even hinting at his own divine identity. He never shied away from offering himself as a role model to aspiring yogis. In one case, he recounted how he counseled happy newlyweds to follow his example. "My love for my Eternal Beloved has deepened and ripened. My eyes are more filled with joy than yours ever were. Wake up, without God's love, your love, which is His reflection will fade away. Feed your love with everflowing power of His love, or it will wither into nothingness."[115] More than a role model, though, he was the guru devotees needed to achieve liberation successfully. Yogananda did not directly equate himself to Krishna, the all-powerful divinity disguised as Arjuna's human companion. But throughout the series Arjuna functioned as the role model for readers, while his mentor, Krishna, and Yogananda were both routinely described as model gurus, thus inviting implicit comparison between the two without asserting deity outright.[116]

JESUS CHRIST AS PERFECT YOGI

Despite Yogananda's long efforts on behalf of "the Hindu Bible," it was not his most remarkable project as a leader of the global interfaith movement. That honor belongs instead to a regular column entitled *The Second Coming of Christ*. The series began in May 1932, ran through July 1942, and included 118 installments.[117] A commentary on the life and teachings of Jesus as presented in the New Testament, this series clearly showed Yogananda's deep interest in Jesus and his desire to draw connections between Christianity's founder and yogic truth.

The Second Coming epitomized Yogananda's version of Hindu-Christian syncretism, a thoroughly inclusivist effort to interpret Jesus and Christianity in light of universal Hindu truth. The title of the series already hinted at Yoganandaʼs legerdemain. In Christian parlance, the Second Coming traditionally identified the apocalyptic return of the resurrected Jesus to earth in the last days. Christian liberals had generally spiritualized Jesus's return and often avoided Second Coming language, but fundamentalists, evangelicals, and Pentecostals generally continued to anticipate Christ's literal return. But Yogananda meant something quite different by his use of the term: the yoga disciple's full experience of self-realization, which he often termed Christ Consciousness. This was a "Second Coming" in which the believer no longer expected to *encounter* Jesus but aspired to eventually *become* Jesus. Through his commentary, Yogananda sought to reach a wide group of Americans, some only loosely tied to the Christian tradition but who retained a sense of reverence for Jesus and the Bible. He wanted to show that Yogoda was not antithetical to Christianity but rather the substance of which Christianity was merely the shadow. In seeking to understand Jesus in light of Hinduism, Yogananda was following the well-trod path taken by many modern Hindu thinkers. Contemporaries such as Vivekananda, Ramakrishna, Sarvepalli Radhakrishnan, and Sri Aurobindo devoted some attention to evaluating Christianity and Jesus. Though their approaches and the level of attention they devoted varied, they all basically distinguished between Jesus, whom they viewed favorably, and Christianity, which they uniformly criticized.[118]

A commentary on the Gospels was a bolder strategy than his exegesis of the *Gītā*. There, Yogananda delved deeply into an ancient Hindu text to explain esoteric truths. Here, he aggressively reinterpreted the core of the Christian Bible *as* Hindu truth. The closest parallel to *The Second Coming* is P. C. Mozoomdar's 1883 *The Oriental Christ*, which follows Jesus's career from baptism through the Crucifixion and Resurrection, drawing connections to Indian traditions. But Mozoomdar's Jesus is still recognizable as the figure from the Gospels.[119] How did Yogananda defend this hermeneutical move? He warned about the danger of literal biblical interpretation, which had "caused great havoc," and instead advocated "intuitional perception of truth."[120] As one SRF monk, Brother Bernard, explained to an unconvinced newcomer, through meditation, Jesus is "becoming a living reality for people—a being with whom they can commune, instead of one whom they merely read about in the Bible. This was what Jesus meant when he said that he would come again. Master often speaks of this work as the Second Coming of Jesus—not to return again outwardly, but in the souls of those who loved him and communed with him." When the newcomer objected that this understanding was not what most Christians believed, Bernard replied that Jesus himself rebuked his disciples "for taking his words literally, when he meant them metaphorically." That newcomer, Donald Walters (later Swami Kriyananda), eventually came to deeply respect his master's exegetical flexibility, but his conversion was gradual. For a long time, Yogananda would write, "'This means so and so,' then turn around—almost, to my mind, as though correcting himself—and say, 'But on the other hand, it also means . . .' and go on to suggest an interpretation which—again, to my way of thinking—bore little relation to the first one. 'Can't he make up his mind?' I marveled. 'How is it possible for the same passage to have both meanings?'"[121] The intuitively perceived meaning of Scripture required a spiritual master.

Yogananda preempted potential criticism of his understanding of Jesus by taking the offensive. He accused Christians of allowing petty denominationalism and dogmatism to destroy genuine Christianity, of which he was the legitimate representative. He denounced Christian doctrinal minutiae and used the derisive term "Churchianity" to deplore the "hackneyed repetition and revamping of the same sermon every Sunday."[122]

Rather than adopting the simple strategy of using a passage from the Gospels as a point of departure for a broad thematic teaching, Yogananda took on the much more daunting challenge of detailed exegesis. Given how far his interpretations diverged from the surface sense of the text, this required him to provide elaborate explanations of symbols, codes, and spiritualized interpretation. John the Baptist's prophecy that Jesus was the "Lamb of God, who takes away the sins of the world" referred not to the Passover sacrifice but to the deeper allegorical truth that "Jesus came as the lamb of spirituality, humble, loyal to God, ready to offer Himself as a sacrifice before the Temple of Truth, so that by His supreme example of purity, humbleness, and meekness He might act as the greatest spiritual light to drive away the dark sins of the world." His expectation of finding yoga meditation techniques in the Gospels led to even more imaginative constructions. When John announced that first-century Jews should "make straight the way of the Lord," Yogananda clarified John's meaning that Christ Consciousness could only be experienced by meditating with a straight spine.[123] Christian exegetes would doubtless have disagreed with Yogananda's interpretation on nearly every point, but a century-long democratization of American Protestantism had fashioned "every man his own interpreter" of the Bible, making idiosyncratic interpretations fair game.[124]

As Yogananda unfolded Jesus's identity, he made it clear that Christ could only be understood in light of India. Yogananda began with a review of Jesus's baptism by John the Baptist, as recorded in the Gospels. The reader soon learned that baptism was originally an Indian practice; the contemporary Christian sacrament preserved only a faint remnant of that ancient tradition. The name Jesus was not a Greco-Latin modification of the Hebrew name Yeshua, as biblical scholars supposed. According to Yogananda, it was a corruption of the Sanskrit Isa, Lord of Creation. Through circuitous argument, Yogananda identified Christ with Krishna. He labeled the state one achieved through meditation Christ Consciousness, which was first achieved by Jadava, a great Indian prophet from 1500 B.C.E. who became the *āvatara* Krishna. Yogananda often spelled the name Christna to heighten the parallel between the two figures. Thus, the Hindu manifestation of Christ preceded the earthly Jesus by more than a millennium. Though Jesus was a divine figure, Yogananda was emphatic that he was *not* God incarnate, as Trinitarian Christians assumed, because "God never created Himself into a human being, subject to the weakness of flesh and mental limitations."[125] Rather, Christ was the fullness of the divine presence—and awareness of that presence—within a human being.

The appearance of the Holy Spirit, which descended on Jesus at his baptism, allowed Yogananda to introduce his understanding of the Trinity directly. He labored valiantly to stuff this Christian tenet into a Hindu Procrustean bed. The Father represented Cosmic Consciousness residing outside the vibratory creation, the Spirit was the "creator of creative vibration," and Christ was present in creation as the manifestation of the Father—divine intelligence "to create, recreate, preserve, and mould it according to its divine purpose."[126] If the real Christ was Krishna, the true Trinity resided in a Hindu universe.

Apart from the Trinity, readers of *The Second Coming of Christ* encountered a number of doctrines they might have heard in more conservative churches, including the historicity of Jesus's miracles and the existence of angelic beings. Though these doctrines had been transformed by Yogananda's interpretive skills, they were nonetheless precisely the tenets that liberal Christians attracted to Yogananda had banished from their creeds.

Yogananda's teaching on Satan fits into this category. Satan was an important figure for Yogananda, who mentioned him nearly three hundred times throughout the series. Yogananda insisted on the reality of metaphysical evil, calling "childish" those who denied its existence and asserting that belief in an "objective Satan," a fallen archangel, explained "the origin of all evil.[127] Demonic spirits were real, and exorcism had long been one key yogic power.[128] In defending this view, he shrilly denounced "modern" theologians in terms that sounded truly fundamentalist. "No amount of skin-deep liberal thinking can explain away these works of Jesus of casting out the devils. Because most modern theologians do not know anything about healing or casting out devils, that does not mean that the physical and mental and spiritual healing of man is impossible or that casting out of devils is superstition."[129] Satan tempted Adam and Eve, whose sin was not disobeying God by eating of the Tree of the Knowledge of Good and Evil, but, in a manner much more in line with Yogananda's own sexual ethic, procreating through sex instead of through willpower.[130] Through a convoluted explanation, Yogananda revealed that Satan created the mechanism of *karma* and the cycles of death and rebirth. He also created *māyā*, the delusion that keeps humans from seeing their true spiritual identity.[131]

Yogananda's discourse about Satan represents a particularly striking example of his complex syncretism, placing a distinctively Christian tenet within a Hindu cosmos. But his demonology required less of a departure from Hinduism than a first glance reveals. There is no direct counterpart to Satan, but evil spiritual forces are part and parcel of Hindu cosmology. Hindu written traditions—including the Vedas, Epics, and Purāṇas—and oral folk traditions include a host of ghosts, spirits, and demons. Ghosts attack victims and cause illness, functioning as one means of implementing karmic justice.[132] The most powerful harmful forces are essentially evil deities, an "inverted pantheon" that regularly battles the gods. Evil forces possess humans and harm them in a variety of ways, causing disease, death, and other misfortunes.[133] Prayer, mantras, and various other remedies can repel such forces. But while Yogananda fought zealously to affirm the ontological existence of evil forces and the efficacy of yogic powers in defeating them, elsewhere he expressed ambivalence about their existence as he strove to reconcile this teaching with the conviction that all reality is ultimately a manifestation of God.[134]

To face Satan's challenges successfully, Jesus had to fast. Great yogis like Jesus had long practiced this physical discipline, tapping into the stored-up energy of their "body battery" (a diagram accompanied this description, showing a large, wired-up battery) to demonstrate their victory over physical bodily needs. Deep meditation must accompany such physical austerity. When Satan tempted Jesus in the desert, Jesus famously retorted, "Man shall not live by bread alone, but by every word that proceeds from the mouth of God." Yogananda's elaborate paraphrase of this retort brought out Jesus's underlying meaning:

> The battery of man's wisdom, intelligence, life, and body shall not live (be sustained) by bread (outer material, solids, liquids, and so forth) alone, but by every word (unit of intelligent living vibration) that proceedeth out of the mouth of God. The Cosmic Energy or Life Energy, as it proceedeth out of medulla, through which mouth or opening, God breathes His breath of life (Cosmic Energy) into the soul, mind, and body battery of man.[135]

When Jesus went up on a mountainside to pray before selecting his apostles, he also took advantage of "the pure oxygen" there and engaged in breathing exercises "calculated to burn the carbon in the system, quiet the heart and switch off the life current from the five sense telephones so that the sensations cannot bother the brain and attention directed to God." He came down the mountain, picked his twelve disciples, and commissioned them to heal the sick and cast out demons.[136]

Jesus's admonition that his disciples be "wise as serpents, and harmless as doves" gave Yogananda an opportunity to introduce *kuṇḍalinī*, the "serpent power" lying coiled at the base of the spine. Yogananda also slipped a discussion of *kuṇḍalinī* into one of the central Gospel texts, where Jesus cryptically informed Nicodemus that a person must be "born again"—that is, from the Holy Spirit—to enter the Kingdom of God. In Yogananda's hands, being "born again" became an endorsement of yoga meditation as the mean of lifting the sleeping *śakti* power. "Jesus said that each Son of Man, or each bodily consciousness, must be lifted from the plane of the senses to the Astral Kingdom by reversing the Life Force through the serpent-like coiled passage at the base of the spine. Every time you mediate deeply, you automatically reverse the Life Force and consciousness from matter to God. This helps to loosen the Astral and physical knot at the base of the spine."[137] As the dialogue between Jesus and Nicodemus continued, it moved to Jesus's climactic statement that "whosoever believes in me shall not perish, but inherit eternal life." Through Yogananda's alchemy this became, "Whosever believes in the doctrine of lifting the bodily consciousness (Son of Man) from the physical to the Astral body reversing the Life Force through the coiled passage at the base of the spine, will not perish, that is, be subject to mortal changes of life and death, but will gradually acquire the changeless Eternal State."[138] Jesus's crucifixion also became a great karmic event, where the "seeds of actions are burned up in the fires of wisdom," leading him to find immortality beyond death.[139]

Yogananda routinely used *The Second Coming* to explore the crucial guru-disciple bond, and hints of Yogananda's own authority were never far from the surface of such texts. The guru best exemplified Jesus's own advanced consciousness, and thus held the greatest likelihood of transmitting that knowledge to eager disciples. As Yogananda explained, "God uses only about-to-be-perfect souls to serve as examples and teachers to deluded humans."[140] A guru was thus essential for one's spiritual journey, someone "who will discipline you and take a personal interest in your spiritual welfare and lead you as far along the spiritual path as you wish to go." Only in obeying him could disciples attain their ultimate goal.[141] The relationship between John and Jesus represented just such a relationship, the only way in which "complete satisfaction, comfort, and God-consciousness" could be found.[142] Conversely, Yogananda warned about the dangers of avoiding transparency before one's guru, the only person who could heal a disciple's illness. "In this way an error-stricken disciple makes his moral transgression grow upon him. To hide the moral disease from the Spiritual doctor is extremely dangerous to Spiritual health."[143]

Though Yogananda held out the theoretical possibility that anyone could be "a Jesus Christ in one life by proper meditation," the harsh reality was that even though disciples could make spiritual progress, achieving Christ consciousness was a truly rare phenomenon.[144] But they could enjoy this achievement vicariously through their affectionate submission to a beloved Christlike guru. Yogananda made abundantly clear that he was one of the rare gurus who possessed Christ Consciousness. Thus, beyond Brother Bernard's explanation of the "Second Coming of Christ," this label very likely bore another meaning. Yogananda, a guru who fully manifested Christ Consciousness, was the Christ who had returned. The veiled character of this assertion blunted its audacity; more direct revelation awaited a more autobiographical vehicle.

AUTOBIOGRAPHY OF A DIVINE GLOBAL YOGI

Of all the texts that established Yogananda's vision of himself and his role in the world, none is more crucial than *Autobiography of a Yogi*. It does not follow conventions familiar to the autobiography genre. Yogananda left out much of his childhood, including games, likes and dislikes, early schooling, and romantic attractions. He was also largely silent about his twenty-five-year ministry in the United States, which constituted nearly half of his life at the time of writing. The narrative concentrates almost exclusively on his quest to become a yogi. Along that path, he enjoyed many fantastic encounters, and these accounts fill most of the book. This is how one chapter begins:

> "I saw a yogi remain in the air, several feet above the ground, last night at a group meeting." My friend, Upendra Mohun Chowdhury, spoke impressively.
>
> I gave him an enthusiastic smile. "Perhaps I can guess his name. Was it Bhaduri Mahasaya, of Upper Circular Road?"
>
> Upendra nodded, a little crestfallen not to be a news-bearer. My inquisitiveness about saints was well-known among my friends; they delighted in setting me on a fresh track.
>
> "The yogi lives so close to my home that I often visit him." My

words brought keen interest to Upendra's face, and I made a further confidence.

"I have seen him in remarkable feats. He has expertly mastered the various *pranayamas* of the ancient eightfold yoga outlined by Patanjali. Once Bhaduri Mahasaya performed the *Bhastrika Pranayama* before me with such amazing force that it seemed an actual storm had arisen in the room! Then he extinguished the thundering breath and remained motionless in a high state of superconsciousness. The aura of peace after the storm was vivid beyond forgetting."

"I heard that the saint never leaves his home." Upendra's tone was a trifle incredulous.

"Indeed it is true! He has lived indoors for the past twenty years. He slightly relaxes his self-imposed rule at the times of our holy festivals, when he goes as far as his front sidewalk! The beggars gather there, because Saint Bhaduri is known for his tender heart."

"How does he remain in the air, defying the law of gravitation?"

"A yogi's body loses its grossness after use of certain *pranayamas*. Then it will levitate or hop about like a leaping frog. Even saints who do not practice a formal yoga have been known to levitate during a state of intense devotion to God."

"I would like to know more of this sage. Do you attend his evening meetings?" Upendra's eyes were sparkling with curiosity.

"Yes, I go often. I am vastly entertained by the wit in his wisdom. Occasionally my prolonged laughter mars the solemnity of his gatherings. The saint is not displeased, but his disciples look daggers!"[145]

Historians have often wondered how to make sense of such a text. Polly Trout canvases the options:

1) The miracles Yogananda describes are veridically, literally true.
2) They did not "really" happen as Yogananda perceived them, but he is genuinely convinced that they did, and is therefore entirely honest in his account of them.
3) They did not "really" happen, and Yogananda knows this, but he is using these stories as metaphorical pedagogical devices. In other words, he is engaging in a mode of discourse in which literalist definitions of truth and falsity are irrelevant.
4) Yogananda was a liar.[146]

While Trout opts for either the second or the third option, some might find her first choice attractive. Similar claims have been made in other historical contexts. Independent scholar Michael Grosso recounts that when seventeenth-century Catholic friar Joseph of Cupertino was ordained, he began to levitate regularly, and "his life was never the same again."[147] Equally bizarre occurrences have been reported in the centuries since. Based on these reports, Grosso makes a case for a "parapsychology of religion" that is open to nonrational phenomena, experiences that have traditionally been explained as the existence of higher beings, the power of belief and prayer, out-of-body experiences, mediums, reincarnation, ghosts and apparitions, and even miracles.[148] He recounts numerous stories from anthropologists and ethnographers—many skeptical of the supramundane by disposition and training—of inexplicable phenomena they encountered in the field in various parts of the world.[149]

Whatever one thinks about the possibility of such phenomena, Yogananda clearly believed them to be literally possible—not mere metaphors, as Trout suggests in her third option. His followers, including his first converts, the Lewises, routinely attributed to him the ability to heal, to intervene for their physical safety, to read their thoughts, and to predict the future. "Miracles," Swami Kriyananda explained, "were part of Yogananda's service to others. He seldom spoke of them, but among those whose lives were associated with his, miracles were common."[150]

Apart from ontological doubts about supramundane deeds, there are more routine reasons for skepticism about at least some of Yogananda's claims. As demonstrated in chapter 1, on the rare occasions where his account can be corroborated—his "chance" meeting with Yukteswar and his presentiments of the death of his mother, brother, and guru—the other source, typically written by a colleague or relative sympathetic to Yogananda, often provides a more mundane explanation. Responding to such divergent accounts, Satyeswarananda cast a jaundiced eye at the *Autobiography*'s miraculous accounts, blaming the book's editors for "mystifying" events to appeal to "Christian seekers" who would be drawn to a more devotional understanding of yoga. The *Autobiography* bore "the character of a spiritual fiction from the standpoint of conservative, serious, seekers of truth of Vedic culture."[151]

Trout's fourth option, the blunt assertion that Yogananda was simply a liar, echoes old tropes about the yogi as charlatan. While anticult myth busters and disgruntled former SRF members have sometimes made precisely this claim, as discussed in the Epilogue, this explanation assumes that Yogananda knowingly perpetrated a fraud for more than three decades and deceived thousands, including his closest disciples, many of whom have continued to keep SRF alive for nearly seventy years since his death. This explanation fails to capture the earnestness, conviction, and consistency Yogananda and his successors have shown.

This leaves Trout's second option, but one that requires some nuance. For Yogananda, the boundary between imagination and reality was fluid. He narrated events from his childhood, not necessarily as they actually happened, but as they might have happened or ought to have happened, in order to bring out the possibilities of an enchanted world. As one scholar of Indian folklore comments, "A story's lifelikeness . . . allows events to become believable within it, even if they should never occur in everyday life. For though the world created by a story is often similar to lived cultural reality, it is also full of boundless possibilities. Within a story, received categories can be combined into fantastic new shapes, and time can jump backward, sideways, or far ahead. . . . By stretching conceptions of the possible, narrative . . . [points] toward transcendent meanings instead."[152]

The *Autobiography* was fundamentally designed to persuade readers to accept his vision of a cosmos suffused with the miraculous—and to reveal himself as a yogi who could perform such deeds. Believing deeply in the power of the word to create reality, he sought to create a shared reality with his readers. In essence, the text functions as a performative speech act, creating through its utterance the reality that it asserts.[153] The *Autobiography*, then, is best understood as a new scripture for the modern world in which Yogananda casts himself as the divine savior sent by God to proclaim self-realization through yoga.

To exegete the *Autobiography* as scripture, this section will begin by applying a drastically simplified model of semiotician A. J. Greimas's structural semantics that focuses on how narratives function within their own self-enclosed universes of meaning. Greimas argued that most stories share a few stock features. A story involves a *sender* commissioning a *subject* to accomplish some *object* (sometimes, as in this case, the delivery of a message) for a *receiver*. Along the way, the subject faces both obstruction from *opponents* and assistance from *helpers*. The story's outcome depends on its genre, a function of the *setting* in which the narrative transpires.[154]

Analysis of the *Autobiography* will begin with a consideration of the *setting*. Yogananda set the story in an imagined India he reappropriated from Western Orientalists. The pure, spiritual India he constructed was untainted by the West, which explains the near total absence of the British Empire in his account. And because the quaint India of Orientalist fantasy was rural and premodern, Yogananda avoided depictions of teeming cities and modern technology as much as possible. India was thus more than an actual place; it was a parallel reality, an alternative to the disenchanted Western world. Readers could experience this alternative reality—wherever they lived—if they sought constant awareness of the spiritual realm. American audiences undoubtedly found it easier to embrace an enchanted universe where astounding miracles transpired every day when it was located in the mystical Orient, far from their own workaday lives.

Yogananda employed an arsenal of strategies to reenchant the world. First, he gave the *Autobiography* the texture of sacred writ. He routinely cited sacred texts in his copious footnotes—the Vedas, Upaniṣads, *Bhagavad Gītā*, *Rāmāyaṇa*, and Patañjali's *Yoga Sūtras*, as well as the Bible, especially the Gospels—as authoritative sources. His writing style imitated Scripture with intentionally archaic language that evoked the English Bible. In 1946, the proliferation of English translations of the Bible had not yet begun; the vast majority of American Protestants knew the Bible through the Authorized, or King James, Version of 1611; Catholics were familiar with the similarly archaic-sounding Douay-Rheims translation. *Autobiography* readers would have been reminded of the Bible because it was the only place they might routinely encounter such dated language. The *Autobiography*'s first chapter, for example, includes the following archaic words found in the King James Bible: "verities," "dwell," "blessings," "bulwarked," and "beguiling." As an English speaker for well over two decades, adept in the use of vernacular English, Yogananda's archaizing seems to be a clearly intentional strategy.

He also imitated common Indian storytelling traditions. The narrative quality of the *Autobiography*, like Yogananda's face-to-face teaching, reflected the hortatory, folkloric character of India's oral tales. Smaller narratives gradually accreted around the main narrative, creating a meandering, nonlinear structure in which one fantastic account segued into another. In this genre, supernatural occurrences routinely take place and historical verifiability is not the point.[155] Yogananda structured his narrative through a series of dialogues with the many strange figures he encountered on his spiritual path. While making his narrative more lifelike and exciting, dialogues created a story-within-a-story or "frame story" pattern familiar to Indians from the great epics, such as the *Mahābhārata* and *Ramayaṇa*, and the Purāṇas.[156]

The *Autobiography*'s narrative trajectory also follows established stages of Indian hagiography:

1) *miraculous origins*: a child is born under unusual circumstances into a well-off family and grows up demonstrating precocious abilities;
2) *spiritual search*: the individual begins a search for spiritual truth,

experiencing humiliation or loss as the trigger for the search or as a consequence of it;

3) *initiation by a guru*: after many adventures, journeys, and guidance by holy men, the individual finds his guru, who initiates him into a formal spiritual path;

4) *growing ministry*: the individual, who displays a commanding personality, grows in independent spiritual authority—usually defying some norm or ruler—founding his own ashram or sect, confounding spiritual rivals, and gathering an increasing number of followers; and

5) *approaching the end*: often near the end of life (which may be supernaturally foreknown), the individual achieves spiritual enlightenment, merging with or becoming God.[157]

The one partial exception is step 5. Yogananda certainly depicted his own spiritual enlightenment, but since he was writing his own hagiography, he could not narrate his own death, though he clearly intimated his own divine spiritual enlightenment. This partial exception points to a unique feature of Yogananda's hagiography. Hagiography is rarely autobiographical. Like the epics, hagiographic accounts typically develop over centuries, becoming more elaborate—and often more fantastic—as later disciples invent new details. Yogananda created a numinous hagiography *about himself* de novo.

He filled this hagiographic narrative world with miraculous events performed by advanced yogis. Though a great many such events fill the book, they fall into a half-dozen different formulaic categories, all of which fit within the expectations of *siddhi* powers described in the *Yoga Sūtras*.[158] Regardless of type, each miracle follows a stock formula:

- The narrative begins with an account of the miracle itself.
- Next, characters who witness the miracle, including Yogananda, express surprise or amazement.
- Finally, expressions of surprise provide an opening for an enlightened figure to utter a divine revelation ultimately designed for the reader's edification. In some cases, the narrative makes clear how the miracle provides practical aid for a certain character; in others, the miracle serves to evoke awe and a concomitant explanation of cosmological truth.

Exploring exemplary accounts of the different miracle types provides an opportunity to examine the spiritual enlightenment the text provides at the narrative climax. The first miracle type, levitation, has already been described.

In that account, the spiritual revelation was that all physical reality—including human beings—is composed of energy and the realized yogi can command energy to do whatever it wishes. Yogananda's second miraculous type was mind reading. As the narrator, Yogananda revealed to the reader something a character (often he himself) was thinking. A yogi would vocalize the secret thought accurately and respond authoritatively to it. Not long after Yogananda and Yukteswar met, for example, the Master provided divinely intuited guidance about Yogananda's life at the Bharat Dharma Mahamandal ashram: "It is time for a change, inasmuch as you are unhappily situated in the hermitage." This announcement surprised Yogananda, since he had shared nothing about his unhappiness with Yukteswar. "By his natural, unemphatic manner, I understood that he wished no astonished ejaculations" about his insight. Yukteswar's authoritative guidance that Yogananda go back to Calcutta to live with his family resolved his dilemma and relieved his secret anguish.[159]

Clairvoyance was the third type of miracle. A spiritual authority would announce some future event in detail, advising an appropriate response or explaining how the person's fate could not be avoided. In one case, for example, Yukteswar announced, "The stars are about to take an unfriendly interest in you, Mukunda. Fear not; you shall be protected. In about a month your liver will cause you much trouble. The illness is scheduled to last for six months, but your use of an astrological armlet will shorten the period to twenty-four days." Yukteswar directed Yogananda to purchase a silver bangle to lessen the severity of the malady. Because of Yogananda's excellent health, however, "Master's prediction slipped from my mind. He left Serampore to visit Benares. Thirty days after our conversation, I felt a sudden pain in the region of my liver." Yukteswar's clairvoyance communicated that fate could be foreknown and, to an extent counteracted, if one responded with the appropriate faith.[160]

The fourth type of miraculous feat was bilocation. A spiritual figure was expected to be in one location, but a trustworthy eyewitness met him simultaneously in a completely different location. The witness remembered some specific detail that irrefutably proved that the saint really had been in two places at the same time. Swami Pranabananda was meeting with Yogananda at his home even while he met Yogananda's friend Kedar Nath Bubu down by the river. When the dual appearances were discovered, Kedar Nath pointed out, "Look, those are the very sandals he was wearing at the *ghat*." Pranabananda turned to Yogananda "with a quizzical smile." He asked, "Why are you stupefied at all this? The subtle unity of the phenomenal world is not hidden from true *yogis*. I instantly see and converse with my disciples in distant Calcutta. They can similarly transcend at will every obstacle of gross matter." Rather than being a simple parlor trick, bilocation revealed, like levitation, profound truth about mastery over physical matter.[161]

Finally, there were the feats of strength: going without food, demonstrating superhuman might, or living without breathing for extended periods of time. The Tiger Swami, a man who subdued wild tigers with his own brute strength, most colorfully illustrates the *Autobiography*'s accounts of superhuman power. Challenged by a maharaja to fight his newly captured tiger, the Tiger Swami prevailed, using uncommon strength. Yogananda vividly relayed the tale as a first-person account in the Tiger Swami's own words. After being injured by the tiger, "I swung my left arm in a bone-cracking blow. The beast reeled back, swirled around the rear of the cage, and sprang forward convulsively. My famous fistic punishment rained on his head." The fight continued as the rivals exchanged blows. "The cage was pandemonium, as blood splashed in all directions, and blasts of pain and lethal lust came from the bestial throat." Finally, "I mustered all my will force, bellowed fiercely, and landed a final concussive blow. The tiger collapsed and lay quietly."[162] While Yogananda did not provide parallels to all the abilities Patañjali attributed to *siddhis* in the *Yoga Sūtras*, the narratives he did offer were clearly designed to evoke their supernatural powers.

Yogananda recognized that canny modern audiences might be skeptical of the veracity of such amazing claims. He created verisimilitude using a variety of subtle, creative strategies, addressing readers' doubts obliquely rather than through blunt assertions of metaphysical fact. Dialogue was an ally in this strategy. Robert Alter's observation about the Hebrew scriptures' penchant for avoiding narration in favor of dialogue applies well to the *Autobiography*: "The primacy of dialogue is so pronounced that many pieces of third-person narration prove on inspection to be dialogue-bound, verbally mirroring elements of dialogue that precede them or that they introduce. Narration is thus often relegated to the role of confirming assertions made in dialogue."[163] Yogananda frequently placed himself into dialogues that allowed him to play the vicarious role of the reader, portraying himself as open but needing confirmation. He disarmed skeptics by putting their putative objections into his own mouth. Conversely, he put important expressions of truth into other people's mouths, allowing them to articulate spiritual truth without being forced to adopt a didactic role directly himself. For example, when Yogananda's friend encountered the bilocating swami, he exclaimed, "Are we living in this material age, or are we dreaming? I never expected to witness such a miracle in my life!"[164] Though Yogananda did not utter this comment, his ventriloquism subtly won readers to his perspective.

Another strategy of verisimilitude was the frequent depiction of prophecy-fulfillment sequences. The content of prophetic announcements was not always intrinsically remarkable. Precise forecasting of even mundane future occurrences, however, underscored the yogi power of clairvoyance. Since all the prophecies Yogananda recounted had found fulfillment by the time he narrated them for the *Autobiography,* a skeptical reader would find it impossible not to wonder whether they were all *vaticinium ex eventu* pronouncements. As Yogananda's Indian antagonist Swami Satyeswarananda comments, "Ideas were interjected to look as if some divine hands were working behind the scenes. Mystifications were well thought out during the ten long years period [*sic*] of editing the forty-nine chapters from the materials Yogananda had collected. It was written with mystic vibrations which would be attractive to Christians."[165] Yogananda addressed this problem by creating long narrative gaps between the announcement of a prophecy and its fulfillment, claiming through the book's dialogue to have forgotten a specific prophecy until after its fulfillment.

Having established the *setting,* it is time to turn to the *subject* or, better, the protagonist. It will be no surprise that Yogananda is the hero of his autobiography, though his full identity does not become clear until the end of the narrative. The early chapters establish his spiritual precocity, including the *siddhi* feat of remembering his previous existence, a memory that faded as his soul awakened in the body of the newborn Mukunda. He also describes being frustrated with his infant body for refusing to cooperate with his mind's knowledge and abilities. He wanted to walk, wanted to speak, but could not make his thoughts coalesce into language until Bengali settled in his mind. Yogananda's frequent descriptions of his unquenchable spiritual thirst would suggest that he was his own *sender*—his yearning for spiritual truth propelled him on his quest. But there are hints throughout, including a prophecy given to his pregnant mother that she would give birth to a great yogi, that his life path was foreordained. This suggests that the narrative's ultimate *sender* is God.

Along the way, Yogananda encountered many spiritual figures who functioned as *helpers* in his spiritual quest. Most of the yogis who performed the miraculous feats described above, for example, guided him into deeper understanding. But Sri Yukteswar, as Yogananda's personal guru, played the most significant role in his spiritual development. Yogananda labored to show the worthiness of his mentor, a wise and powerful yogi. Then he demonstrated the uniquely intimate guru-disciple relationship he shared with this great master. Beyond their dramatic first encounter, Yogananda recounted unusual instances of physical intimacy: touching Yukteswar's feet, being tenderly cared for while ill, and, most strikingly, sharing his master's bed as a rare privilege. When Yukteswar appeared to Yogananda after his death, Yogananda recognized him in part by his distinctive bodily odor. He also related a number of private revelations of privileged information that intimated Yukteswar's trust and his transmission of authority to Yogananda, as the principle vehicle for Yukteswar's message to the West.

Because plot exists only where there is conflict, the *Autobiography* is suffused with *opponents*. From his earliest years, opponents at every level conspired to thwart Yogananda's spiritual journey. But he ultimately prevailed against all odds. Remarkably, his opponents were often his own family members, rather than more sinister figures. Nearly every story he recounted from his childhood involved opposition, skepticism, or doubt from a family member regarding appropriate behavior or underlying spiritual reality. These stories were always resolved through Yogananda's complete vindication, though sometimes only after a delay. For example, when his sister mocked his devotion to the Mother Goddess, Yogananda predicted that the deity would give him victory in a kite battle where Indian children smeared glass fragments on their kite strings and attempt to cut rivals' strings. Needless to say, Yogananda got precisely what he foretold, forcing his sister to confess, "Indeed, Divine Mother listens to you! This is all too uncanny for me!" After this remark, she "bolted away like a frightened fawn."[166]

Yogananda related a number of incidents of opposition from his oldest brother, Ananta, most notably his attempt to keep Yogananda and his friends from escaping to the Himalayas. But there are less dramatic examples. A fortune-teller predicted that Yogananda would marry three times. Ananta accepted this prophecy and teased his brother, whose fate was clearly sealed. But Yogananda rejected the legitimacy of this prediction; although he did receive three marriage arrangements, he turned them all down—and turned the tables on his brother's mockery.

Yogananda even clashed with his father, particularly over the decision whether to depart immediately when news of his mother's illness arrived. Yogananda's prophecy of her death proved prescient, despite his father's dismissal of his fears. Yogananda's conflict with his father is especially surprising, given that his father was not a religious skeptic but a devoted yoga practitioner who followed the same lineage that Yogananda joined.

All of these accounts—a very small sampling of a much larger collection—follow the same pattern: through spiritual immaturity, blindness, or mean-spiritedness, Yogananda's family members all doubted or challenged him. All were eventually compelled to admit their error. And Yogananda was never intellectually or morally in error. The only person free from the taint of opposition was his beloved mother, whose death left him so bereft that he never desired to cast her as a stumbling block on his spiritual path. Although Yogananda undoubtedly experienced real grievances with family members, he also magnified relatively minor tensions to make his life — which was not especially difficult — conform to the hagiographic pattern of struggle.

As the story's *subject* or hero, Yogananda succeeds in his goal of proclaiming the message of yoga not only to spiritually hungry America but also to the world at large. The final chapter finds Yogananda in his beautiful Encinitas ashram, overlooking the great Pacific Ocean, writing the very volume that readers hold in their hand. After surveying his rapid institutional expansion — with new temples in Washington, D.C., Hollywood, and San Diego — he hinted at plans he had hatched with Minott Lewis for a new global venture, a World Colony of All Nations.

> "'World' is a large term, but man must enlarge his allegiance, considering himself in the light of a world citizen," I continued. "A person who truly feels: 'The world is my homeland; it is my America, my India, my Philippines, my England, my Africa,' will never lack scope for a useful and happy life. His natural local pride will know limitless expansion; he will be in touch with creative universal currents."
>
> Dr. Lewis and I halted above the lotus pool near the hermitage. Below us lay the illimitable Pacific.
>
> "These same waters break equally on the coasts of West and East, in California and China." My companion threw a little stone into the first of the oceanic seventy million square miles. "Encinitas is a symbolic spot for a world colony."

The *Autobiography* closes with Yogananda's reflection, "Lord, . . . Thou hast given this monk a large family!"[167] The celibate guru from India had adopted many American children, and he looked forward to adopting many more from all over the world.

A structural reading of the *Autobiography* thus suggests a scriptural account of the divine messenger's successful quest to share yoga with the world. But the *Autobiography*, like the *Bhagavad Gītā* commentary and *The Second Coming of Christ*, points beyond Yogananda's role as a mere missionary of yoga to something more profound. Throughout the book, Yogananda routinely rehearsed his spiritual pedigree through an unbroken line of yogis from the mysterious Babaji, a "deathless" guru in the remote Himalayas; to Babaji's disciple

Lahiri Mahasaya, whose devotees included Yogananda's own parents; and to Yukteswar, Yogananda's personal guru. Those great self-realized yogis merited titles like Yogi-Christ, divine guru, Savior, Divinity Itself in the form of flesh. In the preface W. Y. Evans-Wentz proclaimed the link between Yogananda and these other yogis. "The value of Yogananda's AUTOBIOGRAPHY is greatly enhanced by the fact that it is one of the few books in English about the wise men of India which has been written, not by a journalist or foreigner, but by one of their own race and training—in short, a book ABOUT yogis BY a yogi."[168] As a yogi like his illustrious forebears, Yogananda was at least their equal. But since his global ministry far exceeded theirs, arguably he surpassed them. Given their already exalted status, this could only mean that he was presenting himself as a new Christ figure.

Yogananda mentions Jesus Christ roughly three dozen times in the *Autobiography*. Mostly he presents Jesus as a yogi and describe yoga's goal as the production of "Yogi Christs." Thus, Babaji, Lahiri Mahasaya, and Yukteswar are all described as "Christ-like," as is Ramakrishna, unofficial mentor to Yogananda and official mentor to Vivekananda.[169] Other references imply parallels between events in Jesus's life and Yogananda's. Jesus left his family behind to conduct a ministry of teaching, healing, and discipleship. Jesus suffered in his body as a "ransom for the sins of many," just as Yogananda, who had experienced physical difficulties by the time he wrote the *Autobiography*, suffered in bearing the karmic burdens of his disciples. And when Yogananda claimed, "If Christ returned to earth and walked the streets of New York, displaying his divine powers, it would cause the same excitement," the thinly veiled reference to his own early ministry in America is unmistakable.[170]

Yogananda, then, was not simply the *subject* or protagonist of the *Autobiography* commissioned by God to carry out the *object* of spreading the word about yoga to his *receivers* in America. In the final analysis, the narrative reveals that he was to offer himself—as an exemplar, a faultless guide, and even more a divine presence—to the world. He thus became both *subject* and *object* of his own story. And in revealing this truth about Yogananda, the scripturelike *Autobiography* became the most important medium for disseminating this message.

Given such grand claims by a relatively unknown swami, it is little surprise that critical reception of the *Autobiography* was generally dismissive. There were exceptions, to be sure. *Newsweek* called Yogananda "an authentic Hindu yogi" and praised his efforts to provide an "autobiography of the soul" rather "than of the body," giving him the final word as he expounded on the "consciousness of a perfected yogi."[171] But *Time* was more typical. In a backhanded compliment, its reviewer thought the book showed "exceedingly well how an alien culture may change when transplanted by a businesslike nurseryman from the tough soil of religious asceticism into hothouses of financial wealth and spiritual despair."[172] The book merited only a capsule review in the *New York Times,* which read in its entirety: "A rare account of the Indian cult from within, by one who practices it, with many photographs. An incident is contact with Luther Burbank and his talks with the plants which responded to his conversation."[173] A review in the *Chicago Daily Tribune Review* entitled "Study of Yogi Mysticism and Swami Tricks" described the book as a series of miracles the author attempted to explain in the language of modern science. "Whether he succeeds in this, or merely wraps one mysticism up in another, you will have to judge for yourself."[174] The peer-reviewed *Philosophy East and West* offered the most denunciatory review. "The book, widely advertised and read," University of Hawaii professor S. K. Sachsen commented, "will no doubt acquaint the reader with India, yoga, and Swami Yogananda, but whether it will portray them truly is quite doubtful. Truth never suffers so much from its opponent as from its over-zealous devotee." Sachsen was impatient with the book's frequent descriptions of miracles, but more with Yogananda's self-identification as a yogi, as "it is not traditional for a yogi in India to speak of himself as such; nor does a spiritual man style himself by the highest title 'Paramhansa,' which is reserved for only those rare souls who have attained their liberation from the bondage of earthly life and activity and live in complete equanimity of mind."[175]

International reviews showed only slightly more enthusiasm. A *China Weekly Review* began by noting, "The contents of this book are unusual, to say the least." Yogananda's miracle accounts "arouse curiosity rather than conviction," including his account of passing his university exams without studying, which the reviewer thought "faintly ludicrous." But the reviewer enjoyed the philosophical passages and ultimately found that the book was worth reading. Given recent Western interest in the Orient, "some idea of Eastern spiritual development is essential."[176] A 1950 review of the Dutch translation damned the *Autobiography* with faint praise. Apart from some esoteric content, the book was most interesting "as an intimate description of life in India," and some passages, as when "the young boys set out on their own to become hermits in the Himalayas, are not devoid of humor."[177] Only the *Times of India* provided a gushing, if brief, endorsement: "The autobiography of this sage makes captivating reading, and its value lies in the portrait of saints he has presented to the reader, spiritual giants portrayed with remarkable fidelity to truth."[178]

But professional reviews fail to capture the full picture. Popular interest in the *Autobiography,* both in the United States and abroad, belied these negative assessments. Within eighteen months of its American publication, the *Auto-*

biography had been translated into Bengali, Hindi, Spanish, French, Dutch, and Swedish, and a British edition had been prepared. Global interest was due in no small part to SRF's aggressive promotion of "the book that is awakening thousands." As SRF beamed, "This is the first time that an authentic Hindu *yogi* has written his life experiences for a Western audience. India's great masters live in these unforgettable stories told by Paramhansa Yogananda, chosen to bring their message to all. Entertaining from cover to cover."[179] Enthusiastic responses poured in from all over England, Australia, Germany, Sweden, Austria, Canada, Argentina, Kenya, and Italy thanking SRF for publishing a "wonderful," "marvelous," "fascinating" book, "the greatest reading experience of my life." Some readers wrote in to say that the *Autobiography* provided spiritual truth they had been seeking their whole lives, and others confessed that they did not even know such truth existed before reading the book. Most, however, recognized that the book went beyond revealing truth, whether esoteric or practical. They understood that the *Autobiography*'s central message was about the yogi who told his story within its pages. As one Viennese reader implored Yogananda, "I ask you for help, Divine Master! Don't refuse my request! Teach me Kriya Yoga. Give me a sign of your grace which makes me an accepted disciple of your group. Grant my supplication! Sitting at your sacred feet, I am waiting for a word of response from you."[180]

PARAMAHANSA, GLOBAL GURU AND *GURUDEV*

By the late 1940s, thanks in no small part to the *Autobiography,* Yogananda was at the height of his influence. In 1949, feeling confident and ambitious, Yogananda launched another spiritual business venture. He opened SRF Café along California's Pacific Coast Highway in Encinitas. The prime location along the route from L.A. to San Diego and Mexico provided plenty of free advertising. Travelers' eyes were drawn to the thirty-foot gold-domed facade of Golden Lotus Gateway and then to the sign announcing in bold capital letters, "MUSHROOMBURGERS."[181] A more ambitious venture than Nutritive Nuggets, SRF Café offered a variety of vegetarian items—some unfamiliar to most Americans—in an effort to turn a profit offering healthy food choices. An advertisement announcing the café's opening sounded truly evangelical as it proclaimed, "HERE'S GOOD NEWS!"[182] "You'll be very much pleased," readers were reassured, "with the home cooked foods served here, and with the atmosphere of peace and cheer which pervades this unique establishment."[183] The café's menu offered "the finest foods and juices." The most prominent item was the mushroomburger itself. Other unusual menu options for the era included carrot juice made from "garden-fresh carrots grown in the Colony" and omelets with "special curry sauce." Some foods, though, were much more familiar fare, such as fresh-baked pies and homemade ice cream. Customers could purchase frozen mangoes and coconuts. In short, SRF Café offered a combination of exotic and familiar foods, all of which were flavorful while also being ostensibly healthy. If that combination was not inducement enough, Yogananda resorted to the familiar tactic of testimonial: "Distinguished world-traveled guests have proclaimed our food unexcelled anywhere."[184] The world café seemed a fitting gesture from a global guru.

The growth and expansion of SRF by the late 1940s largely matched Yogananda's global vision. En route to this position, SRF had experienced expansion, contraction, and relocation. At the onset of World War II, there were thirty-four SRF centers, including overseas centers in London, Latvia, Johannesburg, and seven in India. By the late 1940s, at least a dozen centers had closed, including some in prominent cities—many of which had been established for a number of years. Santa Barbara, Fresno, San Francisco, New York, Chicago, Saint Louis, Cincinnati, Dayton, Saint Paul, Milwaukee, and Salt Lake City centers present in 1940 had disappeared by 1948. Some shrinkage likely resulted from negative press surrounding another lawsuit by a former partner. Sri Nerode claimed that Yogananda had been "conducting himself in a matter repugnant to the organization and been teaching doctrines opposed to those of the Hindu self-realization philosophy." Among other things, Yogananda's alleged misconduct included holding himself up as "a sort of deity.'" Nerode also claimed that Yogananda lived in luxurious conditions and was "visited at all times of night by young women." As a coauthor of many SRF materials, Nerode was also upset by being cut out of the ministry's profits, which he calculated at a million dollars. Nerode lost the suit when Yogananda's attorney produced letters proving that no partnership existed between the two. Having learned his lesson from the earlier Dhirananda lawsuit, Yogananda had required Nerode to sign a release indicating that he would never claim "any part of the proceeds derived from Swami Yogananda's Correspondence Course, or his books, magazine, or any income of his whatsoever." He would receive only "free minimum board and lodging for his services," and could be let go at any time.[185]

Whatever the reasons for earlier center closures, SRF experienced consistent post–World War II growth with several notable features. First, Southern California remained the organization's spiritual center, with a new church in Long Beach and a temple in San Diego. The Lake Shrine, a Pacific Palisades meditation site, was dedicated in a public ceremony attended by the California

The Lake Shrine in Pacific Palisades (bottom) and the Encinitas Hermitage, two quintessential SRF sites in prime Southern California locations. The Lake Shrine's Golden Lotus archway frames the Mahatma Gandhi World Peace Memorial, which contains some of Gandhi's ashes. The pedestrian crosswalk is called "Swami's Ped Xing" in reference to nearby Swami's Beach, named in honor of Yogananda.

lieutenant governor.[186] Most significantly, Yogananda oversaw construction of a temple in Hollywood, on the prominent thoroughfare of Sunset Boulevard. Lined by palm trees, it conveyed his aspiration to be at the symbolic center of Southern Californian culture. An "India Center" auditorium was added to the site in 1951. Second, the earlier broad national dispersion of SRF centers disappeared, as major eastern and midwestern cities no longer hosted groups, perhaps as a consequence of lingering patriotism stirred by the war that made a religion with foreign roots less attractive.[187] If nothing else, the closures indicate the tenuous hold many of these centers had. The establishment of new centers offset these losses, with the number of facilities at thirty-five by 1948. Finally, the growth of international centers was quite remarkable. Eight centers in India were complemented by a dozen others: two in England, one in Germany, four in West Africa, two in Mexico, and two in Canada. The importance of the British Dominion is clear, as all but three of the international centers were in current or former British territories. More than half of all Self-Realization Fellowship centers were now located overseas, symbolizing an important international shift in membership and outlook.

E. E. Dickinson, whose receipt of a silver cup confirmed the identity of Yogananda as his true guru, became an exemplar of the many followers around the world who had a similar epiphany in the 1940s. The *Autobiography* clearly did its work well, enlightening readers and drawing seekers from across the country to prostrate themselves at their guru's feet, whether literally or only metaphorically. The book's hints about the author's divine status represented the culmination of a tradition that had been under way for more than a decade. By the time his revised correspondence course was published in the late 1930s, he was already informing disciples that God "can fully manifest through the body of your Guru (preceptor)" and directing them to include him in the pantheon of divine figures they evoked in prayer:

> O Spirit, Sri Krishna, Sri Christ, Saints of All Religions, Supreme Master Babaji, Great Master Lahiri Mahasaya, Master Swami Sriyukteswarji, *Guru-Preceptor Paramhansaji*, I bow to you all. Free my life from all obstacles and give me material, mental, and Spiritual development.[188]

FIVE

The Death of an Immortal Guru

Charisma, Succession, and Paramahansa Yogananda's Legacy, 1946–1952

By 1952, Brahmachari Jotin had enjoyed the longest relationship with Yogananda of any remaining disciple. One of three Self-Realization Fellowship leaders born in India, he had been an ashram student at Ranchi when Yogananda left for the United States in 1920. Summoned by Yogananda, he joined the American ministry in 1928. The other two Indian colleagues, Dhirananda and Nerode, had long ago left after acrimonious disputes with Yogananda about his authority and unwillingness to share ministry proceeds. Jotin served the Washington, D.C., center faithfully, enduring many hardships and ultimately earning Yogananda's admiring acknowledgment: "Jotin, what you have accomplished in Washington, I could not have done."[1] In 1941, during one of the many summers he spent with his guru at Encinitas, Jotin was ordained by Yogananda and took the title Swami Premananda.

Given the long, affectionate relationship the two shared, Yogananda's death on March 5, 1952, came as a heavy blow to Premananda. He wrote in the second person when recounting his final viewing of Yogananda's physical body, a reflection of his belief in his master's continued spiritual presence. "Immersed in etheric radiance your earthly form laid still—still as the summit of the Everest Mount beneath the star-lit heaven of midnight blue. Even in death your countenance was shining in a heavenly glow." Praying for one more encounter with his guru, he "placed my right hand upon your heart and motioned to my fellow sister disciples to do the same. . . . I felt your presence." Then a miracle occurred. "To assure us of your presence among us and the joyousness of your soul you shed tears. Tears of love and joy trickled down the corners of both of your closed eyes. The disciples stood transfixed observing this unbelievable occurrence." Premananda commanded those present not to share what they had witnessed. Shortly thereafter, he witnessed Yogananda's soul departing its body.[2]

The leaders present deliberated over what to do with their master's body, ultimately deciding for local burial. James Lynn asked Premananda to perform Yogananda's funeral, "the holy rite of liberation." This made Premananda "the last hand to touch your sacred body." As he touched Yogananda's shoulders, heart, and forehead, he chanted a *mantra*,

> By the touch of this fire, this body is purified,
> By the touch of this water, this body is returned to its immortal nature,
> By the touch of this sandalwood paste, this body is returned to God
> with devotion.

But however great the honor of conducting his master's funeral rites, the earlier bedside scene held greater significance. Premananda sensed that Yogananda had called him immediately after his *dehatyag*, or renunciation of the body, "that I may receive a small portion of your deathless life to my life. In your death you gave the affirmation of the transitory nature of the body and the immortality of the soul. What greater blessing can a disciple receive from his Gurudeva?"[3] Premananda interpreted the "small portion" of Yogananda's "deathless life" as a unique transfer of charisma from his guru that authorized him to minister with Yogananda's blessing, authority, and prestige.

Premananda would not be the only disciple to make this claim. In the wake of Yogananda's death, many disciples would make similar assertions, both those who remained within SRF and those, like Jotin, who went their separate ways. Whether they had enjoyed lengthy relationships with Yogananda or much shorter training periods, these personal disciples continued to feel equally close to the Master—and equally qualified to wear his spiritual mantle.

Who were the people who chose to follow this Indian guru? They were spiritual seekers who embraced not only Yogananda's instruction in Kriya Yoga but also his call for total surrender to his authority. They became members of a distinctive religious community and, in most cases, abandoned their prior religious commitments in order to follow Yogananda. Given America's continued Christian cultural ethos, discipleship often represented a significant sacrifice.

The first section of this chapter identifies common patterns among those who chose to follow Yogananda, by applying a model of conversion to the profiles of more than a dozen disciples. It concludes with an examination of disciples' experiences, particularly the ways they responded to the intense demands Yogananda placed on their spiritual apprenticeship amid a culture of permissive behavior and exalted individualism.

The circumstances surrounding Yogananda's death are considered in the second section. Yogananda had suffered from poor health for years, so those closest to him may have expected his death. But to most of the community, his passing was a shock—sixty-year-old Yogananda had taught for years about a yogi's ability to increase human longevity through overall health and the destruction of karmic seed, as described in *Yoga Sūtra* II.13—that needed to be explained theologically. This section also examines the way core disciples began to remember Yogananda and his teachings almost immediately after his departure.

The third section explores the crisis in leadership that Yogananda's death produced. Max Weber's model of the routinization of charisma and subsequent modifications offer insight into how SRF coped with the death of their charismatic leader. Yogananda, anticipating the leadership vacuum his death would create, had provided a partial solution by indicating that his writings were to become the "guru." Still, the sprawling international organization required a leader, and finding the right one proved difficult. After a brief period under Lynn's leadership, SRF enjoyed stability and growth through Daya Mata's decades-long presidency.

But this represents the response only within SRF itself. A number of disciples left SRF to form their own organizations, out of dissatisfaction with SRF's leadership or simply a desire to become independent spiritual leaders. The chapter concludes by exploring the organizations formed by a half-dozen different individuals who represented a range of positions on a spectrum—some very faithful to Yogananda and his teachings, others quite different—while all claiming direct authority from their former guru. Some of these organizations died quickly, but those that survived became part of the communal phenomenon of the baby boomer counterculture, thus providing a bridge between Yogananda and later New Age expressions of Hindu-inspired spirituality and yoga.

CONVERTING TO YOGANANDA'S RELIGIOUS VISION

Yogananda's ministry in the United States began in the Roaring Twenties, survived the cataclysms of the Great Depression and World War II, and continued into the dawn of the Cold War. During these three decades, he drew thousands of followers, who ranged widely in their level of commitment. Many individuals were only mildly curious, enrolling in the correspondence course and dropping out after a few lessons. After 1946, some read the *Autobiography* and felt inspired to live according to its insights, becoming followers in a loose sense.

More committed devotees persisted in the lessons until they reached the stage of Kriya Yoga initiation. In some cases, they relied entirely on the lessons as their form of instruction, but those fortunate enough to live near a local SRF center strengthened their faith by attending weekend services.

Those who embraced Yogananda completely often jettisoned their previous religious practices. Though he expressed religious tolerance rather than exclusivism, he also positioned his instruction, not as a supplemental meditative routine one might occasionally practice in an otherwise full life, but as an all-encompassing spiritual vision for life.

Self-Realization Fellowship advertised in newspapers' religion section, and local centers functioned more like churches than local yoga studios or YMCAs, instructing attendees in a range of theological, ethical, and cosmological doctrine. Yogananda went out of his way to emphasize SRF's churchlike features. Unlike Hindu ritual, which was mostly home and family based, Yogananda instituted a strong culture of weekly worship. Services took place on Sunday mornings and featured Scripture-based sermons, singing, and Sunday school classes. Some centers were explicitly named churches, like the Hollywood center, which was dedicated as the Self-Realization Church of All Religions.[4] Christmas and Easter were the most important services of the year, and Yogananda always printed special season-themed talks about the birth of the Christ Child and the Resurrection in his magazine. In his inclusivist vision, Yogananda seems to have seen SRF as a replacement for traditional Christian churches, whose outmoded focus on doctrinal details left them spiritually dead.

Even if that was not Yogananda's intention, in practical terms deep involvement in SRF precluded commitment to another church. Thus, it is instructive to view followers' embrace of Yogananda as a form of conversion. This conversion could incur higher social costs than membership in a more conventional religion, as a Hindu-based movement fell well outside the mainstream of American tradition. As Andrea Jain says in a related context, a "global market for spiritual goods required marketers to calculate the costs for products associated with unpopular ideas or practices."[5] Disciples committed to more than a set of cosmological tenets or spiritual practices. Devotion to Yogananda required deep dedication, as he made extravagant claims about his personal identity and expected exceptional personal loyalty.

Remaining in the religious tradition in which one is raised—or one's lack of tradition, in the rare case of an SRF follower who came from a spiritually uninvolved background—is the default option, and "most people" exposed to a new religion, Lewis R. Rambo points out, "say no to conversion."[6]

To understand Yogananda's ministry, therefore, it is crucial to determine what drew people to him and his teachings. A number of disciples from the earliest days through the late period of his ministry left recollections of their relationship with their guru. Nearly twenty such accounts are considered in this chapter. This does not include the stories of conversions that have already been described, such as Minott and Mildred Lewis and James Lynn. Nor does the chapter explore the biographies of Yogananda's Indian friends Dhirananda and Nerode, who are best understood not as disciples but as colleagues. The accounts explored here include written spiritual biographies and autobiographies, both formally and personally published, and recorded oral recollections. Self-Realization Fellowship sponsored some, others were produced by SRF members independently of the organization, and still others were produced completely independently—without SRF's blessing or approbation. Most were written decades after the events they record; some are hagiographic, others self-serving. Those who took the effort to provide accounts of their experiences with Yogananda were often the most fervent disciples, and this passionate perspective should be kept in mind. Despite these accounts' limitations, together they constitute a group profile of the type of spiritual seeker drawn to Yogananda. Though varying in length of time with the master, gender, or previous station of life, together they attest to his captivating presence, deep wisdom, miraculous power, and spiritual authority. This magnetic guru invited them to swear total devotion, and they obeyed him in matters great and small, submitting to tasks that were a joy to carry out as well as demands that they found hard to accept.

Based on an adaptation of religious sociologists Lewis R. Rambo and Charles E. Farhadian's model of conversion, this chapter traces the typical path of Yogananda's disciples in three stages:[7]

- The first stage includes the *backgrounds* of disciples and the *crisis* that frequently led to their spiritual *quest*.
- The next analyses the disciples' first *encounter* with Yogananda, often a transcendent experience that became the moment of conversion, ending their quest and launching them on the path of discipleship.
- The final stage explores the *relationship* the disciples had with their guru, a relationship marked by deep intimacy, profound spiritual experiences, and even some playfulness. But discipleship fundamentally demanded "attunement," total subjection to Yogananda as a father figure and to his sometimes ruthless "scolding." These disciples recognized both at the time and much later that such rebuke

was unpleasant and often ran counter to their own perceptions about appropriate behavior. Their willingness to submit to such treatment nevertheless testifies powerfully to the trust they accorded their guru and his ability to transform their character.

Scholars of conversion suggest that a crisis—religious, political, psychological, or cultural—often catalyzes a spiritual quest. Although Rambo and Farhadian present crisis and quest as two separate stages, the two cannot be easily separated. These two stages typically happen simultaneously, and seekers' perception of crisis is often retrospective—that is, people do not recognize themselves to have been in crisis until they begin or even complete their quest. Common crises include illness, a "growing sense of dissatisfaction with life as it is," and a restless desire for transcendence.[8]

The seekers whose quest eventually led them to Yogananda fit this pattern. Many experienced at least one substantial hardship early in their lives that could reasonably be seen as a crisis. Several, for example, suffered from a severe childhood illness. Mary Buchanan was ravaged by scarlet fever as a child, and Edith Anne Ruth D'Evelyn suffered a number of serious physical ailments throughout her childhood.[9] These physical maladies often contributed to feelings of emotional distress. Faye Wright, a shy, earnest sixteen-year old the year she met Yogananda, suffered from a disease that caused "blood poisoning," which left her face bandaged and her self-esteem battered.[10] Roy Eugene Davis grew up in the 1930s on an Ohio farm, where he was diagnosed with rheumatoid arthritis as a teen. He was bed-bound for five long, lonely months.[11]

Others suffered the loss of a parent, which created both financial and emotional strain. John Laurence, for example, came of age on a Wyoming Indian reservation, the son of a U.S. Army Medical Corps father and a devoutly Catholic mother. Following his mother's prodding, Laurence went to seminary to prepare for the priesthood. But his father's sudden death in the Great Depression created family havoc and forced a career change.[12] Mary Peck suffered the loss of her father in a different way. An often-absent navy man, he was a raging alcoholic who routinely threatened to kill his family when he was at home.[13]

Several later disciples experienced both a serious illness *and* the loss of a parent, often in quick succession. Florina Darling was born sickly after an outbreak of diphtheria among her family claimed her sixteen-year-old sister's life. Her father left to find a job in Detroit, so she grew up functionally fatherless.[14] D'Evelyn also lost her father when she was young, and her family remained poor after her mother remarried and moved to Minnesota.[15] After Davis recovered from rheumatoid arthritis, his mother died and he became the meal preparer for his father and younger sister.[16]

A few suffered various less severe hardships. Buchanan's parents separated when she was twelve, and she grew up with her mother in an era before divorce was widespread.[17] Mildred Hamilton, a bright girl and good student, had to leave school in eighth grade to help her family survive financially.[18] Like those who suffered harsher adversities, these milder experiences created a sense of restlessness, a search for meaning, and often a hope of healing that eventually led them to Yogananda.

Finding Yogananda was often the end of a spiritual quest that had begun long before. Many of his closest disciples were from Catholic or liberal Protestant families, representing the nation's majority religious tradition. But a disproportionate number relative to their extremely small populations came from such nonmainstream religious traditions as Mormonism, Christian Science, and Theosophy. Many converts were, like Americans who embraced Buddhism around this time, "intellectual nonconformists or cultural dissenters" disillusioned with mainstream Christianity but still drawn to spirituality. But Yogananda's devotees were much less likely to be coastal or urban than Buddhist converts—and much more likely to be female.[19] Yogananda's American followers also parallel the Indians drawn to divine gurus in the past half-century: uprooted individuals, often urban dwellers, disillusioned by modern materialism and longing for reenchantment.[20]

Several later devotees had already developed an interest in Indian spirituality that served as a stepping-stone toward Yogananda's particular brand of Hinduism. Some ventured out from deeply religious nonmainstream spiritual traditions to seek Hindu wisdom. Faye Wright and her sister Virginia descended from the first Mormon families that had settled in Utah in the 1840s. Restless with Mormonism, Faye spent her teen years as a deep seeker after spiritual truth. She had been reading the *Bhagavad Gītā* for at least two years when she heard Yogananda speak.[21] Leo Cocks grew up in San Jose in the 1930s, part of a family that practiced Vedānta.[22] During his convalescence, Davis read extensively about psychology and religion, feeling drawn especially to the Transcendentalists and Indian texts.[23] Donald Walters eagerly consumed books about India—the Upaniṣads, the *Bhagavad Gītā*, the *Mahābhārata*, texts on yoga—before he learned about Yogananda through the *Autobiography*.[24]

By contrast, a few found Hinduism from backgrounds that epitomized American establishment Christianity. D'Evelyn married Clark Prescott Bissett, an Episcopal divinity student who left the clergy for law and, eventually, university teaching. A woman with deep spiritual curiosity, D'Evelyn read Indian texts as a young woman and had the opportunity to meet the poet Rabindranath Tagore when he visited the West Coast. Encountering her "first definite teaching of Hindu truth in 1909," she reflected, "I will never be the same again."[25]

For some, the journey was literal as well as metaphorical. As a young teen, Swiss-born Henry Schaufelberger spent a summer in the mid-1930s with his uncle, who delivered discourses to him on "karma, reincarnation, the astral and causal planes, and particularly on saints." Schaufelberger pressed his uncle on how to achieve bliss, but his uncle could provide no clear direction. "He said that one has to have a guru who could teach everything. When I expressed my great desire to meet one, he just shook his head and smiled. 'My poor boy, there are no gurus in Switzerland!'"[26] When he moved from Switzerland to the United States in 1948 to study architecture under Frank Lloyd Wright, Schaufelberger made a point of tracking Yogananda down at the Hollywood temple.

What transpired when converts first encountered their future guru? Like most Americans, they were struck first by his appearance. In 1931, when Mary Peck was seven years old, she and her mother met Yogananda in San Diego. Young Mary was intrigued by his robe, his brown skin, and his long, dark, wavy hair that he brushed back "with a graceful sweep of his hand."[27] But this first glimpse was no mere novelty. It was an epiphany. Faye Wright thought he glowed in a golden light, dressed in his ocher robe.[28] Most were struck by Yogananda's face and particularly his eyes, which offered a window into his soul. Schaufelberger was transfixed when he "looked into those deep luminous tender eyes" for the first time.[29] At her first encounter with Yogananda, "those brown eyes" mesmerized Corinne Forshee. Photos, she thought, never adequately captured his most perfect face.[30] When Darling saw him in Detroit in December 1927, she was "riveted to the beautiful face," her soul "sensing the God-like soul within the outward form." He was the "most beautiful man I had ever seen, in his orange robe and long black flowing hair on his shoulders, and his large lotus, dark, expressive eyes."[31] Yogananda's physical appearance provided these devotees, men and women, with their first transcendent experience of their Master, which they could describe only in the intimate language of grace, beauty, and attraction.

When they met Yogananda or first heard him speak, future disciples frequently experienced an immediate emotional bond. This phenomenon typically included intense physical symptoms that signaled a transcendent encounter. Meeting Yogananda after a Sunday service, Henry Schaufelberger became spiritually intoxicated. "The moment he touched me, I was drunk, and completely drunk. No that was the real stuff. That was the stuff of the mystics." Leaving the service, he was unable to contain his "unbelievable bliss." He staggered down the street, laughing out loud.[32] The moment Faye Wright heard Yogananda speak, she knew that her spiritual search had ended. All the religious speakers she had heard before faded into insignificance. "He knows God," she thought for the first time about any person, instantly transported into a higher state of consciousness. When she approached Yogananda a few days later, asking to join his ashram, and he replied, "and you shall," a "bolt of lightning" went through her.[33]

This description was not unique. In recounting the moment of transcendent encounter with Yogananda, disciples often evoked the language of power or electricity he often used in his teachings. An "electric wave" went into Darling's arm and through her body when she took Yogananda's hand.[34] Hamilton recalled the "electric shock" she felt when she first looked into his eyes, which followed her from "stem to stern." After that, she belonged to him completely.[35] The first time Cocks met Yogananda, he knew nothing about him. As Yogananda began teaching before a meditation session, Cocks felt profoundly empowered. "It was just like everything opened up! I became my heart, my chest opened up, my heart had wings and I flew up out of my body about eight or ten feet. I could see him, and I instantly just felt, 'Oh, He is my guru! He is my guru!'"[36]

Those whose quest had been launched by their physical suffering often found wholeness in Yogananda's presence. Disciples routinely testified to his ability to heal. This included the physical healing Minott Lewis and his children had experienced and the emotional restoration a world-weary James Lynn had found. Faye Wright's younger brother was delivered from fainting spells. And she was healed of her "blood poisoning" illness within a week of being touched by Yogananda during a class on divine healing. Her illness never returned.[37]

Even when he did not relieve the physical symptoms, Yogananda's detailed explanation of the intricacies of *karma* provided a coherent meaning to suffering. At times, however, understanding the karmic mechanics of suffering proved inadequate. Edith Bissett continued to experience an agony so severe and unrelenting that on at least one occasion she conveyed to Yogananda her wish to die. In response, he encouraged her to view her suffering as a test from God. "You are an example to all; so do not be overpowered by suffering or have self-pity, but smile away all your troubles." She lived for another eight years after this letter, finally dying in 1951. At her memorial service, Yogananda addressed head on the philosophical challenge her unremitting anguish caused.

He explained that Bissett assumed the karmic burden of others and suffered "because of the sins of many others who became saintly through her life. There was not a sin of her own I could find. Such is the mystery of God."[38] Though Bissett was denied physical relief, SRF community members may have found emotional comfort in learning that this kind woman suffered for a reason.

The wisdom of a teacher who understood the great mysteries of life, however difficult to accept, proved irresistible. Those who knew Yogananda personally uniformly attested to his charisma. Max Weber's classic definition is tailor-made for Yogananda: "The charismatic leader may be seen as having special access to the divine realm or special abilities of healing, prophecy. . . . The leader . . . embodies the virtues and powers that are articulated by the religious ideology, or has accomplished particular feats, or has extraordinary powers of discernment and persuasion."[39] Yogananda's charisma was not some serendipitous attribute but a sense of presence he cultivated, a capacity to "elicit from a following deference, devotion and awe toward himself as the source of authority."[40]

Understanding Yogananda's charismatic authority requires moving beyond the demand side of the conversion equation, the motivations of potential converts, to consider the supply side. Yogananda diverged dramatically from conventional Hindu instructors, who rarely sought out disciples, though they often received would-be followers who came unbidden. He did not simply wait passively for disciples to come to him, but like Jesus summoning the apostles, he pursued them actively. In his relentless touring, advertising, publishing, and commodifying of goods, Yogananda was much more like a typical evangelist who "assesses the potential target audience and formulates persuasive tactics to bring converts into the religious community."[41] Yogananda effectively deployed standard evangelistic strategies that emphasized the cognitive, affective, and volitional benefits of his movements, as well as his charismatic leadership.[42]

His charismatic persuasiveness overcame the reluctance of several individuals who chose to follow him despite themselves, making their eventual surrender all the more dramatic. The exoticism of a Hindu movement intrigued many who found Christian traditions unsatisfying, but the deeply unfamiliar elements of his teaching could still be a hurdle. San Diego resident Merna Brown described herself as "very orthodox in the church she was raised in." So when her mother, sister, and sister's friend became interested in Yogananda and began attending the local temple, she remained suspicious and refused to attend. Her mother eventually persuaded Merna to come, encouraging her to bring her Bible with her since Yogananda often taught from it. When Merna attended the first time, she carried her Bible to ward off Yogananda's charm. In the event, her talisman proved ineffective and she yielded to Yogananda.[43]

Although conversion models often privilege individual experience, the influential role of Merna's mother and sister highlight the importance of social networks of family and friends, particularly in the case of reluctant converts. For example, when Edith Bissett first heard about Yogananda in 1925, she was hesitant to attend a talk, fearing that any interest in "the teachings of a long-haired Hindu" would jeopardize her husband's university position. So she first came in contact with Yogananda's teachings through her adult son before she finally met him at her home in July 1925 and discovered that the "Hindu swami in the ochre robe of renunciation" incarnated "the answer to all my prayers and longing."[44] Faye Wright's parents were initially resistant to her interest in a "foreign faith," but after she won them over, her mother and three siblings converted—her sister Virginia and brother Richard both became important leaders in the organization.[45]

Some first encountered their guru not face to face but through his *Autobiography*, a testament to his ability to embody charismatic authority in his spiritual masterpiece. The resulting conversions were as immediate and profound as those who first met Yogananda in person. "*Autobiography of a Yogi* is the greatest book I have ever read," Walters concluded simply in his own spiritual autobiography. "One perusal of it was enough to change my entire life. From that time on my break with the past was complete. I resolved in the smallest detail of my life to follow Paramahansa Yogananda's teaching."[46] Converts often felt a personal devotion to a teacher they had never met. Davis came across an advertisement for *Autobiography of a Yogi* in a health magazine and ordered the book by mail. Reading it multiple times, "I knew that Paramahansa Yogananda was my guru."[47] Some were convinced that divine providence placed the *Autobiography* in their hands to bring them to the Master. Peggy Dietz, a Pasadena native who had had metaphysical experiences from childhood, was praying one day as she crumpled up a piece of paper. Something prompted her to unroll the wad, which turned out to be an advertisement for the *Autobiography*. She promptly got a copy and began reading it. Her reading was interrupted by a call from a friend inviting her to hear a talk: "The speaker's name is something like Param . . . Paramhansa Yogananda."[48] Santa Barbara native Norman Paulsen did not even need to read the *Autobiography* to convert. Working at a job site, he saw the book's cover and recognized the man with long hair and large, dark eyes who had haunted him for years. He asked the owner of the house who the person was. Informed that Yogananda lived a few miles away, Paulsen immediately dropped his work and departed for Mount Washington.[49]

The spiritual journey that led these seekers to the *Autobiography* often became a literal journey as well. Many physically traveled to SRF headquarters, to Encinitas, or to one of the centers in what functioned as a pilgrimage experience, the geographical journey a manifestation of the internal one. Given that SRF sites were imbued with a sense of sacredness—especially Mount Washington and Encinitas—approaching the guru's abode could be a powerful part of the experience. And like traditional pilgrimage, the greater the distance or the difficulty of the ordeal, the more heightened the sense of arrival.

Donald Walters's pilgrimage illustrates this pattern, though Roy Eugene Davis and Norman Paulsen had remarkably similar experiences. When Walters finished the *Autobiography*, he immediately decided to travel to Los Angeles to follow in person the one who had already become his guru on the page. He left a note for his godfather, "I'm going to California to join a group of people who, I believe, can teach me what I want to know about God and about religion." Then he boarded a bus for California. When Walters arrived in Encinitas, he discovered that Yogananda was not there. He would be preaching at the Hollywood temple that Sunday, but unfortunately there was a two-and-a-half-month waiting period before Yogananda would be available to meet with him. Fighting despair, Walters determined to remain hopeful as he went to the Hollywood service. Having been informed of Walters's request, Yogananda arranged to meet with him after service. His first encounter with Yogananda echoed the intimate language of those struck by Yogananda's grace and beauty. "What large, lustrous eyes now greeted me! What a compassionate smile! Never before had I seen such divine beauty in a human face." Yogananda seemed reluctant to take Walters in, as he was accepting fewer disciples at the time. At last he relented, "All right. You have good karma. You may join us." Then came the call to total devotion Yogananda had routinely made for more than a quarter century, since he first asked Minott Lewis to always love him. "Will you do as I ask?" he asked Walters. When Walters was bold enough to ask if he had to obey even when he disagreed with Yogananda, Yogananda replied, "I will never ask anything of you, that God does not tell me to ask."[50] And that settled the matter.

After their quest had led them to an encounter with Yogananda, what was the nature of the relationship they shared with their guru? As Rambo indicates, a religious community envelops new converts in relationships that consolidate emotional bonds, rituals that integrate them into their new way of life, rhetoric that provides guidance and meaning, and roles that give converts a meaningful mission.[51] Those who chose to follow Yogananda as monastics entered into a relationship with him as well as the few dozen other members of the Mount Washington community. Daily meditation practices created a rhythm and reinforced the sense of community. Personal instruction from Yogananda—both formal and ad hoc—provided the organization's core rhetoric. And as both a ministry and a functioning community, every individual had an identifiable role that contributed to the larger sense of mission they shared with their guru—from shopping and preparing food to producing publications to providing for their master's needs. Yogananda was the community's center of gravity, the reason the community existed. Disciples drew inspiration from simply observing Yogananda wandering the grounds and were blessed by being in their guru's presence, as promised in *Yoga Sūtra* II.35.

For many, his supernatural powers authenticated his ministry, authorizing him to take extreme measures. He performed a number of miracles that restored physical health and demonstrated control over the natural world—many strikingly similar to those reported of Jesus in the Gospels. On his trip to India in 1935–36, he raised a sinking steamship at the mouth of the Ganges, then healed the constriction in the throat of the vessel's captain that had prevented him from shouting a warning. At Mount Washington, he caused a freak windstorm to cease suddenly, and at Encinitas he drove away rain so that a monk could take a sunny drive with him. Rather than wine, he multiplied a small amount of freshly squeezed carrot juice to fill the cups of all present. He prevented major car accidents that would have killed Minott Lewis and, years later, Norman Paulsen and Leo Cocks. He rescued a hitchhiking monk from peril. Monks working on construction projects at various SRF sites were saved from serious bodily injury by Yogananda's intervention. In one case, he even restored to life a woman thought to be dead.[52]

But life with Yogananda was not all numinous experiences. As members of the community, monastics had the opportunity to see Yogananda's playful, almost childlike side. Though such behavior can be viewed as a temporary pressure valve for the challenges of an ascetic lifestyle, devotees understood the Master's childlike playfulness through the lens of *līlā*. Often translated as "sport" or "play," *līlā* is an expansive concept that often refers to the spontaneity of divine behavior. The deity's freedom to create or destroy can seem capricious, but it may also suggest a joyful lightheartedness—an example devotees should adopt.[53] Yogananda often exhibited such bliss-filled playfulness.[54] He had a healthy appetite for recreation. The leader who often used motion pictures as a metaphor for the spiritual life enjoyed going to the movies for recreation. He was particularly fond of westerns, horror films, and war films. Disciples frequently witnessed him fall asleep watching them, though perhaps he was meditating as he claimed. Though he never learned how to drive, he enjoyed being taken out for an evening drive, on picnics, and especially for visits to the beach. He loved to "treat his large family" by buying a box of Eskimo pies and passing them around.

Yogananda also had a lively, mischievous sense of humor. He loved to tell jokes and play pranks on the devotees. In the darkened movie theater, he would poke people with his cane and then feign innocence or place pieces of bunched-up tissue on the heads of those sitting in front of him. He would call to disciples from his upstairs window and pour a pan of water on them as they stood below. Once he used a water gun to shoot water onto the ceiling above James Lynn when he was not paying attention. Lynn was surprised and puzzled when the water dripped onto his bald head. In retelling this prank to another disciple, Yogananda "started laughing so hard that I could scarcely understand his words."[55]

The rhythms of life in community—the sublime, the humorous, the quotidian—birthed a surrogate family. In committing to Yogananda and his fellowship, disciples had forsaken family and marriage. They had a deep desire, even a need, for his approval and acceptance. Though Edith Bissett was a generation older than Yogananda, the majority of the monastics were single women, who sometimes related to Yogananda as a sort of surrogate spouse. Despite a number of accusations over the years, there is no credible evidence of sexual impropriety in Yogananda's relationships with these women. But they undoubtedly shared a level of physical intimacy that would have been unacceptable in the outside world. Florina Darling recounted, with pride rather than embarrassment, how she sat patiently for nearly two hours while Yogananda plucked her gray hair out.[56] Such physical interactions were routine, as devotees regularly touched their guru's feet in a sign of deference while he touched their head or body to impart a blessing. Disciples eagerly sought opportunities for one-on-one encounters with Yogananda, where they would lay their souls bare, sharing their most personal thoughts and submitting to his guidance.

More often, however, Yogananda's relationship with his disciples was less spousal than parental, replicating a pattern rooted in Hindu tradition.[57] Disciples openly embraced this relational pattern. Henry Schaufelberger was pleased when Yogananda referred to the male monastics as "my little boys" and vowed to himself that "to my last day, I am one of Master's little boys." Richard Wright, who was his close daily companion throughout the entire 1935–36 overseas journey, referred to him as "Holy Dad."[58] As a father figure, Yogananda was often duty-bound to discipline his children for their own good. Once, when resisting one of Yogananda's many "scoldings," Darling protested, "After all, Sir, I am a grown woman." "His face became crestfallen and he answered,

'I wish you hadn't said that, because I never see you all as grown women but as children of God.'"[59] The editor of Leo Cocks's memoir reflects this paternal outlook in a comment on Cocks's need for discipline, "Leo was utterly devoted to his guru and like a parent who must guide a willful child so it will grow and fulfill its destiny, Yogananda guided Leo with love and discipline."[60]

Yogananda was an authoritarian father, determining his spiritual children's life choices, from the consequential to the mundane. One young devotee shared with Yogananda her plans to enroll in art school. He immediately rejected the idea. Knowing all of her previous lives, he discerned that this career path would not be a good fit for her. She surrendered to his guidance. "He was everything to us," she reflected later after many years as an SRF monastic.[61] Yogananda's veto power ranged from career choices to personal appearance. His decisions often seemed capricious. Male disciples, for example, had to receive express approval to grow facial hair. Yogananda refused to allow Cocks to grow a beard with the terse reply, "Not you, Leo. You'd look like a baboon!"[62] But he actively encouraged Walters to grow one—which greatly surprised Walters, since Yogananda had often warned, "I don't want my boys looking like wild men!"[63] Disciples interpreted his apparent caprice as serving an undisclosed purpose. Facial hair was neither right nor wrong per se; the question was whether it was tailored to a particular disciple's unique spiritual development. For Cocks, Yogananda's insult was an "opportunity to deflate my ego."[64]

As their spiritual father, Yogananda also determined their devotional activities. Yogananda made Cocks, who had grown up in the Vedanta movement, take down a shrine to Ramakrishna and Vivekananda that he had placed alongside a shrine to the SRF masters. This is especially surprising in light of Yogananda's respect for both swamis. Davis was likewise instructed to read only SRF materials, an admonition he ignored to his own detriment. On a whim in a Scottsdale bookstore he bought a spiritual book, probably *Gospel of Ramakrishna,* the collection of Ramakrishna sayings Yogananda had carried around as an adolescent. A fellow disciple reported Davis's misconduct. The following day, Yogananda was gathered with a group of disciples when Davis walked into the room. Davis was greeted by his guru's announcement, "Roy is a spiritual prostitute." Yogananda went on to explain that in a couple of years Davis might be ready for reading from other spiritual masters, when his spiritual discernment was more developed.[65] Devotion to other Hindu masters, which Yogananda regularly endorsed in *East-West,* might seem innocuous. But it could hamper the spiritual development of those committed to the Kriya Yoga path. It was Yogananda's responsibility to provide training that remained firmly within the *paramparā,* or lineage, that ran from Babaji through Yukteswar to himself.

Yogananda reserved his harshest scolding for disciples who failed to display utter subjection to him. Faye Wright experienced several rebukes that left a deep impression on her. Her spiritual father once fashioned a dunce cap and commanded her to put it on in front of the other disciples. She refused, and a battle of wills ensued. Eventually, when everyone had left the room, he called her back to talk. The shy young woman asked him, "Is it really right to make fun, to tease me in front of everyone?" Ignoring her query, he commanded her to stand in a corner with his back to her, where she promptly burst into tears. She turned to him, confessed her gratitude for his discipline, and begged him to put the cap on her. After her submission to his authority, he relented from placing the cap on her.[66] One scholar's evaluation of the Vedanta movement also aptly describes SRF: "Probably few other American religious (or political) movements of the past century have been based so largely upon the notion of willing, steadfast obedience to another person."[67]

Obedience under such conditions could exact a heavy toll, which disciples often described as experiences of dismemberment. These events mirror "degradation ceremonies" in conversion theory, where insulting disciples is a common strategy "designed to break a person down so that the spirit is more malleable by the new group, and/or to break old patterns of behavior considered destructive or counterproductive to the person."[68] Merna Brown bluntly reflected, "You have no idea how difficult sometimes it was to be in that exacting personality, in the presence of that exacting personality. Could you be taken apart, literally, in front of your peers, and still feel not sensitive, but take it with the right attitude, not be critical of the Guru?"[69] Leo Cocks experienced unbearable distress at being subjected to "harsh words like a scalpel, cutting sharply through the layers of my consciousness. . . . Master went on and on. It was so painful that I couldn't take it any more."[70] Apart from the severity of punishment, its arbitrariness was also puzzling. Yogananda yelled at Brown once because she forgot to deliver a phone message; but she experienced his full wrath only when she tried to justify her lapse in memory. "Very often, what we might be scolded or disciplined for was totally insignificant and that's why it was difficult to understand at the moment. But there was an aspect of his training . . . he never explained. He never explained, we never asked."[71]

Convinced that Yogananda's harshness always served a beneficial purpose, disciples became skilled interpreters of his mercurial behavior. He often dismissed them curtly, "Go! Leave my room!"[72] Peremptorily cast from his presence, they went off to meditate until they could discover the secret lesson he doubtless wanted them to learn. This could be confounding when they perceived nothing culpable in their conduct. But Yogananda's self-realized perfection was a basic tenet that trumped their own perceptions. His faultlessness left their error as the only logical conclusion for his anger. "Sometimes it was difficult to understand why we were being scolded or disciplined in a certain way, but I never questioned why or the reason behind it, or that it was right. That, that would never have occurred. The only question was, What did I do? [She laughs] What did I do wrong? Or how do I need to correct myself?" She would go back, kneel at his feet, and put her head on his feet. He would respond graciously, "More sweet than nearest dearest family or friends."[73]

He frequently apologized for his scolding afterward, but disciples understood these apologies the same way Yogananda undoubtedly intended them: as marks of tenderness and humility, rather than admissions of error. Some found proof of Yogananda's benevolent intentions not in his words or any overt behavior but in subtle body language indicators. "Even though he scolded us and showed great anger or anxiety," Darling reflected that if disciples looked directly into his eyes, they could detect "a little glimmer of a smile in the corner of his eyes . . . he couldn't help but smile, because he never had anger inside. It was just a play to be able to correct us, or to teach us a lesson."[74] Employing a complex interpretive strategy, disciples acknowledged Yogananda's manifest wrath but refused to view it as an indication of his interior state.

A few authors address the issue of Yogananda's authority and how difficult it could be for disciples to face. Polly Trout goes out of her way to downplay the severity of his discipline, asserting that "the guru could never hurt or fail the disciple and that apparent failures were misunderstandings on the part of the disciple." She concludes that "no great harm was done by suspending critical reasoning in this manner, for he was generally a kindhearted man."[75] Philip Goldberg suggests that while the attraction of a "genuine holy man" can be "fatal when the magnet is unscrupulous or exploitative," "Yogananda seems to have had little of that dark side." Goldberg acknowledges, however, that the "severity" of Yogananda's leadership was "too demanding for most."[76]

Some disciples found the demands of Yogananda's leadership overwhelming and decided to leave. Cocks ultimately departed because he found Yogananda's severe treatment detrimental. Yogananda acknowledged the harshness of his discipline but assured Cocks of its redemptive purpose. "I have through God saved lives not destroyed them," he explained. "I did not come on earth to do destructive work—you have misunderstood my words and me. Every saint is made of thunder and flower. But in regard to principles, one must be stern."[77] Knowing the benefits of his tutelage, Yogananda viewed the temptation to leave as a sign of spiritual weakness and rarely made it easy for disciples to depart. When a monk named Daniel Boone decided to leave because he found monastic life too difficult, Yogananda summoned him to his room and tried all night to persuade Boone to stay. Boone agreed to try for two more weeks, but at the end of the period he still left.[78] When Cocks wrote that he was tempted to leave, Yogananda told him that Satan was tempting him. Cocks eventually left, regretted his decision, and begged to come back.[79] Paulsen also became restless, in part because of Yogananda's authority. "I seemed to feel strange within whenever I called him Master. To me he was a God-realized elder brother of the highest caliber. . . . The word 'master' seemed to create a barrier for some, making him seem almost unapproachable." Paulsen made the difficult decision to leave in November 1951, along with a few other male disciples.[80] Although Yogananda entreated disciples to stay for their own good, he viewed their departures as a personal affront, interpreting defection as a form of divine testing.[81] He deeply valued loyalty and unswerving commitment. As his dear childhood friend Satyananda recollected later in life, though "he had a loving, affectionate and motherly heart for the people around him, by nature he could not rely on or trust them."[82] Identifying himself as Jesus, Yogananda frequently referred to anyone who betrayed him as "Judas."[83]

There was a gender dimension to contests of power between Yogananda and his disciples. Male arrivals to SRF ashrams in the late 1940s were struck by the preponderance of female devotees, and those who were closest to Yogananda tended to be women. This cannot be explained by an assumption that Yogananda held egalitarian gender views. He characterized gender in dualistic ways: men represented God while women represented Nature; men were rational while women were emotional; sexual temptation resulted from arousal of "the negative feminine instinct of feeling."[84] And some of the choicest SRF properties, such as the Lake Shrine and the ashram in Twenty-Nine Palms, whose "natural surroundings . . . lend themselves admirably to the meditative state," were exclusively available to male monastics.[85] Though nonmainstream religious movements often have high female-to-male ratios, in SRF's case this initial recruitment imbalance was exacerbated by the greater endurance of women in the movement relative to men. In a period before second wave feminism made gender equality a cultural norm, submission to a male authority figure would have been much less challenging for many women, who had often experienced such relationships already. Those who gave up on Yogananda's authority and left the community in the final years of his life were all men. Disciples who stayed, male or female, had learned, in SRF parlance, "attunement" with the Master. They were in harmony with him, which meant that they had surrendered fully to him.[86]

Even disciples who reconciled themselves to Yogananda's purging never found the process easy. They learned to view this routine humiliation not as emotional abuse but as an indispensable step toward their spiritual liberation. Purging the ego was painful, as Cocks discovered when he asked to grow a beard, but it was necessary. When Walters was subjected to the "undeserved humiliation" of a Yogananda "tirade," he eventually concluded that he needed more criticism, not less. "Sir, please scold me more often," he begged.[87] And it was in a tone of great affection that Wright bluntly reflected, "He freely picked me apart in front of others."[88] Those who successfully established an "inner process of commitment," bravely surrendering and enduring harsh treatment, found themselves cleansed of many spiritual impurities.[89]

In abandoning their individual autonomy, disciples believed that, paradoxically, they had found their true selves. Social psychologists who have studied high-demand religious groups find those who pay a higher price for membership value it more highly. They conclude that the harshness of initiation intensifies members' commitment to the organization.[90] Similarly, market theories of religion emphasize rational choices involving the reward for participation. Choosing a nonmainstream religion involved high social costs, from the judging looks of passersby who found it odd to see Yogananda meditate by the side of the road, to family members who worried about the psychological and physical well-being of converts. Walters had a skeptical friend who was disturbed by the authority Yogananda asserted over their lives. "This is a free country!" the friend pronounced. "Americans aren't slaves. And anyway, no one has a right to be the master of another human being." Walters replied that Yogananda's followers had handed him not their freedom but their bondage. "He is a true master of the practices in which we ourselves are struggling to excel. You might say that he is our teacher in the art of achieving true freedom."[91] In the face of outside judgments, SRF disciples continued to insist on the value of their choice.

Disciples' willingness to commit freely to Yogananda stemmed from their conviction that he provided spiritual goods no one else could. In religion as in the marketplace, value is often measured by access to a product that offers immediate, tangible, powerful rewards—limited access to such a good makes it all the more precious.[92] Yogananda knew his disciples perfectly—even better than they knew themselves—and what he did was always for their personal growth, whether they recognized it or not. Henry Schaufelberger believed that even in their first conversation together, Yogananda "knew me better than I did." This attested to Yogananda's supernatural abilities, because "if somebody knows you completely, no ordinary human being can do that." Despite Yogananda's awareness of Schaufelberger's mistakes, he was not judgmental but understanding, displaying "unconditional love."[93] Other disciples confirmed Yogananda's telepathy, a *siddhi* described by Patanjali in *Yoga Sūtra* III.19. Mrinalini Mata said simply, "He knew everything I was thinking," and Cocks recalled Yogananda telling him, "I know everything you think and say."[94]

A Master who had foreknowledge, knowledge of disciples' previous incarnations, ability to read his disciples' thoughts, moral infallibility, and the ability to heal and perform miracles was no mere human teacher. Like many gurus, Yogananda had long claimed divine attributes. As scholar Orianne Aymard explains, in Hinduism "the guru is the radiating mask that God takes to come to us."[95] But Yogananda hesitated to claim divinity outright, perhaps because Christian ideas of utter transcendence made such a claim seem more audacious in an American context, while Hinduism often accepted more porousness between human and divine identities. But in the late 1940s, he began revealing his true status, though only privately to individual disciples and even then with great reticence. He told Darling that in a previous incarnation he had been Arjuna, the warrior hero born of the god Indra and recipient of the great god Krishna's revelation contained in the *Bhagavad Gītā*.[96] Other disciples believed that he had been Jesus in a previous incarnation. Asked about this, Yogananda replied that it was a matter of indifference. But he did not deny the identification.[97] Given his routine hints throughout his major texts, this must be seen as an indication of humility rather than an admission of uncertainty. In discovering that he was an incarnation of Christ, he was only following the lead of Ramakrishna, who had had a similar realization decades earlier.[98]

At one point, Walters asked him point blank, "Sir, are you an avatar?" or incarnation of a deity, a reasonable question to ask of a guru.[99] Yogananda answered humbly but clearly, "A work of this importance would have to be started by such a one." He answered Cocks's query in almost identical fashion. "Whenever a teaching of this magnitude is brought, God always sends it with an avatar."[100] One devotee challenged him to acknowledge his divinity less obliquely. "But if you have no ego left, that means you are God!" Again, Yogananda's answer was humble but clear: "The Scriptures say, "he who knows Brahma becomes Brahma."[101] His divinity explained both his extraordinary powers and the appropriateness of unquestioning devotion.[102]

It is difficult to know how far beyond the inner circle of monastics the intense pattern of discipleship to Yogananda—and the acceptance of his exalted status—extended. As a recent movement, all of its committed members were converts, including thousands of faithful SRF lay members. Intense devotion may have been widespread, since as sociologist Eileen Barker argues, "Converts, having decided to accept a new faith . . . rather than continuing in the one into which they were born and/or which is the norm in their society or subculture, tend to be considerably more enthusiastic about their new beliefs and practices than those brought up in their religion."[103] On the other hand, personal contact with Yogananda was essential to sustaining the passion of his closest disciples, and he was unable to interact personally with thousands of students. Recognizing this, he and SRF worked hard to maintain a sense of guru-disciple intimacy through teachings, poetry, and anecdotes in various forms—radio, magazine, and personal address. And not all devotees thought that Yogananda's physical presence was necessary to experience him fully. "Does one miss out by not having a guru in the physical form on this plane?" Dietz asked. "No, one need not miss out at all. Through right action, meditation, prayer and the power of spiritual love, the devotee will draw the guru's response, from whatever he is. In this manner will the devotee experience the guru's presence, realize peace of mind, and merge with Christ consciousness . . . and the glory of God."[104] Yogananda would be powerfully present even after death. That conviction became more essential in the late 1940s, as Yogananda's worsening health hinted that death might be near.

DEATH OF AN IMMORTAL YOGI

Throughout his career, Yogananda had presented himself as an unofficial ambassador of India to the United States, and although his own nationalism was primarily religious rather than political, he had long advocated autonomy for his beloved homeland. When independence finally came in 1947, he invited readers to "imagine the joy" that "every one of the 400 million Hindus, Moslems, Jains, Parsis, Sikhs" experienced when they finally achieved what they had "wished every moment of their conscious lives."[105] India became a global role model when it achieved independence. Historian John Springhall calls it "one of the most remarkable acts of decolonization in the twentieth century," stirring a "'wind of change,' which dislodged various other European colonial rulers in subsequent years."[106] The collapse of European overseas empires was one of the most momentous changes of the twentieth century, turning the possessions of a handful of European powers into more than one hundred nation-states in a few short years. Though decolonization was a complex phenomenon with many roots, observers both then and since have recognized India's crucial role as catalyst, inspiration, and exemplar for movements throughout Asia and Africa.

The new nation's global stature boosted American popular interest in the subcontinent, though the Cold War tilted American foreign policy away from

India. Yogananda participated in the celebration welcoming the American visit of Jawaharlal Nehru, India's first prime minister, to San Francisco in November 1949. The invitation to this significant event reflected acceptance of his self-appointed role as unofficial Indian ambassador to the United States. Yogananda attended Nehru's public speech, and later the two met in the prime minister's hotel room, where they shared a brief conversation and Yogananda was introduced to some of Nehru's family.[107] Nehru already had some familiarity with the guru before coming to the United States. Yogananda had reached out to him by telegram the previous year with a bold plea that he "save half of Gandhi's ashes, some for India, some for America, to be buried beneath statues erected in two countries."[108]

When Gandhi was assassinated January 30, 1948, less than six months after independence, Yogananda offered himself as curator of the great leader's memory. It was only appropriate, he thought, that America's most notable living Indian saint should commemorate the martyrdom of India's greatest leader. During his regular radio broadcast he paid tribute to Gandhi's legacy, placing him in a global context and assuring listeners of his ongoing influence. "Mahatma Gandhi's passing is a loss not only to India but to the whole world. World leaders and all India mourn for him. We mourn for our loss, but he is freer to work through the Infinite. Jesus Christ and Abraham Lincoln died for the same cause as Mahatma Gandhi has died." In the wake of World War II and the emergence of atomic weapons, Yogananda wrote and spoke publicly about the ongoing danger of war; Gandhi stood out in the movement for world peace.

> By following Gandhiji's nonviolent doctrine, India won her independence without firing a single shot. If the world followed his doctrine, it too could receive its independence from the slavery of destructive and misery-making wars. Gandhiji, limited by his frail body, accomplished much, but his liberated spirit will work more mightily in the hearts of nations and individuals for all time. Let us pay homage to the ever-living great Mahatma Gandhi. He is not dead, for his exemplary life and spirit of goodness are going to work unhampered through the temple of our hearts ever and forever.

This address was reprinted in a Gandhi biography written by prominent occult author Marc Edmund Jones the same year.[109]

Self-Realization Fellowship also conducted memorial services for Gandhi, including a fire ceremony that symbolically consigned his body to the flames while his liberated soul "commingles with the soul of God." In his memorial address, Yogananda called the audience to honor Gandhi's legacy properly. It was appropriate to erect statues to commemorate Gandhi, but it was more vital to "erect in one corner of our heart a statue to nonviolence if Gandhi is to be rightly remembered. We must establish a monument to Gandhi within us if we are to have a world peace. Enemies and friends are all our brothers under the fatherhood of God."[110]

In early 1949, Yogananda finally acquired a portion of Gandhi's ashes through the assistance of a longtime Indian disciple Dr. J. V. Nawle, secretary of the Great Mother Bharat Institute and Society for World Peace. Originally planning to inter the ashes at Encinitas, Yogananda ended up sending them to a new SRF property instead.[111] Through James Lynn's generosity, SRF had acquired a small artificial lake in Pacific Palisades a few blocks from the ocean. Resting in a bowl bordered by a long curve in Sunset Boulevard, the idyllic property had a Hollywood pedigree. A film site in the silent movie era, the land was later purchased by H. Everett McElroy, assistant superintendent of construction for 20th Century Fox studios. The Lake Shrine's official dedication ceremony in August 1950, which brought Lieutenant Governor Goodwin Knight and his wife, commemorated the thirtieth anniversary of Yogananda's ministry in the United States.[112] Yogananda built a World Peace Memorial honoring Gandhi at the lake and deposited the ashes there. In this way, Yogananda successfully associated himself with Gandhi, India, global peace—and Hollywood—at one picturesque site. His own death would shortly transpire, appropriately enough, during a Los Angeles dinner honoring India's first ambassador, Binay R. Sen.

Yogananda had suffered poor health for years, though he kept this from the public and even many of his disciples. The stresses of the ministry—travel, organization, speaking, and, above all, the trial instigated by his former friend and partner Nerode—likely exacted a physiological toll. And despite advocating exercise and a healthy vegetarian diet, he was probably overweight during much of his ministry, a factor that often contributes to heart disease and the likelihood of heart attack.[113] In August 1936, on the eve of his departure for the return voyage to the West, he had a distressing experience:

> Yesterday afternoon as I sat in a half-meditation state, Satan dropped onto my body and pulled my astral body out of my physical body; my heart stopped. Then Guru as an angel of God appeared and warned me, saying, "Look, look what Satan is doing unto thee!" I made an effort; and like a stretched rubberband my astral body slipped back into my

lifeless frame, and I cried out. This happened under the eyes of one of the school boys who was alarmed to see me suddenly grow cold and lifeless and then cry out. I would not understand why this happened on the eve of my departure.

Yogananda portrays this experience as a dramatic demonic attack. But stripping away the spiritual language reveals physical symptoms—a stopped heart, the sudden feeling of a heavy weight, a loud cry suggesting sharp pain, and the physical appearance of death—that suggest that the forty-three-year-old had experienced a severe heart attack. Late that evening Yukteswar appeared to Yogananda in a vision to supply a motive for the spiritual attack. "Satan on this last day wanted to destroy your body that you might not be able to go to America and redeem other souls."[114] As this vision makes clear, Yogananda recognized that he had narrowly avoided death.

Given Yogananda's efforts to conceal his physical problems, it is difficult to know whether he experienced other heart attacks in the decade after his return from India. But an event in 1948, which he described as a particularly intense *samādhi* experience, may have been another heart attack. Though the disciples present thought they were only witnessing deep meditation, some noted that the episode marked a dramatic change in his behavior serious enough that at least one disciple interpreted it as a harbinger of his death. He became reclusive, withdrawing even from his closest disciples. He spoke publicly less frequently and spent more time alone in the desert.[115] A notice subsequently appeared in SRF's publication *Self-Realization* asking correspondents to be patient if Yogananda was slower to respond to mail since "he is now observing a stricter seclusion than he has done in the past. . . . Because of his constant immersion in God, it is not always possible for his secretaries to intrude on his attention."[116] This abrupt notice was replaced two months later by a warmer personal address from Yogananda himself, who explained that "crowds of Souls from all quarters of the globe are coming on pilgrimages to Self-Realization Headquarters—when I have less time. The work has expanded beyond my imagination." As a result, he "humbly" asked that personal letters be "short and to the point" and that, whenever possible, correspondents write directly to his secretaries, who are "equipped and spiritually trained."[117]

His informal addresses to disciples after 1948 were often rambling repetitions of familiar themes and lacked his characteristic vigor. Death seemed often on his mind as he regularly cited a favorite trope about the insignificance of an individual water drop in relation to the vast ocean. He also rehearsed the metaphor about life as a motion picture—his Hollywood-inspired tribute to the Hindu notion of *māyā* that had become a cliché through decades of repetition. Thinking of his own weakening body and impending death, he reminded his flock of the illusory nature of individual human experience, repeatedly telling them that he was not his body. "Oh, it is such a joke . . . that Divine Mother is playing on you all. You think this is so real. It is not real. . . . Don't take it so seriously. It is just a joke she is playing on you." He began to cry, adding, "But I feel so sorry for all of you because to you it is yet real. Don't take it so seriously."[118]

By the fall of 1950, he began to suffer severe leg pain that kept him wheelchair-bound for months. Close disciples interpreted this physical impairment as the result of a master's struggle to bear the karmic burden of his disciples. This was a gift Yogananda, like his alter ego Jesus, had sacrificially bestowed on his disciples at great cost to himself, while "a frightful array of demonic entities" wreaked "havoc on his body."[119] Although Yogananda had taught this familiar Hindu precept,[120] he had also endorsed a countervailing tradition that "the great *yogis*," as Buddhist writer Alexandra David-Neel explains, were "inaccessible to sickness." "These eminent individuals leave our world at the moment they choose, without physical deterioration."[121] Perhaps to avoid unnecessary distress, news of his illness was concealed from the public. Even within the confines of Mount Washington, Yogananda avoided scenes that might diminish his stature. On one occasion, waiting until he was sure no one else was around to see, he asked the six-foot, four-inch Paulsen—whom he had nicknamed Big Boy—to carry him piggyback up the two flights of stairs to his room.[122]

Yogananda's death occurred on the night of a banquet for Binay R. Sen, Indian ambassador to the United States, at the Biltmore Hotel in Los Angeles. Yogananda was to introduce Sen and present a gold medal from SRF to him. During the ceremony, Faye Wright recalled that Yogananda was so "God-intoxicated" that the banquet room, filled with the ambassador, the mayor, and other officials, was "absolutely motionless" while he poured out his heart. He ended his talk by reciting his poem "My India," an autobiographical reflection of his deep affection for India, for "there I learned first to love God": "Her sages taught me to find my Self / Buried beneath the ash heaps / Of incarnations of ignorance." Though his soul had been "garbed sometimes as an Oriental / Sometimes as an Occidental," its extensive travels had led it at last "in India, to find Itself."

His hybrid Indian-American identity was made all the more poignant by his having recently become an American citizen. The 1946 Luce-Celler Act allowed a small number of Filipinos and Indians to immigrate each year by creating a loophole in the Immigration Act of 1917's Asiatic Barred Zone. The law

The iconic "Last Smile" photograph *Los Angeles Times* photographer Arthur Say took of Yogananda just moments before his departure. Though initially caught off-guard by Yogananda's abrupt end, his disciples quickly understood it as his *mahasamādhi*, a yogi's conscious exit from the body. This beatific image provided confirmation that the Master had been perfectly at peace before the dramatic event occurred.

also allowed immigrants from these two groups to become naturalized, in effect reversing the 1923 *Thind* decision. Yogananda began the naturalization process soon after the law took effect and took the oath of allegiance in 1949.[123] Forced to accept the artificial boundaries of nation-states, he had made America his country, but he never forgot his homeland, birthplace of all religions:

Better than Heaven or Arcadia
I love Thee, O my India!
And thy love I shall give
To every brother nation that lives.
God made the earth;
Man made confining countries
And their fancy-frozen boundaries.
But with newfound boundless love
I behold the borderland of my India
Expanding into the world.
Hail, mother of religions, lotus, scenic beauty,
And sages!
Thy wide doors are open,
Welcoming God's true sons through all ages.
Where Ganges, woods, Himalayan caves, and men dream God—
I am hallowed; my body touched that sod.

Shortly after finishing the poem, he slumped to the floor, dead. Press accounts tended to describe the suddenness of the attack, reporting his death due to "acute coronary occlusion," or heart attack.[124] Bearing his disciples' *karma* had taken a heavy toll. The yogi who once touted "perpetual youth" and predicted he would "live forever" was dead at age fifty-nine, seven years short of the average life-span for American males at the time.[125] Devotees later remembered the moment of death as calm and perfectly timed, a reflection of their belief that the guru's time of death was under his control.[126] But that was not their initial reaction. Some disciples found the notion of his death so incomprehensible that they wondered if he was simply in an intense state of *samādhi* at an inopportune moment. So they all repeated the *mantra* he had previously taught them to bring him out of a meditative trance. Gradually they recognized that he was really gone.[127] Once this realization set in, his disciples perceived that their guru's death was indeed under his control, as *Yoga Sūtra* III.22 promised, and therefore perfectly timed. At a very apt moment during the celebration he had achieved *mahasamādhi*, the freely chosen surrender of the fully self-realized soul.[128] This rare phenomenon signaled that their guru had purged himself of all *karma*—including what he had vicariously assumed on behalf of his disciples—and mastered *saṃsāra*. Disciples of a fully self-realized guru who dies often cope by trying to "correlate or reconcile the implicit, hidden knowingness of their guru with his explicit, public unknowingness," retroactively discovering hints that he had provided regarding his impending death.[129] Yogananda's devotees recalled many intimations over the last several years that left no doubt—at least in retrospect—that he had achieved *mahasamādhi*, like his master before him.

As the leaders present at Mount Washington when Yogananda died deliberated over what to do with their master's body, Premananda received a telegram from Yogananda's brother Sananda: "Jotin, send brother's body home." Minott Lewis deferred to Premananda as an Indian and Yogananda's longest friend regarding the disposition of Yogananda's remains. Though burial is a deviation from the general Hindu practice of cremation, it is not an uncommon practice for swamis, who symbolically consign their bodies to be consumed by fire when they take their monastic vows.[130] Premananda reflected on Yogananda's decision in 1936 to bury Yukteswar in Puri and concluded that it would be appropriate to bury their own master as well.[131] The leaders then discussed the possibility of shipping Yogananda's body to Puri to be buried alongside his mentor, but transporting the body back to India did not seem viable. In the end, the yogi who had made his home in the United States for nearly his entire adult life would be buried in his adopted country. Once SRF leadership made the decision to inter Master in California, the next question was the suitable location. Initially, SRF leaders planned to bury him at Mount Washington or the Lake Shrine in Pacific Palisades, but zoning laws did not permit this.[132] Given his prominence, it seemed fitting that he be buried at Los Angeles' most famous cemetery, Forest Lawn. Hundreds attended the funeral held at Mount Washington, including more than one hundred monks, ministers, and sisters, in what the press described as a two-hour "half-Indian, half Christian ceremony" that included both a sacred fire ritual and singing "Ave Maria," chants from the Vedas and readings from the Bible. Words from Gandhi were also spoken.[133] The Indian who routinely compared himself to Jesus was placed in Forest Lawn's replica Gothic cathedral, his vault in the Sanctuary of Golden Slumber bathed in light that streamed in through stained-glass windows.

Forest Lawn staff detected an unusual phenomenon while preparing Yogananda's body. The mortuary director wrote a notarized letter to SRF expressing astonishment at the unprecedented absence of bodily decomposition and desiccation. Between March 11 and 27, "no indication of mold was visible on Paramhansa Yogananda's skin, and no visible desiccation (drying up) took place in the bodily tissues. This state of perfect preservation of a body is, so far as we know from mortuary annals, an unparalleled one."[134] SRF immediately republished this letter in full in a commemorative issue of *Self-Realization*. It also reprinted excerpts that heightened the scale of the miracle by omitting any reference to the embalming performed twenty-four hours after his death.[135] Though

The banquet room in the Biltmore Hotel in Los Angeles where Yogananda left this world on March 7, 1952. Yogananda was a guest speaker at the banquet held in honor of Indian ambassador Binay R. Sen. After delivering a brief address, Yogananda read aloud his poem "My India" and suddenly slumped over.

lack of outward decay is not unusual for embalmed bodies, Yogananda's postmortem preservation quickly became proof that he had been no mere mortal.[136] Self-Realization Fellowship compared this phenomenon to the bodies of such Christian saints as John of the Cross and the Spanish mystic nun Teresa of Ávila, who reputedly remained incorruptible for centuries, her burial place a site of "innumerable miracles."[137] According to Kriyananda, William the Great of Aquitaine and the Ferdinand III of Spain, called el Santo, had also been miraculously preserved. Both men were previous incarnations of Yogananda, prompting Kriyananda to muse, "Was the incorruptible state of their bodies a condition that would always attend this soul?"[138] While SRF disciples reached for parallels in the Christian tradition, they unaccountably ignored the fact that incorruptibility of the guru's body is a common Hindu belief.[139]

The tributes that poured in after Yogananda's death affirmed the Paramahansa's local, national, and international status. California lieutenant governor Goodwin Knight, unable to break away from a difficult legislative session, expressed his "shock and grief" at the sudden death of his "good friend," assuring SRF that his "warm personality and kindly understanding will be sorely missed by all of those who were privileged to know him."[140] Papers across the country reprinted the Associated Press account of his funeral, including the claim that Yogananda had thirty million followers. *Time* magazine ran a short article, providing a summary of his ministry, his two years of illness, and his death from a heart attack, closing with the mortuary's report.

India welcomed their expatriate teacher home as well. Mulk Raj Ahuja, consul general of India in San Francisco, viewed Yogananda as "an apostle of peace and a believer in the brotherhood of man," who saw India and the United States as "not two separate countries but the two component parts of one single plan for the development in harmony of both material and spiritual values of man."[141] Fellow guru Swami Sivananda, leader of the Divine Life Society in Rishikesh, paid tribute to the "eternal, all-pervading, stable, immovable, and ancient" Yogananda, "an ideal representative of the ancient sages and seers, the glory of India."[142] Throughout India, Yogoda Satsanga Society member organizations held their own memorial services, while university officials, church leaders, and other notables mourned his passing.[143]

The death of Yogananda did not end his disciples' relationship with him. Self-Realization Fellowship's official death announcement two weeks later reassured members that although Yogananda "has taken his physical form from this earth, tremendous waves of spiritual upliftment are being felt by disciples and members, a divine assurance of his omnipresent spirit among us still."[144] Like other gurus, he remained near his closest disciples.[145] Donald Walters felt Yogananda's presence while he stood in front of his master's crypt shortly after the interment. He told Walters, "I'm not in there!"[146] Three weeks after his death, Mary Buchanan recorded in her diary, "Master came! Here in my room suddenly *Master was standing right before me*. He was not only dear to my sight but so tangibly here that impulsively I reached forward to put my hand on his arm. He looked at me, said gently, 'Well . . .' Then he began to vanish. I wanted to ask him to stay longer but he was gone."[147]

These experiences were not confined to monastics who had enjoyed close contact with the Master. Within months of his *mahasamādhi*, everyday members were writing in to share their experiences of the guru. One individual from San Francisco, while practicing the correspondence course lessons, "saw Master dressed in pure white, watching me with approval." After adjusting an imperfect technique, the devotee heard a clear affirmation, "Now you do quite well." In the same setting, a Canadian SRF member beheld the Master "dressed in a white robe," "with his hands pointed upward in the position of prayer." The student reflected how wonderful it was to have "a Master who manifests himself with such kind encouragement and loving guidance in the way that is most appropriate to our stage of development." After hearing word of Master's death, a third member finally understood the meaning of a puzzling vision in which Yogananda had been walking alone at Mount Washington. "He seemed much younger, although it appeared to be almost dark and I could barely make out his form. It was not a material form, but a spiritual one" the Master inhabited.[148]

These visions continued sporadically for decades. Yogananda appeared in physical form to Daya Mata years after his *mahasamādhi*. When she touched his feet, "They were as solid as my own." Mary Peck Stockton experienced a vivid vision of Yogananda during colon cancer surgery three decades after his death.[149] In the mid-1980s, a woman stopped by an organization headed by Walters to buy a laminated photograph of Yogananda, though she did not know who he was. She had had a very hard life and, shortly after the visit, decided to commit suicide by driving off a bridge. Walking toward the front door, she had a transcendent experience. Her recently purchased "photograph expanded and became life-sized. It stood in the doorway, and wouldn't let me through. I decided at that point to drop my plan of committing suicide."[150]

Such descriptions closely follow the patterns described in a "large, critical literature on ostensible post-mortem encounters," according to New Testament scholar Dale Allison, in which the departed appears and disappears abruptly; is both seen and heard; appears to individuals who may not have known the person in life; and provides guidance, issues commands, and offers comfort.[151] While these accounts typically involve the postmortem apparition of merely human loved ones, occasionally a divine figure makes a visitation. Perhaps the closest parallel to Yogananda's appearances comes from Theosophy cofounder Henry Steel Olcott, who had a vision of "an immense Hindu man clad in white, his long black hair tumbling from underneath a turban, and his black beard parted at the chin and twisted up and over the ears 'in the Rajput fashion'":

> His eyes were alive with soul-fire; eyes which were at once benignant and piercing in glance; the eyes of a mentor and a judge, but softened by the love of a father who gazes on a son needing counsel and guidance. He was so grand a man, so imbued with majesty of moral strength, so luminously spiritual, so evidently above average humanity, that I felt abashed in this presence, and bowed my head and bent my knee as one does before a god or a god-like personage.[152]

Besides recounting reports of divine encounters, SRF preserved Yogananda's memory in more prosaic ways. Within months of the *mahasamādhi*, SRF published *The Master Said*, a collection of wisdom and advice to disciples with a foreword explaining how Jesus had foretold the existence of a master who would do greater works than he himself had done. Collecting and retelling a guru's stories after his death is a common practice in India; such stories often have a folkloric character and serve a hortatory purpose.[153] The aphoristic accounts in *The Master Said*, rarely more than a brief paragraph, frequently followed a stereotyped structure: an often nondescript setting that gave the account a timeless relevance, a question or challenge to Yogananda about his teachings or practices, and his pithy retort—commonly a metaphor, paradox, or dialectical statement—that always began with "the Master said":

> 1) When a friend criticized the use of advertising to spread the Self-Realization teachings, the Master said, "If Wrigley can use ads to make people chew gum, why shouldn't I use ads to make people chew good ideas?"
> 2) "You are very hard to understand, Master!" a disciple remarked. And the Master said, "There is no need for you to understand me. Follow me. Everyone reads commentaries on Christ, but who does what he told us to do?"
> 3) "How can God, the manifested Absolute, appear in visible form to the devotee?" a disciple asked.
> And the Master said, "If you doubt, you won't see; and if you see, you won't doubt."
> 4) When the Master first came to America he wore the Indian dress, and his hair was long around his shoulders. Someone, fascinated by what was to him a strange sight, inquired, "Are you a fortune-teller?"
> And the Master said, "No, I tell people how to mend their fortunes."

5) A stranger talking to the Master for the first time said, "You seem to believe in Christ, but I thought all Hindus were heathens!"

And the Master said, "Most Christians call the Hindu heathens. But the saints of every faith bow to the God within one another."

Each account ended with Yogananda's final authoritative pronouncement, creating a sense of deep paradoxical wisdom that hearkened back to such ancient sages as Buddha, Jesus, and Confucius.

In *Stories of Mukunda*, published the following year, Walters presented more than a dozen anecdotes Yogananda told to various audience about his childhood that had not made their way into the *Autobiography*, including "The Goldfish Tragedy," in which the death of a pet prompted the six-year-old's diary entry in English, "My red fish is die."[154]

Self-Realization Fellowship published a commemorative volume in 1958, *Paramahansa Yogananda: In Memoriam*, which collected various postmortem tributes to Yogananda, along with his final speech and a narrative of his final days on earth. Following Yogananda's lead in presenting himself as a Christ figure, the narrative included a section entitled "A Last Supper with His Disciples" that described an intimate dinner with his devotees on Wednesday, March 5, two nights before his death. His followers, who noticed how "quiet and thoughtful" he was during the meal, remembered that "Lord Jesus, just before his passing, observed the Oriental custom when he sent Peter and John to prepare, for him and the twelve disciples, a Last Supper." In retrospect, they understood that "in honor of his approaching *mahasamādhi*, he too had arranged a Last Supper."[155]

Disciples who knew Yogananda personally began sharing anecdotes from the stage at various SRF anniversaries and convocations. Every possible recollection was retold, no matter how mundane; every anecdote helped maintain at least a tenuous link with the Master. Self-Realization Fellowship recorded some of these gatherings and eventually offered them for sale, institutionalizing disciples' memories while providing the organization with an ongoing revenue stream.[156]

Important SRF sites have become shrines devoted to Yogananda's memory, not simply functioning religious centers. At Mount Washington, Yogananda's former top-floor bedroom is preserved in the condition it was at his death; the library downstairs includes personal memorabilia. The former India Center at the Hollywood temple functions as a miniature museum displaying a small collection of historical photos. The Lake Shrine contains a small museum with photographs and artifacts. Encinitas, an active retreat center, has a welcome center. Yogananda's childhood home in Calcutta, which remains in the Ghosh family as a private home, preserves his bedroom and meditation room as shrines. Group tours can be arranged to visit the home. Outside, a plaque greets visitors:

HERE LIVED
PARAMAHANSA YOGANANDA
FOUNDER
YOGODA SATSANGA SOCIETY OF INDIA
AND
SELF-REALIZATION FELLOWSHIP

Perhaps most importantly, Yogananda's image joined Krishna, Jesus, Babaji, Lahiri Mahasaya, and Yukteswar in the divine pantheon displayed on every SRF and YSS altar around the world.

THE FATE OF YOGANANDA'S LEGACY

As an organization that epitomized Weber's notion of charismatic leadership, SRF's survival hinged on the question of Yogananda's successor. Weber suggested several ways that succession could be legitimated: a search for a new leader with appropriate charismatic qualities, divine revelation through some oracular means, designation by the original leader, designation by qualified staff, hereditary charisma, and office charisma.[157] Yogananda and, subsequently, SRF experimented with various combinations of these approaches before finding the right mix. Before his death, Yogananda had provided a temporizing solution by appointing James Lynn his successor. Though Lynn was not a natural leader, Yogananda was essentially obliged to select him. Self-Realization Fellowship quite literally owed its continued existence to Lynn's largesse. Yogananda courted Lynn for years, writing him more than seven hundred letters, many of which included requests for donations. Indeed, until the end of his life Yogananda continued to implore Lynn to donate his vast fortune to SRF. Lynn finally did so only in the summer of 1953, more than a year after Yogananda's death and his own accession to the presidency.[158] In gratitude and affection, Yogananda regularly praised Lynn's deep devotion and unparalleled spiritual progress.

Yogananda gradually laid the foundation for Lynn's authority as his successor, bestowing the monastic name Rajarsi Janakananda on him in 1951.[159] He hinted at Rajarsi's advanced spirituality, predicting that he would shortly achieve *nirvikalpa samādhi*, the highest stage of meditation.[160] This was a remarkable achievement for one who came to discipleship in midlife after years as a householder and businessman. To reach an advanced spiritual state, Lynn had to be purged of many imperfections. He was, as Florina Darling put it, "more business than spiritual."[161] His behavior during Encinitas visits reflected the character of an entitled millionaire indulging his material desires as much as that of a spiritual renunciant. He required freshly laundered bedsheets daily and had soiled clothes shipped home to Kansas City in exchange for clean ones. Rather than taming his appetite, he indulged it, eating throughout the day whenever he felt hungry, expecting dinner whenever he chose, and keeping the best portions for himself rather than his Master. He criticized the dietary habits of others so harshly that Merna Brown took to eating in her room to avoid his reproach.[162]

Though Rajarsi grew spiritually, he remained a dubious candidate for spiritual leadership. Monastics may have viewed Yogananda's decision as a reflection of deep affection for his friend or more pragmatically as a calculated reward. Most likely, they simply trusted the unfathomable wisdom of their guru. Though Rajarsi was indisputably earnest and sincere, his understanding was unsophisticated, his addresses were inarticulate, and his presence was underwhelming. In personality and presentation, he could not have contrasted more sharply with the Master. His unassuming nature may have held some charm, especially for a millionaire, but it in no way compensated for his lack of charisma. Undoubtedly recognizing Lynn's limitations as a leader, Yogananda had labored valiantly to steer him toward a figurehead position. He cast a vision for Lynn of his retirement as a life of meditation "free from the entanglements of an organization," that is, devoted to the cause but not involved in leadership.[163]

Rajarsi's lackluster leadership was on full display almost immediately. For his first formal address as head of SRF for its convocation, the annual meeting that celebrated the organization and brought members from all over the world to Mount Washington, he strung together a series of clichés totaling fewer than five hundred words. He announced that Master was still present with the gathering, which explained why "I don't care to talk."[164] Merna Brown attempted to put Rajarsi's leadership in the best possible light by describing him as "that spiritual bridge that we needed between Master and the work" immediately after Yogananda's departure, a necessary but temporary expedient during a crisis. She acknowledged that Lynn was basically a figurehead president and that real responsibility fell to Faye Wright after Yogananda's death, because, as she delicately put it, "Rajasi didn't get a lot into the administration."[165] Lynn's leadership flaws notwithstanding, even a genuinely gifted leader would have struggled to don Yogananda's mantle. In the last few years of Yogananda's life, his intimations of divine status exacerbated the already daunting challenges any successor would confront.

Apart from giving Lynn no real decision-making power, Yogananda limited his authority in another way. Faced with indisputable evidence of his own looming death and canny enough to recognize Lynn's limitations, Yogananda endeavored to secure the legacy he had worked so hard to create. Self-Realization Fellowship members learned that, despite having ordained Lynn into the swami order, the *paramparā* would end with Yogananda. Neither Lynn nor any other disciple would formally succeed him. This was an unexpected strategy for one who relentlessly discussed the importance of the swami order, the guru-disciple relationship, and the unbroken lineage from Babaji, Lahiri Mahasaya, and Yukteswar to himself.[166]

Instead, Yogananda came to view his own teachings themselves as "the guru," a somewhat novel idea at the time, but one that anticipated a recent trend in yoga. Despite widespread belief in the necessity of a physical guru, some have asserted that the guru's part can be played by a "disembodied influence, that is in reality the inner guru, this interiorized and non-materialized aspect of the exterior guru, who is not separated from the Self and who never dies."[167] Yoga scholar Suzanne Newcombe argues that the "institutionalization of charisma away from a direct *guru-sisya* interaction" in recent decades has facilitated the popularization of yoga globally.[168] Arguably, however, reducing the guru's authority is easier in the largely secular world of postural yoga than in a tightly structured religious organization like SRF. Indeed, the survival of a guru's legacy may hinge largely on his teachings, as religious scholar Douglas Barnes notes.[169] Yogananda's articulation of teachings-as-guru reflected a sense of his own unique significance, his reluctance to leave the spotlight, and his reticence about ceding full authority to any of his disciples. Convinced by his declining health that he would not achieve literal immortality, he sought to live on through his writing. The *Autobiography* had already begun the process of his immortalization through text, but he wanted to get the rest of his now voluminous teachings, some only in note form suitable for oral instruction, in order for publication. He began to express great anxiety about having sufficient time to edit this mass of written works. "Where is the time? There is no more time," he lamented.[170]

The notion of Yogananda's teachings as the guru was made plain to SRF followers early in Lynn's presidency. He announced in April, "Master is our guru. There will be no other guru. Is there another preceptor? He will continue as always to be our preceptor."[171] To shore up any doubts, an SRF announcement made clear Lynn's desire "that the SRF teachings and Paramhansa Yogananda remain forever the Guru of the organization." This revelation was presented not as a limitation on Lynn's authority but as an expansion of devotees' freedom to advance in their training and spiritual enlightenment "without dependence on the personalities of the SRF leaders." The guru's eternal nature and omnipresence would steer devotees away from error. "Yoganandaji is their Guru still, watching over them beyond any shadow of doubt, and filled with joy at each step of progress they make along the spiritual path. He promised many times to guard the organization and its members after he had left the body for Omnipresence."[172]

Lynn's stopgap presidency combined with Yogananda's teachings as the true guru did little to resolve SRF's questions of long-term stability. Self-Realization Fellowship's third annual convocation, held at the Hollywood temple four months after Yogananda's death, featured instruction, not by Lynn, but by the temple's resident minister, the Reverend C. Bernard.[173] Lynn was already ill with brain cancer when he became president; he would die in 1955 after several treatments. His rapid decline raised the urgent question of a suitable long-term, authoritative successor. Merna Brown had asked Yogananda shortly before his death who would be president after Rajarsi, an indication that they knew his tenure would be short. "God and Guru already know who they are, and when the time comes, they will be divinely revealed," he reassured her. "There will always be at the head of this organization men and women of divine realization."[174] This vague reassurance offered little direction, however, about who this long-term leader might be. And however divinely realized, this leader would exercise authority through what Weber described as the routinization of charisma, a shift "from a unique, transitory gift of grace of extraordinary times and persons into a permanent possession of everyday life."[175] The next leader—the first not directly designated by the Master—had to be perceived as a consensus appointment, not the result of a majority vote by a board of directors. Self-Realization Fellowship found itself in the position of other Hindu guru traditions that, as philosopher David Lane indicates, often feel pressure to ensure the organization's continued authority by disguising evidence of succession disputes following a leader's death.[176] After Rajarsi's death, Faye Wright and others asked Florina Darling to be president, but she declined.[177] The position ultimately fell to Wright, who was presented to the public on the third anniversary of Yogananda's death as the sole, unanimous choice, "an inspiring example of one-pointed devotion to God and Guru."[178] The taciturn Wright may have lacked charisma, but she possessed a quiet authority acquired through her decades-long intimate relationship with the Master. Though the accession of a woman to SRF's presidency resulted from pragmatism more than progressivism, it was nevertheless remarkable in culturally conservative 1950s America.

Self-Realization Fellowship's survival remained tenuous for the first decade after Yogananda's death. The organization's greatest strength, Yogananda's teaching, was also its greatest constraint. Lane's description of another twentieth-century Hindu organization captures the choice SRF faced: "Turn backwards toward the leader, thereby freeing the founder's ideas as unique and unquestionable; or turn towards the present and future by looking toward the new successor to forge new territory. In the former case, one runs the risk of losing the vitality that personal charisma brings, while avoiding the essential unpredictability (and occasional radicalness) that a new leader may display. In the latter case, the benefit depends largely on the success of the chosen master."[179] Having received the "teachings as guru" principle from Yogananda as a fait accompli, SRF was almost forced into the first choice. Its ongoing legitimacy rested largely on Yogananda's teachings, and the organization became a repository of his instruction, endlessly reprinting his articles and reiterating his sayings. Reliant on his authority, leaders lacked their own vision.

The organization eventually found a renewed vision by emphasizing its Indian identity even more strongly than Yogananda had. *Self-Realization* regularly featured instruction on *āsanas* with photographs depicting proper posture and provided detailed explanations of beliefs like the four *āśramas*. Monastics routinely adopted Indian titles and began wearing ocher robes. President Daya Mata (Faye Wright) sponsored an extended trip to the United States or Shankaracharya, at the time head of the Śankara swami order, which increased SRF's cachet at home and abroad. Daya Mata and other leaders then made a year-and-a-half pilgrimage to India in 1958–59, replicating their guru's earlier journey and strengthening organizational ties between India and the United States. Along with her extended visit to India, Daya Mata poured financial resources into Indian centers, which placed them on a more stable footing.[180] Among other things, Indianizing SRF helped to lessen the awkwardness of an American-based Hindu organization led by a white woman—one founded by an Indian and a nationalist to boot—overseeing a branch in India. In a remarkable shift in its center of gravity, Yogoda Satsanga Society in India became home to twenty-five centers, double the number of American SRF centers. But SRF's growth was not limited to India—in the 1950s, SRF became truly global. By 1960, there were seventy centers in nineteen countries across six continents.[181] Daya Mata gradually grew into her role, and her incredible fifty-five-year tenure ensured that Self-Realization Fellowship—and the guru who founded it—would long remain fixtures of the landscape in California, the United States, and around the world.

But the preservation of Yogananda's legacy did not depend entirely on the survival of SRF, since several disciples ventured outside the organization to form independent endeavors. The death of a charismatic founder often triggers organizational schisms, a tendency exacerbated by personal ambitions, personality conflicts, doctrinal disagreements, and the availability of alternative means of legitimation.[182] Former disciples had several reasons for forming their own organizations. A few, like Norman Paulsen, had left SRF during Yogananda's lifetime, disillusioned by his leadership but still inspired by his instruction, while others, particularly Donald Walters, continued in leadership positions for several years before conflicts within the leadership spurred them to set out on their own. Whatever their reasons for leaving, the survival of the groups they formed was even more tenuous than that of SRF.

Because SRF could make the most plausible claim to be Yogananda's successor, splinter group leaders were forced to work hard to legitimate their claims to authority.[183] Leaders of new movements often identified a self-authenticating charismatic quality or recounted a mystical encounter with Yogananda in which he transferred authority, but this did not resolve matters.[184] These independent communities had to walk a tightrope, celebrating their leaders' heritage as direct disciples of Yogananda's teachings while attempting to offer a compelling explanation for their separation from the very organization their guru founded.

Donald Walters created the most successful independent community. He took his final vows in 1955 under Daya Mata (Wright), becoming Swami Kriyananda and became vice-president of SRF in 1960. In 1958, he traveled to India for the first time promoting Kriya Yoga. His restlessness over the strictures of institutional religion, combined with ongoing tensions with the leadership, particularly Wright, led to his ouster from the organization in 1962. Whereas he saw them as hidebound, they undoubtedly viewed him as an upstart, having known Yogananda for such a short time by comparison with their own much longer relationships.

Though his discipleship had been much shorter than Wright's, Walters had enjoyed a particularly close relationship with the Master during his last few years. Walters traced his spiritual legitimacy chiefly to his personal time with Yogananda in the Twenty-Nine Palms ashram, transcribing his guru's comments for the *Second Coming of Christ* commentary. He claimed that Yogananda had bestowed on him a supernatural ability to recall accurately, years after the fact, the Master's exact words and their tone. And though Yogananda never asked Walters outright, he "intimated strongly that he wanted me someday to write about him." Walters based this impression on Yogananda's lengthy reminiscences about his life, ministry, and plans for SRF's future.[185]

After being forced out of SRF, Kriyananda felt disillusioned, unsure what to do with his life severed from the one who had given that life meaning. As he wandered physically and spiritually, he explored Episcopalian monasteries in three states, lived briefly in a Catholic hermitage near Big Sur, became an ashram minister in San Francisco for a time, and contemplated joining a "little-known religious site in Lebanon."[186]

In 1967, at the height of the counterculture, Kriyananda and a few like-minded individuals began construction of a community in the Sierra Nevadas that epitomized the era's communes. Kriyananda's community embodied all of the features Timothy Miller identified as core values most 1960s communes shared despite a host of variations: a common purpose and separation from society, some level of individual self-denial for the sake of the group, living in geographic proximity, regular personal interaction, economic sharing, real existence (as opposed to only envisioned), critical mass beyond an individual family, and commitment to rural idealism, environmentalism, egalitarianism, and community.[187] Well-known Beat figures Allen Ginsberg, Richard Baker, and Gary Snyder purchased several hundred acres in Nevada City in the mountains northeast of Sacramento for the creation of Ananda, Kriyananda's cooperative community.[188] Ananda matched the communal spirit of the counterculture era and its fascination with Asian traditions, and undoubtedly deepened both.[189]

For Kriyananda, however, this communal vision sprang from the "brotherhood communities" Yogananda had called for decades earlier when he returned from India. Kriyananda envisaged "places to facilitate the development of an integrated, well-balanced life, and as examples to all mankind of the advantages of such a life." Not isolated from the larger world, they would be "an integral part of the age in which we live."[190] Ananda's focus on "householders" offered a sharp contrast with SRF, which devoted substantial attention to strengthening monastic communities, even though the vast majority of rank-and-file SRF members were married devotees. Kriyananda was personally ambivalent about the virtues of a monastic life compared with the attractions of sexual intimacy. He was twice married and divorced, and he admitted to having affairs with women in his community. His personal lifestyle choices aside, by arguing that Ananda had remained faithful to Yogananda's communal vision while SRF ignored it, Kriyananda boosted his claim to be the Master's authentic spiritual descendent.

By the early 1990s, Ananda had grown to more than 350 members and several satellite organizations, including one in Italy.[191] Legal and financial troubles have reduced its ranks over the years, but a half-century after its founding, it continues to exist as a modest community of more than 100 members who support themselves through work in and around the community. Like Yogananda, a good part of Kriyananda's popularity—and his organization's longevity—stemmed from his 1977 book *The Path: A Spiritual Autobiography*. A massive, sprawling, supernatural account largely devoted to his life with Yogananda, the book functioned as a recruitment tool, as *Autobiography of a Yogi* had. Beyond his autobiography, Kriyananda wrote prolifically about Yogananda, community, yoga, meditation, and spirituality in a destructive age. He reprinted numerous Yogananda works that were not copyrighted and published an edition of the *Bhagavad Gītā* in 2006, which he claimed to have reproduced from memory based on his editorial work with Yogananda at Twenty-Nine Palms more than fifty years earlier. In 2012, he published a lengthy biography of Yogananda that included spiritual details, including his identity in previous incarnations.[192] When Swami Kriyananda died in 2013, commemorations of his life and ministry revealed that his flock were as devoted to him as he had been to his own beloved guru.[193]

In 1970, Oliver Black established Song of the Morning Ranch, an independent community in Michigan similar to Ananda. Black's path to yoga gurudom had been long and winding. Born in Ohio in 1893, he had owned a million-dollar auto parts chain. Despite his success, he had been deeply unhappy before he met Yogananda in 1931. A severe hypochondriac, he popped "pills for laxatives, aspirins for headaches, and probably would have taken tranquilizers if they'd had them." And like many disciples, his attraction to Yogananda had been immediate, as he "instantly recognized" Yogananda "for the spiritual giant he was." Black became a disciple that day, and Yogananda changed the entire direction of his life.[194] Though something of a renegade, he became a part-time SRF teacher. But unlike Lynn, he never heeded Yogananda's call to abandon his business life and donate the bulk of his wealth to the higher cause of SRF. Just months before his death, Yogananda wrote to Black, urging him to use his leadership skills to do "something much greater, much more lasting, much easier, and much more secure than present-day business organizations in which one works to pay taxes, ruining his health and happiness." He thought Detroit's location ideal for drawing "true seekers, both from East and West," and wanted Black to establish a center there.[195] Black resisted this call and ultimately lost much of his wealth in a hostile takeover of his company in 1952. Chastened by what he took to be punishment for ignoring God's call through Yogananda, Black finally became a full-time minister.

His relationship with SRF leadership after Yogananda's death was rocky. In the mid-1960s, he established an independent instructional program, Yogacharya Oliver Black's Self-Realization Yoga. A few years later he opened Song of the Morning Ranch on eight hundred acres in Michigan's Pigeon River State Forest. The community was founded to practice meditation, teach yoga, explore philosophy, "investigate unexplained laws of nature and the powers latent in human beings," and "provide people with opportunities and facilities to reach a better understanding of themselves, their environment, the universe and God on an interdenominational, interfaith and international scope."[196]

Claiming the mantle of Yogananda, Black was credited with similar qualities. Believers experienced the power of his lustrous eyes, sensed that he knew their thoughts—in fact, knew them better than they knew themselves—and viewed him as the manifestation of God.[197] Black died in 1989 at age ninety-six while practicing yoga. Like many communal experiments of that era, the community he founded has long since folded; the ranch continues today largely as a "yoga retreat of excellence," providing guests "an environment in which to learn and practice timeless spiritual techniques and principles anchored in the teachings of Paramahansa Yogananda."[198]

Norman Paulsen, undoubtedly the most colorful of all of Yogananda's disciples, received a cosmological revelation that authenticated his independent ministry. While still at SRF he saw UFOs. His visions ultimately landed him in Camarillo State Hospital for psychiatric evaluation. In 1969, he rented a house in downtown Santa Barbara that he dubbed "The House of Aquarius" and began teaching meditation to hippies, surfers, and other seekers. Eventually, "Spirit brought together so many people of varied backgrounds to learn to live and work together in brotherhood" that they decided to create a commune.[199] He formed Sunburst, a community of three hundred on three thousand acres in Santa Barbara. The group operated the nation's largest organic farm, four markets, two restaurants, and a bakery.

Despite some reliance on his short discipleship under Yogananda to establish his spiritual pedigree, Paulsen largely forged his own path. His worldview was built on a narrative about earth's ancient history:

> Five hundred thousand years ago the Earth supported a super civilization. This super race, called The Builders, was invaded by a

malignant, negative force around three hundred and fifty thousand years ago. This invasion was fought out in space for a while, from Earth, Mars, and the moons of Jupiter. The enemy first forced a landing in The Euphrates Valley, bringing the war to Earth's surface. A devastating attack by The Nephilim destroyed the whole continent of Mu finally and generated the great Biblical flood. This flood made the Earth uninhabitable for the invaders as well as most of The Builders.

The Builders were decimated — more than sixty million died in one night — and the survivors fled the earth in their starships, leaving the solar system altogether. The Builders began to return in 1961, "to illuminate all of humanity and destroy the makers of war forever," and Sunburst was one of their base stations.[200]

By the late 1970s, the community began to collapse as Paulsen's erratic behavior drove members away. Anticipating society's collapse, he directed a former Green Beret soldier to stockpile assault rifles and ammunition at Sunburst. Paulsen's serious drug addiction also upset many, who wanted clean bodies along with clean spirits in their community — not least from their leader. Paulsen acknowledged his drug problem, though he explained it as the consequence of absorbing his disciples' bad *karma*. His explanation failed to persuade many. By the late 1980s, his community had largely dissolved and he was living in a waterfront condominium in Oxnard next to his seventy-eight-foot schooner. A few members of the group held on to a sliver of the Santa Barbara land and operated a gas station. Eventually, they reestablished the organic ranch and community.[201] Today, Sunburst describes itself as "a world community of practice dedicated to personal and planetary awakening." The whitewashed description of their founder is brief and upbeat, describing Paulsen as having had "a series of illuminating experiences," "culminating in a journey into cosmic consciousness — a face to face meeting with the ineffable light of God, merging with the eternal Divine Presence." Ignoring its debt to extraterrestrials, Sunburst touts its link to Yogananda: "The teachings of Self-realization that Sunburst offers are based upon the universal lineage of Paramahansa Yogananda and his direct disciple, founder Norman Paulsen, as well as the living guidance of the Christ consciousness Jesus exemplifies unceasingly. These great souls are active in these teachings today, as are many others from the living presence of I Am That I Am."[202]

Like Black, Roy Eugene Davis took an unconventional route to independent spiritual leadership. He joined SRF only in 1949, but shortly after Yogananda's death, he left to serve a short stint in the armed forces. This decision reflected an awareness of "a need to learn to live effectively in the secular world," an oblique criticism of SRF's cloistered monastic lifestyle.[203] Davis also objected to tenets of SRF theology that were essential to Yogananda's glorified status: that a guru has no personal *karma*, that he could avoid personal physical illness, or that he was an *avatāra*.[204] He also strenuously rejected the notion that the lineage of gurus stopped with Yogananda's death. Davis staked his own claim to spiritual legitimacy as Yogananda's "only living guru-successor" and insisted that the Master expected his disciples to train their own disciples.[205] In 1964, he formed an independent organization, the Center for Spiritual Consciousness, on eleven and a half acres in Lakemont, Georgia, a mountainous community ninety miles northeast of Atlanta, with this mission: "All authentic enlightenment traditions are honored and the innate, divine nature of every person is acknowledged. We affirm that it is possible for everyone, by right personal endeavor and God's grace, to have a conscious relationship with the Infinite and to fulfill all of life's purposes in harmony with natural laws."[206]

Not long after Yogananda's death, Mildred Hamilton moved to Seattle. Like Premananda, Hamilton was jolted from head to toe when she touched the Master's body on its deathbed. This was a fitting bookend to her physical relationship with Yogananda, which began with an electric shock when she first met him back in 1925.[207] It was also an authentication of her authority to teach in his name. In 1954, she became a follower of Ram Dass (born Richard Alpert), one of the most influential yogis in the United States of the baby boom era. She visited him in India and began to call him "Papa." Despite her devotion to Ram Dass, she viewed Yogananda as her guru and saw herself as faithful to his teachings. Like many others, she received a postmortem visit from Yogananda in 1956. In this visit, however, "her great Guru" commissioned her "to initiate others, thus carrying on the hallowed guru-disciple relationship."[208] Besides this vision and the electric shock, she traced her authority to her status as "the only woman world-wide whom Yogananda himself ordained to be a Yogacharya, fully transmitting the highest vibration from his unending reservoir of spiritual magnetism."[209] After her return from India, she gathered disciples around herself and eventually formed the Cross and the Lotus, a "Christian Yoga" organization—not an officially incorporated church—"Dedicated to the Realization of God and service to Him in all forms." Despite tension between the Cross and the Lotus and SRF, the two acknowledge the same guru lineage: Jesus and Babaji, Lahiri Mahasaya and Sri Yukteswar, and Yogananda himself.[210] At Hamilton's death in 1991, the mantle passed to David Hickenbottom, a disciple since 1974. Cross and Lotus favors virtual community over literal community. It publishes a journal and a blog, while making publications available to help people practice yoga as a "non-sectarian, non-affiliated group of souls who are sincerely working to manifest the will of these great Masters of Yoga: Union with God."[211]

WHO SPEAKS FOR YOGANANDA?

Swami Premananda, Yogananda's sole remaining Indian friend and the man who conducted his memorial service, outlived his master by more than four decades, finally passing from this life in 1995 at age ninety-two. Since his death, the Self-Revelation Church of Absolute Monism has been run by an American-born white woman, Srimati Kamala. Self-Revelation Church mirrors SRF in that an Indian founder has been succeeded by white disciples who oversee a largely white lay membership—though, given the nation's increased ethnic diversity, both organizations boast more nonwhite members than in previous decades. Self-Revelation Church is also like the surviving independent organizations in another key sense. With the exception of Davis, who remained the director of the Center for Spiritual Awareness in 2018 at age eighty-seven, these organizations have all entered at least their second generation of leadership. The direct disciples of Yogananda passed from the scene long ago.

Few of these organizations have experienced substantial success. They lack access to various resources, tangible and intangible, that have allowed SRF to thrive. The departure of some to found their own organizations was too modest to cause a schism within SRF, whose power continued largely unabated, as is common with "religious groups with centralized authority structures."[212] SRF possesses tremendous financial resources that cushion it from temporal storms. It owns several pieces of valuable property, some of which are tourist destinations at which brochures are distributed about the correspondence course lessons and images, postcards, incense, and various SRF publications are sold. Self-Realization Fellowship sells a host of Yogananda publications in many languages and editions. To SRF's chagrin, some of Yogananda's works are in the public domain, including the *Autobiography*. But SRF retains copyright over several others. Years ago, SRF began including a message of authenticity on the inside covers of its materials, entitled "The Spiritual Legacy of Paramahansa Yogananda." Acknowledging the "increasing variety of sources of information" about Yogananda, SRF was obligated to ensure that "the spiritual legacy he left not be diluted, fragmented, or distorted with the passing of time." The SRF name and logo guarantee that the publication "originates with the organization founded by Paramahansa Yogananda and faithfully conveys his teachings as he himself intended they be given."[213] This message has failed to make SRF the sole authority on Yogananda's image, teachings, and legacy. In the past few decades rival portrayals, both positive and negative, have proliferated, thanks in part to the growth of the Internet.

Epilogue

On December 12, 2010, a solemn group of spiritual devotees convened at the Pasadena Civic Auditorium on the outskirts of Los Angeles, filling the three thousand-seat venue to capacity. The "blessed and sacred occasion" was a memorial service in honor of Sri Daya Mata, SRF's *sanghamata*, or mother of the spiritual community, for more than a half-century. Daya Mata, Faye Wright, had recently "passed," though disciples offered testimonials of her continued presence; the vibrations of her love continued to flow into their hearts, they said.[1] Her death was honored—though not mourned, as participants steadfastly refused to express grief—in an elaborate two-and-a-half-hour ceremony replete with Hindu rituals and affectionate commemorative speeches. The devotees, though well versed in the spiritual lineage of their movement, were nevertheless reminded at the ceremony's outset that their gathering was made possible by the "living spirit of Sri Sri Paramahansa Yogananda," their "*premavatar*," or incarnation of divine love, and "*gurudev*," or personal teacher embodying divinity. The service concluded with audio playback of a talk in which Daya had expressed her "one hunger" that devotees would know the "blissful love" she had experienced with God, "because he is the greatest lover in the world, he is the one love from whence we have all come. We must learn to live and move and have our being in that consciousness of his love and then one day to melt again back into that immortal love, where we will all meet again."

The Hindu character of the event was unmistakable. A banner with SRF's stylized lotus logo, a prominent symbol of Indian spirituality, dominated the flower-festooned stage. The ceremony featured meditation, the intoning of "Om, Shanti, Om," and lengthy *kīrtan* singing, including one of Daya Mata's favorite "cosmic chants." A reading from the *Bhagavad Gītā* reminded devotees that while "the end of birth is death" and "the end of death is birth," the soul is "impenetrable, unentered, unassailed, unharmed, untouched, immortal, all-arriving, stable, sure, invisible, ineffable." Thus, "never the spirit was born; the spirit will cease to be never." Near the end of the service, a "sacred and holy ancient ascension ceremony" was conducted, the fire on stage representing the "soul of the departed, which, free from limitations and physical form," was now "finding its greater existence in spirit." Swami Smaranananda, who led the fire ceremony, was a leader in Yogoda Satanga, the Indian branch of SRF. His presence was a reminder of SRF's Indian roots, its continued ties to India, and its global reach. The memorial service also reflected SRF's engagement with Christianity, selectively incorporating elements of its belief and worship — with use of "Amen" and references to "Heavenly Father" and "Jesus Christ" intertwined with invocations to the Divine Mother, Krishna, and gurus in the movement's lineage — into its larger Hindu vision that fulfilled all spiritual longings.

Daya Mata's death prompted SRF's first leadership replacement since the Eisenhower era. She was succeeded by the seventy-nine-year-old Sri Mrinalini Mata (Merna Brown), SRF vice-president for nearly fifty years. Having long since routinized its charismatic leadership, SRF chose Mrinalini Mata through a businesslike board of directors election in early 2011.[2] Her position seemed largely titular. She rarely appeared in public and did not attend the 2016 memorial service for Brother Anandamoy, a monk for more than sixty-five years. A board member read a letter from her instead.[3]

Yogananda and his ministry have reached the age where milestone celebrations begin to pile up. The year Daya Mata died, SRF celebrated the sixtieth anniversary of the World Convocation in Los Angeles, an annual spiritual conference begun by Yogananda in 1950 at Mount Washington. Where the original convocation drew a few hundred participants, more than four thousand attended the 2010 event held at the Westin Bonaventure Hotel, a premier conference venue in downtown Los Angeles. The following March, SRF and its sister organization in India formally commemorated the sixtieth anniversary of Yogananda's *mahasamādhi* with local celebrations, a commemorative issue of *Self-Realization* magazine, and an audio compact disc of Daya Mata's reminiscences of the Master.[4] Self-Realization Fellowship celebrated the seventieth anniversary of Mrinalini Mata's entrance into the ashram in June 2016.[5] As the introduction indicated, the centenary of Yogananda's work was celebrated in March 2017. And in January 2018, Yogananda devotees around the world commemorated the 125th anniversary of his birth.

The year 2017 also saw a changing of the guard. The centerpiece of that year's convocation was a memorial to the recently deceased Mrinalini Mata. On September 1, SRF announced that Brother Chidananda, a longtime board member and a monk since 1977, would become the organization's fourth president. The first male to head SRF in more than sixty years, he is also the organization's first president who never knew the Master personally, having been born the year after Yogananda died. Following established SRF precedent, the announcement of his appointment was accompanied by testimonials legitimizing his succession: shortly before her death, Daya Mata had confided to Mrinalini that Chidananda would be the next president; Mrinalini had had a similar conviction months before her own death; and the SRF vote was unanimous. At sixty-four, Chidananda could potentially lead the organization for two decades or more, providing stability after the relatively short tenure of the aged leader Mrinalini.[6]

Brother Chidananda's first act as president was to announce the upcoming release of a "comprehensive enhancement and expansion" of the SRF lessons. In their current form, the convoluted, repetitive, and dated-sounding lessons sprawl across more than thirteen hundred pages. The revised lessons will condense Yogananda's instruction "into a more organized and focused presentation" that will provide "clearer and more detailed instruction on the SRF meditation techniques, including Kriya Yoga, and many other subjects." A cause for celebration and possible trepidation, SRF leadership walked a tightrope in their rollout presentation. They sought to assure the faithful of the ongoing validity of the existing lessons, which "have everything a seeker needs to find God," until the new lessons became available. At the same time, they established the new lessons' legitimacy by authenticating their pedigree: Yogananda himself began the revisions before personally commissioning the task to Mrinalini Mata, who labored on the project for decades.[7] In this and his many other endeavors, Chidananda does not have to manage the burden of leadership alone. Gurudev Sri Sri Paramahansa Yogananda will undoubtedly continue to guide the organization, as he done ever since his *mahasamādhi*.

Changes in leadership are not the only hurdles SRF has overcome in the past few decades. Since the 1990s, several controversies have also challenged the identity that Yogananda so carefully crafted for himself and his ministry. In 1995, a man named Ben Erskine began to pursue family hints he had heard since his childhood that Yogananda might be his father. His search became more prominent through the work of the *Los Angeles New Times*, a short-lived publication that prided itself on exposé-style investigative reporting, which published two lengthy articles purporting to prove that Yogananda had fathered Erskine in 1933 with an SRF member named Adelaide Erskine.[8] The credibility of this claim depended in part on earlier rumors and accusations. Besides the allegation of sexual impropriety Nerode made in his 1939 lawsuit, rumors long swirled that Yogananda had fathered a child with Laurie Pratt. Pratt, a devotee since 1924 and editorial assistant to Yogananda for decades, gave birth out of wedlock in 1929, and Yogananda allowed the unmarried mother and child to live at Mount Washington. At best, this evidence was circumstantial and could easily be explained as Yogananda's compassionate response to a vulnerable young mother and child. But if paternity were to be established for Erskine or any other claimant, it would damage Yogananda's reputation, premised on his perfect character. Equally devastating to SRF, the legal rights to his lucrative writings would transfer to his closest blood relative. Self-Realization Fellowship reportedly threatened the *New Times* with multiple lawsuits. In 2002, the conflict concluded when blood tests failed to confirm Erskine's claims, *New Times* folded, and the rumors faded.[9]

Another attack challenged the character of Yogananda's successors. A *New Times* article reported that Daya Mata and her sister had been living in a luxurious home in Sierra Madre for decades and driving a pink Cadillac to Mount Washington—a secret so well kept that even some monastics at Mount Washington were unaware of the women's residence. *New Times* also alleged that SRF paid hush money to a woman who claimed that she became pregnant by Brother Arjunananda.[10] Though inadequately sourced, these accusations nevertheless blackened SRF's reputation.

Even SRF's generally friendly Mount Washington neighbors have sometimes turned hostile. In 1999, SRF resurrected plans to inter Yogananda at Mount Washington, a move the well-off residents of the steep hillside community successfully resisted. Some critics viewed the reburial plan as an effort to control access to the shrine (presently publicly accessible at Forest Lawn Cemetery) and to commercialize it through construction of a museum and gift shop.[11]

Some have accused SRF of being a secretive cult. Geoffrey Falk's *Stripping the Gurus* offered a scathing exposé of SRF from a former member who spent more than a decade with the organization, including time at its Hidden Valley ashram. He found SRF oppressive and invasive.[12] Other former members have sometimes echoed these accusations. A now-defunct long-running online discussion board, SRF Walrus, provided a forum for ex-SRF members to discuss their negative experiences with the organization while defending what they viewed as a more accurate account of Yogananda's character, teachings, and legacy. The introduction to the discussion board avowed that those "using this board are loyal devotees of Paramahansa Yogananda. The board is not intended to be a source of criticism of his message or life. While it is often critical of those currently in leadership positions within Self Realization Fellowship, this should not reflect on the many giving loving service to Master."[13] A successor site launched in 2012, SRF Blacklist, has been more willing to target Yogananda himself, with threads exploring allegations of sexual impropriety and assertions, often with proffered documentation, that he was not sole author of texts attributed to him.[14] Online nonprofit organizations such as Cult Education Institute, which describes itself as a nonprofit public "internet archive of information about cults, destructive cults, controversial groups and movements," monitors SRF—as well as its offspring, Ananda—and posts regular news updates about the organization's activities.[15]

The most impassioned controversies have taken place between rival organizations contesting Yogananda's legacy—and legal right to the lucrative products of that legacy. Hugh Urban notes that as "struggles over intellectual property have become increasingly common with religious movements," disputes over copyright, patent, and trademark have become more common, though some organizations "have resisted the commercialization of traditional spiritual practices, arguing that these are 'public goods' that cannot be privatized and commodified."[16] Self-Realization Fellowship challenged Ananda in a major lawsuit that spanned more than a decade, triggered in part by Ananda's 1990 decision to change the organization's name by adding "Self-Realization," a term SRF claimed to have sole right to as a result of its 1935 incorporation. At stake was SRF's claim to be the sole entity authorized to represent Yogananda. The organization asserted exclusive right to publish Yogananda's writings, even though some texts had never been formally copyrighted and others, like the *Autobiography*, had expired copyrights. It also claimed to own the rights to Yogananda's name and photographs of him. Throughout the lawsuit, Kriyananda sent a raft of open letters to Ananda members and to SRF members, portraying his organization as David to SRF's Goliath and offering to "make friends."[17] Self-Realization Fellowship leaders did not see these unsolicited letters as benign attempts at reconciliation. They sent their own lengthy letter to SRF members clearing up what they viewed as Kriyananda's falsehoods, while clarifying their own position on various issues raised in the litigation.[18]

During this lawsuit, a former member of Ananda, Anne-Marie Bertolucci of Palo Alto, sued senior minister Danny Levin, vice president of Ananda's publishing wing, Crystal Clarity. Later, she added Swami Kriyananda to the suit, allegedly for making unwanted sexual advances toward her when she went to him asking for help with Levin. Ananda acknowledged an affair between Bertolucci and Levin but steadfastly denied the charges against Kriyananda. Ananda believed that SRF had secretly encouraged Bertolucci's suit to destroy Kriyananda's reputation, since the lead attorney, Michael Flynn, was the same in both cases. Self-Realization Fellowship vehemently denied the charge. Seven women ultimately testified under oath to sexual harassment, and a $1.8 million judgment was brought against Ananda.[19]

Ironically, Ananda largely won the copyright lawsuit: the organization was allowed to use Yogananda's name, some photographs of him, and the label "Self-Realization." Also ironically, Ananda now refers to itself as Ananda Sangha Worldwide, adopting the Sanskrit word meaning "community," a term Yogananda employed in the United States in the years before SRF's incorporation in 1935 and which is still incorporated in YSS, the India branch of SRF.[20] More importantly, anyone can publish *Autobiography of a Yogi* and a few other books without threat of suit by SRF. Project Gutenberg, for example, provides an electronic copy of the first edition.[21] Between legal expenses and the judgment in the Bertolucci case, Ananda filed for bankruptcy. Critics viewed this as a cynical effort to avoid paying damages to Bertolucci.[22]

Through the litigation process, it became clear that over the years SRF had altered Yogananda's writings in generally small ways but in countless places. Most notably, the organization made more than a hundred modifications to *Autobiography of a Yogi*, which it justified as expressing the true intent of their guru, who had himself made alterations between the first edition and 1946 and his death in early 1952. Many of these changes were simple updates of information that was no longer relevant or accurate decades after Yogananda's death. Some changes corrected minor errors or clarified statements that Yogananda had worded ambiguously. He was curiously reticent, for example, to credit James Lynn for the Encinitas Hermitage, a vagueness clarified in revised editions.[23] But many changes seem more self-interested, reflecting efforts to portray SRF as the chosen vessel for Yogananda's teachings. For example, the revised text describing learning the Kriya Yoga technique adds that it should be learned "from an authorized Kriyaban (Kriya Yogi) of Self-Realization Fellowship."[24] Editors of the book placed a very convenient declaration into Yogananda's mouth on the eve of his 1935 departure for India, having him announce, "To Self-Realization Fellowship I donated all my possessions, including the rights in all my writings."[25]

If some changes to the *Autobiography* portrayed SRF as Yogananda's unique mouthpiece, other changes seemed designed to discredit independent organizations as legitimate representatives of his teachings. References to groups no longer associated with SRF were purged entirely. Several references to Swami Premananda, a close friend of Yogananda's from India who first came to the United States in 1928, disappeared from SRF's revised *Autobiography*. This is likely because his organization had become the Church of

Absolute Monism, an organization independent of SRF—but continuing to claim direct authority through direct lineage from Babaji, Lahiri Mahasaya, Sri Yukteswar, and Yogananda.[26]

One notable disagreement between SRF and other organizations surrounds the centrality of celibacy. Self-Realization Fellowship has consistently presented monasticism as the preferable form of community. Consequently, SRF staff omitted entirely Yogananda's vision of a brotherhood colony at the end of the *Autobiography* that had inspired Kriyananda, Davis, Black, and others to create their own communities of families rather than monastics. After the *Autobiography* was published in 1946, Yogananda does seem to have shifted to a focus on monastic communities. By 1949, he was "showing a new way of freedom in the West" by envisioning the creation of "simple colonies of approximately 25 acres each in various areas beyond the city limits where taxes are lower." Each community would consist of fifty to one hundred "selfless monks and sisters." Whether young, middle aged, or elderly (as long as they were healthy), Yogananda was quite clear that they would be "renunciants," not householders.[27] Still, even if brotherhood colonies did not reflect Yogananda's mature vision, SRF's elimination of his original words from the *Autobiography* was a bold assertion of interpretive authority.

Later editions also made Yogananda's supernatural qualities more prominent. This included the deletion of his warning about the possibility of World War III, a statement that later readers might have interpreted as a failed prophecy.[28] It also included insertions, such as the lengthy footnote explaining that Yogananda told his students that "after this life, he would continue to watch over the spiritual progress of all Kriyabans (students of Self-Realization Fellowship Lessons who have received Kriya initiation . . .). The truth of his beautiful promise has been proved, since his *mahasamādhi*, by letters from Kriya Yogis who have become aware of his omnipresent guidance."[29]

The most important change to SRF's later editions of the *Autobiography* was the insertion of a publisher's note that explicitly defended the organization's unique authority to propagate Yogananda's teaching. The note accused other unnamed groups of "borrowing the name of this beloved world teacher to further their own societies or interests, or to gain recognition for themselves." Then SRF's explanation went on to justify their changes as a fulfillment of Yogananda's express wishes.

> Others are presenting what is purported to be his "original" teachings, but what is in fact material taken from publications that had been poorly edited by temporary helpers or compiled from incomplete

> notes taken during Paramahansa Yogananda's classes. Paramahansaji was very dissatisfied with the presentation of this material, which came out during his early years in America, when he was often away on lecture tours for months at a time and had very little opportunity to oversee the material being published. He himself later did much work on it and gave specific instructions for its correction and clarification.

The punchline was the explanation that followed, which assured potentially confused readers that the only genuine publications were those bearing the SRF logo. Even though SRF's editors had indisputably altered what the Master wrote, they remained the guarantors of his authentic message: "Paramahansa Yogananda founded Self-Realization Fellowship in 1920 to be the instrument for worldwide dissemination of his teachings. He personally chose and trained those close disciples who constitute the Self-Realization Fellowship Publications Council, giving them specific guidelines for the publishing of his writings, lectures, and Self-Realization Lessons."[30]

The *Autobiography* was only the most prominent of Yogananda's texts to receive a postmortem makeover from SRF. Two other massive works based on his writings were published near the start of the new millennium. *The Bhagavad Gita: God Talks with Arjuna: Royal Science of God-Realization*, appeared in 1995 and totaled more than twelve hundred pages in two volumes. *The Second Coming of Christ: The Resurrection of Christ Within You* followed in 2004, also in two volumes and several hundred pages longer. As systematic treatments of the core texts of Christianity and modern Hinduism, the books represented Yogananda's authoritative treatment of the two great religious traditions that defined his ministry. These lavish publications, with hardback covers, gold lettering, decorative endpapers, and dozens of rich full-color illustrations, both appeared in print for the first time decades after Yogananda's death. Both bore his name as author and were ostensibly based on long-running columns in *East-West*—and both departed dramatically from the text that appeared there.

At the outset of each tome, SRF was obligated to explain the astonishing delay in publication after Yogananda's death—more than forty years in the first case and over fifty in the second. In her preface to the *Gītā*, Daya Mata referred to the *East-West* articles parenthetically and called them merely a "a preliminary serialization." Yogananda's real work, she said, began at Twenty-Nine Palms in late 1948 and required "a review of the material that had been written over a period of so many years, clarification and amplification of many points, abbreviation of passages that contained duplication that had been necessary only in serialization for new readers." But work extended beyond mere editing to the "addition of new inspirations—including many details of yoga's deeper philosophical concepts that he had not attempted to convey in earlier years to a general audience not yet introduced to the unfolding discoveries in science that have since made the *Gītā*'s cosmology and view of man's physical, mental, and spiritual makeup much more understandable to the Western mind." Converting these new insights to book form required extensive labor. Completely ignoring any role by Walters, the preface explained that Tara Mata (Laurie Pratt) edited Yogananda's work as he wrote and, after his death, continued the magazine serialization. She died in 1971, "before she could complete the preparation of the *Gītā* manuscript as he had intended," according to Daya Mata. The baton was then passed to Mrinalini Mata, the only person who, "because of her years of training from the Guru and her attunement with the Guru's thoughts," could have completed the task.[31]

The hints that Pratt's product was inadequate and that Mata uniquely possessed the requisite understanding of Yogananda's teaching together suggest that something more substantive than mere editing of Yogananda's words was involved in bringing the commentary to print. Whatever the disarray of his notes, editing alone cannot explain the decades-long delay in publication. More likely, there was protracted debate within the leadership of SRF about how best to represent the spirit of the Master's words without relying exclusively on extant texts.

Daya Mata seems to suggest this kind of interpretive editorial process in her preface to the other major commentary, *The Second Coming of Christ*. She explains how Yogananda worked on the Gospel commentaries at Encinitas throughout the late 1930s and into the 1940s, though only sporadically, since much of his time was absorbed by other projects, especially the *Autobiography*. After a plan fell through to turn the Gospel series into a book, Yogananda recognized "that for the worldwide public distribution he envisioned, the manuscript would require further attention." For the time being, the Gospel commentary would be available only through the magazine. "Continue to print the articles in our magazine for our readers," he purportedly directed. "Later, I will have to do more work on them." During his final period in Twenty-Nine Palms, when he was at work on the *Gītā* commentary, Yogananda also sought to revise a number of earlier works, including the Gospel commentary. "His instruction for the completion of this present book was to draw on the full measure of material he had given on the life and teachings of Jesus in order to impart to a world audience the comprehensive presentation of the true teachings of the blessed Christ that he had divinely received." This required SRF staff to cull through his years of weekly sermons, since "he often included some commentary on, or applicable to, one or more verses from the Gospels." A review of these materials revealed "freshly expressed concepts, clarification and elaboration of points" not directly addressed in the magazine serialization. The sermon insights, along with "other of Paramahansaji's truth-perceptions, forthcoming during his full lifetime" of ministry, "have been made an integrated whole in this definitive edition of *The Second Coming of Christ*." Thus, the final product was a composite work that stitched together teachings from various texts that the author had never himself combined and, like the *Gītā*, seemed designed to capture the spirit of the Master's teachings, even if some of the particular words had never before appeared in print (preface, *Second Coming*, xvi–xx).

Publication of *The Second Coming of Christ* drew interest from the press in Los Angeles, home of SRF's international headquarters. The *Los Angeles Times* article "A Hindu's Perspective on Christ and Christianity" reported that the work by a "renowned Indian guru" was receiving praise as "the first detailed interpretation of the four Gospels by a Hindu." The article cited praise from two religious scholars. Robert Ellwood called *Second Coming* a "rare bridge-building book," and Arvind Sharma said it was "path breaking." "We have to let go," Sharma continued, vindicating Yogananda's inclusivist adoption of the New Testament, "of the attitude that only Christians have the right to interpret the Bible, that a religion belongs only to its followers."[32]

Given SRF's sense of interpretive license, it is no surprise that the *Bhagavad Gītā* and *Second Coming* are both strikingly different from their early *East-West* serializations. First, the books are considerably longer. For example, the SRF commentary on chapter 1, verse 1, of the *Bhagavad Gītā* contains roughly 50 percent more words. But length alone fails to capture the true differences. The titles, subtitles, organization of material—even the Sanskrit translation of the *Gītā* text—all differ from the magazine articles. The actual wording has also been heavily revised. Consider an example of one paragraph from the magazine followed by another from the commentary with shared words highlighted:

> *The Bhagavad Gita* in the first stanza speaks of the glaring truths of how *life is a series of battles between Spirit and matter, knowledge and ignorance, soul and body, life and death, health and disease, changelessness and* change, *self-control and temptation, discrimination and the* senses. In the mother's body the baby has to battle with disease, darkness, and ignorance. Each child has to fight also the battle of heredity. The soul

has to overcome many hereditary difficulties. It has also to contend with the self-created influencing effect of pre-natal Karma or past actions.[33]

> This is an important point. The timeless message of *the Bhagavad Gita* does not refer only to one historical battle, but to the cosmic conflict between good and evil: *life* as *a series of battles between Spirit and matter, soul and body, life and death, knowledge and ignorance, health and disease, changelessness and* transitoriness, *self-control and temptations, discrimination and the* blind sense-mind. The past tense of the verb in the first stanza is therefore employed by Vyasa to indicate that the power of one's introspection is being invoked to review the conflicts of the day in one's mind in order to determine the favorable or unfavorable outcome.[34]

In this fairly typical example, nearly two-thirds of the words in the book version differ from what Yogananda originally wrote.

Unlike the backlash by Yogananda followers in Ananda and elsewhere over SRF's changes to the *Autobiography,* the editorial liberty SRF exercised with these two publications did not generate significant outrage. It is not hard to see why. The *Autobiography* has been the Bible for Yogananda's followers, within both SRF and other organizations, a role neither commentary ever came close to playing. Also, while many knew the *Autobiography* well and could easily compare differences in published editions, particularly after free versions of the 1946 edition were made available online, relatively few have access to the original magazine articles. Fewer still probably read either the *Gītā* or *Second Coming* articles in sequential order as part of an ongoing series, which is the only way the discrepancies would have stood out.

But unaltered versions of portions of these commentaries were familiar to some of Yogananda's disciples outside SRF. Between 1979 and 1986, the Amrita Foundation published the copyrighted *The Second Coming of Christ: From the Original Unchanged Writings of Paramhansa Yogananda's Interpretations of the Sayings of Jesus Christ* in three volumes, reprinting verbatim text from the magazine articles.[35] The tendentious subtitle suggests the organization's views on SRF's revisions. Something similar happened with the *Gītā* in the Ananda community, though on a much more modest scale, when the monks prepared a mimeographed copy of Yogananda's commentary on the first chapter as a Christmas present to the community in 1980.[36]

In 2006, Swami Kriyananda offered a much more ambitious commentary on the *Gītā* comparable to SRF's two-volume edition. Still, at under seven hundred pages, *The Essence of the Bhagavad Gita* is considerably shorter than SRF's version. Kriyananda and, since his death, Ananda have consistently portrayed themselves as defenders of the original, unexpurgated editions of Yogananda's works. It is ironic, then, that Kriyananda's approach in the *Essence* so closely resembles SRF's. Kriyananda built his authority to publish the *Essence* on the fact that he was with Yogananda in Twenty-Nine Palms as the Master worked on his text. As he explained in the preface,

> I should state that I worked personally with Paramhansa Yogananda during the major portion of his writing of this work. He had told the monks in 1950, before he went out to his desert retreat to begin this labor, "I asked Divine Mother whom I should take out there with me to help with the editing, and your face appeared, Walter [the name by which he called me]. To make extra sure, I asked Her twice more, and each time your face appeared. That's why I am taking you."
>
> I read the original manuscript, and worked on it with him (though not extensively). The copy I worked on still exists in SRF's archives; it contains my handwriting. I was in my early twenties then, however, and a "greenhorn" without proper experience as an editor. Now that I have reached nearly the age of eighty, I might be described as somewhat seasoned in this field—especially with some eight-five books to (what I hope are) my credit.

While criticizing SRF for keeping the original manuscript hidden, Kriyananda found its published commentary wanting, which explained why he produced his own version when he did. Since the 1995 publication of SRF's commentary, he had seen the need for a "simpler and clearer version," and one that "was closer to the original"—an edition that did not eliminate teachings and stories that "do not appear in the first published version."

Even if he could make a case for his authority to publish, he still had to persuade readers of his ability to faithfully reproduce his master's words a half-century later. "Fortunately," he possessed "an exceptionally clear memory." In addition, he had been "teaching these truths for nearly sixty years, as a devoted disciple of my Guru, and have the teachings, so to speak, 'under my belt.'" Now, with more confidence and experience, he had attempted to "reproduce his book in such a way that I think (and certainly hope) has been pleasing to my Guru, with at least some of its impact of immediacy. His insights are the most amazing, thrilling, and helpful of any I have ever read on the Bhagavad Gita."[37] The year after the publication of *The Essence of the Bhagavad Gita,* Kriyananda adopted a similar role as Yogananda's interpreter, this time exegeting his master's teaching on Jesus. *Revelations of Christ: Proclaimed by Paramhansa Yogananda* was a much more modest project than his *Gītā* commentary or SRF's *Second Coming*. Kriyananda did not attempt to provide systematic commentary on specific New Testament passages and settled instead for explaining Yogananda's views, rather than trying to present his actual words.[38]

In the end, then, though SRF and Ananda are bitter rivals in claiming Yogananda's mantle, they have adopted similarly capacious definitions of authorship in which each claims the right to intuitively express the sense of the Master's meaning. The title page of the *Essence* captures this blurring between author and interpreter:

The Essence of the Bhagavad Gita
Explained by Paramhansa Yogananda
As Remembered by His Disciple
Swami Kriyananda
(J. Donald Walters)

Viewed apart from the eyes of faith, both organizations might be seen as asserting the authority to ghostwrite texts by listing the long-departed Yogananda as the author of works he did not compose in their published form. Such boldness stems from parallel theological convictions. Leaders of both organizations treasure their position as direct disciples, believe they have received Yogananda's anointing to carry on his work, and express confidence that his spirit—if not his ghost—remains present after his *mahasamādhi* to guide them and prevent error. Together these principles have bestowed the authority each organization needs to present his teachings more fully. In endeavoring to intuit the Master's deeper meaning by transcending the literal text, they were merely following in his footsteps; he had already charted this hermeneutical path in his interpretations of the New Testament and the *Bhagavad Gītā*.

Self-Realization Fellowship's modification of the *Autobiography* was only the most obvious of its concerted efforts to tidy up Yogananda's reputation. It has never made earlier issues of *East-West* accessible to its members, perhaps out of concern that they might encounter embarrassing content—Yogananda's praise for Mussolini or Nazi Germany, which could undermine perceptions of his divinity among less secure devotees, or his early enthusiasm for atomic energy, which now seems retrograde. The most bizarre example of SRF's obsession with posthumous rectification of their guru's reputation is the decision to change the spelling of his official title. In mid-1958, when Daya Mata and other leaders discovered that "Param*a*hansa" was a more appropriate English rendition of the Master's Sanskrit title than "Paramhansa," the way he had always signed it, they simply adopted the new spelling without making any announcement. More dramatically, they surgically enhanced his original signature by separating the two halves of the title, inserting an "a," and reattaching the parts.[39] Though outsiders rarely notice this difference in spelling, it has become a shibboleth that differentiates SRF members from devotees in other organizations who use Yogananda's actual signature—and deride SRF for what they see as its chicanery.

These bitter disputes testify to the ongoing vitality of Yogananda and his teachings. As Yogananda wooed celebrities during his lifetime, his message of self-realization continued to draw them after his *mahasamādhi*. As discussed in the previous chapter, Beat poets Allen Ginsberg and Gary Snyder collaborated with Swami Kriyananda—whose reputation largely rested on his discipleship by Yogananda—in the creation of Ananda. Reclusive novelist J. D. Salinger and his wife became enamored of Yogananda after reading the *Autobiography* in 1954; they wrote to the publisher asking for a recommendation for a local church and were directed to Swami Premananda's D.C.-area church.[40] Emmy-winning *Gunsmoke* star Dennis Weaver visited the Hollywood temple in 1958, where he met Minott Lewis, who made a pitch to Weaver that would have made Yogananda proud: "Can you give fifteen minutes in the morning and fifteen minutes at night to know God?" Weaver found that "an offer I couldn't refuse," so "from that day, I never failed" to practice Kriya Yoga. He remained a faithful follower until his death nearly fifty years later, often serving as a leader of monthly Sunday services at the Lake Shrine.[41] Actor Woody Harrelson revealed to late-night host Jimmy Kimmel in May 2018 that he had found God after reading the *Autobiography* and deciding that Yogananda was not a "phony and a fraud," but instead "full of integrity and a deeply spiritual man."[42] Doria Loyce Ragland and Thomas Markle—the parents of Meghan Markle, who married Prince Harry in May 2018—met when they were both working on the set of *General Hospital* and were married at Self-Realization's Hollywood Temple in 1979.[43]

Musicians have been especially attracted to Yogananda. He inspired the Beatles' George Harrison for a number of years, which explains why Yogananda, Sri Yukteswar, Lahiri Mahasaya, and Babaji—the entire Kriya Yoga lineage—appear on the cover of the *Sgt. Pepper's Lonely Hearts Club Band* album cover. When Harrison died in 2001, SRF hosted a memorial service for him at the Lake Shrine. His onetime Traveling Wilburys bandmate, rocker Tom Petty, was honored in the same fashion after Petty's 2017 death.[44] Elvis Presley visited the Lake Shrine during filming for *Harum Scarum* in 1965. After reading a number of Yogananda writings, he made several visits to SRF and eventually began Kriya Yoga instruction.[45] John Coltrane's music was inspired in part by Yogananda,[46] and singer-songwriter Kenny Loggins says that the *Autobiography* (along with Herman Hesse's *Siddartha*) prompted him to practice meditation and "helped me see everything in my life—performing, writing songs, relationships—in a more spiritual light."[47]

Perhaps the most famous American to show interest in Yogananda has been Steve Jobs. In 1972, he and his friend Daniel Kottke had spent a lot of time together in the attic crawl space above the dorm room of Kottke's girlfriend. "We took psychedelic drugs there sometimes, but mainly we just meditated," Jobs later recalled. Jobs and Kottke shared an interest in Eastern spirituality, and *Autobiography of a Yogi* was one of the books they discussed. Two years later, Jobs was a sandal-wearing college dropout who wanted a break from his job at Atari, an electronic game maker in Palo Alto, California. He strode into his boss Al Alcon's office announcing his plan to quit and travel to India. As Alcorn recalls, "He comes in and stares at me and declares, 'I'm going to find my guru,' and I say, 'No shit, that's super. Write me!'" An earlier traveler had left an English copy of *Autobiography of a Yogi* in the room Jobs was renting from a local family. He read it through several times as he recovered from severe dysentery.[48] Jobs would embrace an eclectic set of Eastern beliefs throughout his life—derived more from Zen Buddhism than anything else—but he never forgot *Autobiography of a Yogi*. After he returned from India, he began reading it once a year, a practice he continued for the rest of his life. Shortly before Jobs died, biographer Walter Isaacson looked at the contents of Jobs's brand-new personal iPad 2 and discovered just one book: *Autobiography of a Yogi*. Jobs's relationship with Yogananda did not end with his death. The fastidious planner organized all the details of his own memorial service at Stanford University, which included a small wrapped gift for each guest. Salesforce CEO Mark Benioff was excited to open his friend's gift. "I knew this was a decision he made that everyone was going to get this. So whatever this was, it was the last thing he wanted us all to think about." It turned out to be a copy of *Autobiography of a Yogi*.[49]

Yogananda-related material continues to proliferate, driving continued interest in him and, in turn, driven by that interest in a positive feedback loop. Other presses, including Ananda's Crystal Clarity, reproduce Yogananda texts in the public domain such as *Autobiography of a Yogi* and a slate of other texts in which Yogananda figures prominently. Kriyananda published a collection of his reminiscences of anecdotes and instruction from Yogananda in 2004. Five years later, he wrote an updated version of his own spiritual autobiography, in which Yogananda is a near-constant presence. Shortly before his death, Kriyananda also wrote a long biography of Yogananda.[50] But SRF far outpaces Crystal Clarity, regularly publishing various editions of Yogananda texts, sometimes in deluxe hardcover editions with gilt titles.

Yogananda's message has been become available in various formats outside of traditional printed texts. In 1982, he found fame as the subject of a thirty-two-page full-color comic book in the famous Amar Chitra Katha series. Since the late 1960s, Amar Chitra Katha ("immortal illustrated story") has dominated the Indian comic book market, serving as a vital tool for teaching about Indian religion, history, and culture. Individual issues, which often appeal to educated readers at home and in the diaspora, are published in English and translated into regional Indian languages. The series, which has sold more than a hundred million copies, includes more than four hundred titles that introduce classic religious narratives and biographies of Indian national figures.[51] The comic's storyline includes a vision from God telling Yogananda to go to America, for "you are the one I have chosen to spread the message of Kriya Yoga." But interest in his teaching begins to grow only after his move to Mount Washington. In the final panel, his *mahasamādhi* takes place as he promises his disciples, "My body shall pass, but my work shall go on."[52]

More recently, SRF released ten audio compact discs of Yogananda talks from late in his life that they had won exclusive rights to through the lawsuit with Ananda.[53] Unauthorized fan sites hosted by private devotees have sprung up all over the Internet, and YouTube features hundreds of audio, video, and music selections from his ministry posted by individuals alongside formal presentations provided by SRF.

Yogananda has also featured in film. In 2014, *Awake: The Life of Yogananda* was released. This hagiographic documentary presents Yogananda as a prescient global thinker for the twenty-first century. Though filmmakers Paola Di Florio and Lisa Leeman claim that *Awake* represents an "outside point of view" on "the guru who brought yoga to the West," it was produced with the full cooperation of SRF. In fact, the project originated in SRF's outreach to them. Di Florio and Leeman struggled with the challenge of how to "make a film about an exalted master," and the process became their own "voyage of Self-discovery."[54] Despite *Awake*'s support from SRF, the film included interviews with Kriyananda before he died. Some hoped that the project help heal wounds between the two organizations. This turned out to be unduly optimistic; even while filming was under way, Kriyananda criticized SRF for not having any males "at the highest levels" of leadership—comments that seemed insensitive to SRF, coming only a few months after the death of Daya Mata.[55] The film received generally positive press as an "absorbing glimpse into the life and times of the world's first superstar swami," though some were put off by its "feel-good cinematic hagiography."[56] The same year *Awake* was released, Ananda's *The Answer*, a docudrama about Swami Kriyananda's relationship with Yogananda, premiered at Cannes.[57]

In 2018, *The Life of Yogananda: The Story of the Yogi Who Became the First Modern Guru*, a popular biography of Yogananda by spiritual author and teacher Philip Goldberg, was published. Before the book's release, Goldberg asked rhetorically, "Why a biography? Isn't *Autobiography of a Yogi* enough?" His answer, not surprisingly, was "No, it's not. As the terrific documentary *Awake* showed, much of Yogananda's fascinating and influential life is not covered in his iconic memoir." Goldberg aimed to "fill in the many blanks and place Yogananda in historical context."[58] Interest in Yogananda is as lively as it has ever been, so the market for Yogananda-themed products, within SRF and outside it, remains vibrant.

ENSHRINING YOGANANDA

Encinitas remains a sleepy town, a beautiful Southern California location whose beach-casual vibe belies its residents' high income average. On any weekend, this scenic spot is overrun with tourists. Though most just want to enjoy the stunning beach, they cannot avoid hints of Yogananda's imprint, seamlessly integrated into this quintessentially California locale. There is Swami's Café, a stone's throw from the former vegetarian restaurant he ran for years, decorated inside with a mural of a surfing Yogananda. The town's famous surfing spot is named Swami's Beach in his honor. A pedestrian crosswalk spanning Pacific Coast Highway is labeled "Swami's Ped X-ing." More overt signs of SRF's presence include the Encinitas ashram, the adjoining garden with breathtaking bluff-top views, a local SRF temple, and an SRF bookshop.

The SRF store combines shameless Orientalist pandering—incense, textiles, Ganesh statues, Om wall decorations, carved furniture, and expensive musical instruments—with a variety of SRF publications. The shop promises consumers an authentic taste of India while they remain in Southern California comfort. Not surprisingly, the store's most prominent publication is *Autobiography of a Yogi*. Copies in English and a number of foreign languages are available, a testimony to Yogananda's worldwide popularity and a reminder of the ways that, according to Yale theologian Miroslav Volf, "world religions are part of the dynamics of globalization."[59] One of the translations of this English-language classic is in Bengali, Yogananda's native language, a perfect example of the pizza effect.

The Yogananda "shrine" inside the Encinitas Books & Gifts shop in Encinitas, California, a quintessential beach town and magnet for yoga practitioners. The store combines the sale of Orientalist products with the offer of spiritual development. While the lighted Yogananda display is reverential, his framed portrait is also for sale, an example of commodified spirituality that perfectly captures Yogananda's career.

In the center of this lavish Encinitas shop there is an elaborate, lighted shrinelike niche with a large iconic portrait of Yogananda from *Autobiography of a Yogi*. This arrangement conveys his revered, even his divine, status. At first this shrine seems out of place amid the flood of books, pamphlets, and Orientalist decorative items from his homeland. On further reflection, however, the portrait is perfectly suited to this commercial setting. The Hindu missionary to America who taught yoga to countless thousands through a correspondence course looks at home in this affluent, white, Southern California beach town. The polyglot books that surround him simultaneously suggest his status as "the 20th century's first superstar guru," as one *Los Angeles Times* writer labeled him.[60] Posed forever with a serene, beatific smile, he continuously extends the promise of God-contact through yoga, an offer of transcendence as compelling to many twenty-first-century seekers around the world as it was a century ago, when a young Bengali swami first set foot on American soil.

Notes

Unless otherwise indicated, all Web addresses are accurate as of May 2018.

INTRODUCTION

1. "Prime Minister Modi Pays Tribute to Swami Yogananda on the 65th Anniversary of His Passing," *India Down Under*, March 18, 2017, http://www.indiandownunder.com.au/2017/03/prime-minister-modi-pays-tribute-to-swami-yogananda-on-the-65th-anniversary-of-his-passing/.

2. Anthropologist Agehananda Bharati, who coined the term in 1970, offered the example of Maharishi Mahesh Yogi, who gained popularity in India after the Beatles adopted him as their spiritual mentor. See Bharati, "Hindu Renaissance."

3. "Virat Kohli Reveals the Inspiring Source That Changed His Life," *Hindustan Times*, February 19, 2017, http://www.hindustantimes.com/cricket/virat-kohli-reveals-the-inspiring-source-that-changed-his-life/story-UtA6DDUF097mvswkkFMELK.html.

4. "Paramhansa Yogananda: India's First Yoga Guru in the U.S.," *Times of India*, March 6, 2015.

5. Hitendra Wadhwa, "Yoga Modern Civilisation's Great Movement," *Daily Pioneer*, June 21, 2015, http://www.dailypioneer.com/state-editions/ranchi/yoga-modern-civilisations-great-movement.html.

6. Swami Anand Kul Bhushan, "We Should Pay Homage to the Mystic Paramhansa Yogananda," *Coast Week*, n.d., http://www.coastweek.com/3825-kul-bhushan-yogi-Paramhansa-Yogananda-introduced-yoga-in-united-states.htm.

7. "Paramahansa Yogananda," *Self-Realization Fellowship*, http://www.yogananda-srf.org/Paramahansa_Yogananda.aspx; "Paramahansa Yogananda," *Yogoda Satsanga Society of India*, https://yssofindia.org/paramahansa-yogananda/Paramahansa-Yogananda.

8. "Platinum Jubilee: Yogoda Satsanga Math—Dakshineswar," *Yogoda Satsanga Society of India*, https://yssofindia.org/75_years_of_Dakshineswar/.

9. On Vivekananda as a Hindu missionary, see Brekke, "Conceptual Foundation of Missionary Hinduism."

10. Wadhwa, "Yoga."

11. Deepak Chopra, "Why the New Age (Still) Matters," *BeliefNet*, http://www.beliefnet.com/columnists/intentchopra/2008/01/why-the-new-age-still-matters.html.

12. On Modi's daily regimen, see Price, *Modi Effect*, 137.

13. "PM Releases Commemorative Postage Stamp on the Occasion of the 100th Anniversary of Yogoda Satsanga Society of India," *Narendra Modi*, March 7, 2017, http://www.narendramodi.in/pm-modi-releases-special-commemorative-postage-stamp-on-100-years-of-yogoda-satsanga-math-534638.

14. California Department of State, *Articles of Incorporation of Self-Realization Fellowship Church*.

15. De Michelis, *History of Modern Yoga*, 188–89. This is true despite De Michelis's belief that such groups began only in the 1960s.

16. Cited in "Prime Minister of India Meets with YSS Monks," *Self-Realization Fellowship*, April 4, 2016, http://www.yogananda-srf.org/NewsArchive/2016/YSS_meeting_with_Modi.aspx.

17. "Locations," *Self-Realization Fellowship*, https://members.yogananda-srf.org/CenterSearch/SearchMap.aspx.

18. For an introduction to the larger historiographical project of transnationalism, see Bender, *Rethinking American History*. McGreevey, "American Religion," notes a few emerging themes in modern religious historiography that might be considered transnational and transpacific: twentieth-century developments in Catholicism and American overseas missions, particularly among Pentecostals.

19. Waghorne, "Beyond Pluralism," 233.

20. Csordas, "Introduction," 1–2. The contributors to Csordas, *Transnational Transcendence*, place transnational religious experience in the context of "globalization." Failing to historicize the important conceptual term globalization, they simply assert that it is a recent phenomenon and, thus by implication, so is transnational religion.

21. Forstoefel and Humes, *Gurus in America*; Singleton and Goldberg, *Gurus of Modern Yoga*; Gleig and Williamson, *Homegrown Gurus*.

22. Lucia, "Innovative Gurus," 221.

23. David Crumm, "Conversation with an Eastern Voice, Now Part of America's Spiritual Culture," *Read the Spirit*, https://www.readthespirit.com/explore/248-conversation-with-an-eastern-voice-now-part-of-americas/.

24. See Jensen, *Passage from India*. For a recent work exploring less familiar dimensions of the earlier Indian diaspora, including Muslims, see Bald, *Bengali Harlem*.

25. This label comes from Brekke, "Conceptual Foundation of Missionary Hinduism." On an attempt to distinguish a Hindu mission from proselytization, see Sharma, *Hinduism as a Missionary Religion*, esp. 131–38.

26. Dirks, *Castes of Mind*, 146.

27. Lucia, "Innovative Gurus," 222.

28. Race, *Christians and Religious Pluralism*, quotations on 11, 37, 72, 38.

29. Waghorne, "Beyond Pluralism," 231.

30. Thomas, *Hinduism Invades America*, 140. See also L. J. Vandenberg, "Coal to Newcastle," *Los Angeles Times*, January 28, 1925, B4, where the author refers to Yogananda's "reversion of evangelism."

31. Carrette and King, *Selling Spirituality*; Forstoefel and Humes, *Gurus in America*; Lucia, "Innovative Gurus"; Jain, *Selling Yoga*.

32. On negative stereotypes about India and Indians, see Prashad, *Karma of Brown Folks*. For negative stereotypes about yogis in particular, see Singleton, *Yoga Body*.

33. See esp. Carrette and King, *Selling Spirituality*.

34. Indeed, such a move may seem to further the dominance of Christianity within American religious historiography. Despite increased attention to metaphysical traditions and Asian religions, Christian traditions—especially Protestant traditions—still tend to dominate the historiographical landscape. See, e.g., the survey of recent American religious historiography provided by McGreevy, "American Religion," 242–60, which reviews several dozen books that, with a few exceptions, deal with Protestant or Catholic Christianity. On yoga and metaphysics, see De Michelis, *History of Modern Yoga*; and Singleton, *Yoga Body*.

35. *Los Angeles Times*, August 13, 1932, A2.

36. Crumm, "Conversation with an Eastern Voice."

37. The notion of an "accent" inflecting a spiritual "language" is borrowed from Prothero, *White Buddhist*, 69.

38. For a classic statement of seeking among the baby boomer generation, see Wuthnow, *After Heaven*. For more recent trends, see Putnam and Campbell, *American Grace*.

39. Schmidt, *Restless Souls*, 12; for greater elaboration, see esp. 227–68. Though he identifies Transcendentalists and other forerunners, his analysis really begins with the turn of the twentieth century.

40. See, most recently, Dochuk, *From Bible Belt to Sunbelt*. The classic study is McGirr, *Suburban Warriors*.

41. See McWilliams, *Southern California*; and Frankiel, *California's Spiritual Frontiers*.

42. See Engh, "'Practically Every Religion.'"

43. Weber, *Sociology of Religion*, 270.

44. For a classic statement on this view, see Berger, *Sacred Canopy*.

45. For Berger's later views, see Berger, *Desecularization of the World*. For an example of a reassertion of the older view, see Bruce, *God Is Dead*.

46. Strauss, "Adapt, Adjust, Accommodate," 72.

48. Singleton, *Yoga Body*, 131–32.

47. White, *Sinister Yogis*, 246.

49. De Michelis, *History of Modern Yoga*, 196.

50. Smith, *Hinduism and Modernity*, 173. Smith's list begins with Ramakrishna, Vivekananda's mentor, and proceeds to Vivekananda and then to ten other gurus whose lifespans overlapped with Yogananda's.

51. Goldberg, *American Veda*, 109–29.

52. Syman, *Subtle Body*, 170–71.

53. Trout, "Hindu Gurus." Trout's dissertation was published with minor changes as Trout, *Eastern Seeds*.

54. Anderson, "Reimagining Religion."

55. Foxen, *Biography of a Yogi*, 1.

56. For example, SRF provided documentary filmmakers Paola Di Florio and Lisa Leeman archival materials that they incorporated into their documentary *Awake: The Life of Yogananda*. But SRF cosponsored this deferential production and likely handed over preselected items rather than granting the filmmakers direct access to their archives. See "Acknowledgements" and "Texts and Photos" in the companion book published by SRF, Di Florio and Leeman, *Awake*, n.p. Similarly, Philip Goldberg, who was an interviewee for *Awake*, thanks SRF president Brother Chidananda for showing him "key archival documents" for his biography of Yogananda (*Life of Yogananda*, 333).

57. Trout, *Hindu Gurus*, 159.

58. Phyllis Lindeman to Dave Neumann, September 24, 2014, in author's possession; Lindeman to Neumann, October 10, 2014, in author's possession.

59. See, e.g., Sharma, *Neo-Hindu Views of Christianity.*

60. Syman, *Subtle Body*, 171; Yogananda, *Autobiography* (1946), 235. He seems to be referring specifically to the use of *āsanas*, since his Kriya Yoga assumes the importance of *kuṇḍalinī* power, a key teaching of *haṭha yoga*.

61. See, e.g., Bernard, "Sarvangasana," *Self-Realization*, May 1949, 12–15.

62. White, *Sinister Yogis*, 47.

63. Strauss, *Positioning Yoga*, xix, emphasis added. Alter, *Yoga in Modern India*; De Michelis, *History of Modern Yoga*; Singleton, *Yoga Body*.

64. Jain, *Selling Yoga*, 98.

65. Forsthoefel and Humes, *Gurus in America*; Singleton and Goldberg, *Gurus of Modern Yoga*; Gleig and Williamson, *Homegrown Gurus*.

66. A typical example is Amanda Porterfield's *Transformation of American Religion: The Story of a Late-Twentieth Century Awakening*, whose subtitle indicates her assumption that American religious pluralism is a very recent phenomenon.

67. This is the case Diana Eck makes in *A New Religious America: How a "Christian Country" Has Now Become the World's Most Religiously Diverse Nation*.

68. As late as 2008, the Pew Forum on Religion indicated that Buddhists, Muslims, and Hindus together made up less than 2 percent of the American population. See Cohen and Numbers, "Introduction," in *Gods in America*, 8–9.

CHAPTER 1

1. Yogananda, *Autobiography* (1946), 92–94.

2. Satyananda, "Yogananda Sanga," 178.

3. For example, hagiographic accounts complicate efforts to establish the history of the twentieth-century Indian gurus Krishnamacharya, Muktananda, and Satya Sai Baba. See Singleton and Fraser, "T. Krishnamacharya," 85; Jain, "Muktananda," 193; and Srinivas, "Sathya Sai Baba," 264. Yogananda was reluctant to disclose his age or birthdate, as part of his effort to convey a supramundane life story.

4. Self-Realization Fellowship, *Life of Paramahansa Yogananda*. On the introduction of streetcars to Calcutta, see "Engines and Horses," February 6, 1882, in Majumder, *Statesman*, 61–62.

5. See Inden, *Imagining India*. King, *Orientalism and Religion*, worries in particular that downplaying Indian agency may perpetuate "reproduction of colonialist tropes such as the myth of the passive Oriental" (205). More recently, see Adluri and Bagchee, *Nay Science*, which moves beyond the Orientalist critique, arguing that scholarship on India rigidly imposed Protestant (and anti-Catholic) categories on Indian texts, so this scholarship ultimately reveals more about European self-assessment than it does about India.

6. Chattopadhyay, *Representing Calcutta*, 14.

7. Alter, *Yoga in Modern India*, 73.

8. King, *Orientalism and Religion*, 205.

9. Despite the contested, problematic nature of the label "modernity," many historians continue to find it indispensable. For descriptions that largely agree with the assessment offered here, see particularly Thomas, "Modernity's Failings," 737; and Saler, "Modernity and Enchantment," 694.

10. Halbfass, *India and Europe*, routinely uses the label Neo-Hinduism to describe this modern outlook among Indians. Neither the term, which for Halbfass connotes inauthenticity, nor his negative assessment of the phenomenon is embraced in the present work.

11. Yogananda, *Autobiography* (1946), 29. Trout, "Hindu Gurus," 132–33, acknowledged the challenges of working with the *Autobiography* as a source and the dearth of unauthorized sources on his life nearly twenty years ago.

12. A few other sources might ostensibly fit into this category of those who did not know Mukunda during his childhood, but who spent extensive time with him and might have heard him relate childhood events. The most plausible candidate is Swami Kriyananda, who joined SRF in 1948 and spent extensive time, much of it one on one, with Yogananda during the last three years of his life. Kriyananda's lengthy Yogananda biography offers little assistance as a source, since it is more interested in hagiography than historiography. See Kriyananda, *Paramhansa Yogananda*, 1.

13. Ghosh, "*Mejda*," 3.

14. Ibid., 23.

15. See Satyananda, "Yogananda Sanga." Originally written in Bengali, this text was intentionally translated into wooden, literalistic English by a group of American followers who wished to avoid any impression of interpretive license.

16. Satyananda, "Yogananda Sanga," 163.

17. Dasgupta, *Paramhansa Swami Yogananda*, quotation on 79. Dasgupta's account was originally composed in Bengali in 1984 and translated into English only in 2006.

18. In this chapter, I note several examples of Yogananda's penchant for imaginative reconstruction. I limit these examples to cases where the understanding of a major event in his biography hinges on his characterization of the event. In chapter 4, I undertake a systematic discussion of the *Autobiography*'s narrative art.

19. For information about Mukunda's father, "*Mejda*" is far and away the most useful source; it provides specific, concrete details about dates of service, local, office, rank, and so on. Sananda claims that this information derives from *History of Services of the Officers of the Engineer and Accounts Establishment, Government of India, Public Works Department* (Ghosh, "*Mejda*," 10n.). Unfortunately, his bibliographical reference is incomplete, lacking a date of publication and page numbers. *History of Services* was published annually, but extant copies do not provide the information Ghosh reports. Other government sources do provide some record of Bhagabati's career, and these sparse sources uniformly corroborate Sananda's information. For example, *Government of India, Public Works Department, Classified List and Distribution Return of Establishment*, 595, confirms that "Bhaggobaty Charan Ghosh" was a deputy examiner, class I, in the Superior Accounts Establishment of Calcutta Railways. A second-grade accountant, he joined government service in April 1875 and had served for thirty-one years and three months as of June 1906. He had been in his current position since November 1905. Variations in the Anglicization of Indian names create a challenge in tracking down individuals in Indian government sources; the spelling of Bhagabati's name is different from Sananda's spelling, but the date of birth matches Sananda's information, confirming that this is his father, despite the variation in the spelling.

20. In a country with a staggering 94 percent illiteracy rate, just over 1 percent had any education (as opposed to basic literacy skills), and an even smaller fraction completed high school. Bhagabati's ability to speak English put him an elite category of 0.14 percent of the population. See *General Report on the Census of India, 1891*, 224.

21. Kopf, *Brahmo Samaj*, 195. Less than 1 percent of Indians were employed in state service, and the bulk of these were in jobs the census described as "menial"; about 0.2 percent of all employees were in clerical positions such as his. See *General Report on the Census of India, 1891*, 98–99.

22. Kerr, *Engines of Change*, 83. In 1885, he was transferred to the Office of the Government Examiner of Railway Accounts and sent to Saharanpur in the United Province. A year and half later, he was transferred again, this time to Muzaffarpur in Bihar. In October of 1890 he was sent to Gorakhpur to work for the Bengal and North-Western Railway (Ghosh, "*Mejda,*" 13).

23. Lahore, in the Punjab region of northwest India for two years, Bareilly in the United Province, and Chittagong in Burma for one short month (Ghosh, "*Mejda,*" 39, 49, 80).

24. Only twenty-eight towns in all of India had a population of over one hundred thousand at the time, and all of the places Bhagabati worked (with the exception of Gorakhpur, whose unique features are discussed above) fell into that category. The 1891 census indicates that India was over 90 percent rural, but even this statistic underreports the nature of the case. The rural population was composed overwhelmingly of tiny villages numbering fewer than a thousand people—hundreds of thousands of these villages were spread across a vast area largely untouched by direct British influence. See *General Report on the Census of India, 1891*, 42–49.

25. Headrick, *Power over People*, 186–91; Headrick, *Tools of Empire*, 155–60. In an 1853 memorandum that laid the foundation for British rail planning, then governor-general of India Lord Dalhousie wrote that railroads would allow the government to move troops much more rapidly than was currently possible. Quoted in Davidson, *Railways of India*, 87.

26. The phrase "agents of modern transformation" comes from Prakash, *Another Reason*, 144.

27. Kopf, *Brahmo Samaj*, 87. Given the nature of the Indian social pyramid, it makes sense to consider the *bhadralok* elites, and this label is used for them throughout this chapter. More recently, Chattopadhyay, *Representing Calcutta*, 138–39, offers a more nuanced taxonomy that reveals the aspirational character of the *bhadralok*; though they excluded the nobility and the destitute, the *bhadralok* spanned a range of income levels and classes.

28. Joshi, *Fractured Modernity*, 45.

29. Bhattacharya, *Sentinels of Culture*, 156.

30. Yogananda, *Autobiography* (1946), 4; Ghosh, "*Mejda,*" 326–28.

31. As Halbfass, *Tradition and Reflection*, 350–51, shows however, even in some ancient texts the two terms are occasionally used interchangeably.

32. A fifth category was the "untouchables." These people were *avarṇa*, completely outside the caste system, and members of the other castes avoided all physical contact with them.

33. Bayly, *Caste, Society and Politics*, 25.

34. Ibid., 10.

35. On this point, see esp. Dirks, *Castes of Mind*.

36. *Hindustani*, February 20, 1884, 161, quoted in Joshi, *Fractured Modernity*, 45.

37. Kopf, *Brahmo Samaj*, 87.

38. Dirks, *Castes of Mind*, 210.

39. Joshi, *Fractured Modernity*, 26.

40. Yogananda, *Autobiography* (1946), 5.

41. Ghosh, *"Mejda,"* 17.

42. Eck, *Darśan.*

43. Satyananda, "Yukteshvar," 9–29.

44. Satyeswaranda, *Biography,* 73.

45. Ghosh, *"Mejda,"* 23–24.

46. Yogananda, *Autobiography* (1946), 10.

47. According to Halbfass, *Tradition and Reflection,* 1, although the Vedas theoretically form the core orthodox religious texts, in practical terms most Indians generally ignore them.

48. Originally, the *saṃnyāsin* was probably an alternative path to the other three stages of earthly existence—the one who rejected home and family. But these alternate paths were eventually reconciled when *saṃnyāsins* was incorporated as a life stage to create a somewhat uneasy four-part system. Doniger, *On Hinduism,* 28.

49. Yogananda, *Autobiography* (1946), 7.

50. Ibid., 4–6.

51. Moore, *Manual of the Diseases,* 162–63. On modern transport and human migration in the spread of cholera, see McNeill, *Something New under the Sun,* 195.

52. Yogananda, *Autobiography* (1946), 5–6.

53. Ghosh, *"Mejda,"* 74.

54. Yogananda, *Autobiography* (1946), 16, 18.

55. Ibid., 16.

56. Yogananda, "The Lost Two Black Eyes," *East-West,* May 1932, 7. He also referred to India as a mother, thus conflating human motherhood, the divine, and the nation of India, a popular trope in late nineteenth-century Bengali literature, seen, e.g., in Chatterji's *Anandamath* and Rabindranath Tagore's *The Home and the World.*

57. *Census of India, 1911,* 24.

58. Bayly, *Birth of the Modern World,* 172.

59. Roy, *India in the World Economy,* 188; Kumar, *Cambridge Economic History of India,* 397–98. There was a small manufacturing sector. Three major industries accounted for most of the manufacturing output in late nineteenth-century industry: jute, cotton, and iron.

60. "Number of Coolie Emigrants Embarked from Calcutta, Madras, and French Ports in India, to Various Colonies," in *Statistical Abstract Relating to British India,* 276. See also Northrup, *Indentured Labor.*

61. Kopf, *Brahmo Samaj,* 42.

62. According to Sananda, from the day the two met, they were "fast friends." Ghosh, *"Mejda,"* 93–94.

63. They were in close physical proximity and both deeply interested in spiritual matters. Mazumdar provides one of the most important sources of information about Mukunda's early life. Apart from Mukunda's brother Sananda, Mazumdar is the only person with direct knowledge of Mukunda's childhood who provided any record. Mazumdar eventually became Swami Satyananda. See Satyananda, "Yogananda Sanga," 147.

64. Ghosh, *"Mejda,"* 144. Sananda recounts Mukunda's spiritual activities as a young boy: making his own Kali statue, installing a makeshift *puja* room for it, and conducting religious services that the family observed from a distance. This account smacks of hagiography, retrojecting Mukunda's spirituality into the earliest part of his life. In

his *Autobiography*, Yogananda, never reluctant to share about his precocious spiritual tendencies, does not mention this youthful Kali worship.

65. Satyeswarananda, *Biography*, 18, 22.

66. White, "Introduction," in *Tantra in Practice*, 9.

67. See Urban, *Tantra*, chap. 1. On the practitioner becoming divine, see Brooks, *Secret of the Three Cities*, 92.

68. Other Tantric devotees treat the consumption of polluting substances as purely symbolic activities. See Brooks, *Secret of the Three Cities*, xiv.

69. Doniger, *Hindus*, 419–20.

70. Satyananda, "Yogananda Sanga," 158.

71. Ghosh, "*Mejda*," 143–44.

72. Ibid., 144–45; Satyananda, "Yogananda Sanga," 157–58.

73. Yogananda, *Autobiography* (1946), 13.

74. Ghosh, "*Mejda*," 122–27.

75. Satyananda, "Yogananda Sanga," 172.

76. Ghosh, "*Mejda*," 122.

77. Satyananda, "Yogananda Sanga," 170.

78. Ibid., 172.

79. Yogananda, *Autobiography* (1946), 35.

80. Ghosh, "*Mejda*," 104–6; Satyananda, "Yogananda Sanga," 183; Dasgupta, *Paramhansa Swami Yogananda*, 13.

81. Ghosh, "*Mejda*," 119; quotation from Satyananda, "Yogananda Sanga," 183.

82. Dasgupta, *Paramhansa Swami Yogananda*, 12.

83. Sri "M" was responsible for *Kathamrita*, later translated into English as *The Gospel according to Ramakrishna*, a sprawling thousand-plus-page collection of the largely uneducated swami's sayings that Sri "M" recorded as he listened to Ramakrishna in Dakshineswar Temple. It takes the form of a day-by-day narrative of a series of dialogues, including frequent dialogues in which "M" discusses himself in the third person. Nikhilānanda, *Gospel of Sri Ramakrishna*.

84. Dasgupta, *Paramhansa Swami Yogananda*, 12.

85. Satyananda, "Yogananda Sanga," 181.

86. Jones, *Socio-Religious Reform Movements*, 78–82, quotation on 82. For a somewhat later version of the organization's views, see Bharat Dharma Mahamandal, *World's Eternal Religion*.

87. Farquhar, *Modern Religious Movements in India*, 316–23.

88. Yogananda, *Autobiography* (1946), 92.

89. See Satyananda, "Yogananda Sanga," 177.

90. Satyananda, "Yukteshvar," 75–81.

91. Ibid., 108.

92. Dasgupta, *Kriya Yoga*, 1–3.

93. Satyananda, "Yukteshvar," 78.

94. Ibid., 93–94.

95. Yukteswar, *Holy Science*, 51.

96. Ibid., xxii.

97. Yogananda, *Autobiography* (1946), 176.

98. Yukteswar, *Holy Science*, iii.

99. Long, "(Tentatively) Putting the Pieces Together," 161.

100. Panicker, *Gandhi on Pluralism and Communalism*, 48.

101. Dasgupta, *Paramhansa Swami Yogananda*, 20. Dasgupta explains that "in those days all spiritual-minded patriotic Indian youths' ideal was Mother India's valiant son Swami Vivekananda."

102. Satyeswarananda, *Kriya*, 217; Satyeswarananda, *Biography*, 56.

103. Joshi, *Fractured Modernity*, 7, comments that one "objective indicator distinguishing the middle class in colonial India was its exposure to western-style education."

104. Intriguingly, though, the two colleges he dabbled in did ultimately play a role in his life—as a vegetarian who experimented with different recipes and as a physical culturalist who believed that yogic practices healed the body and the mind, not just the spirit.

105. The Orientalist approach was partly inspired by EIC employee William Jones's conclusion that English and Sanskrit were part of a single language family, a conclusion that prompted efforts to preserve Sanskrit texts, to teach the language, and to reinforce a textual understanding of Indian religious traditions. See Jones, *Discourses Delivered before the Asiatic Society*, 28.

106. This analysis relies heavily on Ghosh, *History of Education*, 20–38.

107. Raj, *Relocating Modern Science*, 164.

108. Curtis, *Orientalism and Islam*, 187.

109. Despatch from the Court of Directors of the East India Company to the Governor-General of India, No. 49, 19 July 1854, reprinted in Richey, *Selections from Education Records*, 365, quoted in Bhattacharya, *Sentinels of Culture*, 157.

110. This policy applied directly only to such public universities as Calcutta University, but because local private colleges were all affiliated with them, some trickle-down improvement of instruction resulted. Ghosh, *History of Education*, 103–33.

111. Long, *Hand-Book of Bengal Missions*, 481–82.

112. Kopf, *Brahmo Samaj*, 159.

113. See Ghosh, *"Mejda,"* 184.

114. Long, *Hand-Book of Bengal Missions*, 493.

115. Kopf, *Brahmo Samaj*, 325–27.

116. See Dasgupta, *Awakening*, 2.

117. Chatterjee, *Empire and Nation*, 26–27, 45.

118. Halbfass, *India and Europe*, 341–48.

119. Sen, *Hindu Revivalism in Bengal*.

120. Hacker, *Philology and Confrontation*.

121. Halbfass, *India and Europe*.

122. Larson, *India's Agony over Religion*, 5. For a rejection of this view, see Nicholson, *Unifying Hinduism*, 142–43.

123. Kopf, *Brahmo Samaj*, 157.

124. Jones, *Socio-Religious Reform Movements*, 46.

125. Joshi, *Fractured Modernity*, 182.

126. Kopf, *Brahmo Samaj*, 177, See, e.g., Bharat, *Christ across the Ganges*; Sen, "Jesus Christ."

127. Thomas, *Acknowledged Christ of the Indian Renaissance*.

128. For example, the second century C.E. *Infancy Gospel of Thomas* recounts an event where the boy Jesus turned clay birds into real pigeons.

129. Joseph, "Jesus in India?," 161–99, quotation on 163.

130. See, e.g., Mazoomdar, *Oriental Christ*.

131. Also see King, *Orientalism and Religion*, 136.

132. Satyananda, "Yukteswar," 119.

133. Yogananda, *Autobiography* (1946), 166.

134. Ghosh, "*Mejda*," 184.

135. Satyeswarananda, *Biography*, 33.

136. Dasgupta, *Paramhansa Swami Yogananda*, 50.

137. Satyeswarananda, *Biography*, 13.

138. Ghosh, "*Mejda*," 93–94.

139. Satyeswarananda, *Biography*, 22.

140. Olivelle, "Orgasmic Rapture and Divine Ecstasy."

141. Kripal, *Kali's Child*. While Kripal received extensive criticism from devotees for his inference, in his preface to the revised edition of the book, he stood by his analysis and explained that it implied no disparagement of Ramakrishna. See Kripal, *Kali's Child*, xiii–xix.

142. Satyananda, "Yogananda Sanga," 213–14.

143. Ghosh, "*Mejda*," 186.

144. See Yogananda, *Autobiography* (1946), 237.

145. Ghosh, "*Mejda*," photo insert before p. 171, indicates that a photo of Yogananda was taken expressly for the Japan trip.

146. Satyananda, "Yogananda Sanga," 221.

147. Ibid., 159. On Tirtha's voyage to Japan, see Rinehart, *One Lifetime, Many Lives*, 1.

148. Ghosh, "*Mejda*," 185–86.

149. Dasgupta, *Paramhansa Swami Yogananda*, 36–37.

150. The maharaja's family maintains a website that celebrates this history of charity: "The Cossimbazar Raj Family," *Murshadabad: A Glimpse from the Past*, http://murshidabad.net/history/history-topic-cossimbazar-raj.htm.

151. This paragraph relies on Ghosh, "*Mejda*," 188–90; Satyeswarananda, *Biography*, 40–41; and Dasgupta, *Paramhansa Swami Yogananda*, 38–44, quotation on 39.

152. Yogananda, *Autobiography* (1946), 351.

153. Satyeswarananda, *Kriya*, 146.

154. Satyananda, "Yogananda Sanga," 262.

155. Dasgupta, *Paramhansa Swami Yogananda*, 46.

156. These intellectual traditions are typically divided into six schools of "philosophy," but there has long been significant overlap among schools. For a perceptive introduction to both the *ṣaḍdarśanas*, or "six orthodox schools," and the relations among them, see Flood, *Introduction to Hinduism*, 231–49. "Hinduism" has become a heavily contested label among a variety of scholars. Some think Hinduism is a fictional European entity "the way the 'satyr' and the 'unicorn' are" (Balagangadhara, "Orientalism, Postcolonialism, and Religion," 162). The most radical critics object that the label "Hinduism" is only symptomatic of the real problem. European invention of Hinduism simultaneously imported the category of religion into India. The British, in this view, used Christianity as a model to impose normative assumptions about "religion" on India. David N. Lorenzen pleads for reasoned moderation in defining religion, pointing out that despite the many differences in metaphysics, codes, and rituals, "religions are grounded in a certain type of mental experience or emotion that somehow gives authority to cultural and morel norms without the necessity of strict rational analysis" (Lorenzen, "Hindus and Others," 25–40, quotation on 38). Richard King, "Colonialism, Hinduism and the Discourse of Religion" 111, while cautioning about the potential for anachronism in using Hinduism for

the premodern period, acknowledges that "in the late colonial/modern context, the term 'Hinduism' certainly does take on increasing significance and social power as an indicator of Hindu national identity and has become a powerful cultural vector through which Indian civilizational history has been and is being interpreted." Without getting mired in this debate, the present work generally uses "Hinduism," since most scholars agree that by the nineteenth century, something called Hinduism undeniably existed, whether a recent reification or part of a longer tradition.

157. See Llewellyn, "Gurus and Groups," 228–30.

158. King, *Orientalism and Religion*, 69.

159. Nicholson, *Unifying Hinduism*, 25.

160. Long, *Vision for Hinduism*, 121.

161. Griffin, *Reenchantment without Supernaturalism*, 278–79, cited in Long, *Vision for Hinduism*, 121.

162. Bryant, *Yoga Sūtras*, 105.

163. Bryant comments on the prevalence of belief within Hindu traditions in a creator God and speculates that Patañjali accepted this belief and viewed God as personal. See Bryant, *Yoga Sūtras*, 90–91.

164. Yogananda, *Your Praecepta: Step I*, P17, 3.

165. Satyeswarananda, *Biography*, 23.

166. Ibid., 56.

167. Brekke, "Conceptual Foundation of Missionary Hinduism," 203–14, quotations on 203–4.

168. See King, *Orientalism and Religion*, 207, but note King's bleak assessment about the overall effectiveness in capitulating to Western tropes.

CHAPTER 2

1. This description is based on the photo that graced the inside cover of his first work, Yogananda, *Science of Religion*, likely taken shortly before his departure.

2. Tweed, *Dwelling and Crossing*.

3. Dasgupta, *Paramhansa Swami Yogananda*, 47–48.

4. None of the extant photos of Yogananda as a young man in India—or during his return trip in 1935–36—show him wearing a turban.

5. See Wight, *Trilogy of Divine Love*, 169.

6. Rambo, *Understanding Religious Conversion*, 98.

7. Aravamudan, *Guru English*; "Guru English" is defined on 10; quotation on 59.

8. Gaustad, "Pulpit and the Pews," 21.

9. See Voskuil, "Reaching Out," 74.

10. Sydney Ahlstrom's magisterial classic, *A Religious History of the American People*, appends two chapters on nonmainstream movements at the end of his eleven-hundred-page work; in this section he includes nearly seven pages on Asian religions. For a work narrowly focused on religion in the interwar period that ignores Hinduism and yoga, see Marty, *Modern American Religion*.

11. On the call to embrace a pluralistic narrative, see Seager, "Pluralism and the American Mainstream," 301–24. For more recent surveys, see, e.g., Noll, *History of Christianity*; his newer but briefer *Old Religion in a New World*; and Butler, Wacker, and Balmer, *Religion in American Life*.

12. See Albanese, *Republic of Mind and Spirit*, 368–69.

13. Both Catholic and Protestant bodies grew significantly. See Marty, *Modern American Religion*, 25–26.

14. See Flood, *Importance of Religion*, 153. Catholics did have their own modernist controversy, but theology and church structure made the issue much less prominent than for Protestants. See Jodock, *Catholicism Contending with Modernity*. American Catholics, who amounted to just over one third of the nation's religious adherents, were busier figuring out how to become a part of mainstream American culture while not succumbing to the dangers of "Americanism." See Kane, *Separatism and Subculture*. On statistics, see Department of Commerce and Labor, *Census of Religious Bodies*, 15.

15. Hedstrom, *Rise of Liberal Religion*, 15–16.

16. On fundamentalism as an intellectual movement, see Marsden, *Fundamentalism and American Culture*, 212–21, 14–17.

17. Ibid., 119.

18. "Foreword," in *Fundamentals*, n.p.

19. Marsden, *Fundamentalism and American Culture*, 167, identifies missions as a "crucial factor in the emergence of fundamentalism as an organized movement." On fundamentalist fears of a liberal takeover of foreign missions, see Carpenter, "Propagating the Faith," 28–31. On the question of the theological message of missions, particularly the role of Christ's divinity, see Patterson, "Loss of a Protestant Missionary Consensus," esp. 74–75.

20. Fosdick, "Shall the Fundamentalists Win?," 716–22. I use *liberal*, *mainline*, and *modernist* interchangeably in this book, as all of these terms were in use in the early to mid-twentieth century. Though not identical in meaning, they overlap. *Liberal* is used most often as the broadest term. On the use of these terms, see Hollinger, *After Cloven Tongues of Fire*, xiii–xiv.

21. For an earlier study of secularization in the academy, see Marsden, *Soul of the University*. More recently, Smith, *Secular Revolution*, has extended that analysis to psychology, law, journalism, and moral reform politics.

22. For liberal views of missions in the early decades of the twentieth century, see Wacker, "Protestant Awakening," 259–60; and Wacker, "Second Thoughts," esp. 285, 288–89. On ecumenicalism, see Hollinger, *After Cloven Tongues of Fire*, 21.

23. International Congress, *New Pilgrimages of the Spirit*, n.p.

24. Kopf, *Brahmo Samaj*, 21–23.

25. International Congress, *New Pilgrimages of the Spirit*, 7.

26. Ibid., frontis.

27. Ibid., 8.

28. See "Declares Japan Doesn't Want War," *Boston Daily Globe*, October 7, 1920, 5.

29. International Congress, *New Pilgrimages of the Spirit*, 8.

30. See Kopf, *Brahmo Samaj*, 51–67, quotation on 67.

31. Alter, *Yoga in Modern India*, 32.

32. Yogananda, *Science of Religion*, 54–56.

33. Ibid., 30–31, emphasis in original.

34. See Hollinger, *After Cloven Tongues of Fire*, 6–7, 14, on liberal Protestant Christianity as "accommodation with the Enlightenment." On the notion of a "sacred canopy," see Berger, *Sacred Canopy*.

35. Yogananda, *Science of Religion*, 29–30.

36. Ibid., iv, 48.

37. Ibid., 36–37.

38. Seager, "Pluralism and the American Mainstream," 301–24.

39. See Yogananda, *Autobiography* (1946), 357.

40. "History of Swami Yogananda's Work in America," *East-West*, November–December 1925, 7.

41. Dasgupta, *Paramhansa Swami Yogananda*, 49; Ghosh, "*Mejda*," 12. The estimate of $100 is based on the putative 1920 rate of 10 rupees to one pound sterling, and $4 to one pound sterling. See Eric W. Nye, "Pounds Sterling to Dollars: Historical Conversion of Currency," accessed Monday, May 7, 2018, http://www.uwyo.edu/numimage/currency.htm, and Jevons, *Money, Banking and Exchange in India*, 254.

42. J. W. Hose, India Office, to Angus Fletcher, Director of the British Library of Information, May 15, 1925, in author's possession.

43. *Life Story of Dr. M. W. Lewis*, 8.

44. Rosser, *Treasures against Time*, 3–4.

45. Smith, *Hinduism and Modernity*, 167, points out the cognitive dissonance for Americans drawn to gurus. At the same time, concerns about gurus' authority and the possibilities of abuse have also been expressed by Indians, from members of the Brahmo Samaj to the contemporary Indian press. See Goldberg and Singleton, "Introduction," 7–8.

46. Weber, *Economy and Society*, 242.

47. Rosser, *Treasures against Time*, 49.

48. See ibid., 17.

49. See Swami Yogananda Giri to Dr. and Mildred Lewis, December 13, 1923, in ibid., 65.

50. See Swami Yogananda to Doctor and Mil Lewis, June 24, 1924, in ibid., 77.

51. Swami Yogananda Giri to Doctor Lewis, November 23, 1924, in ibid., 62.

52. Ibid., 6–7.

53. Ibid., 47.

54. Ibid., 53.

55. *In the Footsteps of Paramahansa Yogananda*, n.p.

56. Eventually, the Boston organization had to be shut down. *Life Story of Dr. M. W. Lewis*, 12, 18.

57. Hose to Fletcher, May 15, 1925, in author's possession.

58. There were 125 women for every 100 men in religious organizations across the nation in the 1920s. Marty, *Noise of Conflict*, 31.

59. Schmidt, *Restless Souls*, esp. 227–68, quotation on 228. This term has most frequently been used by religious sociologists describing seekers of the baby boomer generation and, more recently, the millennial generation. For a classic statement of seeking among the baby boomer generation, see Wuthnow, *After Heaven*. For more recent trends, see Putnam and Campbell, *American Grace*.

60. "City College Unveiling—A Swami Comes to Town—Arkansas Travelers Arrive Here—Honored by France," *New York Tribune*, November 18, 1923, 11. Singleton, *Yoga Body*, 64–70.

61. *Boston Daily Globe*, March 3, 1921, 14.

62. Yogananda, *Science of Religion*, after 107.

63. Jung, *Psychological Types*.

64. See Yogananda, *Psychological Chart*, 6.

65. Ibid., 11.

66. Ibid., 10.

67. "History of Swami Yogananda's Work," 7, noted that Rashid had "proved invaluable in the work."

68. Dasgupta, *Paramhansa Swami Yogananda*, 52.

69. "Swami Offers Fount of Youth to New Yorkers," *New York Tribune*, November 25, 1923, 3.

70. Culver, *Frontier of Leisure*, 3.

71. "History of Swami Yogananda's Work," 9.

72. Highway proponents overcame opposition from states' righters, especially strong in the probusiness 1920s, to forge the Federal Highway Act of 1921, which developed a workable partnership among various levels of governmental authority (federal, state, county, and sometimes municipal) to establish road-building standards and begin a nationwide network of narrow concrete highways with gravel shoulders and wire-rope guardrails linking the nation. Seely, *Building the American Highway System*, quotation on 96.

73. S. Yogananda to Doc and Mil Lewis, September 25, 1924, in Rosser, *Treasures against Time*, 81.

74. S. Yogananda to Doctor and Mil Lewis, October 29, 1924, in ibid., 83.

75. "India Educator Visits Denver on Tour of Country; Swami Yogananda to Give Two Lectures before Leaving City," *Rocky Mountain News*, August 2, 1924, and "Swami Yogananda to Lecture in Denver," *Rocky Mountain News*, August 7, 1924, available at http://www.srf-denver.org/History.html.

76. "History of Swami Yogananda's Work," 11.

77. See Sitton and Deverell, *Metropolis in the Making*.

78. U.S. Census Bureau, www.census.gov.

79. Hise, "Industry and Imaginative Geographies," 18.

80. Tygiel, "Metropolis in the Making," 2–3; Starr, *Material Dreams*, 90–104.

81. Even before the turn of the century, important boosters like Charles Fletcher Lummis had promoted the Southland. See Starr, *Inventing the Dream*, 64–98; and Culver, *Frontier of Leisure*, 15–51.

82. Starr, *Material Dreams*, 96.

83. See Kropp, *California Vieja*.

84. Bottles, *Los Angeles and the Automobile*.

85. Singleton, *Religion in the City of Angels*.

86. Engh, "'Practically Every Religion,'" 202.

87. Singleton, *Religion in the City of Angels*, 105, 84, 96.

88. "Los Angeles, the Chemically Pure," *Smart Set* 39 (March 1913): 109, quoted in Starr, *Material Dreams*, 133–34.

89. Engh, "'Practically Every Religion,'" 201–2.

90. Federal Writers Project, *Los Angeles*, 67, 72.

91. Bunch, "'Greatest State for the Negro,'" 129–48.

92. Churches, primarily independent Baptist and American Methodist Episcopal churches, constituted the core of this black public sphere. Flamming, *Bound for Freedom*.

93. See Stokes, *D. W. Griffith's "The Birth of a Nation"*; for discussion of its aid to the Ku Klux Klan's growth, see 231–45; on NAACP resistance, see 129–31.

94. Goff, "Fighting Like the Devil in the City of Angels," 243.

95. Brereton, *Training God's Army*.

96. See Synan, *Holiness-Pentecostal Tradition*, 84–106.

97. Prominent Los Angeles fundamentalist minister "Fighting Bob" Shuler was perhaps McPherson's most visible and persistent critic. See Sutton, *Aimee Semple McPherson*, esp. 36.

98. See Frankiel, *California's Spiritual Frontiers*.

99. While insisting on the uncompromising nature of their own distinctive convictions they pleaded for unity among all Christians. "Last of Series of Talks Given," *Los Angeles Times*, January 23, 1923, II5; "Spiritual Law Basis of Creed," *Los Angeles Times*, July 3, 1923, II8; and "Lectures Draw Large Crowds," *Los Angeles Times*, January 26, 1920, II5.

100. Gottschalk, *Rolling away the Stone*, 141. Eddy allowed an assistant to include an epigraph from the Bhagavad Gita as a chapter epigraph in the sixteenth edition of *Science and Health*, which led some (including Swami Abhedananda, discussed below) to conclude that she was a student of Hindu scripture.

101. "Points Way to General Amity," *Los Angeles Times*, December 20, 1921, II9. Speakers included a longtime former Episcopal priest, a physician, and a judge—as well as some women, such as long-term Los Angeles resident Blanche Corby.

102. After Blavatksy's death, her esoteric ideas became less prominent. Prothero, "From Spiritualism to Theosophy," 197–216.

103. They even considered merging their nascent organization with the Arya Samaj, a Hindu reform organization not unlike the Brahmo Samaj.

104. Kirkley, "'Equality of the Sexes, But . . . ,'" 272–88.

105. "Inspector Coming Tomorrow," *Los Angeles Times*, November 18, 1902, A1.

106. "Pertinent Pulpit Paragraphs," *Los Angeles Times*, January 10, 1921, II3.

107. "Speaker Explains Aim of Theosophy," *Los Angeles Times*, October 24, 1921, II5.

108. Baur, *Health Seekers of Southern California*, 48, 93–96.

109. Sloane, "Landscapes of Health and Rejuvenation."

110. Ibid., 449.

111. "Introduction," in Pitzer, *America's Communal Utopias*, 10.

112. Hine, *California's Utopian Communities*, 165–66.

113. Roof, "Pluralism as a Culture," 82–99, reference on 86–87; Maffly-Kipp, *Religion and Society in Frontier California*, 182–83.

114. See Carroll, "Worlds in Space," 74, where he summarizes the work of William M. Newman, Rhys H. Williams, and others.

115. A point Braudy hints at in "Cultures and Communities," 276, but does not develop.

116. Lindsay, *Art of the Moving Picture* (1915), reprinted in Ulin, *Writing Los Angeles*, 48.

117. "The Rosicrucian Fellowship," n.p.

118. Cited in Engh, "Practically Every Religion," 201.

119. "Sou' by Sou'west," *Los Angeles Times*, January 28, 1900, IM29.

120. "Los Angeles a Microcosm," *Los Angeles Times*, December 15, 1908, II4.

121. Huxley, "Los Angeles: A Rhapsody," in *Jesting Pilate* (1926), reprinted in Ulin, *Writing Los Angeles*, 57.

122. Quoted in Starr, *Material Dreams*, 135.

123. See McWilliams, *Southern California*, 250.

124. This phrase and the framework it represents come from Frankiel, *California's Spiritual Frontiers*.

125. "Los Angeles a Microcosm," II4.

126. See Gokhale, *India in the American Mind*, 35.

127. On violence toward Mexicans, see Deverell, *Whitewashed Adobe*. Though Paddison,

American Heathens, covers an earlier period, the same dynamics remained in play in the early twentieth century. On the Ku Klux Klan, see Davis, "Sunshine and the Open Shop," 117. On its relationship to Protestantism, see Engh, "'Practically Every Religion,'" 207.

128. "Hindus Are Coming South," *Los Angeles Times*, September 25, 1907, I3; "Hegira of Hindus," *Los Angeles Times*, September 27, 1907, I1; "Influx of Hindus: Thousands from Vancouver Now Employed on Western Pacific in California," *Los Angeles Times*, November 10, 1907, II11; "The Secret of the Green Turban," *Los Angeles Times*, November 22, 1907, II4.

129. "Turbans on Heads, Shovels in Hands," *Los Angeles Times*, December 11, 1908, II1.

130. Lewthwaite, "Race, Place, and Ethnicity," 40–55. On the number of Indians, see Singh, Numrich, and Williams, *Buddhists, Hindus and Sikhs in America*, 44–45.

131. "A Hindu Problem," *Los Angeles Times*, April 8, 1910, II13.

132. See "People of the Coast," *Los Angeles Times*, January 30, 1907, II4; "Hindu's Turban Sign of Guilt," *Los Angeles Times*, April 28, 1913, II2; "Judge Scalps Hindu," *Los Angeles Times*, February 17, 1914, I12; and "May Wear Turban," *Los Angeles Times*, May 19, 1916, II9.

133. "Hindu Troops in Mutiny Kill British Officers," *Los Angeles Times*, February 19, 1916, I5. Several months later, the paper gleefully reported the execution of several rebels: "Execute Indians for Rebellion," *Los Angeles Times*, May 13, 1916, I2.

134. See Coulson, "British Imperialism," 1–42.

135. Chase and Pandit, *Examination of the Opinion of the Supreme Court*, 1–18.

136. Swami Yogananda, "Ethnologists vs. the 'Common Man,'" *East-West*, July–August, 1926, 10–13 (quotation on 13).

137. "Citizenship Is Refused Hindu," *Los Angeles Times*, February 20, 1923, I2.

138. See Coulson, "British Imperialism."

139. See "Hindu Case Ends Local Discussion," *Los Angeles Times*, February 21, 1923, I17; "Plea Made for Hindu's Citizenship," *Los Angeles Times*, September 25, 1923, I15; "Citizenship Contest of Hindu Ends," *Los Angeles Times*, November 18, 1923, I5; and "Hindu Status to Be Decided," *Los Angeles Times*, March 24, 1924, A2.

140. The image of the yogi as magician and imposter was a well-established theme in Europe as well. See Singleton, *Yoga Body*, 64–70.

141. "State Prosecutors Ready for Psychic Inquiries," *Los Angeles Times*, November 16, 1924, 14.

142. "Rubel Must Face a Jury," *Los Angeles Times*, March 1, 1905, II2; "Hypnotize the Jury? Nay, Nay!," *Los Angeles Times*, April 26, 1905, II5; "Faker Sentenced," *Los Angeles Times*, May 2, 1905, II2.

143. William T. Ellis, "Christian Endeavor," *Los Angeles Times*, June 1, 1901, 14.

144. "Eyes toward Nose, the Swami Meditated," *Los Angeles Times*, April 4, 1901, 11.

145. Daggett, "Heathen Invasion," quotation on 399–400.

146. Ibid., 401.

147. See Reed, *Hinduism in Europe and America*, esp. 117–22.

148. See, e.g., Randall and Randall, *Religion and the Modern World*, 118–20; and Atkins, *Modern Religious Cults and Movements*.

149. "Hindu Royalty as Los Angeles Guests," *Los Angeles Times*, July 29, 1919, II3.

150. "The Orient Contributes a Fashion," *Los Angeles Times*, October 10, 1915, VII8.

151. Hoganson, *Consumer's Imperium*, deals with a slightly earlier period and does not explicitly address Indian fashions in her assessment of Orientalism, but her argument about wealthy middle-class women's (superficial) aspirations to cosmopolitanism through consumption certainly fits here. Yoshihara, *Embracing the East*, addresses similar themes

and extends her coverage to 1940, but deals exclusively with East Asian Orientalist interests.

152. Edwin Schallert, "A New Circle of Cinema," *Los Angeles Times*, February 29, 1920, III13; and "Orient Spreads Colorful Wings," *Los Angeles Times*, July 11, 1920, III16.

153. See "Whiteside Will Play in 'Hindu,'" *Los Angeles Times*, March 25, 1923, III32.

154. See Grace Kingsley, "At the Stage Door," *Los Angeles Times*, October 1, 1915, III4.

155. See Surendra N. Guha, "A Hindu Girl to Her Betrothed," *Los Angeles Times*, January 22, 1922, VIII23; and Surendra N. Guha, "A Hindu's Love Letter," *Los Angeles Times*, March 26, VIII9.

156. Eugene Brown, "Break o' th' Year," *Los Angeles Times*, December 31, 1920, II4.

157. *The Cheat* ("Pola Negri, Kosloff Dancers Big Lure," *Los Angeles Times*, September 24, 1923, II7) and *Boomerang* ("'Boomerang' Makes Welcome Film Fare," *Los Angeles Times*, June 8, 1925, A7), both with Hindu schemers, reinforced negative stereotypes. In Bombay, the Douglas Fairbanks movie *The Thief of Baghdad* thrilled one Muslim Indian community. See "Hindus Howl over Doug Film," *Los Angeles Times*, October 20, 1925, A11.

158. See "Fitting Introduction," *Los Angeles Times*, September 28, 1924, B27. Early European films portrayed similar images of Hindus. See Singleton, *Yoga Body*, 66–67.

159. "Plan Rajah Dance," *Los Angeles Times*, December 16, 1922, II15. Indian dancer Roshanara, the stage name of Olive Craddock, the daughter of an English mother and an Anglo-Indian father, announced plans in 1916 to feature in a film celebrating Indian culture, but only if she could film in India. Grace Kingsley, "From Stage to Studio: Roshanara May Do the Hindu Dances on the Film," *Los Angeles Times*, January 24, 1916, II14.

160. Lovell is probably most famous today for the "Health House" that noted modernist architect Richard Neutra built for him in the late 1920s. Sloane, "Landscapes of Health and Rejuvenation," 447.

161. For example, *Los Angeles Times*, May 23, 1926, K24; May 6, 1928, L26; July 1, 1928, K26; and September 9, 1928, K26. The column had a similar tone when Harry Ellington Brook covered it. See, e.g., September 24, 1922, XI22.

162. Barclay L. Severns, *Los Angeles Times*, June 26, 1923, II14.

163. "News and Business," *Los Angeles Times*, March 25, 1901, I2.

164. "Pagan Worship in the States," *Los Angeles Times*, August 14, 1910, I7.

165. See "Obituary," *Los Angeles Times*, July 25, 1902, 2.

166. "'Christ, the Messenger': Swami Vivekananda's Views on the World's Redeemer," *Los Angeles Times*, January 8, 1900, I12. See Jackson, *Vedanta for the West*, 108–9.

167. Jackson, *Vedanta for the West*, 50–56.

168. *Los Angeles Times*, January 13, 1917, II2; January 27, 1917, II2; March 3, 1917, II2; March 30, 1918, II2; and January 12, 1918, II2.

169. See Abhedananda, *Vedanta Philosophy: Three Lectures*, 25, 34, 42, 54–55.

170. See Abhedananda, *Vedanta Philosophy: Five Lectures*, 10–12, quotation on 11. He also wrote about Indian history in culture in *India and Her People* and made the first English translation of Ramakrishna's teaching, *The Gospel of Ramakrishna*, in 1907.

171. Abhedananda, *Reincarnation*, 55–56. According to Vedanta, the end and aim of evolution is the "attainment of perfection" (62).

172. Ibid., 75.

173. Abhedananda, *India and Her People*, 227, 244.

174. Ibid.

175. Jackson, *Vedanta for the West*, 63–65, claims that the year was 1915, while French, *Swan's Wide Waters*, 123, gives 1916. No evidence suggests preaching activity by Paramananda before 1916. This was a second West Coast center, as the San Francisco center was one of earliest and most successful.

176. "Cult Will Settle in Hills," *Los Angeles Times*, May 27, 1923, II14.

177. For example, "How to Live?," "What Is Christianity?," "Freedom," "Sin and Salvation," and the "Science of Self-Mastery."

178. "Cult Will Settle in Hills." On the desire for an ashram in warm California, not cold Boston, see Levinsky, *Bridge of Dreams*, 274.

179. See Levinsky, *Bridge of Dreams*, 136–37, 228–29, 209–10, 217–19.

180. Her Los Angeles talks include "Evolution and Reincarnation," "Mind-Control and Character," "Sleep and Superconsciousness," "Realization through Daily Activity," and "Self-Mastery and Self-Surrender." *Los Angeles Times*, June 23, 1917, II2; *Los Angeles Times*, May 12, 1917, II6; *Los Angeles Times*, June 9, 1917, II2; "Spokesman for the Armenians," *Los Angeles Times*, May 26, 1917 II2; and *Los Angeles Times*, June 16, 1917, II2.

181. Levinsky, *Bridge of Dreams*, 206, 163, 370. She explicitly contrasts Yogananda's crass commercial style with the more restrained approach of Paramananda, who "recoiled from the carnival atmosphere of mass movements" (263).

182. Farquhar, *Modern Religious Movements in India*, 296.

183. *Los Angeles Times*, January 29, 1911, IV1.

184. Professor Guy Carleton Lee, "The Field of Fresh Literature—What Authors Are Saying, Doing, and Writing," *Los Angeles Times*, October 22, 1905, VI15.

185. "Venice Stands Up for Old India," *Los Angeles Times*, August 4, 1905, II9.

186. "Baba Bharati Bids Farewell," *Los Angeles Times*, June 22, 1907, II6.

187. "Good-Goods and Now Brahmins," *Los Angeles Times*, June 4, 1910, II10.

188. "Baba Bharati Bids Farewell."

189. "Greatest God Man," *Los Angeles Times*, March 19, 1906, I12.

190. Nelson, "B. Fay Mills," iii.

191. "Baba Bharati Bids Farewell."

192. "Rose Reinhardt Anthon: A Rarely Gifted Woman Now Living in Los Angeles," *Los Angeles Times*, May 13, 1906, VI18.

193. King, *Lotus Path*, n.p.

194. "Reply of Hindoo," *Los Angeles Times*, March 6, 1907, II6.

195. "Baba Bharati Says Not a Language," *Los Angeles Times*, September 19, 1906, II6.

196. Rose R. Anthon, letter to the editor, *Los Angeles Times*, March 2, 1914, II5.

197. "History of Swami Yogananda's Work," 11.

198. Alma Whitaker, "Swami Praising Spiritual Calm," *Los Angeles Times*, January 19, 1925, A18.

199. D. J. Vandenberg, "Coal to Newcastle," *Los Angeles Times*, January 28, 1925, B4.

200. "History of Swami Yogananda's Work," 11.

201. The Electric Railway Historical Association of Southern California provides detailed information about Mount Washington, the hotel, and the incline rail that transported passengers in the early twentieth century: http://www.erha.org/washington.htm.

202. Parsons, *Fight for Religious Freedom*, 67–68.

203. "Opening Festival," *East-West*, January–February 1926, 27.

204. *East-West*, July–August 1926, n.p.

205. Nye, *American Technological Sublime.*

206. Yogananda, *Master Said,* 119.

207. "History of Swami Yogananda's Work," 12.

208. Yogananda, *Autobiography* (1946), 205–6.

CHAPTER 3

1. Yogananda, *Your Praecepta: Step I,* P17, 3.

2. On "Yogoda" as Yogananda's own neologism, see below. For the ad, see *East-West,* May–June 1927, n.p.

3. The value of goods produced in the first quarter of the twentieth century quadrupled. See Presbrey, *History and Development of Advertising,* 598.

4. Scholars who apply a formal market model are mostly sociologists of religion. See, e.g., Iannaccone, "Religious Markets," 123–31; Finke and Stark, *Churching of America;* and, for a model of rational decision-making in a religious market, Stark and Finke, *Acts of Faith.* In *Founding Fathers,* historian Frank Lambert applies informal market insights to the colonial and early republican periods. Roof, *Spiritual Marketplace,* focuses his analysis on the post–World War II period. Stievermann, Goff, and Junker, *Religion and the Marketplace,* illustrates the common focus on recent, and almost exclusively Christian, cases.

5. See Moore, *Selling God,* who analyzes the entwinement between religion and consumption from the antebellum period through the New Age.

6. See Jain, "Muktananda"; and Urban, *Zorba the Buddha,* quotations on 13, 187. In *Selling Yoga,* Jain has also analyzed more broadly the emergence of counterculture-era American postural yoga through a capitalist framework. Carrette and King, *Selling Spirituality,* apply this model to contemporary yoga in a hand-wringing jeremiad.

7. Yogananda, "Creating Your Happiness," *East-West,* September 1932, 13. The quote on religious materialism is from Bryant, *Yoga Sūtras,* 57.

8. Sivulka, *Soap, Sex, and Cigarettes,* 93.

9. Marchand, *Advertising the American Dream,* 9.

10. Scott, *Psychology of Advertising,* 4.

11. Marchand, *Advertising the American Dream,* 271–73.

12. Bush, *Lord of Attention,* 5, Coolidge quoted on 5.

13. See Presbrey, *History and Development of Advertising,* 608–18, quotations on 611, 617.

14. Barton, *Man Nobody Knows,* 126.

15. Lears, *Fables of Abundance,* 177–78.

16. Hedstrom, *Rise of Liberal Religion,* 25.

17. "Book Review: *The Man Nobody Knows,*" *East-West,* May–June 1926.

18. "City College Unveiling—A Swami Comes to Town—Arkansas Travelers Arrive Here—Honored by France," *New York Tribune,* November 18, 1923, 11. Singleton, *Yoga Body,* 64–70. See below for further discussion.

19. Yogananda, *Songs of the Soul,* n.p.

20. *Washington Post,* January 2, 1927, 31.

21. *Los Angeles Times,* January 20, 1925, B11.

22. "Oriental Author Is Berkeley Visitor," *Berkeley Daily Gazette,* November 6, 1924, 5.

23. "India Educator Visits Denver on Tour of Country; Swami Yogananda to Give Two Lectures before Leaving City," *Rocky Mountain News,* August 2, 1924; "Swami Yogananda

to Lecture in Denver," *Rocky Mountain News*, August 7, 1924; both reprinted at http://www.srf-denver.org/History.html.

24. *Washington Post*, January 2, 1927, 31.

25. Yogananda, *East-West*, November–December 1925, n.p. On the relationship between Yogananda and Burbank, see Smith, "Luther Burbank's Spineless Cactus," 66–68. Burbank gained notoriety shortly after this endorsement when he labeled himself an "infidel" for his criticism of existing religions. "Burbank Declares He Is True Infidel," *Baltimore Sun*, January 23, 1926, 1. For his views, see Burbank, *My Beliefs*; and see Clampett, *Luther Burbank*, for a contemporary defense.

26. *Time*, February 20, 1928, 26.

27. Amelita Galli-Curci, "Foreword," in Yogananda, *Whispers from Eternity*, 9–11.

28. "Los Angeles News," *East-West*, July–August 1928, 25.

29. Little, *American Orientalism*, 17. Though Little is referring to American views of the Middle East, his comment remains apropos for views of India.

30. Shohat, "Gender and Culture of Empire," 25; Studlar, "'Out-Salomeing Salome,'" 99.

31. Yogananda, "Watching the Cosmic Motion Picture of Life," *East-West*, May–June 1928, 3–4.

32. Swami Yogananda to James Lynn, July 12, 1936, in *Rajarsi Janankananda*, 121.

33. Miller, *Consuming Religion*, 79.

34. Wight, *Trilogy*, 173.

35. Stockton, *Testimony of Love*, 28.

36. Susman, "'Personality' and the Making of Twentieth-Century Culture," quotation on 276.

37. For Whitefield, see Stout, *Divine Dramatist*; and Lambert, *"Pedlar in Divinity."* For Finney and Dow, see Hatch, *Democratization of American Christianity*.

38. An immediate best seller, the novel deeply shaped the public's perception of evangelical preachers, according to Weaver, *Evangelicals and the Arts*, 51–64.

39. Moore, *Selling God*, 106–12; on commodified religion, see 119.

40. Dorsett, *Billy Sunday*, 95.

41. Moore, *Selling God*, 186–87.

42. Charles Fuller, later founder of Fuller Seminary, might be included in this group as well. See Carpenter, *Revive Us Again*, 78–79. His radio ministry did not begin until 1937, and he pioneered a more moderate fundamentalism. See Goff, "'Fighting Like the Devil,'" 220–52.

43. See Sutton, *Aimee Semple McPherson*, quotation on 76.

44. Thomas, *Hinduism Invades America*, 171.

45. See *Los Angeles Times*, November 7, 1925, A2.

46. "Student Throws Away Crutch at Swami's Healing Meeting," *East-West*, January–February 1926, 31.

47. Leuchtenburg, *Perils of Prosperity*, 197–98.

48. Davis, "Corporate Reconstruction of Middle-Class Manhood," 201–16; for Los Angeles, see 205–6.

49. Yogananda, *Your Praecepta: Step I*, P17, 4.

50. Yogananda, "Who Is a Swami?," *East-West World Wide*, January–February 1926, 16.

51. "Swami Buys Swanky Car," *Los Angeles Times*, December 6, 1925, G3.

52. See French, *Swan's Wide Waters*, 128–38.

53. Lee and Sinitiere, *Holy Mavericks*, 3.

54. This typology borrows from Stolz, "Salvation Goods and Religious Markets," 13–32, which builds off of the insights of Weber, who first conceptualized religion as a commodity.

55. See Satyeswarananda, *Kriya*, 145–46.

56. See Albanese, *Republic of Mind and Spirit*. Benz, *Theology of Electricity*, shows how some Catholics and Protestants had been fascinated by the theological implications of electricity as well.

57. Nye, *Electrifying America*, 155.

58. Regarding electricity and laborsaving devices as consumer products in the 1910s and 1920s, see Sivulka, *Soap, Sex, and Cigarettes*, 126–30.

59. Yogananda, *Yogoda*, 1.

60. Muller, *My System*. His childhood friend and ashram partner, Satyananda, "Yogananda Sanga," 244, seems to report Muller's influence, though with some imprecision. Singleton, *Yoga Body*, 131–32, who briefly discusses Yogananda in the context of the international physical cultural context in which modern yoga practice developed, exaggerates the centrality of muscle control in Yogananda's overall routine.

61. Satyeswarananda, *Kriya*, 258.

62. The content of the original lessons is very difficult to fully reconstruct. The analysis in this chapter is based on the *Praecepta* lessons, a consolidation and enlargement of the lessons that was begun in 1934 and completed in 1938, which provide the most complete, sequential presentation of extant materials. As with virtually all of Yogananda's writings, the lessons have been subjected to SRF's editing since his death; renamed *Self-Realization Fellowship Lessons* and copyrighted in 1956 (and again in 1984), they contain much of the same material in the same number of lessons, but substantially reordered and rewritten.

63. Yogananda, *Your Praecepta: Step I*, P1, 2.

64. Ibid., P12, 4.

65. Yogananda, *Your Praecepta: Step V*, P109, 2.

66. Ibid.

67. Yogananda, *Your Praecepta: Step I*, P3, 3.

68. Ibid., P1, 3.

69. Yogananda, *Your Praecepta: Step V*, P150, 1.

70. Yogananda, *Your Praecepta: Step VI*, P154, 2.

71. Yogananda, *Your Praecepta: Step VII*, P157, 4.

72. Yogananda, *Your Praecepta: Step V*, P105, 4.

73. Yogananda, *Your Praecepta: Step VII*, P166, 4.

74. Yogananda, *Your Praecepta: Step I*, P7, 3.

75. Yogananda, *Your Praecepta: Step V*, P105, 2.

76. Yogananda, *Your Praecepta: Step I*, P7, 3, P5, 4.

77. Ibid., P26, 3.

78. See Nicholson, *Unifying Hinduism*, 36.

79. Yogananda, *Your Praecepta: Step VII*, P181, 4.

80. Sarbacker, "Numinous and Cessative in Modern Yoga," 172; Sarbacker, *Samadhi*. Sarbacker borrows the term "numinous" from Rudolf Otto, who coined it in *The Idea of the Holy*.

81. White, *Sinister Yogis*, esp. 47.

82. Bryant, *Yoga Sūtras*, 472, 254, 169, 171. On a somewhat different interpretation of the *Yoga Sūtras*' theism, see Larson, "Introduction to the Philosophy of Yoga," 91–100, 136–47.

83. Nicholson, *Unifying Hinduism*, 182.

84. Pittman, "University Correspondence Study," 22; Peters, "Most Industrialized Form of Education," 58–59.

85. See McFarland et al., *Encyclopedia of Sunday School and Religious Education*, 23–24. This publication viewed the genesis of the distance learning movement as an outgrowth of the Chautauqua movement (thus rooted in the church), which developed into courses offered by several denominations and/or affiliated seminaries. On Moody, see Pittman, "University Correspondence Study," 24.

86. Jackson, "New Thought Movement," 537–40, quotation on 539.

87. Ibid., 539.

88. For the founding of the correspondence school, see *Echoes from Mount Ecclesia*, June 1914, 1–4, quotation on 3. On the topics for the course, see Heindel, *Birth of the Rosicrucian Fellowship*, n.p.

89. Leland, "Afterword," 109.

90. Strauss, *Positioning Yoga*, 47.

91. Ramacharaka, *Correspondence Class Course*, n.p.

92. Satyeswarananda, *Kriya*, 280.

93. Yogananda, *Your Praecepta: Step I*, P7, 2.

94. Satyeswarananda, *Kriya*, 258; Dasgupta, *Paramhansa Swami Yogananda*, 56.

95. "For Private and Personal Use," *Yogoda Correspondence Course*, n.p., in author's possession.

96. Yogananda, *Your Praecepta: Step VII*, P177, 4.

97. On this combination of traditional focus on secrecy and modern entrepreneurial concern, see a similar example in Waghorne, "Engineering an Artful Practice," 296.

98. Kriyananda, *Kriya*, 324, cited in Trout, *Eastern Seeds*, 121.

99. L. Y. Royston to Miss Mary Friedel, August 6, 1941, in author's possession.

100. "Special Notice to Friends and Students of Swami Yogananda," *East-West*, November–December 1925, n.p.

101. See "Sympathy for Aimee Semple McPherson," *East-West*, September–October 1926, 24.

102. See Love, *The Great Oom*.

103. See, for example, Deslippe, "The Swami Circuit," 11–12.

104. Albanese, *Republic of Mind and Spirit*, 370, describes Yogananda's language about mind and "self-realization" as influenced by New Thought. Realization language, however, was frequently used by modern yoga teachers to describe the process of self-discovery in meditation. See Larson, "Introduction to the Philosophy of Yoga." Trine, "Extracts from 'In Tune with the Infinite,'" *East-West*, September–October 1926, 23–24. "Churches Heed Armistice," *Los Angeles Times*, November 9, 1929, A6.

105. Leadbetter, *Chakras*, 72. See Leland, *Rainbow Body*, for an exploration of Western appropriation of the *cakra* system, esp. 72–76, where he delineates key differences between Indian and Western understandings.

106. Yogananda, "Yellow Journalism versus Truth: Are Eastern Teachings Dangerous?," *East-West*, January–February 1928, 3–8.

107. Yogananda, "Christian Science and Hindu Philosophy," *East-West*, May–June, 1926, 7–9; July–August 1926, 4–7.

108. "Health Hints," *East-West*, January–February 1926, 13.

109. On the growth of home economics amid the early twentieth century's consumer culture, see Goldstein, *Creating Consumers*.

110. Yogananda, "Three Recipes," *East-West*, May–June 1926, 28.

111. Yogananda, "Spiritual Recipe," *East-West*, May 1932, 25.

112. "Three Recipes," *East-West*, May–June 1926, 28.

113. Yogananda, "Four Recipes," *East-West*, May–June 1927, 15.

114. Yogananda, "Three Recipes," *East-West*, November–December 1927, 27.

115. Yogananda, "Three Recipes," *East-West*, July–August 1928, 22.

116. Yogananda, "Three Recipes," *East-West*, September–October 1927, 22.

117. Yogananda, "Recipes," *East-West*, March–April 1930, 22.

118. Ibid.

119. *Inner Culture*, May 1934, 30.

120. *Inner Culture*, December 1936, 32.

121. *Inner Culture*, September 1935, 32; January 1935, 30.

122. *East-West*, January–April 1927, n.p.

123. *Inner Culture*, December 1936, 32.

124. Bryant, "*Ahimsa* in the Patanjali Yoga Tradition," 33–47.

125. "Three Recipes," *East-West*, November–December 1927, 27.

126. Putney, *Muscular Christianity*.

127. Synan, *Holiness-Pentecostal Tradition*, 201.

128. Iacobbo and Iacobbo, *Vegetarian America*, 12, 21, 108, 98; Beecher quoted on 108; quotation about Kellogg on 129.

129. Tweed, *American Encounter with Buddhism*, 81; Iacobbo and Iacobbo, *Vegetarian America*, 112.

130. Iacobbo and Iacobbo, *Vegetarian America*, 130.

131. *East-West*, January–April 1927, n.p.; November–December 1929, n.p.; November–December 1926, n.p.

132. Hudnut-Beumler, *In Pursuit of the Almighty's Dollar*, 115.

133. *East-West*, November–December 1926, 18.

134. Parsons, *Fight for Religious Freedom*, 109.

135. "Meatless Coolidge Meals Prescribed by Yogananda," *Washington Post*, January 15, 1927, 8.

136. George Rothwell Brown, "Post-Scripts," *Washington Post*, January 15, 1927, 1.

137. "Sage Sees Coolidge," *Washington Herald*, January 25, 1927, reprinted in *East West*, January–April 1927, 38–39.

138. Apparently, Mildred Lewis foresaw just such an eventuality earlier in their relationship: see [Swami Yogananda] to Dr. M. W. Lewis, in Rosser, *Treasures against Time*, 103.

139. Ferguson, *New Books of Revelations*, 312.

140. Thomas, *Hinduism Invades America*.

141. Thomas, "Foreword," ibid., n.p.

142. Ibid., 150. The November–December 1928 issue of *East-West*, 14, mentioned twenty thousand followers.

143. Satyeswarananda, *Kriya*, 180.

144. Premananda, "My Gurudev," 5.

145. Ibid.

146. Yogananda named him a *brahmachari*, or student, as a preliminary step before becoming a swami. Anil Nerode, "The Works of My Father, Sri Nerode," http://www.math.cornell.edu/~anil/ad.html.

147. Satyananda, "Yogananda Sanga," 262.

148. Yogananda, *Science of Religion*, n.p.

149. Satyeswarananda, *Kriya*, 173.

150. Nerode, "Works of My Father." More recently, Nerode has claimed that while growing up at Mount Washington, he witnessed James M. Warnack, an author and *Los Angeles Times* editor, ghostwrite the *Autobiography* by weaving together various notes and stories Yogananda had written. See Deslippe, "The Swami Circuit," 38.

151. Satyeswarananda, *Kriya*, 180.

152. Yogananda, "Mahatma Gandhi," *East-West*, April 1932, 9.

153. "Mme. Naidu in America," *East-West*, November–December 1928, 14,

154. Under Secretary of State, Foreign Office, to Under Secretary of State, India Office, June 20, 1927, in author's possession.

155. Gerald Campbell, Consul General, to Secretary of State, Foreign Office, May 12, 1926, in author's possession.

156. Esme Howard, British Ambassador, to Austen Chamberlain, Secretary of State for Foreign Affairs, January 4, 1927, in author's possession.

157. Howard to Chamberlain, April 29, 1926, in author's possession.

158. *East-West*, October 1932.

159. Yogananda, *Songs of the Soul*, 85–87. On Yogananda's inspiration from Tirtha, see Satyananda, "Yogananda Sanga," 159.

160. Mayo, *Mother India*. She was also an advocate of immigration restrictions and critic of independence for the Philippines. See Sinha, *Specters of Mother India*.

161. Natarajan, *Miss Mayo's Mother India*.

162. Iyer, *Father India*.

163. Wood, *An Englishman Defends Mother India*.

164. Dale Stuart, "Some Replies to an American Critic of India," *East-West*, January–February 1928, 23.

165. Two years later, Christy would expand his dissertation into a book, *The Orient in American Transcendentalism*. Carpenter, *Emerson and Asia*, made a similar case in 1930.

166. Alice Hill Booth-Smithson, "Mother India," *East-West*, January–February 1928, 24.

167. Jenkins, *Mystics and Messiahs*, 121–48.

168. "Swami Returns from East," *Los Angeles Times*, January 15, 1928, B2.

169. Godfrey A. Fisher, British Consul, to Esme Howard, British Ambassador, March 1, 1928, in author's possession.

170. Godrey A. Fisher, British Consulate, to Gerald Campbell, Consul General, April 20, 1926, in author's possession.

171. "Fined for Telling Women of Love," *Indiana (Pa.) Evening Gazette*, February 6, 1928.

172. Vice Consul in Miami to Consul in Atlanta, March 1, 1928, in author's possession.

173. "Fined for Telling Women of Love," *Indiana (Pa.) Evening Gazette*, February 6, 1928.

174. "News of the Night in Brief," *Fitchburg (Mass.) Sentinel*, February 4, 1928, 3.

175. Vice Consul in Miami to Consul in Atlanta.

176. "Judge Withholds Ruling on Ouster of Hindu Mystic," *Atlanta Constitution*, February 9, 1928, 16.

177. The *Atlanta Constitution* mockingly reported that Yogananda had indeed conducted one successful healing: he cured a horse of palsy. See "Federal Court Suit Threatened by Hindu Swami," *Atlanta Constitution*, February 8, 1928, 20.

178. "Swami's Lectures to Women Face Ban as Miami Official Foresees Violence," *New York Times*, February 4, 1928, 1.

179. Ferguson, *New Books of Revelations*, 1, 312.

180. *Washington Post*, February 12, 1928, S2.

181. Ibid.

182. Yogananda, "Yellow Journalism versus Truth," 3–8.

183. See "Chief of Police Quigg Arrested in Miami," *East-West*, March–April 1928.

184. "Swami under Investigation," *Los Angeles Times*, October 17, 1925, A1; "Indian Seer in Civil Suit: Action Filed as Yogananda Continues Lectures; Immigration Officers Start Quiz," *Los Angeles Times*, October 18, 1925, 3.

185. Parsons, *Fight for Religious Freedom*, 68.

186. Satyeswarananda, *Biography*, 44.

187. Parsons, *Fight for Religious Freedom*, 40.

188. Swami Yogananda to Dr. Lewis, May 23, 1929, in Rosser, *Treasures against Time*, 112.

189. Yogananda, "Recipe Messages," *East-West*, November–December 1929, 21.

190. "Swami Yogananda Visits Mexico" and "Meets President Portes Gil," *East-West*, November–December 1929, 28.

191. Paramhansa Yogananda to Duj [Durga Mata], October 11, 1935, August 4, 1934, September 4, 1935.

192. "Swami Row to Be Aired," *Los Angeles Times*, August 21, 1935, A8; "Swamis Air Money Row," *Los Angeles Times*, August 22, 1935, A3.

193. Swami Giri-Dhirananda, also known as Basu Kumar Bagchi vs. Swami Yogananda, also known as Mukunda Lal Ghosh, 387391 (S.C. Ca 1936).

194. Masters and Tsomo, "Mary Foster," 235–48. She gave Yogananda twenty thousand dollars and supported at least three other Indian gurus. See Kemper, *Rescued from the Nation*, 110, 363.

195. See Satyananda, "Yogananda Sanga," 208.

196. Daya Mata, *Finding the Joy within You*, 250.

197. Noll, *History of Christianity*, 431–33.

198. Quoted in Hudnut-Beumler, *In Pursuit of the Almighty's Dollar*, 123.

199. Bey, *My Experiences Preceding 5,000 Burials*, 5–14.

200. "Fakir Buried Hours, Beats Houdini Time," *New York Times*, January 21, 1927, 37.

201. Yogananda, "Hamid Bey, 'Miracle Man,'" *East-West*, September–October 1927, 23.

202. "Announcement Extraordinary," in author's possession.

203. *Rajarsi Janakananda*, 29.

204. Yogananda to Lynn, February 27, 1932, ibid., 53.

205. "Foreword," *East-West*, April 1932, n.p.

206. Yogananda to Lynn, February 27, 1932.

207. Yogananda to Lynn, October 13, 1933, ibid., 54.

208. Parsons, *Fight for Religion Freedom*, 40–41.

209. As part of its defense against a Self-Realization Fellowship lawsuit, discussed in chapter 5, attorneys for Ananda cataloged examples of the use of this term from ancient and contemporary times—and from around the world—in such volume that evidence was placed in twelve three-ring binders. See Parsons, *Fight for Religion Freedom*, 64–65.

210. Susman, "'Personality,'" 276, uses this term to capture turn-of-the-century interest in self-cultivation.

211. California Department of State, *Articles of Incorporation of Self-Realization Fellowship Church.*

CHAPTER 4

1. Yogananda, *Autobiography* (1946), 474–76.

2. Satya Sai Baba is one of the most successful contemporary examples. The label "global guru" comes from Palmer, "Baba's World," and Waghorne, "Beyond Pluralism." Alter, "Shri Yogendra," and Jain, "Muktananda," offer similar paradigms, Alter describing "global gurudom" and Jain "a global entrepreneurial godman."

3. Sluga and Horne, "Cosmopolitanism," 369–73; Sluga, *Internationalism in the Age of Nationalism.* For various forms of transnational connections around the turn of the century, see also Conrad and Sachsenmaier, *Competing Visions*; and Rosenberg, "Transnational Currents," 823–48.

4. Iriye, *Cultural Internationalism and World Order.*

5. See White, *Structure of Private International Organizations,* 11.

6. Iriye, *Global Community,* 28.

7. Iriye, *Cultural Internationalism and World Order,* 147.

8. For the Washington, D.C., conference, see "Swami Yogananda Addresses Fellowship of Faiths Meeting," *East-West,* May–June, 1929, 42; for the Los Angeles gathering, see "World Faiths to Be Discussed," *Los Angeles Times,* February 17, 1937, 12; and "Swami Will Address World Fellowship of Faiths," *Inner Culture,* March 1937, 28.

9. Francis J. McConnell, "Explaining the World Fellowship of Faiths," in Weller, *World Fellowship,* 9.

10. Francis Younghusband, "Fellowship with the Universe," ibid., 46–47.

11. Rajah Jai Prithvi Bahadur Singh, "The Most Outstanding Event in the Century," ibid., 10.

12. "Six American Leaders' Greetings," ibid., 13.

13. Yogananda, "What Nineteen Faiths Contribute to Scientific Technique," ibid., 567–73.

14. Dasgupta, *Paramhansa Swami Yogananda,* 72.

15. Dasgupta mentions "the planetarium," which could only mean Griffith Observatory, which opened in 1935. Ibid., 53–54.

16. Satyananda, "Yogananda Sanga," 267.

17. *Times of India,* September 25, 1936, 4. See also Dasgupta, *Paramhansa Swami Yogananda,* 56.

18. "Swami's Fellowship Centres in America," *Times of India,* August 23, 1935, 14.

19. "Union of East and West: Jubilee in London," *Times of India,* July 22, 1935, 14.

20. Satyananda, "Yogananda Sanga," 269.

21. "Discussion with Swami Yogananda," in *Collected Works of Mahatma Gandhi,* vol. 61, 392.

22. He mentioned this claim first shortly after his visit with Gandhi in letters to James Lynn: Swami Yogananda to James Lynn, September 19, October 1, 1935, in *Rajarsi Janakananda,* 75, 79. He repeated this claim in more elaborate form in the *Autobiography* (1946), 444.

23. See "Mahatma Gandhi Is Host to Swami Yogananda," *Inner Culture,* March 1937, 49. *Gandhi,* a nearly seven-hundred-page biography written by his grandson Rajmohan Gandhi, makes no mention of Yogananda or of being introduced to Kriya Yoga.

24. See Yogananda to Lynn, October 1, 1935, in *Rajarsi Janakananda*, 80.

25. Yogananda to Lynn, September 19, 1935, ibid., 76.

26. Reprinted in Yogananda, *Autobiography* (1946), 376–77. Yogananda's younger brother Sananda describes a more grandiose, affective reunion than Yogananda. See Ghosh, *"Mejda,"* 198–99.

27. See Yogananda to Lynn, January 30, 1936, in *Rajarsi Janakananda*, 100.

28. Yogananda, *Autobiography* (1946), 400.

29. Dasgupta, *Paramhansa Swami Yogananda*, 93.

30. Satyeswarananda, *Kriya*, 150, reports this dialogue as an account that Satyananda shared with him late in his life.

31. Dasgupta, *Paramhansa Swami Yogananda*, 94–95. See Yogananda, *Autobiography* (1946), 400n. Richard Wright's travel diary would illuminate many details about the India trip, including this reported altercation, but SRF has never published it.

32. Ghosh, *"Mejda,"* 199.

33. Though Yogananda omitted the mockery from his recollection of the incident, he did confirm that he departed for the *kumbha mela* against Yukteswar's wishes. See Yogananda, *Autobiography* (1946), 401.

34. Ghosh, *"Mejda,"* 224.

35. Yogananda to Lynn, March 17, 1936, in *Rajarsi Janakananda*, 103.

36. Ibid., 104.

37. This prophecy never came true. Both the Serampore ashram and the Puri ashram (where Yukteswar is buried), however, remain outside of SRF ownership.

38. See S. Yogananda to Doc and Mil [Lewis], July 1, 1936, in Rosser, *Treasures against Time*, 143.

39. Yogananda, *Autobiography* (1946), 413–43.

40. Yogananda to Lynn, March 17, 1936, in *Rajarsi Janakananda*, 104.

41. See Yogananda to Lynn, October 1, 1936, ibid., 35. He elaborated on this encounter in his *Autobiography* a decade later (413–33).

42. Yogananda to Lynn, July 28, August 9, 1935, June 26, 1936, in *Rajarsi Janakananda*, 69, 73, 115.

43. Yogananda to Lynn, July 19, 1936, ibid., 122.

44. Yogananda to Lynn, April 6, 1936, ibid., 105–7. In another letter, Yogananda referred to Mount Washington as Lynn's "supreme child." See Yogananda to Lynn, November 16, 1935, ibid., 91–92.

45. Yogananda to Lynn, April 27, 1936, ibid., 108.

46. See Yogananda to Lynn, July 31, 1935, ibid., 69.

47. See Yogananda to Lynn, October 1, 1935, ibid., 80.

48. See Yogananda to Lynn, November 16, 1935, ibid., 90.

49. See Yogananda to Lynn August 20, 1936, ibid., 128.

50. See Yogananda to Lynn, February 21, 1936, ibid., 101.

51. "Sleep 3 Hours: Laugh More," *Daily Mail*, September 23, 1936, 5.

52. Record of Aliens Held for Special Inquiry, October 24, 1936, in author's possession. On boards of special inquiry, see Cannato, *American Passage*, 88–89.

53. "Convocation Banquet Speeches," *Inner Culture*, March 1937, 14ff.

54. This was despite Yukteswar's supposed directive, reported in the *Autobiography* (1946), that this new title "formally supersedes your former title of *swami*" (400). For continued use of swami, see, e.g., *Inner Culture* articles by Yogananda through December 1937.

55. "Golden Lotus Temple of All Religions," *Inner Culture*, December 1937, 59.

56. "Title of 'Paramhansa,'" *Inner Culture*, October–December 1941, 56.

57. Yogananda, *Autobiography* (1946), 477–78.

58. Yogananda to Lynn, 1934, in *Rajarsi Janakananda*, 54.

59. See Wight, *Trilogy*, 99.

60. Wright, "The Spread of Self-Realization Fellowship," *Inner Culture*, March 1937, 44–46.

61. See "Temple and Hermitage Completed near Encinitas," *Los Angeles Times*, November 2, 1937, 9.

62. "Frye Funeral Today," *Los Angeles Times*, November 9, 1937, A1.

63. On sacred regions, see Feldhaus, *Connected Places*, 5–7.

64. Quotations from *Rajarsi Janakananda*, 39–40; Gorsuch, *I Became My Heart*, 59.

65. C. Richard Wright, "The Spread of Self-Realization Fellowship (Yogoda Sat-Sanga) over the Earth," *Inner Culture*, March 1937, 3 ff.

66. Yogananda spoke on "World Fellowship" in October 1937, *Los Angeles Times*, October 16, 1937, A2.

67. Yogananda, "Success through Unity," *Inner Culture*, May 1936, 3.

68. Yogananda, "Nations, Beware," *Inner Culture*, March 1937, 22.

69. "Teachings of Jesus Applauded as Science," *Los Angeles Times*, February 27, 1939, 10.

70. Goldie Laden, "The United States of the World," *Inner Culture*, July–September 1944, inside front cover.

71. Nicholas Roerich, "The Wreath of Unity," *East-West*, January 1945, 13–15.

72. "Prophet Turns Silent on Eve of 'World's End,'" *Los Angeles Times*, September 21, 1945, A1.

73. "Scientific Digest," *Inner Culture*, October–November 1941, 46–47.

74. *Los Angeles Times*, November 6, 1948, A3.

75. A. Lavagnini, "An International Language," *East-West*, April 1945, 4–8.

76. This paraphrases Horne, "Cosmopolitan Life of Alice Erh-Soon Tay," 422, which is in turn adapted from Appiah, *Cosmopolitanism*.

77. See Aravamudan, *Guru English*, 10–11.

78. Yogananda, "Benito Mussolini on Science and Religion," *East-West*, May–June 1927, 10; November–December 1927; Yogananda, "An Interview," *Inner Culture*, February 1934, 3, 25.

79. "Christmas Message to the Nations of the Earth," *East-West*, December, 1933, 25.

80. *Inner Culture*, October 1935, 23.

81. Dasgupta, *Paramhansa Swami Yogananda*, 74.

82. French, "Swami Vivekananda's Use of the *Bhagavadgita*," 134, 144.

83. Yogananda, "Spiritual Interpretation of the Scriptures," *East-West*, April 1932, 9.

84. Davis, *Bhagavad Gita*, 73–80.

85. On the distinction between *Śruti* and *Smṛti*, see the sources cited in Flood, *Introduction to Hinduism*, 11.

86. S. Y., "The Path of Emancipation: Interpretation of the *Bhagavad Gita*," *East-West*, May 1934, 24.

87. Patton, "Introduction" to *Bhagavad Gita*, xxv, offers roughly 150 B.C.E., based on a reading of fifty recent articles addressing the dating of the Gita.

88. It may have originally been an independent composition inserted into this massive

epic, though recent scholars tend to see it as an organic element of the *Mahābhārata*. See Davis, *Bhagavad Gita*, 41.

89. Patton, "Introduction," vii.

90. Davis, *Bhagavad Gita*, 129, 137.

91. See Jordens, "Gandhi and the Bhagavadgita," 88; and Davis, *Bhagavad Gita*, 136–45.

92. Jordens, "Gandhi and the Bhagavadgita," 89, identifies an "allegorical" approach and reliance on the "primacy of 'experience'" as the twin pillars of Gandhi's interpretation.

93. S. Y., "The Soul's Secret Light: Interpretation of the *Bhagavad Gita*," *East-West*, January 1933, 9.

94. Yogananda, "The Second Coming of Christ," *East-West*, May 1932, 9.

95. S. Y., "Obstacles to Meditation: Interpretation of the *Bhagavad Gita*," *East-West*, September 1933, 9.

96. Yogananda, "Interpretation of the *Bhagavad Gita*—The Song of the Spirit," *East-West*, August 1932, 23.

97. Yogananda, "Spiritual Interpretation of the *Bhagavad Gita*," *East-West*, July 1947, 8.

98. Yogananda, "Spiritual Interpretation of the *Bhagavad Gita*," *Inner Culture*, July 1940, 20–21.

99. Yogananda, "Spiritual Interpretation of the Scriptures," 9–10.

100. White, *Alchemical Body*, esp. chap. 2.

101. Yogananda, "Interpretation of the *Bhagavad Gita*—The Song of the Spirit," *East-West*, June 1932, 10; Yogananda, "The Second Coming of Christ," 12.

102. "Inner Light: Interpretation of the *Bhagavad Gita*," *East-West*, November 1932, 21.

103. Yogananda, "A Spiritual Interpretation of the *Bhagavad Gita*," *Self-Realization*, May 1950, 8.

104. Yogananda, "Spiritual Interpretation of the *Bhagavad Gita*," *East-West*, March 1947, 8–9.

105. S. Y., "The Path of Emancipation: Interpretation of the *Bhagavad Gita*," *East-West*, May 1934, 9.

106. S. Y., "The Six Centers: Interpretation of the *Bhagavad Gita*," *East-West*, November 1933, 27.

107. S. Y., "Victory through Meditation: Interpretation of the *Bhagavad Gita*," *East-West*, March 1934, 9.

108. "Six Centers."

109. Yogananda, "Interpretation of the *Bhagavad Gita*—The Song of the Spirit," *East-West*, August 1932, 8.

110. Yogananda, "Spiritual Interpretation of the *Bhagavad Gita*," *Inner Culture*, July 1941, 15.

111. Yogananda, "A Spiritual Interpretation of the *Bhagavad Gita*," *East-West*, October 1944, 18.

112. Yogananda, "Spiritual Interpretation of the *Bhagavad Gita*," *Inner Culture*, December 1937, 32.

113. Yogananda, "Spiritual Interpretation of the *Bhagavad Gita*," *East-West*, April 1945, 15.

114. S. Y., "Your Spiritual Preceptor," *Inner Culture*, June 1935, 28.

115. S. Y., "A Message from the Masters: Interpretation of the *Bhagavad Gita*," *East-West*, December 1932, 25.

116. For Krishna as guru, see, e.g., "The Second Coming of Christ," 11; for Yogananda as

guru, see, e.g., Swami Yogananda, "Spiritual Interpretation of the *Bhagavad Gita*," *Inner Culture*, December 1937, 32.

117. As with all of Yogananda's publications, later editions published by Self-Realization Fellowship have been heavily edited and thus differ dramatically from the texts Yogananda originally produced.

118. Sharpe, "Neo-Hindu Images of Christianity," 15.

119. Mozoomdar, *Oriental Christ*.

120. Yogananda, *The Second Coming of Christ: The Resurrection of Christ within You*, 2:21.

121. Kriyananda, *Path*, 217, 395.

122. Yogananda, "The Second Coming of Christ," *Inner Culture*, January 1939, 26 ff.

123. Yogananda, "The Second Coming of Christ," *East-West*, March 1933, 5 ff.

124. See Hatch, "*Sola Scriptura*," 74.

125. Yogananda, "The Second Coming of Christ," *East-West*, May 1933, 5 ff.

126. Yogananda, "The Second Coming of Christ," *East-West*, June 1932, 5 ff.

127. Yogananda, "The Second Coming of Christ," *East-West*, August 1932, 5; Yogananda, *The Second Coming of Christ: The Resurrection of Christ within You*, 1:37, 47, 2:117.

128. Ibid., 1:101, 138.

129. Ibid., 1:102.

130. Ibid., 1:61.

131. Ibid., 1:40.

132. See Freed and Freed, *Ghosts: Life and Death in North India*, 9.

133. See Bhattacharya, *Indian Demonology*.

134. See, e.g., Yogananda, *The Second Coming of Christ: The Resurrection of Christ within You*, 1:37, 48, 54.

135. Yogananda, "The Second Coming of Christ," *East-West*, January 1933, 5 ff.

136. Yogananda, *The Second Coming of Christ: The Resurrection of Christ within You*, 1:99.

137. Yogananda, "The Second Coming of Christ," *East-West*, November 1933, 5 ff.

138. Yogananda, *Second Coming*, 120.

139. Yogananda, "The Second Coming of Christ," *Inner Culture*, June 1939, 25 ff.

140. "The Second Coming of Christ," *East-West*, May 1933, 5 ff.

141. "The Second Coming of Christ," *East-West*, May 1932, 5 ff.

142. Yogananda, *The Second Coming of Christ: The Resurrection of Christ within You*, 1:15.

143. Yogananda, "The Second Coming of Christ," *Inner Culture*, March 1934, 5 ff.

144. Yogananda, *The Second Coming of Christ: The Resurrection of Christ within You*, 1:161.

145. Yogananda, *Autobiography* (1946), 62–63.

146. Trout, "Hindu Gurus, American Disciples," 133.

147. Grosso, *Man Who Could Fly*, 23.

148. Ibid., 191–215.

149. Ibid., 8, 51.

150. Kriyananda, *Paramhansa Yogananda*, 202. See the next chapter for specific examples.

151. Satyeswarananda, *Kriya*, 183.

152. Narayan, *Storytellers, Saints, and Scoundrels*, 46–47, quotation on 243.

153. See Austin, *How to Do Things with Words*.

154. Greimas, *On Meaning*, esp. chap. 6, "Actants, Actors, and Figures"; Greimas, *Structural Semantics*.

155. See comment and citations in Aymard, *When a Goddess Dies*, 236.

156. On "frame stories" in Indian epics, see Hiltebeitel, *Rethinking the Mahabharata*, 93–97.

157. This sequence is a synthesis based on a number of sources, not all of which include all of the stages: White, "Swami Muktananda," 306–22; Ramanujan, "On Women Saints," 316–24; Jackson, "Life Becomes a Legend," 717–36; Snell, "Introduction," 1–13; and Lorenzen, "Lives of *Nirguni* Saints."

158. Larson, "Introduction to the Philosophy of Yoga," 125–29.

159. Yogananda, *Autobiography* (1946), 95.

160. Ibid., 171–72.

161. Ibid., 24–25.

162. Ibid., 59–60.

163. Alter, *Art of Biblical Narrative*, 81–82.

164. Yogananda, *Autobiography* (1946), 25.

165. Satyeswarananda, *Kriya*, 179.

166. Yogananda, *Autobiography* (1946), 14.

167. Ibid., 484–85.

168. Evans-Wentz, "Preface," in ibid., vii–viii.

169. On Jesus as a yogi, see ibid., 243–44; for Yogi-Christs, see 232. On Babaji as Christlike, see chap. 33; for Lahiri, see esp. chap. 35; for Yukteswar, see 3, 93; and for Ramakrishna, see 81, 475n.

170. Yogananda, *Autobiography* (1946), 88n., quotations on 210, 291. See the following chapter for more discussion of Yogananda's physical suffering as karmic atonement.

171. "Yoga for the West," *Newsweek*, March 10, 1947, 76.

172. "Here Comes the Yogiman," *Time*, March 17, 1947, 110.

173. "Religious Books of Recent Issue," *New York Times*, March 15, 1947, 11.

174. "Study of Yogi Mysticism and Swami Tricks," *Chicago Daily Tribune*, June 15, 1947, C11.

175. Saksena, "Review of 'Autobiography of a Yogi.'"

176. "Sit Lux," *China Weekly Review*, May 3, 1947, VI.

177. "Books in Various Languages," *Books Abroad* 24, no. 4 (Fall 1950): 421.

178. "Yoga," *Times of India*, November 19, 1950, 7.

179. *Los Angeles Times*, December 14, 1947, H6.

180. "Comments on 'Autobiography of a Yogi,'" *Self-Realization*, September 1952, 40–41; "Comments on 'Autobiography of a Yogi,'" *Self-Realization*, November 1952, 37–38; "Comments on 'Autobiography of a Yogi,'" *Self-Realization*, January 1953, 37; "Comments on 'Autobiography of a Yogi,'" *Self-Realization*, May 1953, 35–36. The quotation is from September 1952, 41.

181. See photo in *Self-Realization*, January 1950, 42.

182. *Self-Realization*, January 1949, 13.

183. *Self-Realization*, March 1949, 17.

184. *Self-Realization*, January 1949, 13.

185. See "Swami Sued for $500,000: Action Charges Girls Living at Headquarters of Religious Leader," *Los Angeles Times*, October 24, 1939; "Swami's Share Profits Pledge Told at Trial: Plaintiff Quotes Yogananda as Declaring Their Assets Valued at $1,000,000," *Los Angeles Times*, December 5, 1940, 2; and "Absent Swami Wins in Court: Former Associate's Claim for $500,000 Partnership Denied," *Los Angeles Times*, December 11, 1940, 2. Parsons, *Fight for Religious Freedom*, 94–96.

186. *Los Angeles Times*, August 15, 1950, A2.

187. See Sittser, *Cautious Patriotism*, on ways the war reinforced the perceived link between Christian identity and the American nation.

188. Yogananda, *Your Praecepta: Step I*, P26, 3; ibid., Step I, P1, 3.

CHAPTER 5

1. Premananda, "My Gurudev," 5.

2. Ibid., 6–7.

3. Ibid., 7–9.

4. "All Religions Church Dedication Awaited," *Los Angeles Times*, August 30, 1942, A2.

5. Jain, "Muktananda," 198, makes a similar point when she discusses Muktananda's embrace of more mainstream tenets because the "global market for spiritual goods required marketers to calculate the costs for products associated with unpopular ideas or practices."

6. Rambo, *Understanding Religious Conversion*, 35, points out that while most conversion studies ignore resistance, "most people say no to conversion."

7. The analysis that follows adapts several of Rambo and Farhadian's stages. It excludes their first and last stages, context and consequence, which are largely irrelevant to the actual process of individual conversion presented here. See Rambo and Farhadian, "Converting," 23–24.

8. Ibid., 26.

9. Buchanan's SRF name was Kamala. See Kamala, *Flawless Mirror*, 105–7, 36–37. D'Evelyn became Edith Bissett after marrying Clark Prescott Bissett. At SRF, she was known as Sri Gyanamata. See Gyanamata, *God Alone*, 3–5.

10. Faye Wright, whom Yogananda named Sister Daya, became Sister Daya Mata. As Sri Daya Mata she served as president of SRF for several decades. See *Him Shall I Follow*.

11. Davis, *Paramahansa Yogananda as I Knew Him*, 27–28.

12. Cara, *Light of Christ Within*, 1–5.

13. Stockton, *Testimony of Love and Devotion*, 51–54.

14. At SRF, Darling was known as Durga Mata. See Wight, *Trilogy of Divine Love*, 2–3.

15. Gyanamata, *God Alone*, 3–5.

16. Davis, *Paramahansa Yogananda as I Knew Him*, 27–28.

17. See Kamala, *Flawless Mirror*, 105–7, 36–37.

18. *Mother Hamilton: A Divine Life*.

19. Less than half of Buddhist seekers seem to have been women. See Tweed, *American Encounter with Buddhism*, chaps. 2–4, quotation on 91.

20. See Jain, "Muktananda," 196.

21. Daya Mata, *Finding the Joy within You*, xix–xxiii; *Him Shall I Follow*.

22. Gorsuch, *I Became My Heart*, 11.

23. Davis, *Paramahansa Yogananda as I Knew Him*, 28–29.

24. Kriyananda, *Path*, 159.

25. She records this thought in her first letter to Yogananda, after the two met in Seattle in 1925. See Edith D. Bissett to Swamiji [Yogananda], July 19, 1925, in *God Alone*, 58.

26. "First Encounters: Brother Anandamoy," *Self-Realization Fellowship*, http://www.yogananda-srf.org/ay/First_Encounters.aspx.

27. Stockton, *Testimony*, 27.

28. *Him Shall I Follow.*

29. "In Memoriam: Brother Anandamoy (1922–2016)," *Self-Realization Fellowship*, http://www.yogananda-srf.org/NewsArchive/2016/In_Memoriam__Brother_Anandamoy_(1922–2016).aspx.

30. Mukti Mata, *"Like the Light from Heaven."*

31. Wight, *Trilogy*, 165, 5.

32. Anandamoy, *Experiencing God Within.*

33. *Him Shall I Follow.*

34. Wight, *Trilogy*, 12.

35. The two kept up a correspondence, even though they always lived in two different cities. *Mother Hamilton.*

36. Gorsuch, *I Became My Heart*, 12.

37. *Him Shall I Follow.*

38. See P. Yogananda to Sister, January 28, 1943, in *God Alone*, 261–62; and Yogananda, "The Dewdrop Has Slipped into the Shining Sea," Encinitas Ashram Center, November 19, 1951, reprinted in ibid., 40–53.

39. Rambo, *Understanding Religious Conversion*, 84–85.

40. Willner and Willner, "Rise and Role of Charismatic Leaders," 1–18, quotation on 2.

41. Rambo, *Understanding Religious Conversion*, 66–67.

42. Ibid., 81.

43. Merna Brown's monastic name was Mrinalini Mata. See Mrinalini Mata, *In His Presence.*

44. Gyanamata, *God Alone*, 12.

45. Without downplaying either emotion or individual choice, Jacoby, *Strange Gods*, especially xiv–xxxiii, underscores the social dimensions of conversion.

46. Kriyananda, *Path*, 163. Note that even the subtitle of his book, *Autobiography of a Western Yogi*, pays homage to Yogananda's *Autobiography.*

47. Davis, *Paramahansa Yogananda as I Knew Him*, 29.

48. Dietz, *Thank You, Master*, n.p.

49. Paulsen, *Sunburst*, 139.

50. Kriyananda, *Path*, 165–74.

51. See Rambo, *Understanding Religious Conversion*, 107–8.

52. Kriyananda, *Paramhansa Yogananda*, 203–10; Gorsuch, *I Became My Heart*, 72.

53. See the essays in Sax, *Gods at Play.*

54. Yogananda was apparently not alone in such childish behavior. Vesey, *Communal Experience*, 227, reports occasionally "childlike, spontaneous" behavior by the normally "aloof and dignified" Vedanta leader Swami Paramananda, including his poem about ice cream as a "nice dream."

55. Wight, *Trilogy*, 22–25, 176–78. For the water gun incident, see Dietz, *Thank You, Master.*

56. She had resided at Mount Washington for more than a decade by the time this event happened in 1941. See Wight, *Trilogy*, 31.

57. Mlecko, "Guru in Hindu Tradition," 33–61, see esp. 39.

58. "In Memoriam: C. Richard Wright," *Self-Realization*, Spring 2002, 46.

59. Wight, *Trilogy*, 32.

60. Gorsuch, "Preface" to *I Became My Heart*, 1.

61. Mukti Mata, *"Like the Light from Heaven."*

62. Gorsuch, *I Became My Heart*, 46.

63. Walters, *Path*, 372.
64. Gorsuch, *I Became My Heart*, 46.
65. Davis, *Paramahansa Yogananda as I Knew Him*, 50.
66. *Him Shall I Follow.*
67. Veysey, *Communal Experience*, 214.
68. Rambo, *Understanding Religious Conversion*, 116.
69. *In His Presence.*
70. Gorsuch, *I Became My Heart*, 81.
71. *In His Presence.*
72. Ibid.
73. Ibid.
74. Wight, *Trilogy*, 191.
75. Trout, *Eastern Seeds*, 187–88.
76. Goldberg, *American Veda*, 120; Goldberg, *Life of Yogananda*, 241–42.
77. See Swami Yogananda to Leo Cocks, February 20, 1952, in Gorsuch, *I Became My Heart*, 91.
78. Paulsen, *Sunburst*, 199.
79. Yogananda to Cocks, July 21, 1950, in Gorsuch, *I Became My Heart*, 56.
80. Paulsen, *Sunburst*, 220.
81. Kriyananda, *Path*, 464.
82. As reported by Satyananda's disciple and biographer. See Satyeswarananda, *Biography*, 69.
83. Wight, *Trilogy*, 189. On his loyalty, she comments, "Master was the most loyal person I have ever, and have yet to meet. . . . Master was the very personification of loyalty" (185).
84. Yogananda, *Your Praecepta: Step 1*, P110, 2–4, quotation on 4.
85. "Secret Desert Retreat," *Self-Realization*, September 1949, 28.
86. For one disciple's lengthy exposition of this principle, see Kriyananda, *Path*, 327–39.
87. Ibid., 335.
88. *Him Shall I Follow.*
89. Rambo, *Understanding Religious Conversion*, 132–33.
90. Ibid., 116.
91. Kriyananda, *Path*, 328.
92. This argument is shaped largely by the model of religious participation by Stark and Finke, *Acts of Faith*.
93. Anandamoy, *Experiencing God Within*.
94. *In His Presence*; Gorsuch, *I Became My Heart*, 47.
95. Aymard, *When a Goddess Dies*, 18. Later she explains that the guru is "to a certain extent the very incarnation of God" (23).
96. Wight, *Trilogy*, 50.
97. Swami Kriyananda, "Has Jesus Come Again?," *Ananda Sangha Worldwide*, December 1, 2002, https://www.ananda.org/clarity/2002/12/christ-faith-god-kriyananda/.
98. French, "Swami Vivekananda's Experiences," 70.
99. Aymard, *When a Goddess Dies*, 236. See also Mlecko, "Guru," 33–61.
100. Gorsuch, *I Became My Heart*, 57.
101. Kriyananda, *Path*, 430, 426.
102. Chapple, "Raja Yoga and the Guru," 17.
103. See Barker, "Perspective," 88–102, quotation on 94.

104. Dietz, *Thank You, Master.*

105. "India Free at Last—What Joy!," *East-West*, November 1947, 7.

106. Springhall, *Decolonization since 1945*, 104.

107. Paulsen, *Sunburst*, 162–63.

108. *Paramhansa Yogananda: History, Life, Mission*, 40.

109. Jones, *Gandhi Lives*. Jones, a native of Missouri, was exposed to both Christian Science and Theosophy as a child. Though he wrote a number of books on esoteric subjects, especially astrology, he provided a straightforward narrative account of Gandhi's life, teachings, and death.

110. "Memorial Rites for Gandhi Held in Church Here," *Los Angeles Times*, February 2, 1948, 2.

111. "Mahatma Gandhi's Ashes," *Self-Realization*, January 1949, 4. Based on this description of receiving "some" of Gandhi's ashes, it would seem that Nehru did not honor Yogananda's earlier request and that he acquired the ashes through other means.

112. "Lake Shrine Dedication," *Lake Shrine Self Realization Fellowship*, http://lakeshrine.org/about/history/.

113. Photographs of Yogananda in India show a young man of average build, while most photographs from throughout his career in the United States suggest that he was consistently stocky. In 1946, he weighed 164 pounds, which, at his then-reported height of five feet, eight inches put him on the cusp of being overweight, according to BMI, an admittedly imperfect measure. If his height was actually five feet, three inches, as reported on his passport renewal form in 1925, then he was significantly overweight—nearly obese—at 164 pounds. Since the passport application spells out "three," it seems more likely that the taller height is a typographical error. See Application for Passport Facilities (Indian), Passport No. 3599, 1925, and Declaration of Intention No. 126676, October 11, 1946, both in author's possession.

114. Paramhansa Yogananda to James Lynn, August 20, 1936, in *Rajarsi Janakanada*, 126.

115. On his change in behavior beginning in 1948, see *In His Presence*. The premonition of death comes from Walters, *Path*, 197.

116. "Special Notice," *Self-Realization*, September 1948, 7.

117. "A Special Request to Correspondents," *Self-Realization*, November 1948, 4.

118. Quotation from *In His Presence*. Descriptions of these informal talks come from a "Collector's Series" of ten audio CDs released by SRF in the early 2000s.

119. Kriyananda, *Path*, 487.

120. On this general belief in Hinduism, see Aymard, *When a Goddess Dies*, 147.

121. Cited in ibid., 135.

122. Paulsen, *Sunburst*, 188.

123. Declaration of Intention No. 126676, October 11, 1946 and Petition for Naturalization No. 138548, January 19, 1949, copies of both in author's possession.

124. "Guru's Exit," *Time*, August 4, 1952, 59; "Funeral Rites for Yogananda Set for Tuesday," *Los Angeles Times*, March 9, 1952, 18; "Religious Leader Dies: Paramhansa Yogananda Stricken at Dinner for Indian Envoy," *New York Times*, March 9, 1952, 92.

125. For the first quotation, see "Swami Offers Fount of Youth to New Yorkers," *New York Tribune*, November 25, 1923, 3, and for the second, see Steve Hannagan, "Mental Flip-Flops for Daily Dozen," *Connersville (Ind.) News-Examiner*, December 13, 1923, 6. For life expectancy, see Ryan, *Vital Statistics of the United States*, "Table B-8. Life Expectancy at Birth by Race and Sex, Selected Years, 1940–2007."

126. Aymard, *When a Goddess Dies*, 138.

127. Wight, *Trilogy*, 53.

128. On *mahasamādhi*, see Aymard, *When a Goddess Dies*, 115.

129. Lane, *Radhasoami Tradition*, 192.

130. See Aymard, *When a Goddess Dies*, 76, for references to ancient texts recommending burial for renunciants.

131. Premananda, "My Gurudev," 7–9.

132. For plans to bury Yogananda at Mount Washington, see "The Miracle at Forest Lawn," *Self-Realization*, May–June 1952, 11.

133. "Hundreds Pay Tribute at Rites for Yogananda," *Los Angeles Times*, March 12, 1952, 24; "Gandhi's Words to Mark Services for Yogananda," *Los Angeles Times*, March 10, 1952, 18.

134. Harry T. Rowe to Self-Realization Fellowship, May 16, 1952, in author's possession.

135. "Miracle at Forest Lawn," 10–11.

136. Angel, *Enlightenment East and West*, 296–97.

137. Sister Lauru, "Yoga and the Miracle of Incorruption," *Self-Realization*, May–June 1952, 13.

138. Kriyananda, *Paramhansa Yogananda*, 302.

139. Aymard, *When a Goddess Dies*, 81. She notes Yogananda explicitly as a recent example of this phenomenon.

140. Goodwin Knight to Miss Faye Wright, April 8, 1952, in *Paramahansa Yogananda: In Memoriam*, 117.

141. Mulk Raj Ahuja, "Paramhansa Yogananda: An Appreciation," in ibid., 98–99.

142. "Tribute from Swami Sivananda," in ibid., 49.

143. See ibid., 85–90.

144. Faye Wright to Self-Realization Fellowship Members, March 19, 1952, copy in author's possession.

145. On posthumous encounters with the guru in dreams, see Aymard, *When a Goddess Dies*, 186–87.

146. Kriyananda, *Path*, 548.

147. Kamala, *Flawless Mirror*, 195.

148. "Visions of the Guru," *Self-Realization Magazine*, November 1952, 43.

149. Kriyananda, *Path*, 548; Stockton, *Testimony*, 87–94.

150. Kriyananda, *Paramhansa Yogananda*, 212.

151. See Allison, *Resurrecting Jesus*, 269–82, for an extensive cross-cultural list of appearances and general patterns. Allison himself experienced a similar visitation from his recently deceased friend Barbara, who appeared "beautiful and brightly luminous and intensely real" (275); quotation from Allison, *Night Comes*, 14. Grosso, *Man Who Could Fly*, 108, recounts the reappearance of the seventeenth-century levitating Saint Joseph of Cupertino, who brought peace and physical healing to those he visited.

152. Prothero, *White Buddhist*, 60.

153. Narayan, *Storytellers, Saints, and Scoundrels*, 47.

154. Kriyananda, *Stories of Mukunda*, 5–7.

155. "Mahasamadhi of a World Teacher," 3; *Paramahansa Yogananda: In Memoriam*, 4.

156. A good example of a fairly vapid video is the Lake Shrine commemoration. See Self-Realization Fellowship, *SRF Lake Shrine 50th Anniversary Celebration*.

157. Weber, *Economy and Society*, 246–49.

158. Wight, *Trilogy*, 51–58.

159. He was initially introduced as "Rajasi," meaning "king of the saints." SRF later explained that this was a misspelling and that the proper spelling was "Rajarsi." See *Rajarsi Janakananda*, 47.

160. Ibid., 41–45.

161. Quoted in ibid., 39.

162. Wight, *Trilogy*, 45–49.

163. Yogananda to Lynn, 1934, in *Rajarsi Janakananda*, 54.

164. Rajarsi Janakananda, "Convocation Address," *Self-Realization Magazine*, November 1952, 37–38.

165. See *In His Presence*. One example of such responsibilities was sending the official announcement of Yogananda's death, which Wright did, not Lynn. See Faye Wright to Self-Realization Fellowship Members, March 19, 1952.

166. Aymard, *When a Goddess Dies*, 152.

167. Ibid., 155.

168. Newcombe, "Institutionalization of the Yoga Tradition," 147.

169. Barnes, "Charisma and Religious Leadership," 5.

170. *In His Presence*; for similar recollections, see also Gorsuch, *I Became My Heart*, 100; and Davis, *Paramahansa Yogananda as I Knew Him*, 63.

171. Rajarsi Janakananda speech at India Hall, Hollywood Temple, April 7, 1952, in *Rajarsi Janakananda*, 149.

172. "Rajasi Janakananda, New President of SRF-YSS," *Self-Realization*, May–June 1952, 20.

173. "Fellowship to Hold Third Convocation," *Los Angeles Times*, July 20, 1952, 43.

174. *In His Presence*.

175. Weber, *Economy and Society*, 1121–23.

176. Lane, *Radhasoami Tradition*, 252.

177. Wight, *Trilogy*, 65.

178. Board of Directors of SRF and YSS to members, March 7, 1955, copy in author's possession.

179. Lane, *Radhasoami Tradition*, 205.

180. Brother Chidananda refers to them as having been "moribund" at the time Daya Mata took over. See Self-Realization Fellowship/Yogoda Satsanga Society of India, *Memorial Service: Sri Daya Mata, President and Sanghamata, SRF/YSS* (Los Angeles: Self-Realization Fellowship, 2010), https://www.youtube.com/watch?v=DldQmH7MdoA.

181. "Directory of Centers, Churches, and Colonies," *Self-Realization*, December 1960, 52–55.

182. Lewis and Lewis, "Introduction," in *Sacred Schisms*, 3.

183. Cited in Humes, "Schisms within Hindu Guru Groups," 300.

184. Lane, *Radhasoami Tradition*, xxxi–xxxii.

185. Kriyananda, *Path*, 373.

186. Ibid., 587.

187. Miller, *60's Communes*, xxii–xxiv.

188. Miller, "Evolution of American Spiritual Communities," 14–33, esp. 22.

189. Paglia, "Cults and Cosmic Consciousness," 57–111, identifies the fascination with Asian traditions as a core element of the counterculture, then suggests that the "groundwork for the Asian trend of the American sixties was probably laid by Paramhansa Yogananda" (76).

190. Kriyananda, *Path*, 612.

191. Miller, *60's Communes*, 105–6.

192. Kriyananda and Yogananda, *Essence of the Bhagavad Gita*; Kriyananda, *Paramhansa Yogananda*.

193. See, e.g., "Swami Kriyananda Remembered," *Ananda Sangha Worldwide*, https://www.ananda.org/swami-kriyananda-remembered/.

194. Quoted in Kamala, *Flawless Mirror*, 111.

195. Yogananda to Oliver Black, May 1951, quoted in ibid., 112.

196. Howard, *Angels among Us*, 30–31.

197. Ibid., chap. 1.

198. Song of the Morning, www.songofthemorning.org.

199. Paulsen, *Sunburst*, 485.

200. Ibid., 520–22.

201. Miles Corwin, "20 Years Later, Some Followers of Guru Still Keep the Faith," *Los Angeles Times*, July 10, 1989, http://articles.latimes.com/1989-07-10/news/mn-2633_1_early-years.

202. "Spiritual Lineage, *Sunburst*, http://sunburstonline.org/our-teachings/our-spiritual-lineage/.

203. "Roy Eugene Davis, Director," *Center for Spiritual Awareness*, http://csa-davis.org/sites/roydavis.

204. Davis, *Paramahansa Yogananda*, 72.

205. Ibid., 74, 77.

206. "Center for Spiritual Awareness," *Center for Spiritual Awareness*, http://csa-davis.org/sites/aboutcsa.

207. *Mother Hamilton*.

208. *Memories of Mother*, xv, xx.

209. Barnowe, "Introduction: Yogacharya Mildred Hamilton: Our Divine Teacher," in ibid., 110.

210. On Yogananda as her guru and SRF's opposition, see Win Smith, "Thank You, Mother," in ibid., 79.

211. "This Path," *The Cross and the Lotus*, http://www.crossandlotus.com/this_path.html.

212. Rochford, "Succession, Religious Switching, and Schism," 281. The institutional strength of SRF, of course, has a potential downside of extreme rigidity. See a comment to this effect (specifically about SRF) by a devotee of another tradition in Aymard, *When a Goddess Dies*, 200.

213. See, e.g., *Rajarsi Janakananda*.

EPILOGUE

1. All quotations and other information about the memorial service come from Self-Realization Fellowship/Yogoda Satsanga Society of India, *Memorial Service: Sri Daya Mata, President and Sanghamata, SRF/YSS* (Los Angeles: Self-Realization Fellowship, 2010), https://www.youtube.com/watch?v=DldQmH7MdoA.

2. Mitchell Landsberg, "Religious Group Has a New Leader; The Self-Realization Fellowship Selects Sri Mrinalini Mata, 79, to Succeed Longtime Leader Sri Daya Mata," *Los Angeles Times*, January 12, 2011, AA 3.

3. Self-Realization Fellowship, *Brother Anandamoy Memorial Service*, October 4, 2016, https://www.youtube.com/watch?v=eLfDGUiwoy4.

4. "SRF to Celebrate 60th Anniversary of Paramahansa Yogananda's Passing," *India West*, March 2, 2012, B24.

5. "Sri Mrinalini Mata's 70th Anniversary," *Self-Realization Fellowship*, June 17, 2016, http://www.yogananda-srf.org/NewsArchive/2016/Sri_Mrinalini_Mata's_70th_Anniversary.aspx.

6. "SRF Announces New President," *Self-Realization Fellowship*, https://www.yogananda-srf.org/NewsArchive/2017/SRF_Announces_New_President.aspx.

7. "SRF Lessons – Enhanced and Expanded Edition Planned for Release in 2018," *Self-Realization Fellowship*, https://www.yogananda-srf.org/SRF_Lessons_New_Edition_Announcement.aspx.

8. Ron Russell, "The Devotee's Son," *New Times L.A.*, July 5, 2001; Ron Russell, "Exhuming the Truth," *New Times L.A.*, November 29, 2001.

9. Teresa Watanabe, "DNA Clears Yoga Guru in Seven-Year Paternity Dispute," *Los Angeles Times*, July 11, 2002, http://articles.latimes.com/2002/jul/11/local/me-guru11. On the disappearance of the *New Times*, see Howard Blume, "The End of New Times," *LA Weekly*, October 2, 2012, http://www.laweekly.com/news/the-end-of-new-times-2135371.

10. Ron Russell, "Return of the Swami," *Los Angeles New Times*, July 1, 1999.

11. Bob Pool, "Debate Rises over Plans for Religious Leader's Shrine," *Los Angeles Times*, January 12, 1999, http://articles.latimes.com/1999/jan/12/local/me-62631.

12. Falk, *Stripping the Gurus*.

13. See SRF Walrus, http://www.angelfire.com/blues/srfwalrus/.

14. On allegations of sexual misbehavior, see SRF Blacklist, https://www.tapatalk.com/groups/srfblacklist/yogananda-s-sexual-indiscretions-t2014.html#p4115; on accusations of dishonest claims of authorship, see https://www.tapatalk.com/groups/srfblacklist/science-of-religion-written-by-yogananda-and-dhira-t1860.html#.WTmQR1KZOV5.

15. See Cult Education Institute, http://culteducation.com/. For its information on Self-Realization Fellowship, see http://culteducation.com/group/1143-self-realization-fellowship.html.

16. Urban, *Zorba*, 157.

17. See Swami Kriyananda to SRF Board of Directors, November 1992, http://www.yoganandafortheworld.com/an-open-letter-to-the-srf-board-of-directors/.

18. Self-Realization Fellowship Open Letter, November 1995, in author's possession.

19. Vicky Anning, "Community: Ex-Ananda Devotee Describes Her 7-Year Ordeal," *Palo Alto Weekly*, February 11, 1998, http://www.paloaltoonline.com/weekly/morgue/news/1998_Feb_11.ANANDA2.html; Ron Russell, "Return of the Swami," *Los Angeles New Times*, July 1, 1999.

20. Parsons, *Fight for Religious Freedom*, 72, 168–69.

21. *Autobiography of a Yogi by Paramahansa Yogananda*, Project Gutenberg, available at http://www.gutenberg.org/ebooks/7452.

22. Helen Gao, "Sex and the Singular Swami," *San Francisco Weekly*, March 10, 1999, http://www.sfweekly.com/sanfrancisco/sex-and-the-singular-swami/Content?oid=2136254.

23. Yogananda, *Autobiography* (1981), 459; cf. original *Autobiography* (1946), 478.

24. Yogananda, *Autobiography* (1981), 235.

25. Ibid., 355.

26. *History and Essence of the Self-Revelation Church of Absolute Monism*, 7.

27. "Secret Desert Retreat," *Self-Realization*, September 1949, 28–29.

28. Yogananda, *Autobiography* (1946), 447.

29. Yogananda, *Autobiography* (1981), 464–65.

30. Ibid., ix–x.

31. Sri Daya Mata, "Preface," in Yogananda, *Second Coming of Christ: The Resurrection of Christ within You*, 1:xii–xiv.

32. Teresa Watanabe, "A Hindu's Perspective on Christ and Christianity," *Los Angeles Times*, December 11, 2004.

33. "Intuitional Whispers: Interpretation of the Bhavagad [*sic*] Gita, Karma, Spiritual Diagnosis, Pain Habits," *East-West*, October 1932, 9.

34. Yogananda, *The Second Coming of Christ: The Resurrection of Christ within You*, 1:7.

35. Yogananda, *The Second Coming of Christ: From the Original Unchanged Writings*.

36. Paramhansa Yogananda, *Bhagavad Gita*.

37. Kriyananda, "Preface," in *Essence of the Bhagavad Gita*, xxii–xxiv.

38. Kriyananda, *Revelations of Jesus Christ*.

39. "Yogananda's Signature Changed by SRF," *Yogananda for the World*, n.d., http://www.yoganandafortheworld.com/yoganandas-signature-changed-by-srf/.

40. Salinger, *Dream Catcher*, 86–91.

41. "Dennis Weaver: In Memoriam," *Self-Realization*, Summer 2006, 56.

42. Jeannie Law, "Woody Harrelson Went to College to Become a Minister, but Chose Life of 'Hedonism' Instead," *The Christian Post*, May 12, 2018, https://www.christianpost.com/news/woody-harrelson-went-to-college-become-minister-but-chose-hedonism-instead-223910/.

43. Leslie Carroll, "How Meghan Markle Was Destined for the Spotlight," *Vanity Fair*, April 24, 2018, https://www.vanityfair.com/style/2018/04/how-meghan-markle-was-destined-for-the-spotlight.

44. John Blistein, "Tom Petty Laid to Rest in California," *Rolling Stone*, October 17, 2017, https://www.rollingstone.com/music/news/tom-petty-laid-to-rest-in-california-w509251.

45. Geller, *Leaves of Elvis' Garden*.

46. Berkman, "Appropriating Universality," 41–62, esp. 44.

47. Canfield and Hendricks, *You've Got to Read This Book!*, 9.

48. Isaacson, *Steve Jobs*, 45–46.

49. Alyson Shontell, "The Last Gift Steve Jobs Gave to Family and Friends Was a Book about Self Realization, *Business Insider*, September 11, 2013, http://www.businessinsider.com/steve-jobs-gave-yoganandas-book-as-a-gift-at-his-memorial-2013-9.

50. Kriyananda, *Conversations with Yogananda*; Kriyananda, *New Path*; Kriyananda, *Paramhansa Yogananda*.

51. McLain, *India's Immortal Comic Books*, 1–4; Pritchett, "World of Amar Chitra Katha"; "About Amar Chitra Katha," *Amar Chitra Katha*, https://www.amarchitrakatha.com/us/about.

52. Pai, *Paramahansa Yogananda*.

53. Parsons, *Fight for Religious Freedom*, 168–70.

54. The official website for *Awake: The Life of Yogananda* is http://www.awaketheyoganandamovie.com/. A lavish coffee-table companion book was also published: Di Florio and Leeman, *Awake: The Life of Yogananda*.

55. See Louis Sahagun, "Filmmakers Strive for Peace behind Politics: Devotees of

Mystic Hope New Movie Will Help Close a Divide," *Columbia Daily Tribune*, January 15, 2011, A7.

56. The positive review comes from Michael Rechtshaffen, "'Awake' a Vivid Glimpse of West's 1st Meditation Guru," *Los Angeles Times*, October 16, 2014. Peter Keough, "'Awake' Offers Little Enlightenment, *Boston Globe*, November 7, 2014, disagreed. He also grumbled about the "mystical music, spooky superimpositions of giant staring eyes over dreamy scenery, [and] pop psychedelic imagery."

57. For the official website of *The Answer: A True Story*, see http://www.movietheanswer.com/home.html.

58. From *Philip Goldberg: Author, Speaker, Spiritual Counselor*, philipgoldberg.com (accessed June 2017).

59. Volf, *Flourishing*, 1.

60. Louis Sahagun, "Guru's Followers Mark Legacy of a Star's Teachings," *Los Angeles Times*, August 6, 2006, http://articles.latimes.com/2006/aug/06/local/me-swami6.

Bibliography

PRIMARY SOURCES

Abhedananda, Swami. *The Gospel of Ramakrishna*. New York: Vedanta Society, 1907.

———. *India and Her People*. New York: Vedanta Society, 1906.

———. *Vedanta Philosophy: Five Lectures on Reincarnation*. New York: Vedanta Society, 1902.

———. *Vedanta Philosophy: Three Lectures*. New York: Vedanta Society, 1901.

Albers, Christina A. *Ancient Tales of Hindustan*. Calcutta: A. C. Albers, 1923.

———. *Himalayan Whispers*. Calcutta: N. Mukherjee, 1920.

———. *Palms and Temple Bells*. Calcutta: Burlington Press, 1915.

Anandamoy, Brother. *Experiencing God Within: The Universal Truth behind All Religions*. DVD. Directed by Self-Realization Fellowship. Los Angeles: Self-Realization Fellowship, 2008.

Andrews, C. F. *Mahatma Gandhi's Ideas, including Selections from His Writings*. New York: Macmillan, 1930.

Atkins, Gains Glenn. *Modern Religious Cults and Movements*. New York: Fleming H. Revell, 1923.

Barton, Bruce. *The Man Nobody Knows: A Discovery of the Real Jesus*. Indianapolis, Ind.: Bobbs-Merrill, 1925.

Bharat Dharma Mahamandal. *The World's Eternal Religion*. Lucknow, India: Newul Kishore Press, 1920.

Bharati, Baba Bremanand. *Sree Krishna: The Lord of Love*. New York: Krishna Samaj, 1904.

Bey, Hamid. *My Experiences preceding 5,000 Burials*. Buffalo, N.Y.: Ellicott, 1933.

Burbank, Luther. *My Beliefs*. New York: Avondale Press, 1927.

California Department of State. *Articles of Incorporation of the Self-Realization Fellowship Church*. Los Angeles, 1935.

Carpenter, Frederic Ives. *Emerson and Asia*. Cambridge, Mass.: Harvard University Press, 1930.

Census of India, 1911. Volume I, Part II—Tables. Calcutta: Superintendent of Government Printing, India, 1913.

Chase, Ray E., and S. G. Pandit. *An Examination of the Opinion of the Supreme Court of the United States Deciding against the Eligibility of Hindus for Citizenship*. Los Angeles: Parker, Stone and Baird, 1926.

Chatterji, Bankim Chandra. *Anandamath*. Calcutta: B. S. Mandir, 1900.
Christy, Arthur. *The Orient in American Transcendentalism: A Study of Emerson, Thoreau, and Alcott*. New York: Columbia University Press, 1932.
Clampett, Frederick W. *Luther Burbank: "Our Beloved Infidel": His Religion of Humanity*. New York: MacMillan, 1926.
The Collected Works of Mahatma Gandhi. 98 vols. New Delhi: Publications Division Government of India, 1999. Available at: http://gandhiserve.org/e/cwmg/cwmg.htm.
Curzon, Marquess George Nathaniel of Kedleston. *Notable Speeches of Lord Curzon*. Madras: Arya Press, 1905.
Daggett, Mabel Potter. "Heathen Invasion." *Hampton-Columbian Magazine* 27, no. 4 (October 1911): 399–400.
Das, Sri Ranendra Kumar. *It Can Be Done: The Secret of Success, the Key to Attainment*. Los Angeles: Mount Washington University Press, 1936.
———. *Reincarnation*. Los Angeles: DeVorss, 1943.
Dasgupta, Sri Sailendra Bejoy. *Kriya Yoga*. London: Yoga Niketan, 2006.
———. *Paramhansa Swami Yogananda: Life-Portrait and Reminiscences*. London: Yoga Niketan, 2006.
Davidson, Edward. *The Railways of India: With an Account of Their Rise, Progress and Construction, Written with the Aid of the Records of the India Office*. London: E. and F. N. Spon, 1868.
Davis, Roy Eugene. *Paramahansa Yogananda as I Knew Him: Experiences, Observations, and Reflections of a Disciple*. Lakemont, Ga.: CSA Press, 2005.
Daya Mata, Sri. *Finding the Joy within You: Personal Counsel for God-Centered Living*. Los Angeles: Self-Realization Fellowship, 1990.
———. *Only Love: Living the Spiritual Life in a Changing World*. Los Angeles: Self-Realization Fellowship, 1998.
———. "Preface." In Paramahansa Yogananda, *The Second Coming of Christ: The Resurrection of Christ within You*, vol. 1. Los Angeles: Self-Realization Fellowship, 2004.
Dietz, Margaret Bowen. *Thank You, Master*. Nevada City, Calif.: Ananda Church of Self-Realization, 1995.
Farquhar, J. N. *Modern Religious Movements in India*. New York: MacMillan, 1915.
Ferguson, Charles Wright. *The New Books of Revelations: The Inside Story of America's Astounding Religions and Cults*. Garden City, N.Y.: Doubleday, Doran, 1929.
Fosdick, Harry Emerson. "Shall the Fundamentalists Win?" *Christian Work* 102 (June 10, 1922): 716–22.
The Fundamentals: A Testimony to Truth. Chicago: Testimony Publishing, 1910.
General Report on the Census of India, 1891. London: Her Majesty's Stationery Office, 1893.
Ghosh, Sananda Lal. *"Medja": The Family and Early Life of Paramahansa Yogananda*. Los Angles: Self-Realization Fellowship, 1980.
Gorsuch, Paul, ed. *I Became My Heart—Stories of a Disciple of Paramahansa Yogananda: Leo Cocks*. San Diego, Calif.: Contact Approach Publishing, 2013.
Government of India, Public Works Department, Classified List and Distribution Return of Establishment. Calcutta: Superintendent of Government Printing, India, 1907.
Gyanamata, Sri. *God Alone: The Life and Letters of a Saint*. Los Angeles: Self-Realization Fellowship, 1984.
Hall-Quest, Alfred Lawrence. *The University Afield*. New York: MacMillan, 1926.

Heindel, Augusta Foss. *The Birth of the Rosicrucian Fellowship: The History of Its Inception.* 1923. Reprint ed. Mount Ecclesia, Calif.: Rosicrucian Fellowship, 2012.
"Here Comes the Yogiman," *Time*, March 17, 1947, 110.
Him Shall I Follow: An Informal Talk by Sri Daya Mata. VHS. Los Angeles: Self-Realization Fellowship, 1997.
Howard, Evelyn. *Angels among Us: The Fabulous J. Oliver Black*. Grosse Pointe Woods, Mich.: Golden Lotus Center for Spiritual Awareness, 2001.
In the Footsteps of Paramahansa Yogananda. Boston: Boston Meditation Group, n.d.
International Congress of Free Christians and Other Religious Liberals. *New Pilgrimages of the Spirit: Proceedings and Papers of the Pilgrim Tercentenary Meeting of the International Congress of Free Christians and Other Religious Liberals*. Boston: Beacon Press, 1921.
Iyer, C. S. Ranga. *Father India: A Reply to Mother India*. London: Selwyn and Blount, 1927.
Jones, Marc Edmund. *Gandhi Lives*. Philadelphia: David McKay, 1948.
Jones, Sir William. *Discourses Delivered before the Asiatic Society and Miscellaneous Papers, on the Religion, Poetry, Literature, etc., of the Nations of India*. London: Charles S. Arnold, 1824.
Jotin, Brahmachari. *The Law of Self-Manifestation*. Washington, D.C.: Self-Realization Fellowship, 1940.
———. *The Magnetic Power of Love*. Boston: Christopher Publishing House, 1940.
———. *Prayers of Self-Realization*. Washington, D.C.: Self-Realization Church, 1935.
Jung, C. G. *Psychological Types; or, The Psychology of Individuation*. Translated by H. Godwin Baynes. New York: Pantheon Books, 1923.
Kamala. *The Flawless Mirror*. Nevada City, Calif.: Crystal Clarity, 1992.
King, Elizabeth Delvine. *The Lotus Path*. Los Angeles: J. F. Rowny Press, 1917.
Kriyananda, Brother. *Stories of Mukunda*. Los Angeles: Self-Realization Fellowship, 1953.
Kriyananada, Swami. *Conversations with Yogananda*. Nevada City, Calif.: Crystal Clarity, 2004.
———. *The New Path: My Life with Paramhansa Yogananda*. Nevada City, Calif.: Crystal Clarity, 2008.
———. *Paramhansa Yogananda: A Biography with Personal Reflections*. Nevada City, Calif.: Crystal Clarity, 2012.
———. *The Path: Autobiography of a Western Yogi*. Nevada City, Calif.: Ananda Publications, 1977.
———. *Revelations of Jesus Christ: Proclaimed by Paramhansa Yogananda*. Nevada City, Calif.: Crystal Clarity, 2007.
———, and Paramhansa Yogananda. *The Essence of the Bhagavad Gita: Explained by Paramhansa Yogananda, as Remembered by His Disciple, Swami Kriyananda*. Nevada City, Calif.: Crystal Clarity, 2006.
Leadbetter, C. W. *The Chakras*. Wheaton, Ill.: Theosophical Pub. House, 1927.
The Life Story of Dr. M. W. Lewis: A Faithful Disciple of Paramahansa Yogananda for Forty Years. Los Angeles: Self-Realization Fellowship, 1960.
Long, James. *Hand-Book of Bengal Missions, in Connexion with the Church of England; Together with an Account of General Educational Efforts in North India*. London: John Farquhar Shaw, 1848.
Majumder, Niranjan, ed. *The Statesman: An Anthology*. Calcutta: Statesman, 1975.
Mayo, Katherine. *Mother India*. New York: Harcourt Brace, 1927.
McFarland, John T., Benjamin S. Winchester, R. Douglas Fraser, and J. Williams Butcher,

eds. *The Encyclopedia of Sunday School and Religious Education*. New York: Thomas Nelson and Sons, 1915.
Memories of Mother: Devotees and Friends Remember Mother Hamilton. Seattle, Wash.: Cross and the Lotus, 2011.
Millard, A. Douglas, ed. *Faiths and Fellowship: Being the Proceedings of the World Congress of Faiths Held in London, July 3rd–17th, 1936*. London: J. M. Watkins, 1936.
Moore, W. J. *A Manual of the Diseases of India*. London: John Churchill, 1861.
Mother Hamilton: A Divine Life. DVD. Directed by Mark Hickenbottom. Seattle: Cross and the Lotus, 2004.
Mozoomdar, P. C. *Oriental Christ*. Boston: Ellis, 1883.
Mrinalini Mata. *In His Presence: A Talk by Sri Mrinalini Mata*. VHS. Los Angeles: Self-Realization Fellowship, 2001.
Mukti Mata. *"Like the Light from Heaven": Remembering Life with Paramahansa Yogananda*. CD. Los Angeles: Self-Realization Fellowship, 2007.
Muller, J. P. *My System: 15 Minutes Exercise a Day for Health*. London: Link House, n.d.
Natarajan, Kamakshi. *Miss Mayo's Mother India: A Rejoinder*. Madras: G. A. Natesan, 1928.
Nerode, Brahmacharee. *Teachings of the East*. Detroit, Mich.: Detroit Yogoda-Satsanga Center, n.d.
Nikhilānanda, Swami. *The Gospel of Sri Ramakrishna*. New York: Ramakrishna-Vivekananda Center, 1942.
Noffsinger, John S. *Correspondence Schools, Lyceums, Chautauquas*. New York: Macmillan, 1926.
Otto, Rudolph. *The Idea of the Holy*. Translated by John Wilfred Harvey. London: Humphrey Milford, 1923.
Pai, Anant, ed. *Paramahansa Yogananda: A Saint for East and West*. Mumbai: India Book House, 1982.
Paramananda, Swami. *The Path of Devotion*. New York: Vedanta Society, 1907.
Paramahansa Yogananda: In Memoriam. Los Angeles: Self-Realization Fellowship, 1958.
Paramhansa Yogananda: History, Life, Mission. N.p., n.d.
Paulsen, Norman. *Sunburst: Return of the Ancients*. Santa Barbara, Calif.: Sunburst Farms, 1980.
Premananda, Swami. *The Gayatri Prayer*. Washington, D.C.: Self-Revelation Church, 1958.
———. *Isha Upanishad: The Philosophy of God-Consciousness*. Washington, D.C.: Self-Realization Fellowship, 1942.
———. *Katha Upanishad*. Washington, D.C.: Self-Realization Fellowship, n.d.
———. *Light on Kriya Yoga*. Washington, D.C.: Self-Realization Church, 1955.
———. "My Gurudev: Swami Yogananda Paramhansa." *Mystic Cross*, n.d.
———. *The Path of the Eternal Dhammapada*. Washington, D.C.: Self-Realization Fellowship, 1942.
———. *The Sanctity of the Senses*. Washington, D.C.: Self-Realization Fellowship, 1948.
———. *Srimad-Bhagavad-Gita: The Revelation of the Supreme Self*. Boston: Christopher Publishing, 1949.
———. *"Thine Is the Glory."* Washington, D.C.: Self-Realization Church, n.d.
———. *Three Upanishads*. Washington, D.C.: Self-Realization Fellowship, 1944.
———. *The Way of Wisdom and Self-Liberation*. Washington, D.C.: Self-Realization Fellowship, 1940.

Presbrey, Frank. *The History and Development of Advertising*. Garden City, N.Y.: Doubleday, 1929.

Rajarsi Janakanada: A Great Western Yogi. Los Angeles: Self-Realization Fellowship, 1996.

Ramacharaka, Yogi. *Correspondence Class Course in Yogi Philosophy and Oriental Occultism*. Palmyra, N.J.: Yogi Publication Society, 1903.

Randall, John Herman Jr., and John Herman Randall. *Religion and the Modern World*. New York: Frederick A. Stokes, 1929.

Reed, Elizabeth A. *Hinduism in Europe and America*. New York: G. P. Putnam's Sons, 1914.

Reese, Curtis. *Humanist Religion*. New York: MacMillan, 1931.

"The Rosicrucian Fellowship: Its Message and Mission." *Rays from the Rose Cross*, September 1915, n.p.

Rosser, Brenda Lewis. *Treasures against Time: Paramahansa Yogananda with Dr. and Mildred Lewis*. Borrego, Calif.: Borrego Publications, 1991.

Saksena, S. K. "Review of 'Autobiography of a Yogi' by Paramhansa Yogananda." *Philosophy East and West* 1, no. 2 (July 1951): 78–79.

Satyananda Giri, Swami. "Swami Sri Yukteshvar Giri Maharaj: A Biography." In *A Collection of Biographies of Four Kriya Yoga Gurus*. Battle Creek, Mich.: Yoga Niketan, 2004.

———. "Yogananda Sanga [Paramhansa Yoganandaji as I have Seen and Understood Him]." In *A Collection of Biographies of Four Kriya Yoga Gurus*. Battle Creek, Mich.: Yoga Niketan, 2004.

Schmidt, Nathaniel. *The Coming Religion*. New York: Macmillan, 1930.

Scott, Walter Dill. *The Psychology of Advertising: A Simple Exposition of the Principles of Psychology in Their Relation to Successful Advertising*. 5th ed. Boston: Small, Maynard, 1913.

Self-Revelation Church of Absolute Monism. *History and Essence of the Self-Revelation Church of Absolute Monism*. Washington, D.C.: Self-Revelation Church of Absolute Monism, 1985.

Self-Realization Fellowship. *Life of Paramahansa Yogananda: The Early Years in America (1920–1928)*. DVD. Los Angeles: Self-Realization Fellowship, 2003.

———. *SRF Lake Shrine 50th Anniversary Celebration: Stories of Paramahansa Yogananda by Direct Disciples*. DVD. Los Angeles: Self-Realization Fellowship, 2008.

Self-Realization Fellowship Lessons. Los Angeles: Self-Realization Fellowship, 1956.

Sen, Keshub Chandra. "Jesus Christ: Europe and Asia." In *The Brahmo Somaj: Lectures and Tracts by Keshub Chunder Sen; First and Second Series*, edited by S. D. Collett. London: Strahan, 1866.

Smith, J. Thorne. "Advertising." In *Civilization in the United States, an Inquiry by Thirty Americans*, edited by Harold Stearns. New York: Harcourt Brace, 1922.

Statistical Abstract relating to British India from 1885–86 to 1894–95. London: Her Majesty's Stationery Office, 1896.

Stockton, Mary Peck. *A Testimony of Love and Devotion: My Life Journey with Paramahansa Yogananda*. Portland, Ore.: Tamaltree Books, 2015.

Sunderland, J. T. *India in Bondage: Her Right to Freedom*. New York: L. Copeland, 1929.

Tagore, Rabindranath. *The Home and the World*. London: Macmillan, 1919.

Thomas, Wendell. *Hinduism Invades America*. New York: Beacon Press, 1930.

U.S. Department of Commerce and Labor, Bureau of the Census. *Census of Religious*

Bodies, 1926, Part I: Summary and Detailed Tables. Washington, D.C.: Government Printing Office, 1930.
Veblen, Thorstein. *The Higher Learning in America: A Memorandum on the Conduct of Universities by Business Men*. New York: B. W. Huebsch, 1918.
Weller, Charles Frederick. *World Fellowship: Addresses and Messages by Leading Spokesmen of All Faiths, Races and Countries*. New York: Liveright, 1935.
White, Lyman Cromwell. *The Structure of Private International Organizations*. Philadelphia: George S. Ferguson, 1933.
Wight, Joan. *A Trilogy of Divine Love*. Beverly Hills, Calif.: Joan Wight, 1992.
Wood, Ernest. *An Englishman Defends Mother India: A Complete Constructive Reply to "Mother India."* Madras: Ganesh, 1929.
"Yoga for the West," *Newsweek*, March 10, 1947, 76.
Yogananda, Paramahansa. "Afterword." In Marc Edmund Jones, *Gandhi Lives*. Philadelphia: David McKay, 1948.
———. *Autobiography of a Yogi*. New York: Philosophical Library, 1946.
———. *Autobiography of a Yogi*. Los Angeles: Self-Realization Fellowship, 1981.
———. *Awake in the Cosmic Dream: Collector's Series #2*. CD. Los Angeles: Self-Realization Fellowship, 1987 [originally recorded January 5, 1952].
———. *Be a Smile Millionaire: Collector's Series #4*. CD. Los Angeles: Self-Realization Fellowship, 1987 [originally recorded January 29, 1950].
———. *Beholding the One in All: Collector's Series #1*. CD. Los Angeles: Self-Realization Fellowship, 1985 [originally recorded January 5, 1949].
———. *Cosmic Chants*. Los Angeles: Self-Realization Fellowship, 1938.
———. *Cosmic Mother: One Aspect of God*. Los Angeles: Self-Realization Fellowship, 1945.
———. *Follow the Path of Christ, Krishna, and the Masters: Collector's Series #6*. CD. Los Angeles: Self-Realization Fellowship, 2003 [originally recorded August 26, 1951].
———. *The Great Light of God: Collector's Series #3*. CD. Los Angeles: Self-Realization Fellowship, 1993 [originally recorded December 23, 1951].
———. *In the Glory of the Spirit: Collector's Series #10*. CD. Los Angeles: Self-Realization Fellowship, 2007 [originally recorded January 5, 1949].
———. *Journey to Self-Realization*. Los Angeles: Self-Realization Fellowship, 1997.
———. *Man's Eternal Quest*. Los Angeles: Self-Realization Fellowship, 1975.
———. *One Life versus Reincarnation: Collector's Series #8*. CD. Los Angeles: Self-Realization Fellowship, 2005 [originally recorded December 4, 1949].
———. *Removing All Sorrow and Suffering: Collector's Series #9*. CD. Los Angeles: Self-Realization Fellowship, 2006 [originally recorded January 1, 1950].
———. *The Second Coming of Christ: The Resurrection of Christ within You*. 2 vols. Los Angeles: Self-Realization Fellowship, 2004.
———. *Self-Realization: The Inner and the Outer Path: Collector's Series #7*. CD. Los Angeles: Self-Realization Fellowship, 2005 [originally recorded December 25, 1950].
———. *To Make Heaven on Earth: Collector's Series #7*. CD. Los Angeles: Self-Realization Fellowship, 2004 [originally recorded December 25, 1949].
Yogananda, Paramhansa. *Bhagavad Gita: Spiritual Interpretations, Chapter One*. Nevada City, Calif.: Ananda Community, 1980.
———. *How to Be Happy All the Time*. Nevada City, Calif.: Crystal Clarity, 2006.
———. *The Master Said*. Los Angeles: Self-Realization Publishing House, 1952.

———. *The Second Coming of Christ: From the Original Unchanged Writings of Paramhansa Yogananda's Interpretations of the Sayings of Jesus Christ*. 3 vols. Dallas, Tex.: Amrita Foundation, 1979–86.

Yogananda, Paramhansa Swami. *Your Praecepta: Step I*. Dakshineswar, India: Yogoda Sat-Sanga Press, n.d.

———. *Your Praecepta: Step II*. Dakshineswar, India: Yogoda Sat-Sanga Press, n.d.

———. *Your Praecepta: Step III*. Dakshineswar, India: Yogoda Sat-Sanga Press, n.d.

———. *Your Praecepta: Step IV*. Dakshineswar, India: Yogoda Sat-Sanga Press, n.d.

———. *Your Praecepta: Step V*. Dakshineswar, India: Yogoda Sat-Sanga Press, n.d.

———. *Your Praecepta: Step VI*. Dakshineswar, India: Yogoda Sat-Sanga Press, n.d.

———. *Your Praecepta: Step VII*. Dakshineswar, India: Yogoda Sat-Sanga Press, n.d.

Yogananda, Swami. *Metaphysical Meditations*. Los Angeles: Self-Realization Fellowship, 1932.

———. *OM Song*. Los Angeles: Yogoda Sat-Sanga Headquarters, 1926.

———. *Psychological Chart*. Los Angeles: Yogoda and Sat Sanga, 1925.

———. *Scientific Healing Affirmations: Their Theory and Practice*. Los Angeles: Self-Realization Publishing House, 1929.

———. *Songs of the Soul*. Boston: Sat Sanga, 1923.

———. *The Science of Religion*. 4th ed. Los Angeles: Yogoda and Sat Sanga Headquarters, 1925.

———. *The Science of Religion*. Calcutta: Kuntaline Press, 1920.

———. *Whispers from Eternity: Universal Scientific Prayers and Poems*. Los Angeles: Yogoda and Sat-Sanga, 1929.

———. *Yogoda, or Muscle-Will System of Physical Perfection*. Boston: Sat Sanga, 1923.

Yogananda Giri, Swami. *The Science of Religion*. Calcutta: Kuntaline Press, 1920.

Yukteswar, Swami Sri. *The Holy Science*. Los Angeles: Self-Realization Fellowship, 1949.

SECONDARY SOURCES

Adluri, Vishwa, and Joydeep Bagchee. *The Nay Science: A History of German Indology*. New York: Oxford University Press, 2014.

Ahlstrom, Sydney E. *A Religious History of the American People*. New Haven: Yale University Press, 1972.

Albanese, Catherine L. *A Republic of Mind and Spirit: A Cultural History of American Metaphysical Religion*. New Haven: Yale University Press, 2007.

Allison, Dale. *Night Comes: Death, Imagination, and the Last Things*. Grand Rapids, Mich.: Eerdmans, 2016.

———. *Resurrecting Jesus: The Earliest Christian Tradition and Its Interpreters*. New York: T & T Clark, 2005.

Alter, Joseph S. "Shri Yogendra: Magic, Modernity, and the Burden of the Middle-Class Yogi." In *Gurus of Modern Yoga*, edited by Mark Singleton and Ellen Goldberg. New York: Oxford University Press, 2014.

———. *Yoga in Modern India: The Body between Philosophy and Science*. Princeton, N.J.: Princeton University Press, 2003.

Alter, Robert. *The Art of Biblical Narrative*. New York: Basic Books, 2001.

Anderson, Theodore Marvin. "Reimagining Religion: The Grounding of Spiritual Politics and Practice in Modern America, 1890–1940." Ph.D. diss., Yale University, 2008.

Angel, Leonard. *Enlightenment East and West*. Albany: State University of New York Press, 1994.
Appiah, Kwame Anthony. *Cosmopolitanism: Ethics in a World of Strangers*. New York: W. W. Norton, 2010.
Aravamudan, Srinivas. *Guru English: South Asian Religion in a Cosmopolitan Language*. Princeton, N.J.: Princeton University Press, 2006.
Austin, J. L. *How to Do Things with Words*. 2nd ed. Cambridge, Mass.: Harvard University Press, 1975.
Aymard, Orianne. *When a Goddess Dies: Worshipping Ma Anandamayi after Her Death*. New York: Oxford University Press, 2014.
Babb, Lawrence A. *Redemptive Encounters: Three Modern Styles in the Hindu Tradition*. Berkeley: University of California Press, 1986.
Balagangadhara, S. N. "Orientalism, Postcolonialism, and Religion." In *Rethinking Religion in India: The Colonial Construction of Hinduism*, edited by Esther Block, Marianne Keppens, and Rajaram Hegde. New York: Routledge, 2010.
Bald, Vivek. *Bengali Harlem and the Lost Histories of South Asian America*. Cambridge, Mass.: Harvard University Press, 2013.
Ballantyne, Tony. *Orientalism and Race: Aryanism in the British Empire*. London: Palgrave MacMillan, 2002.
Banerji, S. C. *Tantra in Bengal: A Study in Its Origin, Development and Influence*. New Delhi: Manohar, 1992.
Barker, Eileen. "Perspective: What Are We Studying?" *Nova Religio: The Journal of Alternative and Emergent Religions* 8, no. 1 (July 2004): 88–102.
Barnes, Douglas F. "Charisma and Religious Leadership: An Historical Analysis." *Journal for the Scientific Study of Religion* 17, no. 1 (March 1978): 1–18.
Baur, John E. *The Health Seekers of Southern California, 1870–1900*. San Marino, Calif.: Huntington Library Press, 1959.
Bayly, C. A. *Birth of the Modern World, 1780–1914*. Hoboken, N.J.: Wiley-Blackwell, 2003.
———. *Indian Society and the Making of the British Empire*. Cambridge: Cambridge University Press, 1987.
Bayly, Susan. *Caste, Society and Politics in India from the Eighteenth Century to the Modern Age*. Cambridge: Cambridge University Press, 1999.
Beckerlegge, Gwilym. *The Ramakrishna Mission: The Making of a Modern Hindu Movement*. New York: Oxford University Press, 2000.
Bender, Thomas, ed. *Rethinking American History in a Global Age*. Berkeley: University of California Press, 2002.
Benz, Ernst. *The Theology of Electricity: On the Encounter and Explanation of Theology and Science in the 17th and 18th Centuries*. Princeton, N.J.: Princeton University Press, 1989.
Berger, Peter. *Sacred Canopy: Elements of a Social Theory of Religion*. Garden City, N.Y.: Doubleday, 1967.
———, ed. *The Desecularization of the World: Resurgent Religion and World Politics*. Grand Rapids, Mich.: Eerdmans, 1999.
Berkman, Franya J. "Appropriating Universality: The Coltranes and 1960s Spirituality." *American Studies* 48, no. 1 (Spring 2007): 41–62.
Best, Gary D. *Dollar Decade: Mammon and the Machine in 1920s America*. New York: Praeger, 2003.
Beyer, Peter. *Religions in Global Society*. London: Routledge, 2006.

Bharat, Sandy. *Christ across the Ganges: Hindu Responses to Jesus*. Ropley, U.K.: O Books, 2007.

Bharati, Agehananda. "The Hindu Renaissance and Its Apologetic Patterns." *Journal of Asian Studies* 29, no. 2 (February 1970): 267–87.

Bhattacharya, N. N. *Indian Demonology: The Inverted Pantheon*. New Delhi: Manohar, 2000.

Bhattacharya, Tithi. *The Sentinels of Culture: Class, Education, and the Colonial Intellectual in Bengal (1848–85)*. New Delhi: Oxford University Press, 2005.

Block, Esther Marianne Keppens, and Rajaram Hegde, eds. *Rethinking Religion in India: The Colonial Construction of Hinduism*. New York: Routledge, 2010.

Boli, John, and George M. Thomas, eds. *Constructing World Culture: International Nongovernmental Organizations since 1875*. Stanford, Calif.: Stanford University Press, 1999.

Bose, Sugata. *A Hundred Horizons: The Indian Ocean in the Age of Global Empire*. Cambridge, Mass.: Harvard University Press, 2006.

Bottles, Scott L. *Los Angeles and the Automobile: The Making of the Modern City*. Berkeley: University of California Press, 1987.

Braudy, Leo. "Cultures and Communities." In *A Companion to Los Angeles*, edited by William Deverell and Greg Hise. Chichester, U.K.: Wiley-Blackwell, 2010.

Brekke, Torkel. "The Conceptual Foundation of Missionary Hinduism." *Journal of Religious History* 23, no. 2 (June 1999): 203–14.

Brereton, Virginia Lieson. *Training God's Army: The American Bible School, 1880–1940*. Bloomington: Indiana University Press, 1990.

Brockington, J. L. *The Sacred Thread: Hinduism in Its Continuity and Diversity*. Edinburgh: Edinburgh University Press, 1989.

Brooks, Douglas Renfrew. *The Secret of the Three Cities: An Introduction to Hindu Sakta Tantrism*. Chicago: University of Chicago Press, 1990.

Bruce, Steve. *God Is Dead: Secularization in the West*. Malden, Mass.: Blackwell, 2002.

Bryant, Edwin F. "*Ahimsa* in the Patanjali Yoga Tradition." In *Food for the Soul: Vegetarianism and Yoga Traditions*, edited by Steven J. Rosen. Santa Barbara, Calif.: ABC-CLIO, 2011.

———. *The Yoga Sūtras of Patañjali: A New Edition, Translation, and Commentary*. New York: North Point Press, 2009.

Bunch, Lonnie G., III. "'The Greatest State for the Negro': Jefferson L. Edmonds, Black Propagandist of the California Dream." In *Seeking El Dorado: African Americans in California*, edited by Lawrence B. de Graaf, Kevin Mulroy, and Quintard Taylor. Seattle: University of Washington Press, 2001.

Burley, Mikel. *Classical Samkhya and Yoga: An Indian Metaphysics of Experience*. New York: Routledge, 2007.

Burton, Antoinette. *At the Heart of the Empire: Indians and the Colonial Encounter in Late-Victorian Britain*. Berkeley: University of California Press, 1998.

Bush, Gregory W. *Lord of Attention: Gerald Stanley Lee and the Crowd Metaphor in Industrializing America*. Amherst: University of Massachusetts Press, 1991.

Butler, Jon, Grant Wacker, and Randall Balmer. *Religion in American Life: A Short History*. 2nd ed. New York: Oxford University Press, 2011.

Campbell, C. "The Easternization of the West." In *New Religious Movements: Challenge and Response*, edited by Bryan Wilson and Jamie Cresswell. London: Routledge, 1999.

Canfield, Jack, and Gay Hendricks. *You've Got to Read This Book! 55 People Tell the Story of the Book That Changed Their Life*. New York: William Morrow, 2006.

Cannato, Vincent J. *American Passage: The History of Ellis Island*. New York: HarperCollins, 2009.

Cara, Elana Joan. *The Light of Christ Within: Reverend John Laurence, a Direct Disciple of Paramhansa Yogananda*. Nevada City, Calif.: Crystal Clarity, 2013.

Carpenter, Joel A. "Propagating the Faith once Delivered: The Fundamentalist Missionary Enterprise, 1920–1945." In *Earthen Vessels: American Evangelicals and Foreign Missions, 1880–1980*, edited by Joel A. Carpenter and Wilbert R. Shenk. Grand Rapids, Mich.: Eerdmans, 1990.

———. *Revive Us Again: The Awakening of American Fundamentalism*. New York: Oxford University Press, 1997.

Carrette, Jeremy, and Richard King. *Selling Spirituality: The Silent Takeover of Religion*. London: Routledge, 2005.

Carroll, Bret E. "Worlds in Space: American Religious Pluralism in Geographic Perspective." In *Gods in America: Religious Pluralism in the United States*, edited by Charles L. Cohen and Ronald L. Numbers. New York: Oxford University Press, 2013.

Chang, Robert S. *Disoriented: Asian Americans, Law, and the Nation-State*. New York: New York University Press, 1999.

Chapple, Christopher Key. "Raja Yoga and the Guru: Gurani Anjali of Yoga Anand Ashram, Amityville, New York." In *Gurus in America*, edited by Thomas A. Forsthoeffel and Cynthia Ann Humes. Albany: State University of New York Press, 2005.

Chatterjee, S. Partha. *Empire and Nation*. New York: Columbia University Press, 2010.

Chattopadhyay, Saayan. "Performative Modernity: Journalism and the Colonial Public Sphere." In *Colonial Modernity: Indian Perspectives*, edited by Pradip Basu. Calcutta: Setu Prakashani, 2011.

Chattopadhyay, Swati. *Representing Calcutta: Modernity, Nationalism, and the Colonial Uncanny*. New York: Routledge, 2005.

Clarke, J. J. *Oriental Enlightenment: The Encounter between Asian and Western Thought*. New York: Routledge, 1997.

Coben, Stanley. *Rebellion against Victorianism: The Impetus for Cultural Change in 1920s America*. New York: Oxford University Press, 1991.

Coburn, T. B. *Devi-Mahatmya: The Crystallization of the Goddess Tradition*. New Delhi: Motilal Banarsidass, 1988.

———. "'Scripture' in India: Towards a Typology of the Word in Hindu Life." *Journal of the American Academy of Religion* 52, no. 3 (1984): 435–59.

Cohen, Charles L., and Ronald L. Numbers. "Introduction." In *Gods in America: Religious Pluralism in the United States*, edited by Charles L. Cohen and Ronald L. Numbers. New York: Oxford University Press, 2013.

Cohn, Bernard. "Regions Subjective and Objective: Their Relation to the Study of Modern Indian History and Society." In *An Anthropologist among the Historians and Other Essays*. New Delhi: Oxford University Press, 1987.

Coluson, Doug. "British Imperialism, the Indian Independence Movement, and the Racial Eligibility Provisions of the Naturalization Act: *United States v. Thind* Revisited." *Georgetown Journal of Law and Modern Critical Race Perspectives* 7, no. 1 (Spring 2015): 1–42.

Conrad, Sebastian, and Dominic Sachsenmaier. *Competing Visions of World Order: Global Moments and Movements, 1880s–1930s*. London: Palgrave Macmillan, 2012.
Copley, Antony, ed. *Gurus and Their Followers: New Religious Reform Movements in Colonial India*. Oxford: Oxford University Press, 2000.
Cotkin, George. *Reluctant Modernism: American Thought and Culture, 1880–1900*. New York: Twayne, 1992.
Coward, Howard, ed. *Modern Indian Responses to Religious Pluralism*. Albany: State University of New York Press, 1987.
Coward, H. G., J. R. Hinnells, and R. B. Williams, eds. *The South Asian Diaspora in Britain, Canada, and the United States*. Albany: State University of New York Press, 2000.
Crunden, Robert. *Body and Soul: The Making of American Modernism*. New York: Basic Books, 2000.
Csordas, Thomas J. "Introduction: Modalities of Transnational Transcendence." In *Transnational Transcendence: Essays on Religion and Globalization*, edited by Thomas J. Csordas. Berkeley: University of California Press, 2009.
Culver, Lawrence. *The Frontier of Leisure: Southern California and the Making of Modern America*. New York: Oxford University Press, 2010.
Curtis, Michel. *Orientalism and Islam: European Thinkers on Oriental Despotism in the Middle East and India*. Cambridge: Cambridge University Press, 2009.
Cushman, Philip. *Constructing the Self, Constructing America: A Cultural History of Psychotherapy*. Boston: Addison-Wesley, 1995.
Dasgupta, Subrata. *Awakening: The Story of the Bengal Renaissance*. Gurgaon: Random House India, 2010.
Davis, Clark. "The Corporate Reconstruction of Middle-Class Manhood." In *The Middling Sorts: Explorations in the History of the American Middle Class*, edited by Burton J. Bledstein and Robert D. Johnston. New York: Routledge, 2001.
Davis, Mike. "Sunshine and the Open Shop: Ford and Darwin in 1920s Los Angeles." In *Metropolis in the Making: Los Angeles in the 1920s*, edited by Tom Sitton and William Deverell. Berkeley: University of California Press, 2001.
Davis, Richard H. *The Bhagavad Gita: A Biography*. Princeton, N.J.: Princeton University Press, 2015.
De Michelis, Elizabeth. *A History of Modern Yoga: Patanjani and Western Esotericism*. New York: Continuum, 2004.
———. "Modern Yoga." In *Yoga in the Modern World: Contemporary Perspectives*, edited by Mark Singleton and Jean Byrne. New York: Routledge, 2008.
Desai, P. N. *Health and Medicine in the Hindu Tradition: Continuity and Cohesion*. New York, Crossroad, 1989.
Deslippe, Philip Roland. "The Swami Circuit: Mapping the Terrain of Early American Yoga." *Journal of Yoga Studies* 1, no. 1 (2018): 5–44.
Deverell, William. *Whitewashed Adobe: The Rise of Los Angeles and the Remaking of Its Mexican Past*. Berkeley: University of California Press, 2004.
Dhar, Niranjan. *Vedanta and the Bengal Renaissance*. Calcutta: Minerva Association, 1977.
Di Florio, Paola, and Lisa Leeman. *Awake: The Life of Yogananda*. Los Angeles: Self-Realization Fellowship, 2015.
Dirks, Nicholas B. *Castes of Mind: Colonialism and the Making of Modern India*. Princeton, N.J.: Princeton University Press, 2001.
———. "Castes of Mind." *Representations*, no. 37 (Winter 1992): 56–78.

Dochuk, Darren. *From Bible Belt to Sunbelt: Plain-Folk Religion, Grassroots Politics, and the Rise of Evangelical Conservatism*. New York: W. W. Norton, 2011.

Doniger, Wendy. *The Hindus: An Alternate History*. New York: Penguin Press, 2009.

———. *On Hinduism*. New York: Oxford University Press, 2014.

Doniger-O'Flaherty, Wendy. *Women, Androgynes, and Other Mythical Beasts*. Chicago: University of Chicago Press, 1980.

Dorsett, Lyle W. *Billy Sunday and the Redemption of Urban America*. Grand Rapids, Mich.: Eerdmans, 1991.

Dumenil, Lynn. *The Modern Temper: American Culture and Society in the 1920s*. New York: Hill and Wang, 1995.

Ebaugh, H. R., and J. S. Chafetz, eds. *Religion and the New Immigrants: Continuities and Adaptations in Immigration Congregations*. Walnut Creek, Calif.: Alta Mira, 2000.

Eck, Diana L. *Darśan: Seeing the Divine Image in India*. Chambersburg, Pa.: Anima Books, 1981.

———. *A New Religious America: How a "Christian Country" Has Now Become the World's Most Religiously Diverse Nation*. San Francisco: Harper, 2001.

Eisenstadt, S. N. "Multiple Modernities." *Daedalus* 129, no. 1 (Winter 2000): 1–29.

Eliade, Mircea. *The Sacred and the Profane: The Nature of Religion*. San Diego, Calif.: Harcourt Brace Jovanovich, 1987.

———. *Yoga: Immortality and Freedom*. Princeton, N.J.: Princeton University Press, 1958.

Ellwood, Robert. *Alternative Altars: Unconventional and Eastern Spirituality in America*. Chicago: University of Chicago Press, 1979.

Emmott, D. H. "Alexander Duff and the Foundation of Modern Education in India." *British Journal of Education Studies* 13, no. 2 (November 1965): 160–69.

Engh, Michael E. "'A Multiplicity and Diversity of Faiths': Religion's Impact on Los Angeles and the Urban West, 1890–1940." *Western Historical Quarterly* 28 (Winter 1997): 463–492.

———. "Practically Every Religion Being Represented." In *Metropolis in the Making: Los Angeles in the 1920s*, edited by Tom Sitton and William Deverell. Berkeley: University of California Press, 2001.

Falk, Geoffrey D. *Stripping the Gurus: Sex, Violence, Abuse and Enlightenment*. Toronto: Million Monkeys Press, 2009.

Federal Writers Project. *Los Angeles: A Guide to the City and Its Environs*. New York: Hastings, 1941.

Feldhaus, Anne. *Connected Places: Region, Pilgrimage, and Geographical Imagination in India*. Gordonsville, Va.: Palgrave Macmillan, 2003.

Fenton, J. Y. *Transplanting Religious Traditions: Asian Indians in America*. New York: Praeger, 1988.

Feuerstein, Georg. *The Yoga Tradition: Its History, Literature, Philosophy and Practice*. Prescott, Ariz.: Hohm Press, 1998.

Fields, G. *Religious Therapeutics: Body and Health in Yoga, Ayurveda, Tantra*. Albany: State University of New York Press, 2001.

Finke, Roger, and Rodney Stark. *The Churching of America, 1776–2005: Winners and Losers in Our Religious Economy*. New Brunswick, N.J.: Rutgers University Press, 2005.

Fitzgerald, Timothy. "Hinduism and the 'World Religion' Fallacy." *Religion* 20, no. 2 (April 1990): 101–18.

Flamming, Douglas. *Bound for Freedom: Black Los Angeles in Jim Crow America*. Berkeley: University of California Press, 2005.

Flood, Gavin. *The Ascetic Self: Subjectivity, Memory, and Tradition*. Cambridge: Cambridge University Press, 2004.

———. *The Importance of Religion: Meaning and Action in Our Strange World*. Hoboken, N.J.: Wiley-Blackwell, 2011.

———. *An Introduction to Hinduism*. Cambridge: Cambridge University Press, 1996.

———. *The Truth Within: A History of Inwardness in Christianity, Hinduism, and Buddhism*. New York: Oxford University Press, 2013.

Forsthoefel, Thomas A., and Cynthia Anne Humes, eds. *Gurus in America*. New York: State University of New York Press, 2005.

Foulston, Lynn. *At the Feet of the Goddess: The Divine Feminine in Local Hindu Religion*. Portland, Oreg.: Sussex Academic Press, 2002.

Foxen, Anna P. *Biography of a Yogi: Paramahansa Yogananda and the Origins of Modern Yoga*. New York: Oxford University Press, 2017.

Frankiel, Sandra Sizer. *California's Spiritual Frontiers: Religious Alternatives in Anglo-Protestantism, 1850–1910*. Berkeley: University of California Press, 1988.

Freed, R. S., and S. A. Freed. *Ghosts: Life and Death in North India*. Seattle: University of Washington Press, 1993.

French, Harold W. "Swami Vivekananda's Experiences and Interpretations of Christianity." In *Neo-Hindu Views of Christianity*, edited by Arvind Sharma. New York: E. J. Brill, 1988.

———. "Swami Vivekananda's Use of the *Bhagavadgita*." In *Modern Indian Interpreters of the Bhagavadgita*, edited by Robert N. Minor. Albany: State University of New York Press, 1986.

———. *The Swan's Wide Waters: Ramakrishna and Western Culture*. Port Washington, N.Y.: Kennikat Press, 1974.

Frykenberg, Robert Eric, ed. *Christians and Missionaries in India: Cross-Cultural Communication since 1500*. Grand Rapids, Mich.: William B. Eerdmans, 2003.

Fuller, C. J. *The Camphor Flame: Popular Hinduism and Society in India*. Princeton, N.J.: Princeton University Press, 1992.

Fuller, Robert C. *Alternative Medicine and American Religious Life*. New York: Oxford University Press, 1989.

———. *The Body of Faith: A Biological History of Religion in America*. Chicago: University of Chicago Press, 2013.

Gallagher, Eugene V. *The New Religious Movements Experience in America*. New York: Greenwood, 2004.

Gandhi, Rajmohan. *Gandhi: The Man, His People, and the Empire*. Berkeley: University of California Press, 2008.

Gaustad, Edwin S. "The Pulpit and the Pews." In *Between the Times: The Travail of the Protestant Establishment in America, 1900–1960*, edited by William R. Hutchison. Cambridge: Cambridge University Press, 1989.

Geller, Larry. *Leaves of Elvis' Garden: The Song of His Soul*. Beverly Hills, Calif.: Bell Rock, 2008.

Ghosh, Suresh Chandra. *The History of Education in Modern India, 1757–2012*. 4th ed. New Delhi: Orient Black Swan, 2013.

Giddens, Anthony. *Modernity and Self-Identity: Self and Society in the Late Modern Age*. Stanford, Calif.: Stanford University Press, 1991.
Gilbert, James. *Redeeming Culture: American Religion in an Age of Science*. Chicago: University of Chicago Press, 1997.
Gleig, Ann, and Lola Williamson, eds. *Homegrown Gurus: From Hinduism in America to American Hinduism*. Albany: State University of New York Press, 2014.
Gokhale, Balkrishna Govind. *India in the American Mind*. Bombay: Popular Prakashan, 1992.
Goff, Philip. "Fighting Like the Devil in the City of Angels: The Rise of Fundamentalist Charles E. Fuller." In *Metropolis in the Making: Los Angeles in the 1920s*, edited by Tom Sitton and William Deverell. Berkeley: University of California Press, 2001.
Gold, Daniel. *Comprehending the Guru: Towards a Grammar of Religious Perception*. Atlanta, Ga.: Scholars Press, 1988.
———. "Guru's Body, Guru's Abode." In *Religious Reflections on the Human Body*, edited by Jane Marie Law. Bloomington: Indiana University Press, 1995.
———. *The Lord as Guru: Hindi Sants in North Indian Tradition*. New York: Oxford University Press, 1987.
Goldberg, Ellen, and Mark Singleton. "Introduction." In *Gurus of Modern Yoga*, edited by Mark Singleton and Ellen Goldberg. New York: Oxford University Press, 2014.
Goldberg, Philip. *American Veda: From Emerson and the Beatles to Yoga and Meditation—How Indian Spirituality Changed the West*. New York: Harmony Books, 2010.
———. *The Life of Yogananda: The Story of the Yogi Who Became the First Modern Guru*. Carlsbad, Calif.: Hay House, 2018.
Goldstein, Carolyn M. *Creating Consumers: Home Economists in Twentieth-Century America*. Chapel Hill: University of North Carolina Press, 2012.
Gottschalk, Stephen. *Rolling Away the Stone: Mary Baker Eddy's Challenge to Materialism*. Bloomington: Indiana University Press, 2006.
Greimas, Algirada Julien. *On Meaning: Selected Writings in Semiotic Theory*. Minneapolis: University of Minnesota Press, 1987.
———. *Structural Semantics: An Attempt at a Method*. Lincoln: University of Nebraska Press, 1966.
Griffin, David Ray. *Reenchantment without Supernaturalism: A Process Philosophy of Religion*. Ithaca, N.Y.: Cornell University Press, 2000.
Grosso, Michael. *The Man Who Could Fly: St. Joseph of Copertino and the Mystery of Levitation*. Lanham, Md.: Rowman and Littlefield, 2015.
Hacker, Paul. *Philology and Confrontation: Paul Hacker on Traditional and Modern Vedanta*. Edited by Wilhelm Halbfass. Albany: State University of New York Press, 1995.
Halbfass, Wilhelm. *India and Europe: An Essay in Understanding*. New York: State of University of New York Press, 1988.
———. *Tradition and Reflection: Explorations in Indian Thought*. New York: State University of New York Press, 1991.
Hall, Catherine. *Civilizing Subjects: Metropole and Colony in the English Imagination, 1830–1867*. Cambridge: Cambridge University Press, 2002.
Hammer, Olav. *Claiming Knowledge: Strategies of Epistemology from Theosophy to the New Age*. Leiden: Brill, 2001.
———, and Mikael Rothstein, eds. *Cambridge Companion to New Religious Movements*. Cambridge: Cambridge University Press, 2012.

Hardy, F. *The Religious Culture of India: Power, Love and Wisdom*. Cambridge: Cambridge University Press, 1995.

Hatch, Nathan O. *The Democratization of American Christianity*. New Haven: Yale University Press, 1989.

———. "*Sola Scriptura* and *Novus Ordo Seclorum*." In *The Bible in America*, edited by Mark Noll. New York: Oxford University Press, 1982.

Headrick, Daniel R. *Power over Peoples: Technology, Environments, and Western Imperialism, 1400 to the Present*. Princeton, N.J.: Princeton University Press, 2009.

———. *The Tools of Empire: Technology and European Imperialism in the Nineteenth Century*. New York: Oxford University Press, 1981.

Hedstrom, Matthew S. *The Rise of Liberal Religion: Book Culture and American Spirituality in the Twentieth Century*. New York: Oxford University Press, 2012.

Hexham, Irving, and Karla Poewe. *New Religions as Global Cultures: Making the Human Sacred*. Boulder, Colo.: Westview, 1997.

Hiltebeitel, Alf. *Rethinking the Mahabharata: A Reader's Guide to the Education of the Dharma King*. Chicago: University of Chicago Press, 2001.

Hine, Robert V. *California's Utopian Communities*. New York: W. W. Norton, 1953.

Hinnells, John R. "Introduction: South Asian Religions in Migration." In *The South Asian Religious Diaspora in Britain, Canada, and the United States*, edited by Harold Coward, John R. Hinnells, and Raymond Brady Williams. Albany: State University of New York Press, 2000.

Hise, Greg. "Industry and Imaginative Geographies." In *Metropolis in the Making: Los Angeles in the 1920s*, edited by Tom Sitton and William Deverell. Berkeley: University of California Press, 2001.

Hoganson, Kristin L. *Consumers' Imperium: The Global Production of American Domesticity, 1856–1920*. Chapel Hill: University of North Carolina Press, 2007.

Hollinger, David. *After Cloven Tongues of Fire: Protestant Liberalism in Modern American History*. Princeton, N.J.: Princeton University Press, 2013.

Horne, Julia. "The Cosmopolitan Life of Alice Erh-Soon Tay." *Journal of World History* 21, no. 3 (September 2010): 419–46.

Hudnut-Beumler, James. *In Pursuit of the Almighty's Dollar: A History of Money and American Protestantism*. Chapel Hill: University of North Carolina Press, 2007.

Humes, Cynthia Ann. "Schisms within Hindu Groups: The Transcendental Meditation Movement in North America." In *Sacred Schisms: How Religions Divide*, edited by James R. Lewis and Sarah M. Lewis. Cambridge: Cambridge University Press, 2009.

Hutchinson, Brian. "The Divine-Human Figure in the Transmission of Religious Tradition." In *A Sacred Thread: Modern Transmissions Hindu Traditions in India and Abroad*, edited by Raymond Brady Williams. New York: Columbia University Press, 1996.

Hutchison, William R., ed. *Between the Times: The Travail of the Protestant Establishment in America, 1900–1960*. Cambridge: Cambridge University Press, 1989.

Iacobbo, Karen, and Michael Iacobbo. *Vegetarian America: A History*. Santa Barbara, Calif.: Praeger, 2004.

Iannaccone, Laurence. "Religious Markets and the Economics of Religion." *Social Compass* 39, no. 1 (March 1992): 123–31.

Inden, Ronald. *Imagining India*. Bloomington: Indiana University Press, 1990.

Iqbal, Iftekhar. *The Bengal Delta: Ecology, State and Social Change, 1840–1943*. New York: Palgrave MacMillan, 2010.

Iriye, Akira. *Cultural Internationalism and World Order*. Baltimore: Johns Hopkins University Press, 1997.

———. *Global Community: The Role of International Organization in the Making of the Contemporary World*. Berkeley: University of California Press, 2002.

Isaacson, Walter. *Steve Jobs*. New York: Simon and Schuster, 2011.

Jackson, Carl T. "The Influence of Asia upon American Thought: A Bibliographical Essay." *American Studies International* 22, no. 1 (April 1984): 3–31.

———. "The Meeting of East and West: The Case of Paul Carus." *Journal of the History of Ideas* 29, no. 1 (January–March 1968): 73–92.

———. "The New Thought Movement and the Nineteenth Century Discovery of Oriental Philosophy." *Journal of Popular Culture* 9, no. 3 (Winter 1975): 523–48.

———. *The Oriental Religions and American Thought*. Westport, Conn.: Greenwood, 1981.

———. *Vedanta for the West: The Ramakrishna Movement in the United States*. Bloomington: Indiana University Press, 1994.

Jackson, William J. "A Life Becomes a Legend: Sri Tyagaraja as Exemplar." *Journal of the American Academy of Religion* 60, no. 4 (Winter 1992): 717–36.

Jacoby, Susan. *Strange Gods: A Secular History of Conversion*. New York: Pantheon Books, 2016.

Jain, Andrea R. "Muktananda: Entrepreneurial Godman, Tantric Hero." In *Gurus of Modern Yoga*, edited by Mark Singleton and Ellen Goldberg. New York: Oxford University Press, 2014.

———. *Selling Yoga: From Counterculture to Pop Culture*. New York: Oxford University Press, 2015.

Jayawardena, Kumari. *The White Woman's Other Burden: Western Women and South Asia during British Rule*. New York: Routledge, 1995.

Jenkins, Philip. *Mystics and Messiahs: Cults and New Religions in American History*. New York: Oxford University Press, 2000.

Jensen, Joan M. *Passage from India: Asian Indian Immigrants in North America*. New Haven: Yale University Press, 1988.

Jevons, H. Stanley. *Money, Banking, and Exchange in India*. Simla: Government Central Press, 1922.

Jodock, Darrell. *Catholicism Contending with Modernity: Roman Catholic Modernism and Anti-Modernism in Historical Context*. Cambridge: Cambridge University Press, 2000.

Jones, Kenneth N. *Socio-Religious Reform Movements in British India*. Cambridge: Cambridge University Press, 1989.

Jordens, J. T. F. "Gandhi and the Bhagavadgita." In *Modern Indian Interpreters of the Bhagavadgita*, edited by Robert N. Minor. Albany: State University of New York Press, 1986.

Joseph, Simon J. "Jesus in India? Transgressing Social and Religious Boundaries." *Journal of the American Academy of Religion* 80, no. 1 (March 2012): 161–99.

Joshi, Sanjay. *Fractured Modernity: Making of a Middle Class in Colonial North India*. New York: Oxford University Press, 2001.

Kaminsky, Arnold. *The India Office, 1880–1910*. New York: Greenwood, 1986.

Kane, Paula M. *Separatism and Subculture: Boston Catholicism, 1900–1920*. Chapel Hill: University of North Carolina Press, 1994.

Kemper, Steven. *Rescued from the Nation: Anagarika Dharmapala and the Buddhist World*. Chicago: University of Chicago Press, 2015.
Kerr, Ian J. *Building the Railways of the Raj, 1850–1900*. New Delhi: Oxford University Press, 1995.
———. *Engines of Change: The Railroads That Made India*. New York: Praeger, 2006.
———, ed. *Railways of Modern India*. New York: Oxford University Press, 2001.
Khilnani, Sunil. *The Idea of India*. New York: Farrar, Straus and Giroux, 1997.
King, Richard. "Colonialism, Hinduism and the Discourse of Religion." In *Rethinking Religion in India: The Colonial Construction of Hinduism*, edited by Esther Block, Marianne Keppens, and Rajaram Hegde. New York: Routledge, 2010.
———. *Indian Philosophy: An Introduction to Hindu and Buddhist Thought*. Edinburgh: Edinburgh University Press, 1999.
———. *Orientalism and Religion: Postcolonial Theory, India and "the Mystic East."* New York: Routledge, 1999.
Kinsley, D. *Hindu Goddesses: Visions of the Divine Feminine in the Hindu Religious Tradition*. Berkeley: University of California Press, 1988.
Kirkley, Evelyn A. "'Equality of the Sexes, But . . .': Women in Point Loma Theosophy, 1899–1942." *Nova Religio: The Journal of Alternative and Emergent Religions* 1, no. 2 (April 1998): 272–88.
Kopf, David. *British Orientalism and the Bengal Renaissance: The Dynamics of Indian Modernization, 1773–1835*. Berkeley: University of California Press, 1969.
———. *The Brahmo Samaj and the Shaping of the Modern Indian Mind*. Princeton, N.J.: Princeton University Press, 1979.
Kramer, Joel, and Diana Alstad. *The Guru Papers: Masks of Authoritarian Power*. Berkeley, Calif.: Frog, 1993.
Kripal, Jeffrey J. *Kali's Child: The Mystical and the Erotic in the Life and Teachings of Ramakrishna*. Chicago: University of Chicago Press, 1995.
Kropp, Phoebe S. *California Vieja: Culture and Memory in a Modern American Place*. Berkeley: University of California Press, 2006.
Kumar, Deepak. *Science and the Raj, 1857–1905*. New Delhi: Oxford University Press, 1995.
Kumar, Dharma, ed. *The Cambridge Economic History of India*. Vol. 2. Cambridge: Cambridge University Press, 1983.
Kurien, Prema A. "Becoming American by Becoming Hindu: Indian Americans Take Their Place at the Multicultural Table." In *Gatherings in Diaspora: Religious and the New Immigration*, edited by S. Warner and J. Wittner. Philadelphia: Temple University Press, 1998.
———. "Being Young, Brown, and Hindu: Identity Struggles of Second Generation Indian Americans." *Journal of Contemporary Ethnography* 34, no. 4 (August 2005): 434–69.
———. *A Place at the Multicultural Table: The Development of American Hinduism*. New Brunswick, N.J.: Rutgers University Press, 2007.
Ladd, T., and J. A. Mathisen. *Muscular Christianity, Evangelical Protestants and the Development of American Sport*. Grand Rapids, Mich.: Baker Books, 1999.
Laird, M. A. *Missionaries and Education in Bengal, 1793–1837*. New York: Oxford University Press, 1972.
Lambert, Frank. *The Founding Fathers and the Place of Religion in America*. Princeton, N.J.: Princeton University Press, 2003.

———. *"Pedlar in Divinity": George Whitefield and the Transatlantic Revivals, 1737–1770*. Princeton, N.J.: Princeton University Press, 1993.
Lane, David Christopher. *The Radhasoami Tradition: A Critical History of Guru Successorship*. New York: Garland, 1992.
Larson, Gerald James. "Introduction to the Philosophy of Yoga." In *Encyclopedia of Indian Philosophies*, Volume 12: *Yoga: India's Philosophy of Meditation*, edited by Gerald James Larson and Ram Shankar Bhattacharya. New Delhi: Motilal Banarsidass, 2011.
———. *India's Agony over Religion*. Albany: State University of New York Press, 1995.
Lavan, S. "The Brahmo Samaj: India's First Modern Movement for Religious Reform." In *Religion in Modern India*, edited by R. D. Baird. New Delhi: Manohar, 1981.
———. *Unitarians and India: A Study in Encounter and Response*. Boston: Skinner House, 1977.
Lawrence, Bruce B. *Defenders of God: The Fundamentalist Revolt against the Modern Age*. San Francisco: Harper and Row, 1989.
———. *New Faiths, Old Fears: Muslims and Other Asian Immigrants in American Religious Life*. New York: Columbia University Press, 2004.
Lears, Jackson. *Fables of Abundance: A Cultural History of Advertising in America*. New York: Basic Books, 1994.
Leland, Kurt. "Afterword." In C. W. Leadbetter, *The Chakras*. Wheaton, Ill.: Theosophical Publishing House, 2013.
———. *Rainbow Body: A History of the Western Chakra System from Blavatsky to Brennan*. Lake Worth, Fla.: Ibis, 2016.
Leuchtenberg, William. *The Perils of Prosperity, 1914–32*. Chicago: University of Chicago Press, 1958.
Levinsky, Sara Ann. *A Bridge of Dreams: The Story of Paramananda, a Modern Mystic, and His Ideal of All-Conquering Love*. West Stockbridge, Mass.: Lindisfarne Press, 1984.
Lewis, James R., and Sarah M. Lewis. "Introduction." In *Sacred Schisms: How Religions Divide*, edited by James R. Lewis and Sarah M. Lewis. Cambridge: Cambridge University Press, 2009.
Lewthwaite, Stephanie. "Race, Place, and Ethnicity in the Progressive Era." In *A Companion to Los Angeles*, edited by William Deverell and Greg Hise. Chichester, U.K.: Wiley-Blackwell, 2010.
Liberman, Kenneth. "The Reflexivity of the Authenticity of Hatha Yoga." In *Yoga in the Modern World: Contemporary Perspectives*, edited by Mark Singleton and Jean Byrne. New York: Routledge, 2008.
Lindberg, David C., and Ronald L. Numbers, eds. *God and Nature: Historical Essays on the Encounter between Christianity and Science*. Berkeley: University of California Press, 1986.
Little, Douglas. *American Orientalism: The United States and the Middle East since 1945*. Chapel Hill: University of North Carolina Press, 2002.
Llewellyn, J. E. "Gurus and Groups." In *Contemporary Hinduism: Ritual, Culture, and Practice*, edited by Robin Rinehart. Santa Barbara, Calif.: ABC-CLIO, 2004.
Long, Jeffery D. "(Tentatively) Putting the Pieces Together: Comparative Theology in the Tradition of Sri Ramakrishna." In *The New Comparative Theology: Interreligious Insights from the Next Generation*, edited by Francis X. Clooney. London: Bloomsbury, 2010.
———. *A Vision for Hinduism: Beyond Hindu Nationalism*. New York: I. B. Taurus, 2000.
Lorenzen, David N. "Hindus and Others." In *Rethinking Religion in India: The Colonial*

Construction of Hinduism, edited by Esther Block, Marianne Keppens, and Rajaram Hegde. New York: Routledge, 2010.

———. "The Lives of *Nirguni* Saints." In *Bhakti Religion in North India: Community Identity and Political Action*, edited by David N. Lorenzen. Albany: State University of New York Press, 1995.

Love, Robert. *The Great Oom: The Improbable Birth of Yoga in America*. New York: Viking, 2010.

Lucia, Amanda. "Innovative Gurus: Tradition and Change in Contemporary Hinduism." *International Journal of Hindu Studies* 18, no. 2 (2014): 221–63.

MacLeod, Roy, and Deepak Kumar, eds. *Technology and the Raj: Western Technology and Technical Transfers to India, 1700–1947*. New Delhi: Sage, 1995.

Maffly-Kipp, Laurie F. *Religion and Society in Frontier California*. New Haven: Yale University Press, 1994.

Majumdar, Rochona. *Marriage and Modernity: Family Values in Colonial Bengal*. Durham, N.C.: Duke University Press, 2009.

Majumder, Niranjan, ed. *The Statesman: An Anthology*. Calcutta: Statesman, 1975.

Manela, Erez. *The Wilsonian Moment: Self-Determination and the International Origins of Anticolonial Nationalism*. New York: Oxford University Press, 2007.

Marchand, Roland. *Advertising the American Dream: Making Way for Modernity, 1920–1940*. Berkeley: University of California Press, 1985.

Marsden, George M. *Fundamentalism and American Culture*. 2nd ed. New York: Oxford University Press, 2006.

———. *The Soul of the American University: From Protestant Establishment to Established Nonbelief*. New York: Oxford University Press, 1994.

———. *Understanding Fundamentalism and Evangelicalism*. Grand Rapids, Mich.: Eerdmans, 1991.

Marshall, P. J. *Bengal: The British Bridgehead: Eastern India, 1740–1828*. Cambridge: Cambridge University Press, 1987.

———. *The British Discovery of Hinduism in the Eighteenth Century*. Cambridge: Cambridge University Press, 1970.

Marty, Martin E. *Modern American Religion*, Volume 2: *The Noise of Conflict, 1919–1941*. Chicago: University of Chicago Press, 1991.

Masters, Patricia Lee, and Karma Lekshe Tsomo. "Mary Foster: The First Hawaiian Buddhist." In *Innovative Buddhist Women Swimming against the Stream*, edited by Karma Lekshe. Richmond, U.K.: Curzon, 2000.

Mazumdar, Shampa, and Sanjoy Mazumdar. "Creating the Sacred: Altars in the Hindu American Home." In *Revealing the Sacred in Asian and Pacific America*, edited by Jane Naomi Iwamura and Paul Spickard. New York: Routledge, 2003.

———. "Hindu Temple Building in Southern California: A Study of Immigrant Religion." *Journal of Ritual Studies* 20, no. 2 (2006): 43–57.

———. "Of Gods and Homes: Sacred Space in the Hindu House. *Environment* 22, no. 2 (1994): 41–49.

Mazumdar, Sucheta. "Racist Responses to Racism: The Aryan Myth and South Asians in the United States." *South Asia Bulletin* 9, no. 1 (1989): 47–55.

McClintock, Anne. *Imperial Leather: Race, Gender, and Sexuality in the Colonial Context*. New York: Routledge, 1995.

McDaniel, June. *The Madness of the Saints: Ecstatic Religion in Bengal*. Chicago: University of Chicago Press, 1989.

———. *Offering Flowers, Feeding Skulls: Popular Goddess Worship in West Bengal*. New York: Oxford University Press, 2004.

McDermott, Rachel Fell. *Singing to the Goddess: Poems to Kālī and Umā from Bengal*. New York: Oxford University Press, 2001.

McGirr, Lisa. *Suburban Warriors: The Origins of the New American Right*. Princeton, N.J.: Princeton University Press, 2001.

McGreevy, John T. "American Religion." In *American History Now*, edited by Eric Foner and Lisa McGirr. Philadelphia: Temple University Press, 2011.

McLain, Karline. *India's Immortal Comic Books: Gods, Kings, and Other Heroes*. Bloomington: Indiana University Press, 2009.

McNeill, J. R. *Something New under the Sun: An Environmental History of the Twentieth-Century World*. New York: W. W. Norton and Co., 2000.

McWilliams, Carey. *Southern California: An Island on the Land*. 1946. Reprint, Santa Barbara, Calif.: Peregrine Smith, 1973.

Miller, Timothy. "The Evolution of American Spiritual Communities, 1965–2009." *Nova Religio: The Journal of Alternative and Emergent Religions* 13, no. 3 (February 2010): 14–33.

———. *The 60's Communes: Hippies and Beyond*. Syracuse, N.Y.: Syracuse University Press, 1999.

———. *When Prophets Die: The Postcharismatic Fate of New Religious Movements*. Albany: State University of New York Press, 1991.

———, ed. *America's Alternative Religions*. Albany: State University of New York Press, 1995.

Miller, Vincent J. *Consuming Religion: Christian Faith and Practice in a Consumer Culture*. New York: Bloomsbury Academic, 2005.

Mitra, Ananda. *India through the Western Lens: Creating National Images in Film*. Thousand Oaks, Calif.: Sage, 1999.

Mlecko, Joel D. "The Guru in Hindu Tradition." *Numen* 29, no. 1 (July 1982): 33–61.

Moore, R. Laurence. *Selling God: American Religion in the Marketplace of Culture*. New York: Oxford University Press, 1994.

Mukherjee, S. N. *Calcutta: Myths and History*. Calcutta: Subarnarekha, 1977.

Narayan, Kirin. *Storytellers, Saints, and Scoundrels: Folk Narrative in Hindu Religious Teaching*. Philadelphia: University of Pennsylvania Press, 1989.

Narayanan, V. "Embodied Cosmologies: Sights of Piety, Sites of Power." *Journal of the American Academy of Religion* 7, no. 3 (2003): 495–520.

Nelson, Daniel Wilhelm. "B. Fay Mills: Revivalist, Social Reform and Advocate of Free Religion." D.S.S., Syracuse University, 1964.

Neufeldt, R. W. "The Response of the Ramakrishna Mission." In *Modern Indian Responses to Religious Pluralism*, edited by Harold Coward. Albany: State University of New York Press, 1987.

Newcombe, Suzanne. "Institutionalization of the Yoga Tradition: 'Gurus' B. K. S. Iyengar and Yogini Sunita in Britain." In *Gurus in America*, edited by Thomas A. Forsthoeffel and Cynthia Ann Humes. Albany: State University of New York, 2005.

Nicholson, Andrew J. *Unifying Hinduism: Philosophy and Identity in Indian Intellectual History*. New York: Columbia University Press, 2010.

Noll, Mark A. *A History of Christianity in the United States and Canada*. Grand Rapids, Mich.: Eerdmans, 1992.
———. *The Old Religion in a New World: The History of North American Christianity*. Grand Rapids, Mich.: Eerdmans, 2002.
Northrup, David. *Indentured Labor in the Age of Imperialism, 1834–1922*. Cambridge: Cambridge University Press, 1995.
Nye, David E. *American Technological Sublime*. Cambridge, Mass.: MIT Press, 1994.
———. *Electrifying America: Social Meanings of a New Technology*. Cambridge, Mass.: MIT Press, 1990.
Oddie, Geoffrey A. "Constructing 'Hinduism.'" In *Christians and Missionaries in India: Cross-Cultural Communication since 1500*, edited by Robert Eric Frykenberg. Grand Rapids, Mich.: Eerdmans, 2003.
Olivelle, Patrick. *Ascetics and Brahmins: Studies in Ideologies and Institutions*. Cambridge: Anthem Press, 2011.
———. *The Asrama System: The History and Hermeneutics of Religious Institution*. New York: Oxford University Press, 1996.
———. "Orgasmic Rapture and Divine Ecstasy: The Semantic History of Ānanda." *Journal of Indian Philosophy* 25 (1997): 153–80.
Olson, Carl. *The Many Colors of Hinduism: A Thematic-Historical Introduction*. New Brunswick, N.J.: Rutgers University Press, 2007.
Paddison, Joshua. *American Heathens: Religion, Race, and Reconstruction in California*. San Marino, Calif.: Huntington Library Press, 2012.
Paglia, Camille. "Cults and Cosmic Consciousness: Religious Vision in the American 1960s." *Axion* 10, no. 3 (Winter 2003): 57–111.
Palmer, Norris W. "Baba's World: A Global Guru and His Movement." In *Gurus in America*, edited by Thomas A. Forsthoeffel and Cynthia Ann Humes. Albany: State University of New York Press, 2005.
Panicker, P. L. John. *Gandhi on Pluralism and Communalism*. New Delhi: ISPCK, 2006.
Parsons, Jon R. *A Fight for Religious Freedom: A Lawyer's Personal Account of Copyrights, Karma and Dharmic Litigation*. Nevada City, Calif.: Crystal Clarity, 2012.
Patterson, James Alan. "The Loss of a Protestant Missionary Consensus: Foreign Missions and the Fundamentalist-Modernist Conflict." In *Earthen Vessels: American Evangelicals and Foreign Missions, 1880–1980*, edited by Joel A. Carpenter and Wilbert R. Shenk. Grand Rapids, Mich.: Eerdmans, 1990.
Patton, Laurie L. "Introduction." In *The Bhagavad Gita*, translated by Laurie L. Patton. New York: Penguin Classics, 2008.
Peters, Otto. "The Most Industrialized Form of Education." In *Handbook of Distance Education*, edited by Michael G. Moore. 2nd ed. Mahwah, N.J.: L. Erlbaum Associates, 2007.
Pittman, Von V. "University Correspondence Study: A Revised Historiographic Perspective." In *Handbook of Distance Education*, edited by Michael G. Moore. 3rd ed. New York: Routledge, 2013.
Pitzer, Donald E., ed. *America's Communal Utopias*. Chapel Hill: University of North Carolina Press, 1997.
Porter, Andrew. *Religion versus Empire? British Protestant Missionaries and Overseas Expansion, 1700–1914*. Manchester, U.K.: Manchester University Press, 2004.

Porterfield, Amanda. *The Transformation of American Religion: The Story of a Late-Twentieth-Century Awakening.* New York: Oxford University Press, 2001.
Potts, E. D. *Baptist Missionaries in India, 1793–1837: The History of Serampore and Its Missions.* Cambridge: Cambridge University Press, 1967.
Prakash, Gyan. *Another Reason: Science and the Imagination of Modern India.* Princeton, N.J.: Princeton University Press, 1999.
Prasad, Bishwanath. *The Indian Administrative Service.* New Delhi: S. Chand, 1968.
Prashad, Vijay. *The Karma of Brown Folk.* Minneapolis: University of Minnesota Press, 2000.
Pratt, Mary Louise. *Imperial Eyes: Travel Writing and Transculturation.* London: Routledge, 1992.
Prentiss, Karen. *The Embodiment of Bhakti.* New York: Oxford University Press, 1999.
Price, Lance. *The Modi Effect: Inside Narendra Mod's Campaign to Transform India.* London: Quercus, 2015.
Pritchett, Frances W. "The World of Amar Chitra Katha." In *Media and the Transformation of Religion in South Asia,* edited by Lawrence A. Babb and Susan S. Wadley. Philadelphia: University of Pennsylvania Press, 1995.
Prothero, Stephen. *American Jesus: How the Son of God Became a National Icon.* New York: Farrar, Straus and Giroux, 2003.
———. "From Spiritualism to Theosophy: 'Uplifting' a Democratic Tradition." *Religion and American Culture* 3, no. 2 (Summer 1993): 197–216.
———. "On Hindu-Bashing in Early 20th Century USA: 'Mother India's Scandalous Swamis.'" In *Religions of the United States in Practice,* edited by Colleen McDannell. Vol. 2. Princeton, N.J.: Princeton University Press, 2001.
———. *White Buddhist: The Asian Odyssey of Henry Steel Olcott.* Bloomington: Indiana University Press, 1996.
Putnam, Robert, and David E. Campbell. *American Grace: How Religion Divides and Unites Us.* New York: Simon and Schuster, 2010.
Putney, Clifford. *Muscular Christianity: Manhood and Sports in Protestant America, 1880–1920.* Cambridge, Mass.: Harvard University Press, 2001.
Race, Alan. *Christians and Religious Pluralism: Patterns in the Christian Theology of Religions.* London: SCM, 1983.
Radice, William, ed. *Swami Vivekananda and the Modernization of Hinduism.* New Delhi: Oxford University Press, 1998.
Raj, Kapil. *Relocating Modern Science: Circulation and the Construction of Knowledge in South Asia and Europe, 1650–1900.* New York: Palgrave-MacMillan, 2007.
Ramanujan, A. K. "On Women Saints." In *The Divine Consort: Radha and the Goddesses of India,* edited by J. S. Hawley and D. Wulff. Berkeley, Calif.: Asian Humanities Press, 1982.
Rambo, Lewis R. *Understanding Religious Conversion.* New Haven: Yale University Press, 1993.
———, and Charles E. Farhadian. "Converting: Stages of Religious Change." In *Religious Conversion: Contemporary Practices and Controversies,* edited by Christopher Lamb and M. Darroll Bryant. London: Cassell, 1999.
Ram-Prasad, C. *An Outline of Indian Non-Realism: Some Central Arguments of Advaita Metaphysics.* Oxford: Oxford University Press, 1991.

Richardson, E. Allen. *East Comes West: Asian Religions and Cultures in North America*. New York: Pilgrim Press, 1985.

Rinehart, Robin. *One Lifetime, Many Lives: The Experience of Modern Hindu Hagiography*. New York: Oxford University Press, 1999.

Rochford, E. Burke. "Succession, Religious Switching, and Schism in the Hare Krishna Movement." In *Sacred Schisms: How Religions Divide*, edited by James R. Lewis and Sarah M. Lewis. Cambridge: Cambridge University Press, 2009.

Roof, Wade Clark. "Pluralism as a Culture: Religion and Civility in Southern California." *Annals of the American Academy of Political and Social Science* 612, no. 1 (July 2007): 82–99.

———. *Spiritual Marketplace: Baby Boomers and the Remaking of American Religion*. Princeton, N.J.: Princeton University Press, 1999.

Rosaldo, Renato. "Imperialist Nostalgia." *Representations* 26 (Spring 1989): 107–22.

Rosenberg, Emily S. "Transnational Currents in a Shrinking World." In *A World Connecting, 1870–1945*, edited by Emily S. Rosenberg. Cambridge, Mass.: Belknap Press of Harvard University Press, 2012.

Rothstein, Mikael. *Belief Transformation: Some Aspects of the Relation between Science and Religion in Transcendental Meditation (TM) and the International Society for Krishna Consciousness (ISKCON)*. Aarhus, Denmark: Aarhus University Press, 1996.

Roy, Tirkthankar. *India in the World Economy: From Antiquity to the Present*. Cambridge: Cambridge University Press, 2012.

Ryan, Mary Meghan, ed. *Vital Statistics of the United States: Births, Life Expectancy, Death, and Selected Health Data*. 4th ed. Lanham, Md.: Bernan Press, 2010.

Saler, Michael. "Modernity and Enchantment: A Historiographic Review." *American Historical Review* 111, no. 3 (June 2006): 692–716.

Salinger, Margaret A. *Dream Catcher: A Memoir*. New York: Washington Square Press, 2000.

Sarbacker, Stuart Ray. "The Numinous and Cessative in Modern Yoga." In *Yoga in the Modern World: Contemporary Perspectives*, edited by Mark Singleton and Jean Byrne. New York: Routledge, 2008.

———. *Samadhi: The Numinous and Cessative in Indo-Tibetan Yoga*. Albany: State University of New York Press, 2005.

Satter, Beryl. "Emma Curtis Hopkins and the Spread of New Thought, 1885–1905." In *Each Mind a Kingdom: American Women, Sexual Purity, and the New Thought Movement, 1875–1920*. Berkeley: University of California Press, 1999.

Sax, William S., ed. *The Gods at Play: Līlā in South Asia*. New York: Oxford University Press, 1995.

Schmidt, Leigh Eric. *Restless Souls: The Making of American Spirituality*. San Francisco: HarperOne, 2005.

———, and Edwin S. Gaustad. *The Religious History of America: The Heart of the American Story from Colonial Times to Today*. San Francisco: HarperOne, 2004.

Seager, Richard Hughes. "Pluralism and the American Mainstream: The View from the World's Parliament of Religions." *Harvard Theological Review* 82, no. 3 (July 1989): 301–24.

Seely, Bruce E. *Building the American Highway System: Engineers as Policy Makers*. Philadelphia: Temple University Press, 1987.

Sen, Amiya P. *Hindu Revivalism in Bengal, 1872–1905: Some Essays in Interpretation*. New Delhi: Oxford University Press, 1993.
Sharma, Arvind. *The Experimental Dimension of Advaita Vedanta*. New Delhi: Motilal Banarsidass, 1993.
———. *The Hindu Gita: Ancient and Classical Interpretations of the Bahagavadgita*. La Salle, Ill.: Open Court, 1986.
———. *Hinduism as a Missionary Religion*. Delhi: Dev Publishers, 2014.
———. *Neo-Hindu Views of Christianity*. New York: E. J. Brill, 1988.
Sharma, Malti. *Indianization of the Civil Services in British India*. New Delhi: Manak, 2001.
Sharpe, Eric J. "Neo-Hindu Views of Christianity." In *Neo-Hindu Views of Christianity*, edited by Arvind Sharma. New York: E. J. Brill, 1988.
———. *The Universal Gita: Western Images of the Bhagavadgita*. London: Duckworth, 1985.
Shayne, Lee, and Phillip Luke Sinitiere. *Holy Mavericks: Evangelical Innovators and the Spiritual Marketplace*. New York: New York University Press, 2009.
Shils, Edward. *Tradition*. Chicago: University of Chicago Press, 1981.
Shohat, Ella. "Gender and Culture of Empire: Toward a Feminist Ethnography of the Cinema." In *Visions of the East: Orientalism in Film*, edited by Matthew Bernstein and Gaylyn Studlar. New Brunswick, N.J.: Rutgers University Press, 1997.
Shontell, Alyson. "The Last Gift Steve Jobs Gave to Family and Friends Was a Book about Self Realization." *Business Insider*, September 11, 2013.
Silburn, Lilian. *Kundalini: Energy of the Depths*. Albany: State University of New York Press, 1998.
Singal, Daniel. "Modernism." In *A Companion to American Thought*, edited by Richard Wightman Fox and James Kloppenberg. Cambridge, Mass.: Blackwell, 1995.
———. "Towards a Definition of American Modernism." *American Quarterly* 39, no. 1 (Spring 1987): 7–26.
———. *Modernist Culture in America*. Belmont, Calif.: Wadsworth, 1991.
Singh, Gurinder, Paul Numrich, and Raymond Williams. *Buddhists, Hindus and Sikhs in America: A Short History*. New York: Oxford University Press, 2007.
Singleton, Gregory. *Religion in the City of Angels: American Protestant Culture and Urbanization, Los Angeles, 1850–1930*. Ann Arbor, Mich.: UMI Research Press, 1979.
Singleton, Mark. "Suggestive Therapeutics: New Thought's Relationship to Modern Yoga." *Asian Medicine* 3, no. 1 (May 2007): 64–84.
———. *Yoga Body: The Origins of Modern Posture Practice*. New York: Oxford, 2010.
———, and Ellen Goldberg. *Gurus in America*. New York: Oxford University Press, 2014.
Singleton, Mark, and Jean Byrne, eds. *Yoga in the Modern World: Contemporary Perspectives*. New York: Routledge, 2008.
Singleton, Mark, and Tara Fraser. "T. Krishnamacharya, Father of Modern Yoga." In *Gurus of Modern Yoga*, edited by Mark Singleton and Ellen Goldberg. New York: Oxford University Press, 2014.
Sinha, Mrinalini. *Colonial Masculinity: The "Manly Englishman" and the "Effeminate Bengali" in the Late Nineteenth Century*. Manchester, U.K.: Manchester University Press, 1995.
———. *Specters of Mother India: The Global Restructuring of an Empire*. Durham, N.C.: Duke University Press, 2006.
Sinha, Pradhip. *Calcutta in Urban History*. Calcutta: Firma KLM, 1978.

Sinha, Vineeta. *Religion and Commodification: "Merchandizing" Diasporic Hinduism*. New York: Routledge, 2011.
Sitton, Tom, and William Deverell, *Metropolis in the Making: Los Angeles in the 1920s*. Berkeley: University of California Press, 2001.
Sittser, Gerald. *A Cautious Patriotism: The American Churches and the Second World War*. Chapel Hill: University of North Carolina Press, 1997.
Sivulka, Juliann. *Soap, Sex, and Cigarettes: A Cultural History of American Advertising*. Belmont, Calif.: Wadsworth, 1998.
Sjoman, N. E. *The Yoga Tradition of Mysore Palace*. New Delhi: Abhinav, 1999.
Sloane, David. "Landscapes of Health and Rejuvenation." In *Companion to Los Angeles*, edited by William Deverell and Greg Hise. Chichester, U.K.: Wiley-Blackwell, 2010.
Sluga, Glenda. *Internationalism in the Age of Nationalism*. Philadelphia: University of Pennsylvania Press, 2013.
———, and Julia Horne. "Cosmopolitanism: Its Pasts and Practices." *Journal of World History* 21, no. 3 (September 2010): 369–73.
Smith, Christian, ed. *The Secular Revolution: Power, Interests, and Conflict in the Secularization of American Public Life*. Berkeley: University of California Press, 2003.
Smith, David. *Hinduism and Modernity*. Oxford: Blackwell, 2003.
Smith, Jane S. "Luther Burbank's Spineless Cactus: Boom Times in the California Desert." *California History* 87, no. 4 (2010): 26–47, 66–68.
Smith, Philip. "Culture and Charisma: Outline of a Theory." *Acta Sociologica* 43, no. 2 (2000): 101–11.
Snell, Rupert. "Introduction: Themes in Indian Hagiography." In *According to Tradition: Hagiographical Writing in India*, edited by Winand M. Callewaert and Rupert Snell. Wiesbaden, Germany: Harrassowitz, 1994.
Springhall, John. *Decolonization since 1945: The Collapse of Overseas Empires*. London: Palgrave, 2001.
Srinivas, Smriti. "Sathya Sai Baba and the Repertoire of Yoga." In *Gurus of Modern Yoga*, edited by Mark Singleton and Ellen Goldberg. New York: Oxford University Press, 2014.
Stark, Rodney. "Why Religious Movements Succeed or Fail: A Revised General Model." *Journal of Contemporary Religion* 11, no. 2 (1996): 133–46.
———, and Roger Finke. *Acts of Faith: Explaining the Human Side of Religion*. Berkeley: University of California Press, 2000.
Starr, Kevin. *Inventing the Dream: California through the Progressive Era*. New York: Oxford University Press, 1985.
———. *Material Dreams: Southern California through the 1920s*. New York: Oxford University Press, 1990.
Stievermann, Jan, Philip Goff, and Detlef Junker, eds. *Religion and the Marketplace in the United States*. New York: Oxford University Press, 2015.
Stokes, Melvyn. *D. W. Griffith's "The Birth of a Nation."* New York: Oxford University Press, 2007.
Stoler, Barbara Miller, trans. *Yoga: Discipline of Freedom: The Yoga Sutra Attributed to Patanjali*. Berkeley: University of California Press, 1995.
Stolz, Jorg. "Salvation Goods and Religious Markets: Integrating Rational Choice and Weberian Perspectives." *Social Compass* 53, no. 1 (2006): 13–32.

Stout, Harry. *The Divine Dramatist: George Whitefield and the Rise of Modern Evangelicalism*. Grand Rapids, Mich.: Eerdmans, 1991.

Strauss, Sarah. "Adapt, Adjust, Accommodate: The Production of Yoga in a Transnational World." In *Yoga in the Modern World: Contemporary Practices*, edited by Mark Singleton and Jean Byrne. London: Routledge, 2014.

———. *Positioning Yoga: Balancing Acts across Cultures*. Oxford: Berg, 2005.

Studlar, Gaylyn. "'Out-Salomeing Salome': Dance, the New Woman, and Fan Magazine Orientalism." In *Visions of the East: Orientalism in Film*, edited by Matthew Bernstein and Gaylyn Studlar. New Brunswick, N.J.: Rutgers University Press, 1997.

Susman, Warren. "'Personality' and the Making of Twentieth-Century Culture." In *Culture as History: The Transformation of American Society in the Twentieth Century*. New York: Pantheon, 1984.

Sutton, Matthew Avery. *Aimee Semple McPherson and the Resurrection of Christian America*. Cambridge, Mass.: Harvard University Press, 2007.

Satyeswananda Giri, Swami. *Biography of a Yogi: Swami Satyananda Giri Maharaj*. 2nd ed. San Diego, Calif.: Sanskrit Classics, 2002.

———. *Kriya: Finding the True Path*. San Diego, Calif.: Sanskrit Classics, 1991.

Syman, Stefanie. *The Subtle Body: The Story of Yoga in America*. New York: Farrar, Straus and Giroux, 2010.

Synan, Vinson. *The Holiness-Pentecostal Tradition: Charismatic Movements in the Twentieth Century*. 2nd ed. Grand Rapids, Mich.: Eerdmans, 1997.

Taylor, Charles. *A Secular Age*. Cambridge, Mass.: Belknap Press of Harvard University Press, 2007.

Teodorowicz, Josef. *Mystical Phenomena in the Life of Theresa Neumann*. London: B. Herder, 1947.

Thomas, Lynn M. "Modernity's Failings, Political Claims, and Intermediate Concepts." *American Historical Review* 111, no. 3 (June 2006): 727–40.

Thomas, Madathilparampil Mammen. *The Acknowledged Christ of the Indian Renaissance*. London: SCM Press, 1969.

Tirthankar, Roy. *India in the World Economy: From Antiquity to the Present*. Cambridge: Cambridge University Press, 2012.

Trautmann, Thomas. *Aryans and British India*. Berkeley: University of California Press, 1997.

Trout, Polly. *Eastern Seeds, Western Soil: Three Gurus in America*. Mountain View, Calif.: Mayfield, 2001.

———. "Hindu Gurus, American Disciples, and the Search for Modern Religion, 1900–1950." Ph.D. diss., Boston University, 1998.

Tweed, Thomas A. *American Encounter with Buddhism, 1844–1912: Victorian Culture and the Limits of Dissent*. Bloomington: Indiana University Press, 1992.

———. *Dwelling and Crossing: A Theory of Religion*. Cambridge, Mass.: Harvard University Press, 2000.

Twitchell, James B. *Shopping for God: How Christianity Went from in Your Heart to in Your Face*. New York: Simon and Schuster, 2007.

Tygiel, Julius. "Metropolis in the Making." In *Metropolis in the Making: Los Angeles in the 1920s*, edited by Tom Sitton and William Deverell. Berkeley: University of California Press, 2001.

Ulin, David, ed. *Writing Los Angeles: A Literary Anthology*. New York: Library of America, 2002.

Urban, Hugh B. *Tantra: Sex, Secrecy, Politics and Power in the Study of Religion*. Berkeley: University of California Press, 2003.

———. *Zorba the Buddha: Sex, Spirituality, and Capitalism in the Global Osho Movement*. Berkeley: University of California Press, 2016.

van der Veer, Peter. "The Global History of 'Modernity.'" *Journal of the Economic and Social History of the Orient* 41, no. 3 (1998): 285–94.

———. *Imperial Encounters: Religion and Modernity in India and Britain*. Princeton, N.J.: Princeton University Press, 2001.

———. "Syncretism, Multiculturalism and the Discourse of Tolerance." In *Syncretism/Anti-Syncretism: The Politics of Religious Synthesis*, edited by Charles Stewart and Rosalind Shaw. New York: Routledge, 1994.

Versluis, Arthur. *American Transcendentalism and Asian Religions*. New York: Oxford University Press, 1993.

Veysey, Laurence. *The Communal Experience: Anarchist and Mystical Communities in the Twentieth Century*. Chicago: University of Chicago Press, 1973.

Voskuil, Dennis N. "Reaching Out: Mainline Protestantism and the Media." In *Between the Times: The Travail of the Protestant Establishment in America, 1900–1960*, edited by William R. Hutchison. Cambridge: Cambridge University Press, 1989.

Volf, Miroslav. *Flourishing: Why We Need Religion in a Globalized World*. New Haven, Conn.: Yale University Press, 2015.

Wacker, Grant. "The Protestant Awakening to World Religions." In *Between the Times: The Travail of the Protestant Establishment in America, 1900–1960*, edited by William R. Hutchison. Cambridge: Cambridge University Press, 1989.

———. "Second Thoughts on the Great Commission: Liberal Protestants and Foreign Missions, 1890–1940." In *Earthen Vessels: American Evangelicals and Foreign Missions, 1880–1980*, edited by Joel A. Carpenter and Wilbert R. Shenk. Grand Rapids, Mich.: Eerdmans, 1990.

Waghorne, Joanne Punzo. "Beyond Pluralism: Global Gurus and the Third Stream of American Religiosity." In *Gods in America: Religious Pluralism in the United States*, edited by Charles L. Cohen and Ronald L. Numbers. New York: Oxford University Press, 2013.

———. "Engineering an Artful Practice: On Jaggi Vasudev's Isha Yoga and Sri Sri Ravi Shankar's Art of Living." In *Gurus of Modern Yoga*, edited by Mark Singleton and Ellen Goldberg. New York: Oxford University Press, 2014.

Washington, Peter. *Madame Blavatsky's Baboon: A History of the Mystics, Mediums, and Misfits Who Brought Spiritualism to America*. London: Bloomsbury, 1993.

Watanabe, Teresa. "A Hindu's Perspective on Christ and Christianity." *Los Angeles Times*, December 11, 2004.

Weaver, John. *Evangelicals and the Arts in Fiction: Portrayals of Tension in Non-Evangelical Works since 1895*. Jefferson, N.C.: McFarland, 2013.

Weber, Max. *Economy and Society: An Outline of Interpretive Sociology*. Edited by Guenther Roth and Claus Wittich. 2 vols. Berkeley: University of California Press, 1978.

———. *The Sociology of Religion*. Translated by Ephraim Fischoff. Boston: Beacon Press, 1963.

Weightman, B. A. "Changing Religious Landscapes in Los Angeles." *Journal of Cultural Geography* 14, no. 1 (Fall–Winter 1993): 1–20.

Wessinger, Catherine. "Hinduism Arrives in America: The Vedanta Movement and the Self-Realization Fellowship." In *America's Alternative Religions*, edited by Timothy Miller. Albany: State University of New York Press, 1995.

White, Charles, S.J. "Swami Muktananda and the Enlightenment through Sakti-Pat." *History of Religions* 13, no. 4 (May 1974): 306–22.

White, David Gordon. *The Alchemical Body: Siddha Traditions in Medieval India*. Chicago: University of Chicago Press, 1996.

———. *The Kiss of the Yogini: "Tantric Sex" in Its South Asian Contexts*. Chicago: University of Chicago Press, 2003.

———. *Sinister Yogis*. Chicago: University of Chicago Press, 2009.

———, ed. *Tantra in Practice*. Princeton, N.J.: Princeton University Press, 2000.

Williamson, Lola. *Transcendent in America: Hindu-Inspired Meditation Movements as New Religion*. New York: New York University Press, 2010.

Willner, Ann, and Dorothy Willner. "The Rise and Role of Charismatic Leaders." *Annals of the American Academy of Political and Social Science* 358 (1965): 77–88.

Woodhead, Linda, ed. *Peter Berger and the Study of Religion*. New York: Routledge, 2001.

Wuthnow, Robert. *After Heaven: Spirituality in America since the 1950s*. New ed. Berkeley: University of California Press, 1989.

Yoshihara, Mari. *Embracing the East: White Women and American Orientalism*. New York: Oxford University Press, 2003.

Yu, Henry. *Thinking Orientals: Migration, Contact, and Exoticism in Modern America*. New York: Oxford University Press, 2001.

Zavos, John. *The Emergence of Hindu Nationalism in India*. New Delhi: Oxford University Press, 2000.

Index

Page numbers appearing in *italics* refer to figures.